The Revised Relative Hills of Britain:

The Marilyns

Alan Dawson

2025

with contributions from

Ann Bowker, Hamish Brown, Colin Crawford, Audrey Litterick,
Jon Metcalf, Paul Richardson and several others

A Pedantic Press publication

PPB006

Published in Great Britain in 2025 by Pedantic Press

pedantic.org.uk

ISBN 978-1-9163662-5-1

Front cover: Stac an Armin, St Kilda
Back cover: Beinn Choradail, South Uist

Subject matter

Tables and tales

Preface

Welcome to the second edition of RHB, which may become known as RRHB. It seems long overdue, sorry about that. Other books and projects delayed progress. Also, the drive for perfectionism provided an incentive to wait until the data was good enough to produce a final, definitive list of eligible hills that would never have to be updated. In theory anyway. If anyone does find an error in the data it would be helpful if they would kindly not mention it for a while, so that the satisfaction of publication and the illusion of pedantic perfection may be preserved for a little longer.

The opening chapters are written for the benefit of those who may not be familiar with the first edition or the concept of relative height. Seasoned hill baggers will be familiar with this stuff except perhaps for the chapter on cartography and topography, which explains why the hills have been organised into topographic areas rather than the original 42 sections. This change will take some getting used to and may be unpopular at first but it has been necessary in order to bring the overall structure up to date as well as all the hill data.

One notable error in the first edition was the inclusion of the Isle of Man. This is a self-governing crown dependency that is not part of the United Kingdom, so it is separate from Britain politically and geographically. It had less right to inclusion than Northern Ireland, which is not part of Britain either but is part of the UK. The Isle of Man was included owing to a lapse in pedantry and because it was part of the Ordnance Survey Landranger series of maps (sheet 95). The anomaly is corrected in this edition, although the hills on the island are still there and can still be climbed.

There are lots of other data changes too. The most notable ones are highlighted in the Tables and summarised in the chapter on Revision, which does list the Manx Marilyns. It was also tempting to omit St Kilda, which has not had any permanent inhabitants since 1930 and in some ways resembles South Georgia more than the rest of Britain. Its omission would have made it far more feasible to climb all the Marilyns, but feasibility has never been a factor in the classification of relative hills. It would have been convenient to exclude St Kilda on practical grounds but it could not be justified geographically, politically or socially.

Another major change from the first edition is the inclusion of lots of notes and stories, as well as a few articles. Many of these were written several years ago but it does not matter if some of the hill details are out of date because the experiences described remain valid. They captured the reality of climbing these hills in a genuine and understated manner with little emotional fluff. We all have moments of splendour and exhilaration to compensate for mundane reality, but these are relatively rare and usually less interesting to read about than tales of bewilderment and misery.

There is only one name on the front cover but this edition is the outcome of a collective effort by numerous writers and researchers. Two of the most significant contributors, Paul Richardson and Ann Bowker, are no longer with us, as Paul died in 2003 and Ann in 2021. Other contributors have been contacted before publication where possible, but some may be surprised to find their own long-forgotten words appearing in print.

When the first edition was published it was impossible to know how many people might be interested in a long list of relative hills, with no notes or guidance. The number of enthusiasts has risen slowly from a handful to a few thousand, but Marilyn bagging is still far from being a mainstream activity. Most people are not interested in hills or hill bagging, which is not great for book sales but is beneficial for walkers, as it would be a pity if these hills became too popular for quiet appreciation by the enlightened minority.

With a huge number of hills and not many people climbing them, the scope for solitude, adventure, variety, uncertainty, enjoyment, satisfaction and frustration remains as great as ever. There are not likely to be any more new Marilyns discovered in the near future, but there will always be more surprises and rewarding experiences available for those who choose to take advantage of the relatively interesting potential offered by a relatively large list of relative hills.

Hensbarrow Downs, near St Austell

On the summit area of Mynydd y Grug, near Caerphilly

Geography

For millions of people in Britain and around the world, one of the simple pleasures in life is to walk to the top of a hill and look around at the landscape to see a small part of our precious planet. The best views are usually those where you can see a fair distance in all directions, with nothing getting in the way. You don't have to be on top of a high mountain, just higher than the land around. You need to be relatively high. This concept encapsulates the essence of the Marilyns. They are the most prominent 1550 summits in the country, the relatively high hills of Britain. This book provides a list of all of them, with notes and stories about some of them.

Most land is lumpy. Higher bits of land are called hills and the highest points of them are called summits. The words mountain and peak are sometimes used to add variety and make them sound more interesting, but essentially they are all hills.

The height of hills is measured against sea level. The sea is not flat or level but it does provide a useful standard baseline for measurements. In the olden days, before 1992, sea level was the only commonly used reference point. Relative hills are also measured against the land, with reference to a specific point of land known as the key col, which separates a summit from a higher hill. Every hill has a key col and most of them are unique points, but for the highest point of islands the key col is the sea. For example, Sgurr Alasdair on Skye is 992 metres high and its relative height is also 992 metres because Skye is an island. It does have a bridge, but the key col is at sea level not bridge level. The crucial factor in determining summits and key cols is their topography – the nature of the landscape – not any man-made structures. Things get more complicated in cases where the landscape has been altered by deep cuttings, large cairns and other human interventions, but the essential principle remains even when it requires interpretation by a surveyor or list compiler.

Relative hills can be defined by any consistent criteria. In the flat lands of Lincolnshire, Lincoln Castle is relatively high. It is only 78 metres above sea level but it is 65 metres higher than its key col, so its relative height is 65 metres.

This book tabulates all hills that have summits at least 150 metres higher than their key col. They are known as Marilyns. The current total is 1550, which is eight more than in 1992 when the first edition of the book was published. There have been more than eight changes, as several new Marilyns have been identified and some others have been excluded because they do not meet the qualifying criteria. Details of these changes are given later, in the chapter on Revision.

As well as a catalogue of hills, this book includes notes and reports about some of them, from numerous contributors. Perhaps that sounds rather dull. To put it another way, this book holds the key to a lifetime of exploration and adventure in all areas of Britain, from mountains in the north to mounds in the south, with scope for a satisfying range of experiences from exhilarating to exhausting, enjoyable to endurable, uplifting to upsetting. Some novelty has been lost now that so much is known and shared about most of these hills, but that can help walkers avoid some of the setbacks and surprises that lay in store for the explorers of little-known hills in the early years of Marilyn bagging.

History

Size, scope and scale, variety, unpredictability and occasional absurdity. These are some of the characteristics that set the Marilyns apart from any other list of hills when the first edition of *The Relative Hills of Britain* was published. It has taken 33 years for the revised edition to appear. The advent of hill surveying introduced the possibility of obtaining data that was accurate enough to avoid the need for any future changes. The optimistic aim was to publish a list of hills that would never have to be updated. This book does contain a far more accurate catalogue of hills than the first edition, but the data will not remain valid for ever. At present we know precisely where the qualifying hills are, how high they are and how prominent they are. The accuracy and precision are excellent, but long-term certainty will remain out of reach, because sooner or later something will change. This is more likely to be the result of human activity rather than earthquake, volcano or asteroid strike. In the meantime, this is the best that can be done by assessing data from map research, satellite-assisted surveying and other sources.

The widespread use of digital information has made a printed book seem less than essential. If all the data is freely available online and accessible via a small hand-held device, with maps and trip reports, then a book may not be necessary, but it can be desirable. The inclusion of photographs, notes, stories and articles adds value to the printed pages. Some of the contributions date from the 1990s when little was known about most of these hills. They are included for entertainment rather than guidance, to give a flavour of the experience of Marilyn exploration that was missing from the first edition. Many of these contributions are drawn from the pages of Marhofn magazine, which was published annually from 1999 to 2016. The words often convey a sense of detached amusement that encapsulated the mentality of Marilyn bagging in the 1990s and early 2000s.

A notable omission from the first edition was a figure for the relative height of each hill, also known as drop or prominence. This number gives an indication of the significance of a summit in the landscape, along with its height above sea level. Another important feature of this edition is the inclusion of hills that just miss out on qualification for the main list. These 99 near misses are known as Submarilyns and have relative height under 150 metres. Ten of these hills were included in the first edition, but surveys have shown their relative height to be under 150 metres. Their inclusion in the tables shows that they have not been forgotten.

The first person to climb 1000 Marilyns was Rowland Bowker, less than three years after the book was first published. Another nineteen years passed before Rob Woodall and Eddie Dealtry reached the top of Stac Lee and became the first people to climb all the Marilyns. By the end of 2024 only nine others had been able to climb them all. The St Kilda sea stacks, with their hostile conditions and hostile access policies, remain formidable physical and bureaucratic obstacles. Various expeditions to the island group have generated a rich set of contrasting experiences, and some of the stories from these trips are included in the chapter on the Western Isles.

Science and technology

Advances in technology in recent years have made it possible to produce far more accurate lists of hills. Four main types of technology have been used for measuring the heights of summits and cols:

1. Ground surveying using levelling and triangulation. This was the main method used by Ordnance Survey to produce spot heights. The heights shown on maps are often remarkably accurate but they do not always refer to the highest point of a hill.

2. Aerial photography and photogrammetry. This method has allowed OS to survey large areas more efficiently than before but the spot heights generated are not usually as accurate as those from ground surveying.

3. Global Navigation Satellite System (GNSS) and Global Positioning System (GPS). This technology can be highly accurate but is labour intensive for hill surveying. It is widely used by amateur surveyors (rarely by OS) to measure the heights of summits and cols. GNSS is the term used for the overall system while GPS is the best-known example of it. GPS is to GNSS as Hoover is to vacuum cleaner or iPhone is to phone.

4. Lidar. This is a method for determining distance by targeting an object with a laser and measuring the time taken for light signals to reach the target and return to the receiver. The use of Lidar in aerial surveys enables surface heights to be measured.

Cairns, trees, buildings, vegetation and other obstacles can all impede measurement accuracy, but in general GNSS can produce heights accurate to within 5-10cm, Lidar to within 20-30cm, ground surveys to within 1-3m and aerial surveys within 2-4m. Heights of triangulation pillars are more accurate than other spot heights shown on OS maps. Evidence from GNSS surveys has shown they are usually accurate to within about 25cm.

All heights require a reference point and in Britain this is the official sea level (OSGB36), which has not been changed since 1936. However, most relative heights are not dependent on sea level, as the vertical distance between summits and cols remains the same even when sea level changes. The exceptions are the highest points of islands, for which the key col is sea level.

Accurate heights and coordinates also require a simplified model of the surface of the Earth, which is an oblate spheroid rather than a perfect sphere (it bulges slightly at the equator and is a little flatter at the poles). The model used in Britain is occasionally updated by OS, most recently in 2015, when it adopted OSGM15 to replace OSGM02. As a consequence, the heights of numerous hills changed by one or two centimetres, while a few on Mull and further west changed by up to 15cm.

The application of all this technology means that the heights and locations of summits are known far more accurately than when the list of Marilyns was published in 1992. The first edition of RHB relied entirely on OS maps, whereas GNSS and Lidar have made it possible to justify publishing decimal points showing heights to the nearest 10cm. There are however still sources of potential error. Aerial photographs and Lidar data may fail to identify summit rocks and therefore produce figures that are too low, or they may measure summit cairns and generate figures that are too high. A surveyor with GNSS equipment can overcome these problems but results may still be subject to uncertainty. More detail about GNSS surveying is given on page 344.

Cartography and topography

Figures for the heights of over half the Marilyns have been obtained by using GNSS or Lidar, but maps are still hugely important for researching and compiling lists of hills. Contours provide vital information about the location and height of cols. Online digital mapping with contours at five-metre intervals has made it easier to estimate col heights when there are no spot heights or survey data. Paper maps are still valuable for obtaining an overview of the landscape and tracing contour lines over long distances.

Maps are also vital for helping to arrange the landscape into regions and areas. The relative heights of hills are determined by their topography and the same principle can be applied to the grouping of hills, with the boundaries between groups defined by the landscape rather than man-made features or political divisions. Consequently, sections 1 to 42 used in the first edition have been superseded by applying topographic criteria to organise the mainland of Britain into 23 regions and 138 hill areas, all including at least one Marilyn. Some of these regions cross political borders because the landscape is independent of political authorities. The mainland regions are listed on the Contents page and form the main chapters of the book, along with the island groups. Islands are organised into fourteen main groups: twelve for Scottish islands and one each for England and Wales. Many small islands have no Marilyns but are included in the overall scheme. The aim has been to define hill areas that are practically useful but based on topographic principles, with all boundaries defined by natural features. These are the rules that have been applied to meet this aim:

— Hills with over 700m drop must have their own hill area. There are 52 of them.

— Hills with under 700m drop may have their own area.

— All land in Britain must be covered. This allows the scheme to be used for all hills.

— Area boundaries may follow coasts, lochs, rivers and glens but not roads or counties.

— The same hill areas should be usable for hills and islands of any height or size.

For hill walkers familiar with regions 1 to 42 the hill areas (also called topo areas) will seem strange, but the topographic scheme has several notable advantages:

— It fits the landscape, not man-made features and political divisions.

— It is designed to cover all categories of hill, whereas the older scheme was designed only for Munros (sections 1 to 17), with other sections tagged on later.

— All island hills are in separate areas from mainland hills.

— It is arranged in a reasonably logical system, from north to south and west to east, rather than starting with region 1 in the Southern Highlands.

— Hill areas can be combined into larger regions to suit smaller hill lists, but the area boundaries, names and identifiers will remain the same.

— The scheme uses helpful area identifiers, such as HN for Northern Highlands and SS for Southern Scotland, rather than arbitrary numbers.

— The scheme includes meaningful descriptive labels based on hill or island names, as well as identifiers, to help indicate the location of the area.

Many of the topographic groupings are very similar to some of the 42 regions. The Northern Highlands region covers the old regions 15 and 16, Eastern Highlands includes regions 6, 7 and 8, while Southern Scotland covers most of regions 27 and 28. In England, region EL is almost the same as section 34 and region EP covers sections 35, 36 and 37.

Giving priority to topography means that some hills in England are grouped with areas in Wales, while a few in Wales are grouped with central England. Similarly, region SE covers the Cheviot Hills, which lie on part of the border between Scotland and England. OS maps also straddle political borders and this is widely accepted.

Hill areas

Hill areas have been given both names and identifiers, to try to make them more memorable for walkers and efficient for digital applications. For example, HN06 is fine as an identifier but **HN06 Culmor-coigach** gives a concise yet meaningful indication of the area of land covered. The scheme is similar to that used by Ordnance Survey for its Landranger maps, whereby each map has a name as well as a number.

Mainland area names are taken from the highest hill in an area and one other hill, to create a unique compound name that conveys location and where possible sounds nice too. For example, Tirran-wirren (HE13) is taken from Ben Tirran and Hill of Wirren, while Scafell-illgill (EL03) is taken from Scafell Pike and Illgill Head. Area names for islands use the island names except for Skye and Lewis-Harris, which are so large and complex that they are both subdivided into smaller areas.

The hill areas organise the landscape more clearly than maps, with no overlaps or omissions. For example, all the Torridon hills are in area HW04 Spidean-alligin, though the area extends beyond Torridon and Gairloch to the coast at Rubha Reidh. On Skye, area SK01 Alasdair-gillean includes the Cuillin hills but extends well beyond the Cuillin to include all the land west of Glen Brittle and Loch Harport.

In Wales, hill area WN04 Llewelyn-elen includes the Carneddau but extends as far as the coast at Conwy. Yr Elen is not a Marilyn but its name is used because there is not much choice in that area and it sounds better than the alternative options. In order to assist the transition from section numbers to hill areas, the original section numbers are shown at the top of each table, as well as the relevant OS Landranger map numbers.

Submarilyns

Submarilyns are hills that miss out on qualification by a small margin. The concept was introduced in the 1990s to identify potential Marilyns and was extended to include all hills with 140-149.9m drop. Almost all of these have since been surveyed using GNSS and some have been promoted. Their relative heights are now known accurately, so there should be no new Marilyns unless there are significant changes to the landscape.

The original purpose of the Submarilyns no longer applies but the concept still has value in identifying hills with Marilynesque qualities, notably those that are the highest point in a large area, such as Raw Head in Cheshire and Cheriton Hill in Kent. The definition has been updated using a proportional scale, so that lower hills require a greater relative height. There are now 99 Submarilyns, including all the hills listed in the first edition that are no longer Marilyns, apart from Scafell and Cunnigill Hill. The formula used to produce the updated set of Submarilyns is given on page 317.

An Teallach from Meall Glac Tigh-fail (HW01), with Sgurr Fiona (left of centre), a Submarilyn with 141.7m drop, and Bidean a Glas Thuill (right of centre), a Marilyn with 757m drop

Yewbarrow (EL02), a Submarilyn with 143.9m drop. Its parent Marilyn is Pillar.

Tables and Tales

The list of hills is arranged into 23 mainland regions and 14 island regions, further divided into 177 hill areas, with one table for each area. These tables provide accurate data for 1550 Marilyns and 99 Submarilyns. Each area includes some notes, anecdotes or short stories that provide an evocative or eccentric description of climbing one or more of the hills. Names and dates are given where relevant to show that these contributions relate to the experience at the time and are not intended to provide guidance. Some of the hills and hill names have inspired songs and quatrains (simple four-line poems), a few of which have been included after the relevant table.

The maps show the approximate location of the Marilyns in each region, with the different colours of triangles indicating different hill areas. More details about the summit locations are available by looking at printed maps or the more precise digital maps that are available via the Hill Bagging website and other online sources.

Like the OS map numbering system, the tables begin with Shetland and end with the south of England. Within each table the ordering of summits begins with the highest hill. Other hills in the same area may be clustered into small groups to indicate ridge lines or proximity, with groups separated by horizontal lines. Submarilyns are not shown on the maps but are listed after their parent summit, with name indented. Some of them are a long way from the main summit.

The tables have seven columns:

Number: This is the hill number used in the Database of British and Irish Hills and on the Hill Bagging website. The numbers provide unique identification and have no intrinsic meaning, though numbers over 19000 are relatively recent additions.

Source: This column has no heading but shows the source of the precise height data where available, using these abbreviations:

A   GNSS survey by Alan Dawson
C   GNSS survey by CMRC Ltd
G   GNSS survey by G&J Surveys
J   GNSS survey by Jon Metcalf
M   GNSS survey by Myrddyn Phillips
O   GNSS survey by Ordnance Survey
L   Lidar
T   OS triangulation point (trig pillar)

If there are two letters in the column it means that two sources of data have been used. If there is no letter code then the height is taken from an OS map at 1:25000 or 1:50000 scale.

Height: This is the height of the summit in metres above British sea level. If a hill has been surveyed using GNSS or Lidar then the height is given to the nearest 0.1m unless there is too much uncertainty (such as a large cairn) to justify that precision. Summits with trig pillars have a decimal point if there is evidence, from ground inspection or photographs, of the height of the OS flush bracket above the summit. In rare cases with a difference of more than 10cm between data sources then the mean figure is used.

Numerous heights in the tables are different from those shown on OS maps. In such cases the maps are wrong and the surveyed heights are correct.

Name: Names of almost all the hills are taken from OS maps. They may be in English, Gaelic, Welsh, Norse or some odd combination of languages. This rich variety of names adds to the exotic appeal of many hills but makes pronunciation a challenge for hill walkers. Most names are shown as on OS maps but accents are not included as they complicate digital applications and have no value for the vast majority of walkers. Where there are two hills in the same area with the same name then the rounded height is appended to the name, e.g. Beinn Tharsuinn 711 in area HN08.

If a map gives alternative names or spellings, the one more commonly used and recognised is included, for example Ben Nevis not Beinn Nibheis, Ben Lui not Beinn Laoigh, Gulvain not Gaor Bheinn. In a few cases where the hill has two names in regular use then two names are given, with a slash symbol separating them, e.g. Snowdon / Yr Wyddfa. In other cases a dash symbol is used to separate a hill name from a summit name, with the hill name shown first, e.g. Beinn Alligin – Sgurr Mor.

Symbols after a name are used to indicate significant changes from the first edition of the book, with the number of applicable hills shown in brackets below.

*** new Marilyn discovered since 1992 (25)

** new hill name and location, replacing a hill listed in the first edition (15)

* same hill name but a significant relocation to a new grid reference (27)

new hill name at the same location (25)

¬ hill that was listed in the first edition but is now a Submarilyn (10)

Drop: This figure shows the relative height of the hill, also known as prominence. It is calculated by subtracting the col height from the summit height. Figures are given to the nearest 0.1m if both summit and col have been surveyed with GNSS or Lidar.

Location: The eight-figure grid references in the tables identify a square of ten metres by ten metres around the highest point. For surveyed summits, the grid reference is guaranteed to be correct. For other summits, grid references are taken from large-scale OS maps or from readings submitted by users of the Hill Bagging website. These are likely to be correct but are not guaranteed. It is now common to see ten-figure grid references, which identify a single square metre of ground. Modern portable GPS devices make this feasible but perhaps too precise. Many summit cairns are more than a square metre in area and survey points are not always on exactly the highest point, for various reasons. Also, slight variations in grid reference systems used by different types of GPS device mean that an eight-figure grid reference is more widely applicable.

Summit: This comment summarises the feature at the surveyed point or that reported by hill walkers as being the highest point. These features may change over time as cairns are built or removed. On cairned summits the survey point is usually the ground next to the cairn. For simplicity, this feature is usually shown as 'Cairn'. **Vrock** means 'vegetated rock' and **Voutcrop** means 'vegetated outcrop'. The terms boulder, rock and outcrop are not precisely defined. A boulder is usually at least one metre long or high and may or may not be embedded, while an outcrop is a continuous area of exposed rock a few metres wide. Rocks are smaller than boulders but must be embedded or immovable to be accepted as summit features.

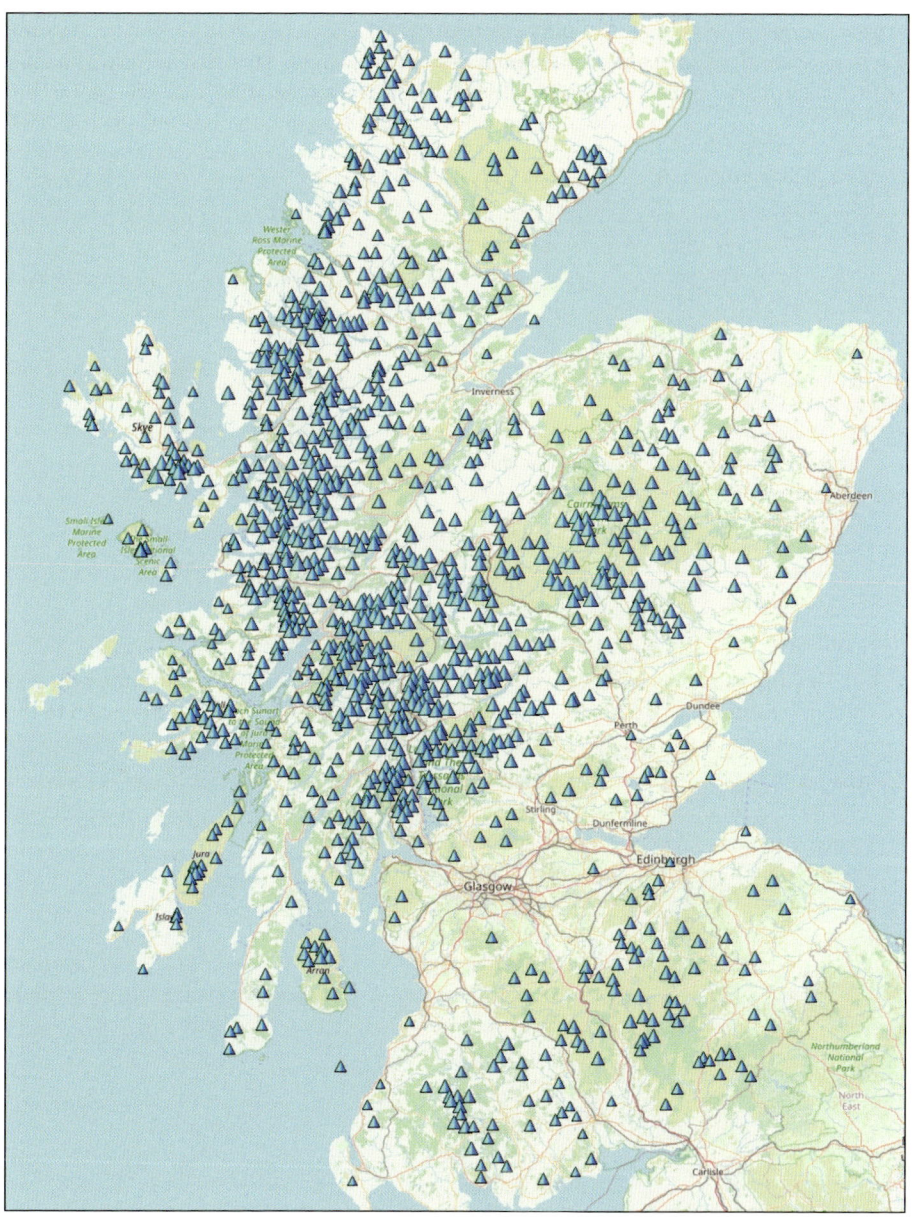

Distribution of the Marilyns of Scotland, excluding the Northern Isles (shown on pages 10-17) and Western Isles (shown on pages 20-35)

——— Shetland Islands ———

Large island group, with Marilyns on nine of the islands

Marilyns: 19
Highest and most prominent: Ronas Hill, Mainland, 450m
Lowest and least prominent: Vord Hill, Fetlar, 159m

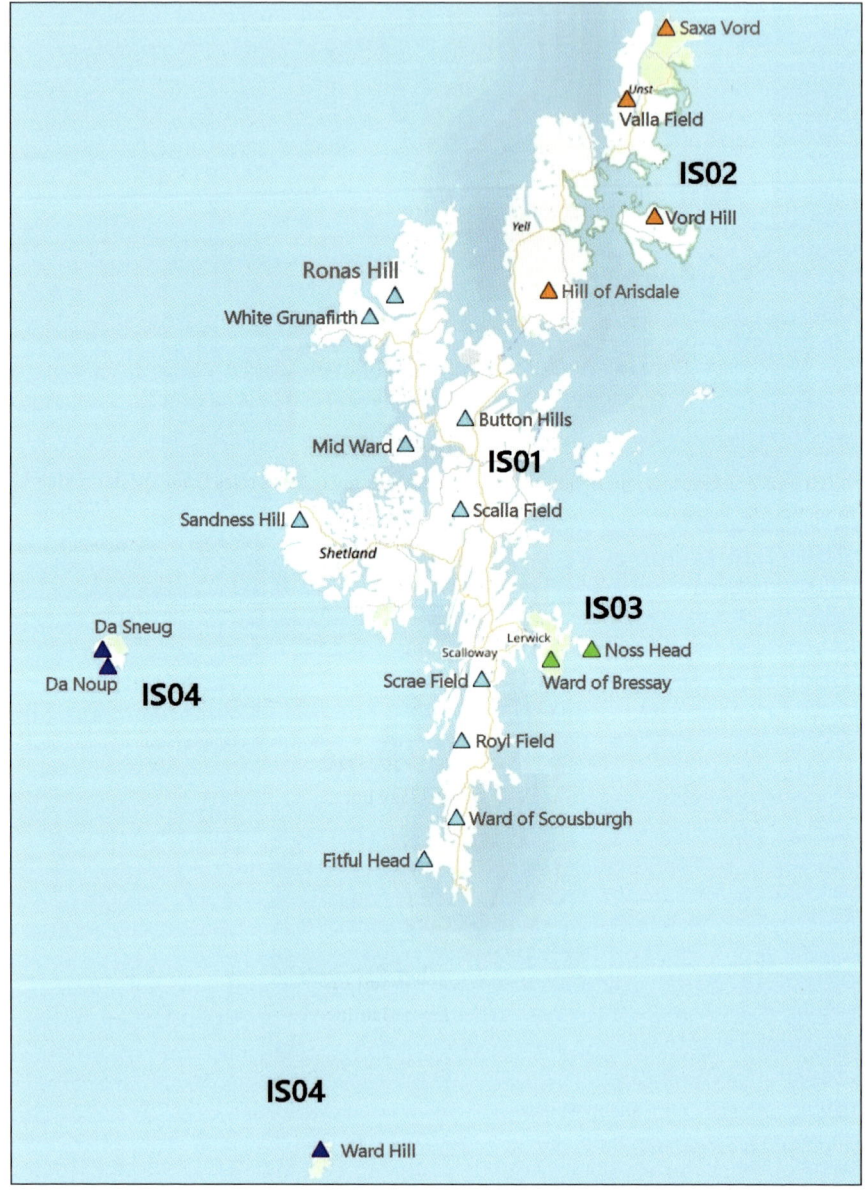

IS01 Mainland-muckleroe

The small island of Muckle Roe is connected by a road bridge to Shetland Mainland

RHB section 22

OS maps 1, 2, 3, 4

Number		Height	Name	Drop	Location	Summit
1527		450	Ronas Hill	450	HU 3050 8347	Rock near trig
1545	A	171.9	Faan Hill	149.4	HU 3447 8020	Tussock
1544	T	173.4	White Grunafirth	158	HU 2756 8072	Grass near trig
1532	T	281.0	Scalla Field	268	HU 3893 5725	Trig
1534		252	Button Hills #	205	HU 3931 6843	Cairn on peat hag
1535	T	249.3	Sandness Hill	235	HU 1916 5570	Trig
1529	T	293.2	Royl Field	288	HU 3959 2851	Trig
1531	T	283.6	Fitful Head	272.9	HU 3462 1353	Grass by trig
1533	T	262.8	Ward of Scousburgh	169.9	HU 3879 1879	Trig
1539	T	215.8	Scrae Field	181.4	HU 4179 3614	Trig
1546		172	Mid Ward, Muckle Roe	172	HU 3201 6521	Cairn on rock

All the Marilyns on Shetland Mainland are so well separated that it is not possible to climb two in one walk without crossing a public road. Eight of the summits have a triangulation pillar on or close to the highest point. The name Dalescord Hill does not appear to apply to the highest point of Button Hills so has not been retained.

IS02 Unst-fetlar

The islands of Unst, Yell and Fetlar can be reached by regular car ferries from Shetland Mainland

RHB section 22

OS maps 1, 2, 3

Number		Height	Name	Drop	Location	Summit
1530	T	284.4	Saxa Vord, Unst	284.4	HP 6312 1662	Trig
1547	A	160.5	Hill of Clibberswick, Unst	148.8	HP 6624 1267	Mound near trig
1540	T	216.1	Valla Field, Unst	203	HP 5846 0786	Trig
1541		210	Hill of Arisdale, Yell	210	HU 4945 8415	Cairn
1548		159	Vord Hill, Fetlar	159	HU 6225 9350	Cairn near trig

IS03 Bressay-noss

There are frequent car ferries from Lerwick to Bressay but access to Noss is seasonal and uncertain

RHB section 22

OS map 4

Number		Height	Name	Drop	Location	Summit
1537	T	226.5	Ward of Bressay	226.5	HU 5028 3872	Trig
1542	T	181.5	Noss Head	181.5	HU 5538 3987	Grass by trig

IS04 Foula-fairisle

Foula and Fair Isle can be reached by air or sea from Mainland but high wind often disrupts services

RHB section 22

OS map 4

Number		Height	Name	Drop	Location	Summit
1528		418	Da Sneug, Foula	418	HT 9478 3950	Grass near trig
1536		248	Da Noup, Foula	181	HT 9544 3751	Grass
1538		220	Ward Hill, Fair Isle	220	HZ 2086 7338	Rocks by cairn

Saxa Vord, Unst

The northernmost Marilyn has received plenty of attention in recent years. The radar station on its summit closed from 2006 to 2019, making it easy to reach the triangulation pillar, though slightly higher man-made ground may exist near the buildings. Access has been more awkward since the base re-opened, with robust new fencing. The situation changes periodically but it is usually possible to drive up the private road to a parking area at the final bend before the base. A short stroll from there leads to a view of Out Stack, the northernmost outpost of the British Isles, just beyond the island of Muckle Flugga and nearby Skerries and Rumblings.

In 2023 the Saxa Vord spaceport was under construction on Lamba Ness peninsula, 5km east of the summit. Other recent developments include the Saxa Vord distillery and the Saxa Vord sky stop on the Wild Skies Shetland Sky Trail. However, the tiny golf course at nearby Burrafirth, shown on older maps, has long since disappeared.

Contestants on University Challenge have extensive knowledge of a wide range of subjects, but in August 2023 none of the team from the University of East Anglia (UEA) were able to answer a question about the location of Saxa Vord, despite being told that it is on the northernmost inhabited island in Britain. They were also unaware that Detling Hill and the North Downs are in Kent and that Brown Willy is on Bodmin Moor in Cornwall, not Dartmoor in Devon. To be fair, the UEA students did choose to attend the university most inconveniently situated for Marilyn bagging and they were well informed about quantum mechanics, video games and crop rotation in the fourteenth century. They also scored more points than the team from the University of Strathclyde, whose best subject was the names of captains of the German national football team.

Hill of Arisdale, Yell

JENNIFER THOMSON, 2003

A bus–ferry–bus journey took me to Otterswick on the island of Yell for a planned meander over Hill of Arisdale followed by a bus north to B&B accommodation in Gutcher and the morning ferry to Fetlar. This meander was to become one of my most scary hill walking experiences ever. Coming down a path into a dip between two lochans, I was lifted sideways by a sudden strong gust of wind and dumped feet first up to my neck, rucksack and all, in a lochan. My boots didn't reach the bottom as I doggy-paddled in a panic to the side. Soaked to the skin – even my camera contained brown peaty water – I dried out during the remainder of the walk, but while water evaporates peat does not, and my B&B landlady was not impressed, especially as the change of clothes in my rucksack had suffered the same fate as those I was wearing.

I escaped on the 7:30 ferry to Fetlar and was given a lift by the schoolteacher. She had just had an excellent inspector's report on her work with all five pupils and took me to view the school, which was conveniently situated at the foot of Vord Hill. The walk to the trig pillar on tussock grass and crowberries was thankfully uneventful. I headed back to the only road and got a lift to the ferry in the back of a van whose most recent occupants had been sheep. This left me three hours to wait for the school bus, but I was offered a lift on one of the five vehicles on the ferry all the way back to Lerwick.

The Shetland Islands, the cliffs, seabirds and people all left a lasting impression after twenty Marilyns in fifteen days on eight islands, all on my own. The hills were not difficult, although on some the peat hags became frustrating. Organising a practical schedule of buses and ferries, while hoping for a lift, was more of a challenge.

Cunnigill Hill and Faan Hill

There were twenty Shetland Marilyns listed in the first edition of RHB but it soon became clear that Cunnigill Hill was included in error, as its relative height is only 127 metres. Research started with OS Landranger map 1 and some contours were misread on map 3, but it was the only such obvious error in the original list. Scafell was included owing to an error of judgement, not an error in research. Cunnigill Hill and Scafell are the only two hills from the first edition that do not qualify as Marilyns or Submarilyns.

Faan Hill seemed to be a strong candidate to replace Cunnigill Hill, but a survey in 2023 showed that it falls short of Marilyn status by 60cm. Its heathery summit can be reached fairly easily from a nearby road and the views are good, but the hill has less to recommend it than the Submarilyn on Unst. The summit of Hill of Clibberswick is on the edge of cliffs that make it feel wilder than most of the Marilyns on Shetland Mainland. Fitful Head at the south end is close to the cliff edge but has a road to the top and an assortment of masts and buildings that detract from its wildness.

Ronas Hill

The highest point on Shetland is bleaker and stonier than the other Shetland Marilyns. It is on North Roe, a bulging peninsula separated from the rest of Mainland by a narrow strip of land called Mavis Grind, which passes between the Atlantic Ocean and the North Sea. Mavis Grind is also the name of a singer on *Road Of Dreams*, the nineteenth track on an album by Julian Cope called *20 Mothers: Better To Light A Candle Than Curse The Darkness*. The Road of Dreams may be the A970 that passes through Mavis Grind. Or it may not.

South of Mavis Grind lies the island of Muckle Roe, easily reached by a low and fairly modern bridge. Near the highest point, Mid Ward, is a lochan called Loch of Bottoms. As all lochs have bottoms, it is unclear what makes this one worthy of its splendid name.

Scalla Field

This summit of this hill is in the middle of an enormous wind farm that now dominates the central part of Shetland Mainland and has had a drastic impact on its character. The huge network of broad tracks has made access simpler but uglier and more depressing.

Ward of Scousburgh

BRIAN EDRIDGE, JUNE 2009

My 600th Marilyn was Ward of Scousburgh in Shetland on 7 June 2009. Regrettably, this was the worst Marilyn to date, littered with communications masts, buildings, ruins, roads and a scrap car. At Saxa Vord we ignored the dire warning notices, went through the open gate, passed a service van and a parked car, found the summit, took photos and left without any challenge.

White Grunafirth

AUDREY LITTERICK, MARCH 2011

The Shetland Marilyns were memorable because I was being paid to be in Shetland and crammed in the hills around my work, but also because the wind never dropped below about 35mph at sea level during the entire four-day visit. I have never crawled into the teeth of a gale for so long on so many hills in such a short time. White Grunafirth was a horizontal, tussock and bog-covered rock-climb in a hurricane and may not have been achieved without the aid of teeth as well as hands and feet.

Saxa Vord from near Hermaness Head

Summit area of Vord Hill, Fetlar

Noss Head

14

Noss Head, Noss

TONY ROGERS, AUGUST 2007

It seemed that most people in Lerwick knew somebody who knew a man who had a boat to take people to the island of Noss. Two of our group spent many evenings in the bars of Lerwick trying to find one of these men, including an 80-year-old who never answered his phone. They later found out that he had died. Some of our party met the local MP on their flight back from Foula and explained the problem to him. On their return to Lerwick they were taken to the constituency office, where he made numerous phone calls to people who might be able to help. Like most MPs he did not have a magic wand. During the week most people visited all the islands with Marilyn summits except Noss.

GRAHAM ILLING, MAY 2008

A new jetty enabled the island warden to ferry us over in a little inflatable boat. The bird life on Noss was fantastic, with puffins as the stars. We made an anti-clockwise circuit of the island, rounding a corner for the magnificent view of Noss Head. It looked like the north face of the Eiger but the smell of ammonia confirmed that it wasn't snow covering the cliffs. The summit view over the massive colony of gannets was truly impressive.

Da Sneug and Da Noup, Foula

JON METCALF, 2002

Already a strong contender for trip of the decade, in a place I would never have dreamed of visiting before succumbing to the influence of RHB. The flight was delayed by three hours but when we finally got underway I had the good fortune to sit next to the pilot for the fifteen-minute flight as the plane was full. I need not have worried about getting round the two sensational hills and a good bite of the soaring cliffs within the available four hours. There was even time in hand for a leisurely sunbathe away from the bonxies at the top of the lost-world-like Sneck o' da Smallie. At the landing site a local came by to tell us it was too misty for the plane to take off from Lerwick. All I had was a day-sack and the clothes I stood up in. I just managed to get a phone signal to let the family know.

Along with two German tourists, I made for the island's only B&B accommodation. The hospitality was amazing, and after a sound dinner most of the party repaired to a living room. Mine host, however, asked me if I would like to come out to set the world to rights with a friend. There is no pub so I couldn't stand my round, which didn't seem to bother him at all. His friend turned out to be a man of 75, who produced a litre-and-a-half of Glen Morangie. Come the end of the evening I could have slept very comfortably on the airstrip. The next thing I knew there was a loud thump at the bedroom door, with a shout of 'forty-five minutes to eat breakfast and get to the plane'.

This visit was a rare privilege. A place already blessed with staggering cliffs and hill-scape also turned up a brilliant evening with exceptional people who I would not have met in other circumstances. The strongest common view they expressed was that, while anyone who made the effort to get to Foula was most welcome, they did not want to publicise its qualities to the wider world in case the place got swamped.

JENNIFER THOMSON, 2003

Our two-day visit to Foula was on the eight-seater plane as the sea was too stormy for the ferry. We stayed at the B&B and the next day were followed up Da Sneug by three of the multi-coloured native Foula sheep that made walking easy. Shortly beyond the summit cairn, the seabird colonies and cliffs of Da Kame were spectacular.

The warden accompanied us over the Daal to look down the dank and treacherous rock fault known as the Sneck o' da Smallie to the teeming seabird colonies under the cliffs. We then made our way up Da Noup and experienced the only mist and rain in my fifteen days on Shetland. Back at the B&B we watched the famous film by Michael Powell which immortalised the evacuation in 1930 of St Kilda but was actually filmed on Foula in 1936, with many islanders taking part.

GARY JONES, 2014

Imagine a small area of pleasant and shapely but unremarkable hills rising from rough fields and scattered houses. Then cut around this on three sides, straight through the highest point on the fourth, and drop the resulting portion into the north Atlantic Ocean. The result is the most stupendous sea-cliffs, 400m high and close to vertical. The Conachair cliffs are slightly higher but photographs suggest that they are less sheer than those of Da Kame on Foula. Lying on the summit of Da Kame with my head over the edge, it slowly dawned that the tiny white dots far below were not gulls but gannets.

URSULA STUBBINGS, MAY 2015

I flew to Shetland for a week and on the fourth attempt managed to reach Foula in the wonderful little plane. The perfect weather made it well worth waiting for and both the Marilyns were a joy. There was also time to visit the fantastically-equipped primary school with sadly at present only one pupil, nine-year-old Jack. He had written a guide to the island that mentioned there are many bonxies: 'they are very fierce, they can kill you'.

I persuaded some other hostellers from the excellent Lerwick hostel to take part in a local quiz evening. A member of the team on the next table came and greeted me like a long-lost friend, and it turned out we had taught together in Cambridge. He had married the sister of the Foula pilot and was now the local minister.

Ward Hill, Fair Isle

Knitwear, seabirds and the shipping forecast have made Fair Isle far more well-known than Foula, and it has been used to welcoming visitors for many years, with the chance for birders to glimpse a rare migrant. For many years the traditional way of reaching the island has been on the Good Shepherd from Grutness on Shetland Mainland, which often provided visitors with a roller-coaster ride through the wild Atlantic for over two hours. In 2016 a study recommended its replacement with a more accessible ferry service, but this long-term project was still in progress in 2024. For those able to afford the fare and take their chances with wind and availability, the aerial route offers a shorter and more appealing altenative.

ALAN DAWSON, AUGUST 2007

A lovely island, reached by a brilliant flight, with wonderful cliffs and coastal scenery. The summit was a rubbish dump of large ugly concrete blocks, apparently the result of the destruction of wartime relics so that they would not detract from a fleeting royal visit in 1959. The island residents had been trying to decide what to do about the resulting mess ever since and did not want to be rushed into a decision. The highest point amongst all the rubble has no spot height on OS maps but is about three metres higher than the trig pillar.

——— Orkney Islands ———

Large island group, with Marilyns on four of the islands

Marilyns: 9
Highest and most prominent: Ward Hill, Hoy, 481m
Lowest: Fitty Hill, Westray, 169.4m
Least prominent: Keelylang Hill, Mainland, 160m drop

IO01 Hoy

The island of Hoy, served by ferry from Orkney Mainland

RHB section 23   OS maps 6, 7

Number	Height	Name	Drop	Location	Summit
1549	481	Ward Hill	481	HY 2286 0224	Cairn near trig
1550	435	Cuilags	319	HY 2099 0336	Cairn
1551	399	Knap of Trowieglen	354	ND 2397 9846	Boulder near trig

The most famous feature of Hoy is its Old Man, a tottering pinnacle of rock on the west coast. Its relative height is only 118 metres, so it is well short of Marilyn status. It is easier to reach than the sea stacks of St Kilda but not easier to climb. The three Hoy Marilyns offer the only significant hill walking in the whole island group, but Orkney Mainland and some of the smaller islands are not short of other attractions.

IO02 Mainland-ronaldsay

Orkney Mainland and the islands of Burray and South Ronaldsay, connected by road bridges

RHB section 23   OS maps 6, 7

Number		Height	Name	Drop	Location	Summit
1552		275	Mid Hill	275	HY 3353 0870	Mound
1554	T	225.6	Wideford Hill	170	HY 4114 1161	Viewfinder near trig
1556		221	Keelylang Hill	160	HY 3780 1025	Cairn
1555		224	Milldoe	188	HY 3582 2070	Mound near trig

IO03 Rousay-westray

The islands of Rousay and Westray, both served by ferries from Orkney Mainland

RHB section 23   OS maps 5, 6

Number		Height	Name	Drop	Location	Summit
1553		250	Blotchnie Field, Rousay	250	HY 4181 2892	Grass
1557	T	169.4	Fitty Hill, Westray	169.4	HY 4297 4487	Trig

Wideford Hill, Mainland

PAUL RICHARDSON, AUGUST 1999

Kirkwall youth hostel had bikes for hire, so this was my first hill climbed by bike. Two miles on a minor road brought us to a narrow lane that climbed steeply towards the hill. We were soon pushing the bikes but easier gradients later gave us the chance to cycle parts of the road. From the trig pillar and masts at the top, the view was a patchwork of sea and land. We swooped down to a bend in the road and branched off to a chambered cairn, which we accessed through a hole in its roof, a trap door and a ladder. A box near the entrance housed a torch, which helped us descend into the 4500-year-old tomb.

Blotchnie Field, Rousay

AUDREY LITTERICK, 2004

What a magic place Orkney is. It has nine Marilyns, most of them easy, some spectacular scenery, especially on Hoy, and enough history and wildlife to keep me mesmerised for our week-long visit. I wanted an unusual hill for my 600th and Blotchnie Field provided a brilliant day out.

The morning dawns clear and bright and I set off past a prehistoric chambered cairn and up past a heavily-wooded dell around a substantial but ruined Victorian mansion. Up through the heather onto the hill. At a shallow angle of peat hags near the top, I decide to sunbathe for a short while, laying my head on my rucksack.

WHOOSH! I open my eyes and sit up, to locate a seabird wheeling round, eyeing me all the time. It is coming at me. And then it is practically about to hit me. I duck.

WHOOSH! Inches from my head. Its dead, black eye like a shark. The bonxie. Known outside the Northern Isles as the great skua. They attack walkers and kill other seabirds, don't they? Or is it the other way around? It's coming at me again and I am angry, my peace disturbed. I jump and swing my camera case at it. It sees this and effortlessly wheels out the way. But instead of giving up, it just keeps on coming. I pick up some stones and crouch so it attacks low. I like wildlife, but something about this bird, pirate of the sea, killer of other birds, engenders a great dislike in me. Britain is a country of passive wildlife, and the bonxie is a shock. If it hit my head with that beak at that speed, it would make a fair old hole. I flee for the summit, and the bonxie does not follow.

A fine summit, with Orkney Mainland and other islands surrounding – green, smooth, streamlined swellings – and browner moors north and west on Rousay itself. I don't want to head downhill so soon on such a fine day, so I continue the walk round to Knitchen Hill, an even better viewpoint back to Mainland, dodging bonxies again.

Rousay is fantastic. I have caught this small community on a good day. I walk round to the island shop, a place with just about everything for sale and adverts for a local dance and many other activities. On the walk back to the hostel a car stops to offer a lift and I squeeze in the back, the driver a teenager home for the summer from university, with his happy, Orcadian-accented granny in the back.

Cuilags, Hoy

Rackwick was almost, but not quite, a ghost village, with few permanent residents and only a scattering of houses. It is dominated by two features – cliffs and hills. In a tight cirque above the curve of shingle and bookend headlands, all three Marilyns were in monolithic mode. On a morning of rare perfection I wanted a greedy round of the lot.

An anti-clockwise direction seemed best, leaving the Old Man as a coda for the walk. Steep grass had the merit of elevating me quickly to the high moorland of the Knap of Trowieglen. I threaded my way between numerous bogs and small pools to attain the walled trig on the summit. I was almost back at sea level, so the re-ascent up to the Howes of Quoyawa looked intimidating. This shoulder of Ward Hill has a much more evocative name than the summit, which reprised the wonderful views already witnessed.

All of the lost height had to be regained on the trudge up to Cuilags. The going underfoot was easy despite the steepness, vegetation being short cropped. I enjoyed a sensational airy prospect across the low-lying green archipelago. A moorland plod on easy ground took me over Sui Fea to the abrupt end of the moor and a transition to an entirely different landscape. I was promenading along the edge of red sandstone cliffs with the top of the billing directly ahead. The Old Man of Hoy adds an element of fantasy to an already incredible vista. Viewed from above, the most fascinating aspect of this celebrated rock stack is its apparent fragility – it appears top-heavy and taunting reality, a natural Leaning Tower of Pisa. Any thought of climbing the thing verged on the insane.

—— Lewis and Harris ——

Large island group, with forty Marilyns on the main island and five on small uninhabited islands

Marilyns: 45
Highest and most prominent: An Cliseam, 800m
Lowest and least prominent: Mullach Buidhe, Garbh Eilean, 161.8m

LH01 Cliseam-conostom

North Harris and the central part of Lewis, either side of Loch Langabhat

RHB sections 24A, 24B   OS maps 13, 14

Number		Height	Name	Drop	Location	Summit
1587	A	800.0	An Cliseam	800.0	NB 1547 0732	Rock
1588	A	730.1	Uisgneabhal Mor	483	NB 1209 0858	Rock by cairn
1591		579	Stulabhal	224	NB 1334 1222	Rock by trig
1589	A	680.0	Tiorga Mor	590	NB 0555 1151	Rock by trig
1590	A	662.2	Oireabhal	420	NB 0839 0998	Rock near cairn
1593	A	556.9	Ceartabhal	146.5	NB 0425 1269	Rock
1596		489	Huiseabhal Mor	272	NB 0226 1160	Cairn
1592		559	Sgaoth Aird	373	NB 1658 0398	Shelter cairn
1594	T	528.3	Todun	390	NB 2102 0296	Trig
1564		492	Liuthaid	307	NB 1753 1362	Cairn on rock
1571		378	Cearnabhal	160	NB 1864 1574	Outcrop by cairn
1576		281	Roineabhal	203	NB 2330 2122	Shelter
1580	L	246.5	Sleteachal Mhor	160.4	NB 2133 1878	Boulder
1578		256	Conostom	211	NB 1665 2996	Outcrop near trig
1581		228	Coltraiseal Mor	161	NB 1587 2278	Cairn

LH02 Mealaisbhal-tathabhal

The hilly western part of Lewis, to the north of Loch Reasort and west of Loch Rog Beag

RHB section 24A   OS map 13

Number	Height	Name	Drop	Location	Summit
1559	574	Mealaisbhal	516	NB 0220 2703	Cairn
1561	515	Tathabhal	252	NB 0423 2634	Cairn
1562	514	Cracabhal	221	NB 0297 2528	Cairn
1563	497	Griomabhal	179	NB 0120 2200	Rock near trig
1570	397	Beinn Mheadhanach	253	NB 0905 2358	Cairn
1567	428	Suaineabhal	313	NB 0779 3087	Rock near cairn
1583	205	Forsnabhal	163	NB 0614 3587	Cairn

LH03 Beinnmhor-gormol

The Pairc peninsula, east of Loch Seaforth and south of Loch Eireasort

RHB section 24A   OS maps 13, 14

Number		Height	Name	Drop	Location	Summit
1560		572	Beinn Mhor	558	NB 2544 0953	Cairn
1566		449	Caiteseal	285	NB 2421 0438	Cairn
1568		424	Muaitheabhal	207	NB 2579 1145	Cairn
1569	A	405.2	Guaineamol *	167	NB 2604 1339	Rock
1573		336	Cipeagal Bheag	173	NB 2476 0646	Outcrop by cairn
1574	T	327.5	Feiriosbhal	252	NB 3012 1462	Trig

1565		470	Gormol	322	NB 3018 0691	Cairn
1572		374	Uisinis	231	NB 3374 0561	Cairn
1584		191	Beinn Bhreac	158	NB 4068 1210	Cairn

LH04 Beinndhubh-roineabhal

South Harris, south of Tarbert

RHB section 24B   OS maps 14, 18

Number		Height	Name	Drop	Location	Summit
1595	T	506.4	Beinn Dhubh	493	NB 0896 0063	Rock near trig
1597		460	Roineabhal	408	NG 0425 8608	Boulder near trig
1599		398	Bleabhal	335	NG 0304 9144	Rock by trig
1602		368	Ceapabhal	363	NF 9720 9243	Rock
1605		280	Greabhal	194	NG 0038 8916	Cairn
1600		389	An Coileach	326	NG 0862 9278	Cairn
1601		384	Heileasbhal Mor	177	NG 0735 9274	Cairn

LH05 Mholach-muirneag

The northernmost and flattest part of Lewis, west and north of Stornoway

RHB section 24A   OS map 8

Number		Height	Name	Drop	Location	Summit
1575		292	Beinn Mholach	253	NB 3556 3870	Cairn
1577	A	261.9	**Beinn Bhragair *****	150.9	NB 2668 4326	Cairn
1579		248	Muirneag	170	NB 4796 4893	Cairn near trig

LH06 Scarp-taransay

The uninhabited islands of Scarp, Taransay and Pabbay, to the west of Lewis-Harris

RHB sections 24B, 24C   OS maps 13, 18

Number		Height	Name	Drop	Location	Summit
1603	T	308.5	Sron Romul, Scarp	308.5	NA 9686 1582	Rock by trig
1606		267	Beinn Ra, Taransay	267	NB 0344 0190	Cairn near trig
1621		196	Beinn a' Charnain, Pabbay	196	NF 8939 8847	Rock near trig

LH07 Seaforth-shiant

Seaforth Island in Loch Seaforth and the Shiant Islands to the east of Lewis-Harris

RHB section 24A   OS maps 13, 14

Number		Height	Name	Drop	Location	Summit
1582		217	Seaforth Island / Eilean Shiophoirt	217	NB 2075 1104	Rock
1586	L	161.8	Mullach Buidhe, Garbh Eilean	161.8	NG 4148 9864	Mound

Beinn Bhragair

This hill was one of fifteen Marilyns added in 1995 after detailed research on large-scale maps. Its status was confirmed by a GNSS survey in 2015. Three of the fifteen were later demoted after a survey (Giur-bheinn and Lovely Seat) or Lidar data study (Cheriton Hill).

An Cliseam

ALAN DAWSON, SEPTEMBER 2021

Western Isles weather does not always follow the same pattern as the mainland. While the Highlands were having a heatwave, rain and wind pounded Harris for six days in a row. On three of the better days I went up Tiorga Mor, Oireabhal and Uisgneabhal Mhor, keeping each walk as short as possible, but the weather was dismal on each of them. On my final day I blinked my way up An Cliseam and along its excellent western ridge in unfamiliar sunshine. Was the sky really blue or was it illusion?

The walk proved to be worthwhile as well as rewarding, for I found that a rock 25 metres from the trig pillar was a metre higher than the OS map figure. My survey result was 799.99 metres, but it is not realistic to claim accuracy to the nearest centimetre, so it has been rounded up to 800m. A sea level rise of only 5cm would be enough to round it down to 799.9m but it should not be rounded down to 799m until the sea has risen by half a metre. Probably not the most serious consequence of global warming.

Tiorga Mor, Oireabhal and Uisgneabhal Mhor

COLIN CRAWFORD, OCTOBER 2005

A week was surely time enough to gather in a few summits in the Western Isles, but the weather laughed in my face as the isles were swept by the autumnal fronts. Three challenging hills on Harris remained outstanding with only one day remaining. I could, of course, have left them for another time, but the day began with the barest hint of promise. By the time the bus had delivered me to Abhainn Suidhe, the fair-weather window was already passing. I splashed my way up the track, then up tolerable slopes to reach the moss-enveloped trig point on Tiorga Mor, where I was met with a gale-force wind. I thumped the trig before diving for cover down the eastern slopes.

I crossed from Ulabhal to Oireabhal like a scuttling beetle below the crest of the ridge. The tops cleared but it was no time for halting to admire the view. I plummeted down the corrie to the base of Sron Scourst, glad to be in a relative calm, then fought my way up Gleann Uisleitir and on to Uisgneabhal Mhor. Somehow I found the determination to add Teileasbhal before enduring the long boggy miles out to the road. The day had moments of blustery exhilaration but could not be called enjoyable, yet it was remarkably satisfying in retrospect. It was a grim little expedition in the execution, but in hindsight I felt vindication in having claimed the summits against the odds.

Uisgneabhal Mhor

AUDREY LITTERICK, 2007

This walk (or rather stagger, grunt and crawl) was completed with two relatively novice hill walking colleagues who had never experienced anything quite like it. Harris was in the throes of an extremely wild Scottish winter day. Snow was down to about 150m and there was a considerable amount of it – deep and slabby lower down, brick hard higher up. Demonstrating good sense, my friends bailed out in zero visibility a few hundred metres from the summit and crouched down behind a boulder, sheltering from the teeth of a violent, screaming, hail-laden gale. They struggled to believe that they had allowed themselves to be dragged up there and at a loss as to why anyone should wish to waste time, let alone risk life and limb crawling with the aid of an ice-axe, to the summit precipice. It felt more like an alpine peak than a medium-sized hill on Harris – magic!

An Cliseam

Taransay and South Harris from the slopes of An Cliseam

On Pabbay, west of Harris, waiting for the boat to return

Huiseabhal Mor

LESLIE BARRIE, JULY 2001

Lunch was taken near the summit in a sheltered spot above the crags, in a rock seat perfectly sculpted by nature. The view from this perch was magnificent, with a fine sandy beach far below and the sun shimmering on Loch Crabhadail. The walk from that beach around the headland to Huisinis was truly memorable. The colours were vivid, the sea turquoise, the machair carpeted in wild flowers, so it was no surprise to come across an artist who was busy capturing the scene in oils.

Ceapabhal

LESLIE BARRIE, JULY 2001

This is truly a gem of a hill, with the machair on the approach a carpet of wild flowers and one of the finest viewpoints from any of the Marilyns I've climbed so far. The clarity of visibility was exceptional. The tide was out, showing the surrounding white beaches in all their splendour. The peaks of Skye and Torridon were sharp in the excellent light, as was the equally fine view down the chain of islands that form the Uists.

Greabhal

CHRIS PEARSON, MAY 2001

Greabhal was a strong contender for view of the year award, with hills, golden sandy beaches, green fields, shapely mountains, moors, glinting lochans, white scattered crofts, shimmering sea, little islands, big islands, waves, blue empty sky and a dipping sun.

HELEN MCLAREN, JULY 2002

The day was truly miserable. It was also World Cup Final day. However, Pete and I agreed that any hill is preferable to any football match so we headed for Greabhal as it was the only thing not lost in clag. By some curious coincidence, there we were, with our copy of The Relative Hills of Britain lying on the dashboard, getting ready to climb one of Alan Dawson's hills in the rain, just about the time Alan was letting himself and others into our warm, dry house to put his feet up in front of the television with a few beers.

Caiteseal to Guaineamol

PHIL COOPER, MAY 2006

After a deal with a boatman to take us to Seaforth Island had fallen through, some fish farmers agreed to ferry two boat-loads to Seaforth Island and on to Pairc across the loch. We all climbed Caiteseal but only Alison Richardson, Alan Dawson and I were up for the long walk out of this superb area, over Ciopeagal Bheag, Beinn Mhor, Muaitheabhal and Guaineamol to Seaforth Head, where Alan had left his car in the morning. We were so happy at salvaging a superb afternoon's walk from a day starting with disappointment.

Beinn Mholach

CHRIS PEARSON, MAY 2000

The view was extensive and superb, but the approach over 5km of flat pathless bog and peat hags must surely deter recreational walkers. Most hills slope upward from the start so that you feel like you are actually getting somewhere. After two hours of desert-like solitude on my lonely mission I finally returned to the oasis of the road, only to be shouted at by an irate fisherman sitting in a hut by a loch. Having apparently never seen anyone set off for the hill in the past twenty years, he had had to contend with people going past his hut window all afternoon and was rather cheesed off. The summit of Beinn Mholach was a checkpoint on a three-day Western Isles Challenge event.

Muirneag and Beinn Mholach

ALAN DAWSON, MAY 2006

It was 6pm by the time I got to NB532486. With mist down to the road and intermittent rain, it took a lot of willpower to get going, but I had nowhere to stay and nothing else to do. The first 500 metres along the track-cum-pier were fine, but after that it was a grim wade, with an odd glimpse of distant land ahoy as Muirneag loomed out of the mist and vanished again, never seeming to get any nearer. When a slight incline was finally reached, the going was even worse. The muddy mess at the summit was a fittingly filthy anti-climax, though I did find two full cans of fizzy drink amongst the piles of rubbish.

I landed back at the car after 3½ hours that felt like a week and moved on. North Lewis was redeemed by Beinn Bhragair later that same night. The next day, the relentless lumpiness of Beinn Mholach made me appreciate the wet flatness of the approach to Muirneag. The terrain on Cairnsmore in Galloway was worse but it did not last for long, so Beinn Mholach received my vote for the least enjoyable Marilyn.

Beinn Bhragair

VICTORIA REID, 2005

The weather for the first two days was pretty dire, with rain and clag down to about 150 metres. Hardly attractive hill walking weather. A brief window in the weather after a trip to Stornoway gave us the chance to bag our first hill of the trip. After driving out to Siabost, we drove along a small straight road to Pairc Shiaboist, where there was a dead-end with a gate, but a full view of our hill – Beinn Bhragair. We left the car at this gate and walked the 2km to the foot of the hill, though you could actually drive along this road, something we never worked out until we realised it led straight up to the hill. Beinn Bhragair is a very rocky hill, and so held a little more excitement than the usual Lewis abundance of heather and bogs. It was a fairly easy ascent, and we were at the top in no time. The views from Beinn Bhragair were spectacular. On one side were mountains rising to the clouds, whereas on the other side was the complete opposite, the landscape being one of the flattest I have ever seen, with the only bump in the horizon being the most northerly Lewis Marilyn – Muirneag. My father described this hill as a heathery bump in the middle of nowhere when he went over it during the Western Isles challenge.

Sron Romul, Scarp

JON METCALF, 2005

Scarp was far more like it after mundane Seaforth Island, although it was a real rush to get from the drop-off slipway to the top and back in the three hours available. The excellent deserted village near the start merited far more time than we were able to give it, but the striking views of St Kilda and the Monach Islands were superb compensation from the summit. Afterwards we took in the nearby island of Mealista, too low for Marilyn status but large enough to be listed in the Hamish Haswell-Smith islands guide. This has become another list to tick which I would never have picked up if I had not stumbled across Alan's book on a wet afternoon in Fort William.

BRENT LYNAM, MAY 2006

Forgetting to take your compass and getting lost on a small island for two hours in low cloud wouldn't be so bad, but keeping the boatman waiting and avoiding a coastguard call-out by ten minutes was not good. The worst bit was taking thirty minutes to walk round in a circle, yet this was my favourite island of the whole Western Isles trip.

Beinn Ra, Taransay

CHRIS PEARSON, MAY 2001

We were joined by a group of five tourists going across for the day. As well as Beinn Ra we bagged the treble-zero point NB000000 and some stunning beaches, and were able to spy on the making of the film Rocketman on the beach below. Apparently it was telling the true story of a German who tried to get mail from Scarp to the mainland by rocket. From what we could see they were filming the bit where the rocket man wanders around for a while then lies in the sun all day. We also wandered around the recently abandoned Castaway 2000 buildings from the televised year-long experiment where 36 strangers lived together to build a self-sufficient community, including then unknown Ben Fogle.

Mullach Buidhe, Garbh Eilean

JON METCALF, 2005

Basking sharks on the way out from Stornoway were all good and fine, but it wasn't until the Shiant Islands finally loomed out of the sea haze that I started to believe we would finally land there. And yet horrors! On all sides the main island, Garbh Eilean, seemed to be flanked by precipitous drops. As we went through the pantomime of landing the party by toy dinghy, the boatman darkly warned of there being only one way up.

A series of twisting ledges and gullies were negotiated using wisps of vegetation, then I missed an easy traverse into a gully and was faced with a horrid line up through crags at the bounds of my psychological comfort. I didn't find a ledge big enough to recover on until the top. The rewards for the climb included stunning cliff views and a fine dram from Ann Bowker to celebrate what she thought would be her last new Marilyn. Back at the cliff we elected to descend a grass gully that would have been suicidal if the grass were damp. Thankfully, it led down fairly simply to an enjoyable scramble round the coastal boulders back to the landing point. Our trip back was blessed with easy and plentiful mackerel fishing, which provided a splendid supper back at the cottage.

PHIL COOPER, JUNE 2006

After a voyage from Stornoway by RIB, three of us struggled up the steep ascent to the plateau and on to the summit. We then made our way down steep grassy slopes on the east side, leading to a boulder-field inhabited by vast colonies of seabirds, including fulmar, great skua, great black-backed gull, herring gull, shag, puffin, guillemot and razorbill. We were there on the first permitted public access day as the nesting season drew to a close, and the last entry in the bothy book was the previous July. A pleasant stroll on Eilean an Taighe, with its 125m summit, almost concluded a brilliant outing, before fishing lessons from the skipper and a bumpier and wetter return to Stornoway.

PETER MALONE, JUNE 2006

A close friend with 55 years of boating experience offered to take me from Lochcarron to the Western Isles. After loading vast quantities of food and drink aboard his converted fishing boat, we set sail for Harris and anchored at a safe sheltered mooring on the idyllic Loch Bhalamuis, east of Loch Seaforth. This natural harbour is five hours walking from the nearest road. We watched otters and seals play while enjoying our drams. Gormol, Caiteseal and Ciopeagal Bheag involved spectacular walking to splendid isolated hills. Next it was on to the Shiant Islands for Mullach Buidhe. A steep but easy grassy gully led to the summit plateau, where I came across the entire bleached skeleton of a ewe in a bog, still standing where she had become trapped, to suffer a slow and painful death.

—— North and South Uist ——

Large pair of islands linked by causeways, together with Benbecula and Eriskay

Marilyns:	17
Highest and most prominent:	Beinn Mhor, South Uist, 620.5m drop
Lowest and least prominent:	Crogearraidh na Thobha, North Uist, 151m drop

IU01 Southuist-eriskay

The islands of South Uist and Eriskay, connected by a causeway opened in 2001

RHB section 24C

Number		Height	Name	Drop	Location	Summit
1608	AL	620.5	Beinn Mhor	620.5	NF 8085 3110	Rock near trig
1609	A	606.6	Heacla / Thacla	309.0	NF 8255 3449	Outcrop by cairn
1610	AL	525.7	Beinn Choradail	226.4	NF 8196 3285	Cairn
1611	T	374.7	Stulabhal	370	NF 8068 2411	Grass by trig
1612		357	Triuirebheinn	256	NF 8127 2126	Cairn
1615		276	Beinn Ruigh Choinnich	170	NF 8065 1967	Cairn on outcrop
1617	L	254.9	Airneabhal	175.7	NF 7851 2559	Rock
1618	L	242.5	Easabhal	238.3	NF 7740 1582	Cairn
1620	T	201.5	Roineabhal	152.6	NF 8169 1404	Rock by trig
1623		186	Beinn Sgritheann, Eriskay	186	NF 7952 1122	Outcrop by trig

IU02 Northuist-benbecula

The islands of North Uist and Benbecula. All seven Marilyns are on North Uist.

RHB section 24C

Number		Height	Name	Drop	Location	Summit
1613	T	347.5	Eabhal	347.5	NF 8989 6051	Trig
1614		281	South Lee / Li a' Deas	275	NF 9187 6532	Cairn on outcrop
1616		263	North Lee / Li a' Tuath	175	NF 9270 6601	Outcrop by cairn
1619	T	230.8	Maireabhal	223	NF 8086 7002	Grass near trig
1622	T	190.3	Beinn Mhor	185	NF 8980 7616	Trig
1624		180	Crogearraidh Mor	169	NF 8678 7317	Outcrop
1626	T	153.7	Crogearraidh na Thobha	151	NF 9747 7242	Trig

Heacla / Thacla

This hill is shown as Hecla on older OS maps and Hecla / Thacla on more recent maps, but in 2024 OS changed it again, to Heacla / Thacla. Numerous hill names in the Western Isles were Gaelicised on OS maps during the 1990s and 2000s, but for most walkers the names such as North Lee and Crogary na Hoe are easier to remember than the Gaelicised versions.

Roineabhal, South Uist

PHIL DANT, 2007

What I've loved about the Marilyns is the opportunity to bag some smaller peaks as my family have grown up. We climbed a fantastic hill in South Uist, Roineabhal, right on the southern tip overlooking Eriskay. We asked a retired English couple if we could go through part of their garden to access the beach, and they recommended walking along the beach as far as possible before climbing up the hill. It was an absolute delight, much better than slogging through long wet grass and heather, which I had originally planned. It kept the kids amused and they loved cliff-jumping onto the soft sand on the way back. The views across to Eriskay and Barra were stunning, which made up for the gale-force winds, making it difficult for my usual pedantic searches for the actual highest point.

Eabhal

ALAN DAWSON, AUGUST 2001

Sometimes you can take things for granted and not appreciate how lucky you are. Foot and mouth disease made it a difficult year for hill walking generally, and it was a difficult year for me personally, but my first trip to Barra and Uist was a remarkable success, as I climbed all 26 Marilyns in ten days of reasonable weather. Eabhal was the last of them and I certainly did not take it for granted as it was obviously a remarkable hill in a unique landscape. It was no surprise to learn later that some experienced hill baggers had nominated it as their favourite hill.

ANDREW TEMPLETON, 2004

An utterly absorbing hill. The approach from Sidinish ended with a dash to the summit before the incoming shower cheated us of the view. On North Lee later we met an Aussie staring incredulously over the loch-studded interior, which he likened to a film set.

PHIL DANT, 2007

The highlight of the year was undoubtedly Eabhal on North Uist. This hill has got to be the best I've ever climbed anywhere. Yes, I've done An Cliseam, Suilven, A' Mhaighdean and Beinn Sgritheall and the Cuillin, but Eabhal would get my vote for the best view in Britain. We climbed it on a perfect warm day with blue skies, crystal clear water and no clouds. Less than 350m high but a remote walk via some tricky tidal stepping stones, skirting a lochan over the purple heathery moorland, near gorgeous seascapes, and ascending steep tussocky slopes to a rocky summit vista with thousands of lochans spread beneath our feet. Near the summit the cliffs fall away almost vertically, offering a fantastic platform for spectacular shots of the unbelievable landscape and water-scape, with views across to Harris, Skye, the rest of Uist and St Kilda out to the west.

MILES HUTCHINSON, SEPTEMBER 2012

After climbing my 1000th Marilyn at age 90, I reckoned my favourite Marilyn of all was Eabhal on North Uist. Being perched up there above that maze of lochans was magical.

North Lee and South Lee (Li a' Deas and Li a' Tuath)

BERT BARNETT, MAY 2003

The 2pm ferry to Lochmaddy sailed out of the rain into the sunshine, and I headed over fine moorland to bag the Lees, with greylag geese overhead calling their passage. Despite the lochs on the map this was an excellent outing and navigation was no problem. Views of Eabhal and the Benbecula lochs dominated, with dog violet bright. Maireabhal was a dull-looking lump, but halfway up I turned to see an amazing view of St Kilda. I could identify Dun, Conachair, Stac Lee, Boreray and Stac an Armin. Camped nearby with snipe and lapwing for company.

AUDREY LITTERICK, 2010

A summer work trip took me to North Uist. North and South Lee just sat there in the sun, waiting to be climbed on my day off. Characterful wee mountains, rocky in places, with good scrambling here and there. The day was clear and breezy to keep down the midgies, and the views were stunning in every direction. Countless lochans all around the mountains, glinting black and silver, with the Cuillin and Rum off to the south-east and St Kilda clearly visible out to the west.

Crogary na Hoe (Crogearraidh na Thobha)

Victoria Reid, 2005

Dad had said there were easy pickings on North Uist and that we could do four hills in the one day. I agreed with my younger brothers, Cameron and Fraser, that two would be a more realistic target, as we wanted to go horse riding as well that day. According to my dad, the first hill we would go up was the second lowest Marilyn on the list – Crogary na Hoe, a boggy little flog. The most amazing thing about this hill was the road you had to drive to reach it. It was almost lower than sea level and you felt like you were in a boat rather than in your car. If global warming continues this road will probably disappear! After a quick bite of lunch at the car, it was off again to do Beinn Mhor. This was an easy straight-up-and-down-from-the-road kind of hill, but when we had finished, that was enough for us juniors. We waited in the car while dad bagged his third hill, Crogary Mor, and while we were horse riding he did the last hill of the day, Marrival.

Eabhal and Harris from the slopes of Heacla on South Uist (Robert Poole)

Beinn Sgritheann on Eriskay

──── Barra and nearby islands ────

The islands of Barra, Vatersay, Mingulay, Sandray, Berneray, Pabbay and Muldoanich

Marilyns: 9
Highest and most prominent: Heabhal, Barra, 384m
Lowest and least prominent: Muldoanich, 153.7m

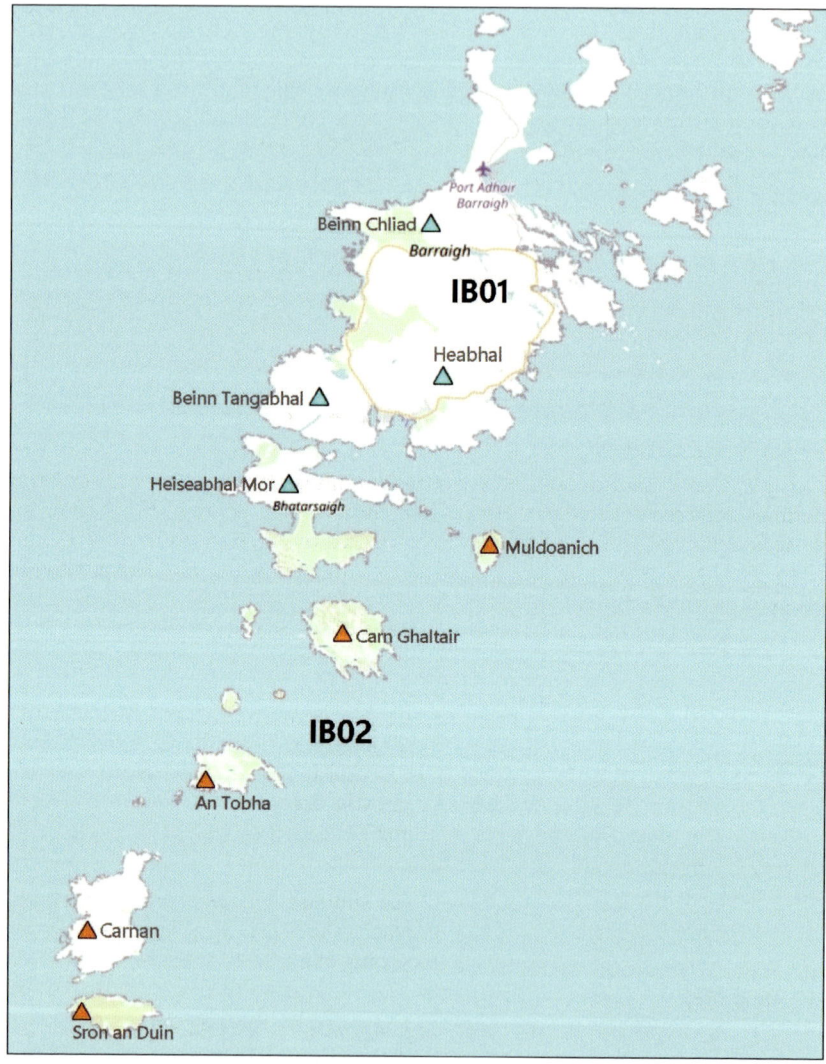

There's an absence of comfortable furniture, between Vatersay and Berneray
These islands have no chairs or couches, the landings will not suit slow slouches
Castlebay has a castle, but to get there is rather a hassle
It's easier to wander up Hecla, or sit by the shore in a deckchair

IB01 Barra-vatersay

The islands of Barra and Vatersay, connected by a bridge

RHB section 24D   OS map 31

Number		Height	Name	Drop	Location	Summit
1627		384	Heabhal	384	NL 6781 9941	Rock by trig
1631		206	Beinn Chliaid	159	NF 6780 0428	Cairn on rock
1628		332	Beinn Tangabhal	309	NL 6388 9906	Trig
1633	T	190.5	Heiseabhal Mor, Vatersay	190.5	NL 6266 9635	Trig

IB02 Mingulay-sandray

The small, uninhabited islands of Mingulay, Sandray, Berneray, Pabbay and Muldoanich

RHB section 24D   OS map 31

Number		Height	Name	Drop	Location	Summit
1629	T	273.4	Carnan, Mingulay	273.4	NL 5530 8280	Trig
1630		207	Carn Ghaltair, Sandray	207	NL 6402 9154	Trig on outcrop
19345		197	Sron an Duin, Berneray **	197	NL 5486 8023	Rock by wall
1634	T	171.4	An Tobha, Pabbay	171.4	NL 5938 8725	Rock by trig
1635	T	153.7	Muldoanich / Maol Domhnaich	153.7	NL 6889 9402	Rock by trig

Sron an Duin, Berneray

Berneray is the southernmost of the five main uninhabited islands south of Barra, It is sometimes referred to as Barra Head, the southernmost point of the island. In 2017, large-scale mapping with 5-metre contours showed the highest point to be by the cliffs next to the lighthouse, and about 600 metres further west than Sotan, the summit location originally listed.

Carnan, Mingulay

JON METCALF, 1999

Mingulay needs much more than the scant two hours available to us, owing to the boatman's immutable 10:30 start. Sandwiches shared with puffins at five feet away was magical. Ace cliffs and stacks and views of Berneray, but no time to poke around the village. On Berneray an easy track led to ghostly deserted lighthouse buildings – fine outside but crumbling internally, with a gannet's eye view down on bird city.

JONATHAN APPLEBY, 2005

Carnan on Mingulay was the highlight of the summer, with the boat trip, the basking sharks, the ruined village, the sheltered beach, the walk along the sea cliffs and the multitude of seabirds. A great day, with something of interest for all the family.

PHIL COOPER, 2006

One of the highlights of the year was Mingulay, with seals basking on the beach, a fine horseshoe walk to include the summit, and the story of MacPhee who was abandoned alone on the island when visitors feared he had been in contact with deceased residents who had the plague. Our group sang the Mingulay Boat Song as we approached the island. It tells how the community fought against the odds to sustain itself and eventually had to give up in 1912.

Carn Ghaltair, Sandray

JON METCALF, 1999

Brilliant walking in strong sun and a welcome wind shadow. Easy-angled rock plates made for pleasant going, and good sunbathing, looking over a clump of four ruins not on the map. No clumpy, straggly grass due to the harsh climate, but a real wealth of orchids and other flora. A walk through from one bay to another was arranged and the boatman picked us up from the far side of the island.

ALAN DAWSON, JULY 2001

The islands trip was so enjoyable that I became engrossed in the superb surroundings and forgot to keep track of various landmarks until the summit of Sandray, which turned out to be a 500th, a 1200th and a 1300th Marilyn for various members of our group, as well as Ann Bowker's 1545th. It was probably my favourite island of the group – not as rugged as Muldoanich but with a lovely beach and little sign of human influence.

CAMPBELL SINGER, MAY 2009

After a very wet trip to Skye in early May I was recompensed by good weather on Barra later in the month. I enjoyed the amazing experience of being taken through the natural arch on the west coast of Mingulay by expert boatman Donald McLeod. The day got even better as we witnessed eagles within 50 metres of us on Berneray and Mingulay and then within ten metres on Sandray. I don't know who got the bigger shock as the huge bird rose from beneath the crags, with me standing a few feet away on the summit, observing the stunning views of the chain of little islands. Days just don't get any better than this.

An Tobha, Pabbay

JON METCALF, 1999

Highlight of the best day's walking I could remember for ages was Pabbay. More of the same great platey rock to walk on, great views north and south, a shag parliament on the way into the landing bay, a confluence of eroded dykes, and the burial mound and rune stone in the settlement.

Muldoanich

JON METCALF, 1999

Muldoanich was hardest of the five islands to access – up steep rocks and steeper grass for 30-40 metres to a more level area. Good stuff once you avoid the back-flip into the sea. There was a two-room ruin which the boatman told us used to be a jail.

ALAN DAWSON, JULY 2001

The combination of a rarely-visited island, difficult landing, steep ascent and lowest hill in the list all helped to give a buzz of excitement along with enjoyment and satisfaction.

IAIN BROWN, JULY 2010

Michael Earnshaw had organised an islands trip but the wind and rain were horrendous when we arrived in Castlebay. We arranged to meet the boatman at 3pm the next day to discuss the chances of the boat sailing at all. One of the party had given up and was heading for Eriskay when a stranger he was giving a lift to told him about the meeting with the boatman. He turned around and arrived just in time. The weather had improved dramatically by then so it was decided to go for all five islands. We set off at 3.15pm and returned to Castlebay at 11.35pm, just as it was getting dark.

——— IX01 St Kilda ———

Small group of four islands and two sea stacks in the Atlantic Ocean, over 60 km from North Uist

Marilyns: 6
Highest and most prominent: Conachair, Hirta, 430.0m
Lowest and least prominent: Stac Lee, 172.2m

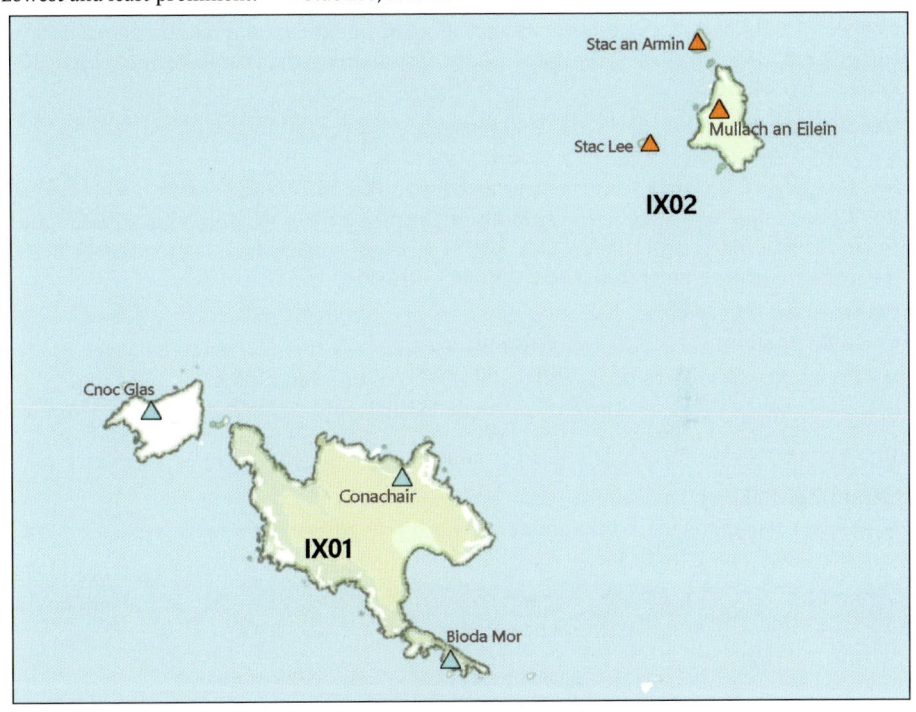

IX01 Hirta-soay

The islands of Hirta, Soay and Dun

RHB section 25   OS map 18

Number		Height	Name	Drop	Location	Summit
1636	L	430.0	Conachair, Hirta	430.0	NA 0998 0022	Cairn
1638	L	379.5	Cnoc Glas, Soay	379.5	NA 0625 0161	Cairn
1640	L	178.5	Bioda Mor, Dun	178.5	NF 1042 9734	Mound

IX02 Boreray-lee

The island of Boreray and two nearby sea stacks

RHB section 25   OS map 18

Number		Height	Name	Drop	Location	Summit
1637	L	384.3	Mullach an Eilein, Boreray	384.3	NA 1536 0534	Grass
1639	L	197.3	Stac an Armin	197.3	NA 1513 0641	Outcrop
1641	L	172.2	Stac Lee	172.2	NA 1422 0491	Cairn

Conachair, Hirta

BARBARA JONES, 2002

David and I had a relatively smooth crossing to St Kilda in our own yacht. We got a grilling from the guy in charge and weren't sure if we would be allowed to land, as foot-and-mouth restrictions had only been lifted the day before. We had an evening ashore round the military bit, a morning doing the round of Conachair, then sailed round the smaller islands and stacks before anchoring again in Village Bay and heading back to North Uist. Looking back, it is the military installations that come to mind first, and I have to work quite hard to conjure up the native St Kildan remains and the natural surroundings. I find that really 'special' places that have been hyped up often disappoint.

KEN WHYTE, JUNE 2002

My most vivid memories from the trip are of two things – coming across an abandoned JCB digger while approaching the summit of Conachair from the direction of the highest radar paraphernalia, and that monstrosity of a power house which is so carefully edited from official photographs. Talk about double standards!

BERT BARNETT, MAY 2003

Saturday 3 May, beautiful day. At Miabhaig harbour at 2.30pm were the Bowkers and the MV Cuma, a twelve-berth boat with double-bunk rooms, toilets, lounge and showers. On board we met the skipper, Murdo, first mate Findlay, and Cathy the cook. Our team was Rowland Bowker, Ann Bowker, Alan Dawson, Mary Cox, Rob Woodall, Chris Upson, Dave Butterfield, myself and Michael, a German living on Berneray. We weighed anchor and made for Loch Resort. Life on the ocean wave was fun.

After a hefty breakfast on Sunday we were put ashore and teams headed off their own ways. We chose Taran Mor – rough ground and breezy but enjoyable. Back on board, after tea and drams, Murdo brought the news that the weather was turning even windier, and he had to return to port, a four-hour trip. As we left the sea loch into the open sea, we had our first taste of big seas. The swell was side on, and the boat made some crazy dives. This was not pleasant and people were looking green.

On the Monday the boat is going nowhere so fresh plans are hatched. Dave and I head off in the rain to featureless Beinn Mholach and Conostom, a fine rocky traverse. Back on board for a big meal and whisky. Michael had abandoned ship due to the weather.

After breakfast on the Tuesday, Murdo reckoned that the force 5/6 forecast was worth a try for St Kilda, as the rest of the week was likely to be worse. As we headed out of the loch, the boat took on a life of its own and we dived inside. People turned green, some went below, some lay down and some buried their heads. Big degradable sick bags were brought out, and Findlay threw the full ones over the stern as required. I stood holding on to two tables, whooping when the boat dipped to a scary angle. Findlay, Alan and I talked cheerily. I suspect the others were beyond help. As we approached Boreray, Findlay encouraged me to peek round the side of the boat. Both hands were needed to stand up, and photos were difficult as we neared the stacks, shining in the sun and spray.

The run up to Hirta was a bit easier and the bay was flat, but it was already 6pm. We had sandwiches before taking the inflatable dinghy to the pier, where we were met by the warden, a new boy who was keen to stamp his authority. As the light began to fade he suggested a tour of the village. I politely advised him that we all intended to climb the hill without delay, and we left in a cloud of dust, with the runners going via Oiseabhal.

We briefly visited cleits and gazed down the cliffs, but were intent on Conachair. The evening light was dimming as we reached the top, but we were grateful for the good visibility. Tomorrow would be the day for absorption of landscape and history.

Looking out on the Wednesday morning, we were struck by the huge detrimental impact of the military establishment, the water storage up the hill and the numerous portakabins, the monstrous electricity generator building, the fuel-storage compound and the radar spheres on the hill. The place is a mess and undermines the potential for historic ambience in the village. Before the crew surfaced, channel 16 called out 'coastguard must speak to Murdo, strong winds approaching'. Force 11 had been mentioned. Before the toast was eaten, Murdo had the engine running and moved over to Dun. Puffins, fulmars, kittiwakes and gannets wheeled about. Disappointment was tempered by a tour of the Hirta cliffs and Soay channel, followed by close-ups of Stac Lee, Boreray and Stac an Armin. The sea was moderate, and one-handed camera shots were possible. As we moved away from the stacks the swell was not so bad and the wind was at our tail. We were heading for Scarp and a possible Marilyn, but the swell was high and the boat was pitching around, so a landing was not on. In the shelter of Scarp, Murdo told us we would have to head for port due to the threat of a north-east wind. The run home was not too bad, and we had a late meal, wines and whisky.

ANN BOWKER, MAY 2003

As obsessive travellers, Rowland and I had embarked on many a voyage heralded as our 'trip of a lifetime', but none deserved this accolade more than the prospect of a visit to St Kilda. It was indeed the culmination of a lifetime of peak-bagging, a chance to snatch one last summit and to see those rocky islands and stacks destined to elude me for ever.

On Tuesday morning we headed for St Kilda. The least said about that crossing the better. At last the violent lurching subsided and we anchored in Village Bay. Despite obvious relief at getting there, the scenery was disappointing with the hills presenting a bland and grassy face to the bay and the village dominated by ugly military buildings. The landing took two trips in the inflatable dinghy and we then had to stand around like schoolkids awaiting the bell while the newly-appointed warden read out the rules from his crib sheet: don't bring any cats and dogs or other animals on to the island, don't leave litter, not even food scraps, avoid disturbing birds, watch out for bonxies, and it is forbidden 'for your own safety' to walk alone.

He then started to tell us about the layout of the village and threatened us with the museum as the sun sank all too fast behind the hills. At last Bert Barnett broke in with: 'Now we'll tell you something. We are off up Conachair now while the sun is shining.'

To our relief, the warden accepted this and we were on our way, with Rob Woodall and Chris Upson running round all the hills in the two hours of remaining daylight and the rest of us content just to reach St Kilda's highest summit. I have to admit that I found Conachair a disappointing grassy plod. The summit was also an anti-climax after having read glowing descriptions of spectacular views of the highest cliffs in Britain. The reality was that a cautious peep over the rim revealed only the sea far below and compared unfavourably with the sensational Biod an Athair on Skye and my all-time favourite island summit on the Isle of Noss. At least there were lovely views of a stormy sunset behind Soay on the descent. I know I shall never go back. Although I was very glad in retrospect to have visited St Kilda, I failed to fall under that spell which all the literature claims inevitably draws visitors back to these islands again and again.

The crossing was as rough and unpleasant as we had feared. The first hour out from Miabhaig was not too bad but as we hit shallower water over the Flannan ridge the winds and waves notched up a few gears and it seemed stupid to be at sea for eight hours in a howling gale, with monstrous waves and a cyclonic swell. By the time we sighted Stac an Armin and Boreray, Bert and Rowland were the only others of our party still standing and well enough to have a look. The scene was sensational, surreal and stupendous. The massive cliffs belonged to the sea, the wind and the birds, so it was laughable to imagine that occasional landings by a few responsible enthusiasts would have any effect at all on this raw marine environment.

We were ashore for only two hours but there was plenty to see. We listened dutifully as the warden emphasised the unique natural and cultural heritage of the island. We were asked to tread gently and to show due respect. As time ticked on and he was stressing the importance of the by-laws and not leaving so much as a breadcrumb or an apple core to interfere with the delicate island ecosystem, I noticed over his shoulder a new van driving down the tarmac road towards the military installation.

Finally the lesson ended and we set off up Conachair, with strict warnings about staying inside the wall and not going near the edge. We were directed to head for some large metal storage tanks near a barn with a corrugated iron roof. The going was easy all the way and we reached the top before dark, so were rewarded with a fine view of the masts and buildings of the rocket-tracking station on the summit of Mullach Mor to the west. Time was short so we took a direct descent to the disused quarry and walked down the road toward the helipad. We headed across an expansive concrete apron adorned by two large rusting containers and hurried past a row of oil drums towards the large generator building with squat blackened chimneys. It was getting dark, so we didn't pay much attention to the grey rows of utilitarian barracks and sheds or the brightly-lit pub where we could see a game of pool in progress and some QinetiQ contractors enjoying a smoke and a pint. The warden intercepted us to check we had behaved ourselves. We assured him we had not left any crumbs on his pristine island.

A squall earlier that day had made it difficult for the helicopter to drop off its twice-weekly payload for the military base. As the unsettled weather was due to continue, it was possible that rough seas might deter some of the 600 tourists expected at the weekend from a visiting cruise ship. We would have liked more time for further insights, but the dinghy was approaching so we said goodbye and headed past the bulky gabions to the concrete steps and choppy sea. The next day's exploration was thwarted by storm warnings and a swift departure, but the brief visit left us in no doubt that Hirta was fully entitled to its place alongside Blaenafon in the world industrial heritage rankings.

EDDIE DEALTRY, SEPTEMBER 2009

The worst moment of the trip was forming a circle to pay homage to the administrator's representative on Earth, in the dusk with your tent still waiting to be unpacked.

ALAN DAWSON, SEPTEMBER 2009

One of the few walks that I would be tempted to describe as magical. It began in damp mist and improved with every step as the sun broke through to highlight the land and reveal a shimmering sea that gradually emerged through the cloud inversion. The summit view, with Boreray and the stacks slowly becoming clear, was one to remember forever.

Village Bay and Dun from the slopes of Conachair

On Dun, returning from the summit to the landing site

Mullach Buidhe, Boreray

ALAN DAWSON, SEPTEMBER 2009

Six years after the disappointment of a short and stormy trip, the sea around St Kilda was about as tranquil as it gets. The landing on Boreray and the initial ascent were not that scary, then the summit ridge and panorama made me feel privileged to be there and unusually emotional. This seemed to be one of the most amazing places on Earth. The green of the grass, blue of the sea and white of the gannets all seemed supernaturally vivid. The exhilaration of the ascent, the near-vertical cliffs, the surreal pyramid of Stac an Armin and the dewy dampness all helped to evoke a dizzying, dream-like atmosphere.

Descent of the steep grassy slopes felt secure, but harsh reality returned when I was faced with the final slithery descent to the boat. A safety rope had been set up and I was torn between trying to climb down and half-abseiling using the rope. I ended up sliding pathetically in full view of amused faces on the boat. Exhilaration became humiliation by the time I leapt aboard. At least I avoided landing in the sea. I thought that I would like to return one day via another landing site, though I never did.

STEVE GILLIONS, 2013

Someone had said that I should be prepared for a shock if the Boreray cliffs were the first thing I saw of St Kilda. They were spot on. One look at the alleged landing point – a narrow, damp line running just above the Atlantic – was enough to make me think there was no way I was going to get onto that one. But I did.

Bioda Mor, Dun

ALAN DAWSON, SEPTEMBER 2009

There were no dogs and no guns involved, but the worst GOML (Get Off My Land) encounter I ever had was in trying to gain access to Bioda Mor on Dun. A diplomatic delegation of four was selected to negotiate with the warden on Hirta, who remained hostile throughout the discussion, even though we were so deferential that it felt almost humiliating. We had advance permission from senior NTS staff and we had a senior RSPB expert in our party, but it was clear that the warden did not want any of us on the island, which he seemed to regard as his personal property. He followed the classic GOML tactic of changing the grounds for objection. We offered to walk in line, following in each other's footsteps. He didn't like that. We offered to spread out. He didn't want that either. We offered to record plant species. He liked that idea but then reconsidered when it transpired that the botanist was Rob, who had been on Dun before and was therefore barred from stepping ashore again. The warden's negative and hostile attitude spoiled what should have been a brilliant experience and in my opinion was a disgrace to NTS, an organisation whose motto was 'a place for everyone'.

When we finally landed, the ascent, the ridge walk and the views were all fabulous. My overall impression from St Kilda was a weird conglomeration of exhilaration, awe, anger, frustration, joy, embarrassment, relief and disappointment.

IAN TEASDALE, 2009

I was unable to disentangle feelings between the three trips that I made in 2009, but all were great expeditions in the truest sense of the word – exposure to new things, uncertain outcome, team spirit. I recovered a feeling that I hadn't had since I used to go off to far-flung corners of the world, but also a feeling that what once seemed remote and strange now seemed easier and achievable.

Stac an Armin and Stac Lee

RICHARD MCLELLAN, OCTOBER 2014

After ten years of waiting and four visits to St Kilda, finally I feel the rough rock of Stac an Armin and Stac Lee, a magical day where, after a gloomy grey start, cloud clears to a give a few hours of blue skies and bright sunshine. We teeter over the slabs at the base of Stac an Armin, the sea waiting for victims of a misplaced step, then it is up steep grass and rock outcrops to the naked boulder of the summit. Stac Lee is more forbidding. Even on landing it is hard to imagine a way up the towering rock face, but step by step progress is gained and one soon learns to enjoy rather than fear the exposure, right to the guano-covered rocks of the summit. The slimy ledges, foul-smelling pools of gloop and decaying nests of gannets will never make it a classic climb, but it must rate as one of the best days out the UK has to offer. In darkness I leap from the rocky ledge into the little tender lit by a pool of torch light as it rises and falls on the swell.

DENISE MCLELLAN, OCTOBER 2014

The St Kilda stack ascents really were as fantastic as expected. My strongest memories are of standing on the tiny summits, with seabirds whirling around and calling hauntingly, looking out across a huge expanse of calm sea. The other isles looked spectacular but insignificant from my vantage point. Stepping between the dinghy and the stacks was my greatest concern, but after the first transfer to Stac an Armin went ok I was free to worry about the climbing on Stac Lee.

I enjoyed creeping along the guano-filled ledges, realising I was one of the few in over fifty years to have been so privileged. It is hard to describe the feeling of elation when driving home the following day. I really could not believe I had finally done them. They had seemed so impossible when viewed from boats in previous years in conditions of higher swell. The careful weather watching had paid off and we caught a tiny window of mild weather with low swell and little wind. The delicate scent of guano lingered in the car for several weeks.

EDDIE DEALTRY, OCTOBER 2014

Scrambled left up first gallery on Stac Lee, which was free of the guano to come. Round a corner with a step right up onto a narrow but solid ledge. Took ledge to the end and belayed then up the crux pitch – mild severe, definitely no more than severe, holds good on left then friction with small holds over a curve to a ledge. The rest was easy or moderate climbing but crappy with guano and some rubble. Top was rubbish and muck. Seconded on rope with Richard and Denise Mclellan.

MARTIN RICHARDSON, OCTOBER 2015

I did not really want to come home. I was not looking forward to experiencing yet another aborted trip to St Kilda. Three years running of curtailing my European travels was enough. I decided that this was going to be the final bid and, if it failed, I would just book myself on one of the tourist boat trips from Skye and be satisfied with Conachair. I did not even bother to book a ferry and just hovered on Skye, bagging Humps.

Then came the call – the swell was promising to be not too bad at the end of the week. Still thinking I was wasting the fare, I went over to Harris. To my surprise, we had a window of calm weather long enough to bag all four of the islands. I had done it and would never have to go through the process again. I had finished with St Kilda and I was satisfied. I had seen the stacks and they looked impossible.

It was back to the mainland and working through some remote north-west Scotland Marilyns. In the midst of daily forays in Strathfarrar, a call came from Rick Salter saying that later in the week there was a forecast for a couple of days of fine weather with little sea swell, and was I interested in bagging the stacks? I should have said no. I could not afford the cost or the disappointment of not being able to summit and we were supposed to be going to Ballater anyway for a week. However, the disease of summit fever clouded my judgement. The stacks proved to be a great place to practise abseiling, and I joined that select group of people who go from having never been to St Kilda to summiting all six Marilyns within six weeks.

Stac an Armin from near the top of Boreray

Boreray and the stacks from Conachair

Stac Lee

DAVE MCGIMPSEY, DECEMBER 2023

A brief window of unusually calm seas and good weather in early December inspired our small team to drop everything for an attempt on the St Kilda stacks. We left Leverburgh just after 6am and landed on Stac Lee about three hours later. Weak winter sunshine greets us on arrival but the reality of climbing this impressive piece of rock subdues the group's mood as we try to imagine a likely line through Stac Lee's winter coat of lush green slime at the base. The swell is obviously higher than forecast but our skipper Iain Angus is undeterred as he busies himself preparing the tender for a landing.

Dan and I decide we have to at least attempt the green slabs before conceding defeat, so a reconnaissance is agreed on first before landing any more of the group. After some discussion we agree on a less slimy short wall furnished with good holds. Dan leads off, quickly climbing up to and gaining the starting gully. We then swing leads up to the top of the pitched climbing section, realising that conditions are too serious for most of the group to climb the route. After more discussion we decide to abseil back down for Dan to attempt Stac an Armin while Derek and Calum join me for an attempt to reach the top.

What unfolds is one of the best adventures I've enjoyed while climbing in Scotland. Derek and Calum are great company and careful, steady climbers. None of the climbing is technically difficult but the overall challenge is significant, with limited daylight and lots of poorly-protected traversing on damp, greasy rock. Conditions did improve in the upper reaches of the climb but the lower section was still just as green and slimy when we got back down. It is a serious, impressive place and not to be underestimated, a fitting crux on the journey to completing the varied list of Marilyn summits.

After an intense four hours, Iain Angus skilfully manoeuvres the tender in between the bigger waves to get us all safely back on board by about 3:30pm. In no time we're back enjoying warm coffees on the boat, elated but disappointed for the rest of the group who were unable to land on Stac an Armin.

Figures on the summit of Stac Lee in December 2023, with Hirta beyond

—— Northern Highlands ——

North of Loch Broom, Loch Glascarnoch, Loch Garve and the River Conon to the Cromarty Firth

Marilyns:	120
Highest:	Beinn Dearg (HN07), 1081.7m
Lowest:	Meall an Fheadain, 204m
Most prominent:	Ben More Assynt, 838m drop
Least prominent:	Beinn Dearg (HN01), 150.7m drop

Number		Height	Name	Drop	Location	Summit
1124	CA	911.2	Foinaven	687	NC 3151 5069	Cairn
1129		787	Arkle	392	NC 3027 4616	Cairn
1130	A	776.7	Meall Horn	264	NC 3526 4492	Cairn
1134	A	730.4	Sabhal Beag	167.5	NC 3730 4291	Rock near cairn
1126	T	872.8	Ben Hee	607	NC 4265 3394	Trig
1138		553	Creag Dhubh Mhor	154	NC 4588 3368	Rock by cairn
1141		472	Meall an Fhuarain	215	NC 5132 3053	Cairn
1142		472	Creag Dhubh Bheag	203	NC 4748 3075	Cairn on rock
1128		801	Cranstackie	560	NC 3506 5559	Cairn
1131		773	Beinn Spionnaidh	211	NC 3619 5728	Rock near trig
1144		423	Meall Meadhonach	196	NC 4100 6278	Rock by cairn
1127	A	800.8	Meallan Liath Coire Mhic Dhughaill	349.8	NC 3572 3915	Trig
1133	A	758.5	Carn an Tionail	209	NC 3923 3903	Rock
1135	A	688.9	Beinn Direach	152.0	NC 4061 3806	Rock
1113		521	Farrmheall	363	NC 3082 5877	Rock
1114	T	485.3	Creag Riabhach	349	NC 2788 6380	Trig
1115		467	An Grianan	154	NC 2646 6269	Cairn
1116		460	Fashven	212	NC 3138 6750	Cairn
1117	J	423.8	**Beinn Dearg *****	150.7	NC 2797 6581	Boulder
1118	T	370.7	Sgribhis-bheinn	217	NC 3193 7135	Trig
1119		362	An Socach	165	NC 2654 5860	Cairn
1120		333	Ghlas-bheinn	156	NC 3321 6144	Cairn
1122		288	Beinn Akie	161	NC 3409 6499	Cairn on rock
1140		521	An Lean-charn	329	NC 4198 5256	Rock by cairn
1143		465	Feinne-bheinn Mhor	178	NC 4344 4626	Rock

This area includes three more Marilyns than any other hill area apart from Mull, which also has 25. It includes the northernmost mainland Marilyn (Sgribhis-bheinn), the northernmost hills over 700m, 800m and 900m, and the hill with the longest name (30 letters). The nine hills on the Cape Wrath peninsula include one of the newest Marilyns. Beinn Dearg was added to the list in 2018 following a GNSS survey by Jon Metcalf. Farrmheall is the highest hill in this group but Creag Riabhach is more impressive and almost as prominent. An Grianan qualifies for the list with only four metres to spare yet it is acclaimed as one of the gems of the list. It is not easy to reach but its steep cliffs, isolated location and outstanding views offer rich reward for the effort involved in reaching its summit.

Foinaven

ALAN DAWSON, MAY 2017

When I began researching the Marilyns in the 1980s, I looked at Ordnance Survey 1:50000 Landranger maps. With 204 maps to work through, the task seemed too enormous to refer to larger scale maps. After the first pass I did refer to some 1:25000 maps to try to resolve the status of several marginal hills, but I did not study all the relevant large-scale maps before RHB was published in 1992. During the 1990s I had access to Scottish maps at 1:10000 scale in the map library at Glasgow University, where I spent many lunch breaks and evenings. I noticed a 914m spot height for Foinaven and drew this to the attention of The Angry Corrie magazine. This generated a flurry of interest and several ascents of Foinaven, but the matter was not resolved until a GNSS survey in May 2007, carried out by CMRC Ltd. This was the first in a series of 'heightings' arranged by The Munro Society, described in their book *Scaling the Heights*, published in 2019. The height obtained by the survey was 911.05m, showing the OS 914m figure to be wrong. However, the photo in the Munro Society book showed the survey point as the base of a large cairn on the summit. Ten years after the first survey, I removed most of the cairn to reveal two small embedded rocks as the natural highest point. My survey result was 911.18m, enough to nudge the rounded height up to 911.2m. In this case 13cm was not significant, but on some summits it could alter the hill classification. None of us could have foreseen that within twenty years half of the Marilyns would be surveyed using GNSS equipment.

Meallan Liath Coire Mhic Dhughaill

The word Meallan is usually translated as a knoll or small hill, but that is not applicable to a hill over 800m high. The word mealladh seems more suitable, meaning charming or beguiling. OS Landranger maps make it difficult to visualise or plan a route over all the interesting outlying summits, as they are spread across sheets 9, 15 and 16. They form a large X shape, with an eastern flourish out to Carn Dearg, which is only 3.5m lower than the main summit. Frank Zappa once wrote a song about dental floss because no-one else had done so, and the same principle has been applied to MLCMD, which looks plausible as a Roman numeral but is not valid. The song has been offered to Taylor Swift but as yet she has not recorded it as she has had some difficulty with the pronunciation.

Unremarkable, unrememberable
Unexceptional, far away hill
Unpronounceable, unannounceable
Too denounceable, far away hill

Meallan Liath Coire Mhic Dhughaill
Needs no magazine approval

No-one writes about it, no-one fights about it
No-one delights about it, no-one but me
No-one knows about it, no long prose about it
No TV shows about it, not worth a thing
No range of clothes about it
No song to sing

Meallan Liath Coire Mhic Dhughaill
Needs no magazine approval
Most ignorable, far away hill
Rather wonderful, far away hill

Arkle

Surveying the summit of Beinn Dearg (Jon Metcalf)

Creag Riabhach and An Grianan (Jon Metcalf)

Creag Riabhach and An Grianan

ANN BOWKER, JUNE 1995

The day was worse than ever. We decided to walk to Strathan bothy. Rowland, being a member of the MBA, had a subsidiary ambition to visit every bothy. After lunch in the bothy, brightening weather lured us up An Grianan, a hill to which the OS does scant justice, giving no inkling of its spectacular summit crags. Looking back from the col with Creag Riabhach, it presented a truly dramatic aspect. The higher hill retained its cover of cloud until we reached the trig point, when it cleared partially to reveal a glimpse of its eastern cliffs and Sandwood Bay far away to the west. The traverse there was not too difficult and proved less arduous than expected.

We arrived at this delectable place in brilliant evening sunshine. The day trippers had departed, leaving us to enjoy the beauty in perfect solitude. We had previously visited this bay on days of less than perfect weather. It had still enchanted, with a very special sort of light which seems to dance off the dunes. Tonight it was pure magic. The combination of sea, sky, sand and the perfectly proportioned sea stack set against the sinking sun confirmed our conviction that this was one of the most beautiful places on Earth. Since we might not have come here tonight without these two Marilyns to lure us, I rated Alan Dawson's book worth the money for this one perfect walk alone.

Beinn Dearg

ALAN DAWSON, JUNE 2005

My Suunto altimeter recorded a difference of 151-152m between the summit of Beinn Dearg and the col at NC278647. At the top of Creag Riabhach the height reading was accurate to within a metre. I was in the middle of an eleven-hour walk over six Marilyns (or was it seven?), so I did not feel like going back up Beinn Dearg to check the readings again. However, I knew that further measurements would be very useful, if one day anyone happened to be near Cape Wrath with more accurate equipment. Thirteen years later, Jon Metcalf used Leica GNSS equipment to confirm that Beinn Dearg was indeed prominent enough to qualify as a Marilyn.

JON METCALF, JULY 2018

I carried a bivvy bag as it was a challenging route at my pace (25km, 1050m ascent, two hours for recording data plus time for setting up equipment etc). I had pre-warned my house mates, so no worries for them. I ended up bivvying on the beach of Loch a' Phuil Bhuidhe. The sand was comfortable, sheltered and free from clegs and midges. Rain for two hours in the night was a bit of a bore as I had to cover the rucksack and head torch.

The practicalities all seemed to work fine. I used twelve rather than fifteen degrees as the default satellite cut-off angle. Lower-angle readings travel through more atmosphere so are less accurate, but the lower the cut-off angle the more satellites you see. The wind vibration of the tripod at the summit may have affected precision a little. At the col the drainage patterns isolated the key survey point to a few square metres of peaty terrain. After the survey I was on the move at 5am and back at base by 9am before anyone else had got up. Curry for breakfast was well deserved.

To climb the hill on its own it would be most efficient from the north, by getting the Cape Wrath bus driver to drop you at about NC286175. This is not to dismiss the logistical issues of getting to Durness, getting the boat and bus and then getting back out if a return bus can't be arranged.

Number		Height	Name	Drop	Location	Summit
1123	T	927.2	Ben Hope	772	NC 4775 5014	Trig
1136	A	599.7	Meallan Liath	147.3	NC 5145 5037	Boulder
1145		414	Meadie Ridge	159	NC 4993 4379	Rock near cairn
1146		408	Ben Hutig	196	NC 5387 6524	Rock rib
1132	A	764.2	Ben Loyal	609	NC 5781 4886	Rock near trig
1137		558	Cnoc nan Cuilean	208	NC 5974 4617	Cairn
1139		535	Ben Hiel	210	NC 5958 5003	Rock near cairn
1147		357	Cnoc an Daimh Mor	165	NC 5331 4270	Cairn on rock
1164		336	Meall nan Clach Ruadha	171	NC 6051 5698	Cairn on rock
1155		527	Beinn Stumanadh	389	NC 6408 4988	Cairn near trig

Ben Hope and Ben Loyal

How would we cope if instead of Ben Hope
This northern hill was called something silly
Like the name of a horse that had won the Grand National
Or something worse, like Botley or Black Willy

Ben Hope and Ben Loyal are by far the most dominant and prominent hills in this compact area. As well as their obvious attractions, the easily pronounced names provide extra appeal. The names are memorable and inspiring but the original meanings had nothing to do with hope or loyalty. According to Peter Drummond's book on Scottish hill names, the name Hope is derived from the Norse *hop*, meaning a bay. The same root is used in the Gaelic Ob, as in Oban and An t-Ob (Leverburgh). The name Loyal is thought to be derived from *laoghail*, meaning legal, at a time when hills were used more for proclamation than recreation.

A full circuit over Ben Hiel, the summits of Ben Loyal and Cnoc nan Cuilean can be a classic day's hill walking, though a strenuous diversion is required to include the striking 568m summit of Sgor Fhionnaich, which falls only eight metres short of Marilyn status but fails to qualify as a Submarilyn under the revised definition.

Meadie Ridge

ALAN DAWSON, 1970

In 2010 the isolated Beinn Stumanadh was my 1542nd Marilyn, a significant landmark as the original RHB book listed 1542 Marilyns. I had been near the top of Meadie Ridge forty years earlier, during a chaotic birding weekend. Our group had dispersed and spent a few fruitless hours wandering around and looking for greenshank before it became apparent that one of us was missing. We spent most of the night searching for him. My boss at the Borough Treasury found a phone box and called for help. A mountain rescue team from Dingwall arrived just as a lone figure turned up uninjured after walking cluelessly through the summer night. I felt embarrassed by the unnecessary call-out and ashamed by our failure to offer a suitable apology. I was only seventeen but was left to drive the hired van to Inverness when everyone else fell asleep. I was not bothered about seeing greenshank or other birds but it had been an excuse to escape from Wirral for a weekend adventure and provided good experience at trudging over tussocks in the dark.

Ben Hutig

This has become one of the most intriguing Marilyns, with the proposed construction of a spaceport on A' Mhoine peninsula. The launch-pad was due to be sited south of the summit, which is usually approached from the east. One day Ben Hutig may offer the possibility of watching a rocket launch while on the summit, but during 2024 the plans were paused, with investment switching to the Saxa Vord spaceport on Unst.

Beinn Stumanadh

Summit tor of Smean, reachable via an easy scramble

Number		Height	Name	Drop	Location	Summit
1150	A	705.5	Morven	575.9	ND 0046 2853	Rock by cairn
1151	JA	626.3	Scaraben	333.2	ND 0660 2684	Trig
1156	A	510.8	Smean	212	ND 0326 2763	Grassy tor
1157		484	Maiden Pap	169	ND 0483 2935	Heather
1152		590	Ben Griam Mor	432	NC 8065 3892	Cairn
1162	A	403.1	Beinn a' Mhadaidh	146.8	NC 7689 4150	Heather near trig
1153	J	579.8	Ben Griam Beg	335	NC 8318 4117	Cairn
1154		555	Creag Scalabsdale	200	NC 9700 2405	Cairn
1159		417	Beinn Dubhain	224	NC 9368 2070	Cairn
1158	A	423.7	Braigh na h-Eaglaise	185.1	ND 0648 2209	Cairn
1160	A	404.5	Creag Thoraraidh	155.1	ND 0406 1875	Tussock by fence
1163	A	401.1	Cnoc na Maoile	152.5	ND 0079 2121	Tussock

Cnoc na Maoile and Creag Thoraraidh

These hills required many hours of surveying to prove that Cnoc na Maoile qualified for the list and that Creag Thoraraidh was higher than nearby Cnoc Coir a' Phuill (by 18cm). It was necessary work but the tussocky terrain offered little enjoyable walking.

Ben Griam Mor and Ben Griam Beg

ALAN DAWSON, MAY 2010

This pair of hills loom large above a flat landscape, making them look higher than they are. They were as good as they looked when I finally climbed them in 2010, but more memorable than the walk was a surreal hour in the bar of the Garvault Hotel watching Chelsea beat Wigan 8-0 on a tiny portable television, in the company of a keen angler and Chelsea supporter from the Czech Republic who lived in Kinbrace.

Creag Scalabsdale

ANDREW TEMPLETION, 2003

This hill provided a grand trek along the edge of Caithness, also taking in Creag nan Gearr, Suidhe an Fhir Bhig and Cnoc an Eireannaich. Overlooked by many I suspect in favour of Morven or Sutherland gems, these were fine hills in their own right.

Beinn Dubhain

RODERICK MANSON, SEPTEMBER 2015

Scotrail Club 50 offers £10 returns anywhere in Scotland. I decide to see how far north I can go, climb a Marilyn and return to Dunkeld and Birnam in a day by rail. The answer was Kildonan, the Marilyn was Beinn Dubhain. Only 96 passengers alighted at that halt all year. On another day, station to station over Beinn a' Bhragaidh and Beinn Lunndaidh en route to Achnagarron standing stones and Rogart, and station to station from Rogart over Ben Horn. This was going so well that I took in a hill fort to the north, diverted to Brora from Dunrobin Castle, missed the last train south by five minutes, took two hours to hitch a lift and overnighted at Inverness youth hostel.

HN04 Klibreck-dhorain

Number		Height	Name	Drop	Location	Summit
1165	A	962.1	Ben Klibreck	819	NC 5853 2992	Rock near trig
1166	JA	712.7	Creag Mhor	367	NC 6984 2401	Trig
1167	JA	705.3	Ben Armine	243.0	NC 6948 2733	Cairn
1173	T	434	Cnoc an Liath-bhaid Mhoir	158	NC 7593 2913	Trig
1168	A	628.3	Beinn Dhorain	416	NC 9254 1565	Cairn
1169		592	Beinn Mhealaich	256	NC 9609 1495	Cairn
1170		545	Carn Garbh	167	NC 8927 1377	Mound
1174	T	387.5	Creag nam Fiadh	173	NC 8411 2371	Trig
1171		520	Ben Horn	354	NC 8072 0633	Cairn
1172	T	446.3	Beinn Lunndaidh	223	NC 7911 0198	Trig
1175		372	Meall a' Chaise	205	NC 6511 1190	Cairn
1180		323	Meall Dola	158	NC 6200 0693	Tussock
1176	A	349.1	Beinn Domhnaill	200	NH 6796 9667	Cairn
1179	A	336.3	An Stoc-bheinn	146.9	NC 6415 0251	Cairn
1177	A	345.4	Creag a' Ghobhair *	174.6	NH 6597 9406	Outcrop
1182	A	260.9	**Creag an Amalaidh *****	151.2	NH 7587 9752	Cairn on cairn

Ben Armine, Creag Mhor and Cnoc an Liath-bhaid Mhoir

COLIN CRAWFORD, JULY 2005

No doubt the use of a bike could have eliminated the need for an overnight stop, but I enjoy the thrill of a remote hill from a camp in the wilderness. I left Lairg in indifferent weather and was soon enveloped by forestry, not shown on my elderly map. Luck and guile saw me through the trees without going seriously astray, and Meall a' Chaise was crossed without problems (another of those teasers whose trig fails to mark the highest point). Reaching the farm at Dalnessie, I joined a series of old paths which suggested relatively easy access, but the paths were so rarely used that they were being reclaimed by the moorland. Their surfaces were rough indeed, the only advantage being an aid to navigation. My speed of travel proved infuriatingly slow, but by the onset of evening I was on top of Creag Mhor and then Ben Armine. Rounded lumps they may be, but the view over uninhabited wasteland offered that sense of delicious isolation which can be absent amongst more dramatic hills.

I found a luxurious haven for the night in this empty quarter. The track to Loch Choire Lodge offered a temptingly easy exit, but I held to the spirit of the outing and forged a route directly towards Cnoc an Liath-bhaid Mhoir. I was thankful that it was a dry spell, as this terrain would be a true slough of despond after rain. From the summit I could see Badanloch Lodge on the B871 and dropped down to a good track leading to the tarmac. I reached the stark outpost of Kinbrace before a single vehicle passed.

The outing was wonderful, both in memory and in actuality. A series of understated, lonely summits were treated with respect. It seemed right to reach them at the cost of some hardship, and the difficulty added to the allure. For me the challenging overnight expedition trumps the long drive or long day. Perhaps one day I will change my ways.

Ben Klibreck

GRAHAM ILLING, MAY 2016

I was lucky to walk away from a minor navigational error and fell through a cornice on Ben Klibreck as I was walking out to Meall Ailein in a white-out. I fell nine metres through the air and had a slide of fifteen metres down the northern snow slope, with wet snow helping to arrest my slide. It took twenty minutes to work my way across the face back to the ridge and tunnel through the cornice to get back onto the ridge. My partner had a long wait in the snow on top of Ben Klibreck, but we are still married.

Creag nam Fiadh

ANN BOWKER, 1999

This must really come into the category of a hill which no sane person would bother with. The bog at the western end of Loch Ascaig is ghastly. We were surprised to see another walker on the skyline but when he turned back to his quad-bike we realised that we had not encountered another Marilyn bagger. We had become so used to solitary hills that we would be amazed to meet another walker, especially on one like Creag nam Fiadh.

ERIC YOUNG, DECEMBER 2007

My conscience blushes to think of what I have done. I chose the drive-in option for Creag nam Fiadh, with keeper's permission. It had an interesting private railway level crossing to negotiate, and hut circle archaeology.

Creag an Amalaidh

ALAN DAWSON, JUNE 2014

This hill required one of my most difficult surveys. The summit was unhelpful, with a new cairn on top of an old one, but the col presented the main problem. Locating a critical point at the junction of four gentle slopes (two going up, two going down) can be difficult enough on open ground. In dense trees with no obvious water course it can be almost impossible. Even if you can find the optimum col location, the GNSS receiver will struggle to detect enough satellites to record valid data. Any signals that do get through may be bounced around by trees on the way. On my first attempt I was not convinced that I was in the right place and the data quality was rubbish anyway. Two days later I went back and found an open stretch of midge-infested grass to set up the equipment. From there I had to do some line surveying using walking poles and a laser level to work out the difference between the survey point and what seemed the correct col location. This added to potential error and uncertainty, but the data was convincing enough to declare Creag an Amalaidh to be a new Marilyn, with at least a metre to spare.

Creag a' Ghobhair

ALAN DAWSON, JULY 2016

The location of the highest point of this hill was uncertain for many years, requiring hill baggers to make sure they went to both candidates. OS map heights were inconsistent but in 2016 I resolved the matter with a survey showing the more easterly top to be higher by 40cm. Not a huge difference but enough to be conclusive.

The terrain between the summits was better than I remembered, but perhaps the most interesting feature was a sign declaring that the Bonar Bridge water treatment works had cost £1,111,439. I admired the precision of the figure but was sceptical about its accuracy. Was it really possible to measure the amount spent to the nearest pound?

Number		Height	Name	Drop	Location	Summit
1183	A	998.9	Ben More Assynt	838	NC 3183 2015	Outcrop
1187		815	Breabag	307	NC 2867 1572	Cairn
1204	A	398.4	Cnoc na Stroine	146.4	NC 2543 1285	Cabin
1191		776	Glas Bheinn	162	NC 2548 2649	Rock near cairn
1197	T	544.8	Beinn an Eoin	271	NC 3895 0827	Rock near trig
1188	A	808.8	Quinag – Sail Gharbh	550	NC 2094 2920	Boulder
1190		776	Sail Ghorm	158	NC 1984 3041	Cairn
1192	A	764.7	Spidean Coinich	192.8	NC 2060 2774	Rock by cairn
1189		792	Beinn Leoid	498	NC 3202 2948	Rock near trig
1193	A	750.5	Meallan a' Chuail	205	NC 3446 2924	Cairn
1195	A	613.0	Meall an Fheur Loch	164.8	NC 3619 3106	Rock
1199	A	512.2	Ben Dreavie	240	NC 2609 3984	Boulder
1198		511	Maovally	200	NC 3782 2119	Stone near cairn
1202		476	Beinn Sgeireach	157	NC 4535 1182	Rock by trig
1194	A	721.0	Ben Stack	531.0	NC 2693 4229	Cairn
1206		847	Canisp	689	NC 2029 1872	Rock
1209	A	731.4	Suilven	496	NC 1532 1836	Cairn
1214		567	Beinn Reidh	172	NC 2112 2122	Cairn

Glas Bheinn

PAUL RICHARDSON, AUGUST 1984

It was a dreary, grey August day, but there was no rain when we chose the highest waterfall in Britain as the objective for a family day out. As an alternative to a walk in and out by the same track, a circuit from Unapool seemed a long, tough trip. Enquiry at the stores seemed to provide the ideal solution – a lift by boat to the head of Loch Beag. We loaded a loaf and some smaller goodies into rucksacks while the proprietor of the stores went off to get his boat. For £6, the four of us enjoyed a pleasant trip up Loch Glencoul into Loch Beag, passing several seals. As we made a rather awkward disembarkation onto seaweed-strewn rocks at the head of Loch Beag, it began to rain quite heavily.

Most of the fall was already in view, but to gain a complete sighting required the roughest walking I had encountered anywhere – trackless heather, grass tussocks and broken rock, all overgrown and very wet underfoot. The rain stopped but progress was very slow until at last we stood opposite the fall, able to see the whole of it. I had found most waterfalls to be a disappointment, and this highest of all I thought hardly justified the trip. It was certainly high, but otherwise unspectacular. It did not detain us long.

We continued beside the burn. Sheep tracks gave us a little respite from time to time, but there was not much relief from the laborious underfoot conditions. It started to rain again. I decided to continue well up the glen. The burn split into five tributaries, and a path from the south-west crossed all five as it traversed the lower slopes of Beinn Uidhe. We could follow any one of these tributaries and therefore find the path so we continued, with the map inside my shirt for protection and me working from memory.

We were well up the glen when we discovered the path, but it was sketchy and we soon lost it again. We were forced to traverse the slopes towards the point where we had seen the path from below. The going remained rough and wet in the extreme. Cloud lay low on the hill and it rained unrelentingly. On we went, heads down, though I realised we now had little hope of meeting the estimated time I had given to the boatman for our return to Glencoul Stores.

There was a spot where the path passed between two lochans, and when we reached it I remembered this feature from the map. We pressed on as fast as we could. Barbara began to complain of being cold. Soon we were on a steep, narrow ridge. Barbara had been given my emergency body-warmer, but now she began to cry with cold and fatigue. I struggled to carry her up the ridge and had to put her down at the top. She was feeling better, but what was this ridge? I took out the map, which was quickly soaked. I could see no ridge marked. But we were on the path and had just passed a lochan. We must soon pass the top of the fall. The writing on the map obscured some of the features at this point. All would be okay. Press on.

A little further. No more ridge, but flat and featureless ground. I can no longer deny that there is no path here at all. All is not well. We have gone astray. Another look at the map, which gets even wetter. We must have strayed on to Cnoc na Creige. A course west will regain the path. But the slope is extremely steep and stony. It is not safe to descend. Visibility is very limited, for we are well into the cloud by now. We are not on Cnoc na Creige. I do not know where we are. We are lost. We are lost in the hills, cannot see fifty yards, and we are wet and tired and hungry.

We cannot be more than two miles from the road. Wherever we are, going west will bring us to it. But west is too steep. Map out again. No idea. Lost and not a little scared, we wander around aimlessly. North seems flatter, but then steep slopes again. Barbara is bearing up well, warmer now, but tired and frightened. Alun insists he is fine but clearly he is not. He is tired and struggling to keep up. He has carried my rucksack for a while, while I carried Barbara. He is reluctant to give it back, but needs a rest. He is persuaded to put on my pile jacket. The rain continues. The mist confounds us.

The map out again. So wet, the cover falls off. Still no clue. In a surge of despair and self-recrimination, I close my eyes. Hopelessly lost, we are probably out for the night in the pouring rain, the clag, the cold. Rescue teams searching. How could I be so stupid? We would probably survive, but it would be hell. Let us get out of this. I will never go on a hill again. Why did I bring the family? Why didn't I pay more attention to the map?

The map. If there is any hope at all, it is there. I open my eyes. The map is soaked. A lochan. Dozens of lochans. There is one by a ridge. Beneath the ridge, a path. The combination brings hope flooding back. Everything fits. Find that flat bit again. Back up the slope. Here it is. I am running now, out of sight of the rest. Frantic shouting back and forth until we are re-united. The level bit. Suddenly, a large cairn, on a large plateau. My god, it's Glas Bheinn. It must be. To test the theory, walk north-west. It's flat, then it begins to descend, at first steadily, then steeply and stonily. Then it flattens out again. Yes, this is Glas Bheinn. I think I know where we are, but there are crags. I can avoid them. Now north down the ridge, steeply. Then another flat bit. No doubt now. Suddenly, a break in the cloud. I see nothing useful. Perhaps I'm still lost after all. The cloud closes in again, then breaks, and we can see the road below. The ridge ends in crags, but now I can see them, and we turn east, down into the corrie, then north.

We are very wet, but we are safe. It is a long, wet haul down to the path and Loch na Gainmhich, but the rain has stopped and we can see we are safe. When everyone is on the path, I rush off ahead to reach the road, then dash north along it as fast as I can go, cutting across corners wherever possible, trying to reach Glencoul Stores before the mountain rescue team is alerted. At last I'm there, three hours later than the estimated time given to the boatman. It is now clear that, because I had failed to look at the map, I had not noticed that at the two lochans which the path passed between, there was a junction of two paths, and we had taken the wrong one. We had then left this to go up the east ridge of Glas Bheinn. I explain. He has not called the rescue team. Boots off, into the car, and I race back up the road again to collect the family, who I can now see coming along the road. Now at last I can relax. Alun takes off his boots and pours water out of them, confessing that he had been unable to feel his feet for some time. But already, the wounds are healing and the clothes are drying.

We are safe. At the hotel in Drumbeg, the process of recuperation continues. I have nearly forgotten what I had said about not going on the hills again. I feel a bit more moderate now. In future, I would keep an eye on the map, rain or no rain. The map lay on the table, spread out to dry. Checking the drying progress, I was seeing possibilities for tomorrow's route...

Beinn Reidh

ALAN DAWSON, JUNE 2004

I was struggling with a torn calf muscle but this hill seemed fairly close to the road and not all that high. Wading the River Loanan at the start was easy, but a thunderstorm near the summit turned it into a raging torrent by the time we got back down. Crossing it would have been suicidal. OS Landranger 15 came to the rescue. The map showed a vital footbridge about two kilometres further south. A retreat several hundred metres back uphill was required to cross some swollen burns. The extra exertion of a diversion uphill was inconvenient and a setback to my recovery but it was safe and avoided benightment.

Ben Stack

PETER MALONE, NOVEMBER 2007

I attended a meeting of the Mountain Bothies Association at the Crask Inn, followed by an ascent of the delightful Ben Stack, where politician Robin Cook sadly met his demise. At almost the exact same spot, my friend also suffered a heart attack. Fortunately his outcome was much more successful, after carefully descending the hill and getting safely to Raigmore Hospital in Inverness.

Maovally

CAMPBELL SINGER, AUGUST 2009

I know that Marilyn bagging is done to various standards of integrity but I feel I may have compromised my own standards when I decided to bag Maovally, on the south side of Loch Shin. From the map it did not look an attractive hill, with uniform heathery slopes, but it looked like there was an excellent hydro track which climbed close to the summit. The bike would be great on descent so I decided to use it. As I was negotiating the large gate at the entrance to the track to Corriekinloch, a white van pulled up and the driver got out to open the gate. I was feeling tired after three hard days and so I cheekily asked him if he could he give me a lift as I was climbing a nearby hill? Yes, he could. I decided to push it a bit further.

'Any chance of my bike fitting in the back?'

The rear doors swung open to reveal an empty space. The bike went in. He was a delight and laughed sympathetically at the concept of Marilyn bagging. At the fork in the track to the power station, I suggested that this was where to drop me off, but:

'No, it's all right. I'll take you up the hill. It's a grand morning'

He then proceeded to bomb up the track to within 100 metres of the summit. I got my bike out and, as I thanked him, he swore that he wouldn't tell anybody about my lift up the hill. I was at the summit in ten minutes, smiling but feeling somewhat guilty at the assistance. What is more, I had a twenty-minute free-wheel back to Corriekinloch before putting in a bit of effort cycling against the wind along the track back to the road.

Spidean Coinich, Quinag

Summit boulder on the flat and stony top of Ben Dreavie, with the top of Ben Stack beyond

Number		Height	Name	Drop	Location	Summit
1205	A	849.7	Cul Mor	652	NC 1620 1191	Trig
1215	A	546.6	An Laogh	147.3	NC 1617 1022	Cairn on outcrop
1207	A	769.4	Cul Beag	546	NC 1403 0883	Rock by cairn
1212	AG	612.4	Stac Pollaidh	439.8	NC 1071 1061	Grass by cairn
1208	A	743.4	Ben More Coigach	656	NC 0939 0425	Shelter
1210	A	703.9	Sgurr an Fhidhleir	160.3	NC 0944 0545	Outcrop
1211	A	617.9	Beinn an Eoin	354	NC 1049 0643	Boulder by cairn
1213	A	587.5	Sgorr Tuath ¬	149.0	NC 1103 0749	Grass
1217		204	Meall an Fheadain	179	NB 9988 1095	Outcrop by trig
1080		578	Meall an Fhuarain	341	NC 2805 0236	Mound near trig
1083		517	Meall Coire an Lochain	182	NC 2118 0651	Rock by cairn

Cul Mor

I think I'll go and climb Cul Mor, cried Rupert Bear one day
And Tiger Lily tagged along too
They were fully unprepared for the magic land they saw
They've got Ben Mor Coigach still to do

Cul Beag

PAUL RICHARDSON, MAY 1984

We flogged up the slopes of Cul Beag to a shallow corrie. My route up the south ridge became steep and stony but gave good views over to Ben Mor Coigach, a magnificent miniature massif. At the summit the hills had lost the clinging clag. The profile of Stac Pollaidh was familiar from dozens of photographs, but more impressive yet was the dramatic profile of Cul Mor, looking like a miniature Torridon hill. Beyond this, the amazing form of Suilven looked like a sleeping dragon. And there was Canisp and Breabag, and dozens of hills besides. It was the most magnificent mountain prospect I had ever seen. In the distance, the bulk of An Teallach was still swathed in cloud.

Meall an Fheadain

NEIL STEWART, JUNE 2007

The best viewpoint of all during a few days in Ullapool was from Meall an Fheadain above Achiltibuie. In one direction I could see all of the individualistic hills of the north-west and in the other, over the Summer Isles, the coastline of the Outer Hebrides. What a view for minimal effort.

JOHN ABBOTT, MAY 2013

The best view of the year was from the smallest Marilyn of the year – the stunning Meall an Fheadain, above Achiltibuie. It was a hot and sunny day with good visibility despite haze over the sea, spilling onto the coast in places. The unusual view of the hills of Skye, Torridon and Fisherfield to the south and Coigach, Assynt and Sutherland to the north was mesmerising, and all for a short walk along the track serving the mast.

Number		Height	Name	Drop	Location	Summit
1062	A	1081.7	Beinn Dearg	807.5	NH 2594 8118	Cairn
1063	A	977.8	Cona Mheall	164.8	NH 2750 8164	Cairn on outcrop
1068		927	Eididh nan Clach Geala	167	NH 2579 8420	Rock by cairn
1073	A	889.7	Beinn Enaiglair	234.9	NH 2250 8052	Rock by cairn
1075	A	728.8	Meall Doire Faid	174.9	NH 2208 7921	Rock by cairn
1077	A	666.3	Beinn Bhreac #	158.8	NH 2257 8865	Cairn on outcrop
1066	A	952.8	Am Faochagach	367	NH 3036 7937	Cairn
1070	A	908.9	Carn Gorm-loch	146.1	NH 3189 8008	Rock by cairn
1078	A	631.1	Meall a' Chaorainn	156	NH 3601 8273	Rock near cairn
1069		927	Seana Bhraigh	252	NH 2818 8787	Rock on cliff
1074	A	843.3	Carn Ban	205	NH 3384 8756	Rock near cairn
1076	A	701.3	Carn a' Choin Deirg	319	NH 3975 9235	Trig
1087		415	Creag Loisgte	177	NH 3676 9577	Cairn
1079		588	Cnoc Damh	367	NH 2704 9622	Outcrop
1082		549	Meall Liath Choire	255	NH 2269 9618	Rock by cairn
1081		559	Beinn Eilideach	185	NH 1706 9266	Rock rib
1084		506	Meall Dheirgidh	303	NH 4731 9434	Tussock near fence
1085		464	Breac-Bheinn *	157	NH 4981 9507	Rock by post

This extensive area includes hundreds of hills but only seventeen Marilyns, all of them over 400m high. Beinn Dearg is over two metres lower than the map height of 1084m, possibly because aerial surveys have measured the top of the large summit cairn.

Carn Gorm-loch

This is the highest of three Submarilyns between 900m and 915m, along with Bowfell and Beinn a' Chumhainn. It is the most topographically significant hill that does not qualify as a Marilyn, Munro or Munro Top, and is more prominent than 77 Munros.

Beinn Bhreac

This hill was listed as Meall Dubh until 2014, when the Scottish Mountaineering Club found someone with local knowledge who reckoned this inconspicuous summit was called Beinn Bhreac, thereby replacing one commonplace name with another. A different name was certainly needed, as OS maps show that the name Meall Dubh applies to a summit 1.5km to the north-east of Beinn Bhreac.

Carn Ban

JONATHAN APPLEBY, 2013

Highlights of the year were Carn Ban, Meall a' Chaorainn and Beinn Tharsuinn. Getting on a bike at misty Black Bridge allowed some respite from the midges and speeded progress to beyond Lubachlaggan. Climbing onto Carn Ban was a revelation – one minute grey damp mist then glorious Technicolor, emerging from a cloud inversion onto a warm summit plateau, bathed in early morning sunshine with inspirational views to north and west. The route over Meall a' Chaorainn and Beinn Tharsuinn involved dipping back into the mist and then climbing back out again, maximising the cloud inversion experience.

Cul Mor and Cul Beag from Sgurr an Fhidhleir

Creag an Duine and the slopes of Seana Bhraigh from the north

The southern slopes of Carn Ban and Loch Sruban Mora

Number		Height	Name	Drop	Location	Summit
1088	T	1046.4	Ben Wyvis	693	NH 4629 6837	Trig
1097	G	763.0	Little Wyvis	251	NH 4296 6447	Cairn
1095	A	838.7	Carn Chuinneag	461	NH 4836 8333	Boulder by trig
1103	A	648.0	Carn Salachaidh	235	NH 5188 8744	Tor
1096	A	787.2	Beinn a' Chaisteil	280	NH 3699 8011	Rock near trig
1100	A	711.2	Beinn Tharsuinn 711	177.3	NH 4125 8293	Cairn
1098	J	743.1	Beinn nan Eun	254.7	NH 4481 7598	Outcrop
1099	A	738.0	Meall Mor	263	NH 5152 7456	Trig
1101	JA	697.4	Carn Loch nan Amhaichean	205.0	NH 4113 7576	Rock near cairn
1104		523	Cnoc Ceislein	240	NH 5891 7062	Trig
1102	A	692.0	Beinn Tharsuinn 692	354	NH 6063 7928	Tussock
1107		373	Struie	157	NH 6584 8498	Cairn
1105		396	Cnoc Corr Guinie	183	NH 6717 7546	Heather
1106		380	Cnoc an t-Sabhail 380	209	NH 6944 7869	Heather by trees
1108		322	Cnoc an t-Sabhail 322	174	NH 7215 8170	Heather near trig
1109		269	Cnoc Mor	161	NH 4902 5694	Grass near trig
1111		205	Hill of Nigg *	191	NH 8206 7053	Grass

Ben Wyvis

Ben Wyvis looks monolithic from a vantage point near Garve
It's possible that that will be the only view you have
But if you take the eastern way from somewhere nearer Evanton
You'll find that it appears to be a complicated mountain

Little Wyvis

PAUL RICHARDSON, JUNE 2003

Despite the climb required, we regard Little Wyvis as an easy option, based on underfoot conditions and lack of navigational problems. The start is not propitious. A big gate has a No Access sign, but it's open. We walk through into something resembling a junk yard. Another sign lying on the ground says access to the Wyvis hills should be made from a spot a couple of miles away.

There are several dilapidated buildings, rusted machines and derelict vehicles at the side of the track. Ahead of us one vehicle is clearly in use but we pass by unhindered from within its tinted windows. We go on up the track to a gate which has to be climbed. We see a couple of wheatears, some starry saxifrage and butterwort to enliven a dull plod. There is a flash of sunshine but its promise is unfulfilled.

There is a cool breeze on the summit. A cairn appears from the mist but it offers no view. We wander about a bit to make sure this is the top, then set off back down. I cannot shake off the thought that this might be my last hill and I have a little regret that we didn't pick a more exciting one. Still, it's good to be out. I strive to savour the experience.

Down below the cloud base, we see the vehicle with tinted windows drive up to one of the gates, but we pass through a gate apparently unnoticed. The other gates are also open apart from the final one. It proves easy to scale and we return to the car without the expected conflict. Our weekend is over. Tomorrow, it's the hospital again for me.

Carn Salachaidh

ANN BOWKER, APRIL 1994

It is a subject for interesting discussion amongst hill walkers. Should one only ascend mountains in good weather to enjoy the view from one's hard-won summit, or are there rewards to be gained from setting out in less favourable conditions? Was it insane to set out in falling snow with a forecast of it turning to persistent rain later. However, here we were, heading north.

Our original plan to follow the forest track from Gledfield over various subsidiary bumps was, perhaps fortunately, thwarted by lack of parking. The closer approach from Gruinards Lodge was almost abandoned for the same reason, but one kilometre westwards we managed to deposit the vehicle and set out in gentle but persistently falling snow. This track emerged vaguely from the forest but soon became clear as it led straight up the hill and then undulated across a boggy area, becoming very boggy itself in places. As it dropped towards the Allt a' Ghlinne it became a pleasant and well-engineered track, then a sheep track continued for some distance up towards the mountain. It petered out in bog, heather and soft snow.

The going quickly became dreadful, with every step a gamble. We fell into peat hags and holes in the heather as we struggled onto the vague north ridge of the mountain. As the slopes steepened the snow became deeper and, apart from some apprehension of avalanche, less hazardous. As the map indicated, the highest ground lay eastwards and the trig point was soon located. Despite the mist we could see that the true summit lay on top of a large block of rock a short distance eastwards, and from there we could vaguely make out the slightly lower eastern top Carn Bhrain beyond.

We returned by exactly the same route, avoiding only those spots where we had fallen into holes on the way up. The snow was just turning to rain as we emerged back on the road, quite content with our expedition, for the beauty of the immediate snowy hillside had amply compensated for the lack of distant views.

Hill of Nigg

The summit of this hill was relocated in 1999, with the new summit position shown as 205m on OS maps compared to 203m at the original location. The change has not been confirmed by a GNSS survey but the trig pillar is only 203.01m according to OS data, so the old summit is likely to be around 202.7m.

BOB KERR, JULY 2006

While taking a photograph from the summit, a herd of about twenty highland cows started charging towards me from about 500 metres away. According to the GPS my maximum speed was 19.6km per hour as I ran for the nearest fence and only just managed to get over it in time, with a few deep cuts on my legs from rusty barbed wire to show for the ordeal.

Carn Chuinneag

The east face of Beinn a' Chaisteil

Meall Mor and Loch Glass

—— Western Highlands: North ——

Land between Loch Broom and Glen Carron, south of Dirrie More and north of Strath Bran

Marilyns: 74
Highest: Sgurr Mor, 1108.9m
Lowest: Torr Achilty, 256m
Most prominent: Liathach - Spidean a' Choire Leith, drop 957m
Least prominent: Sithean Mor, drop 150.8m

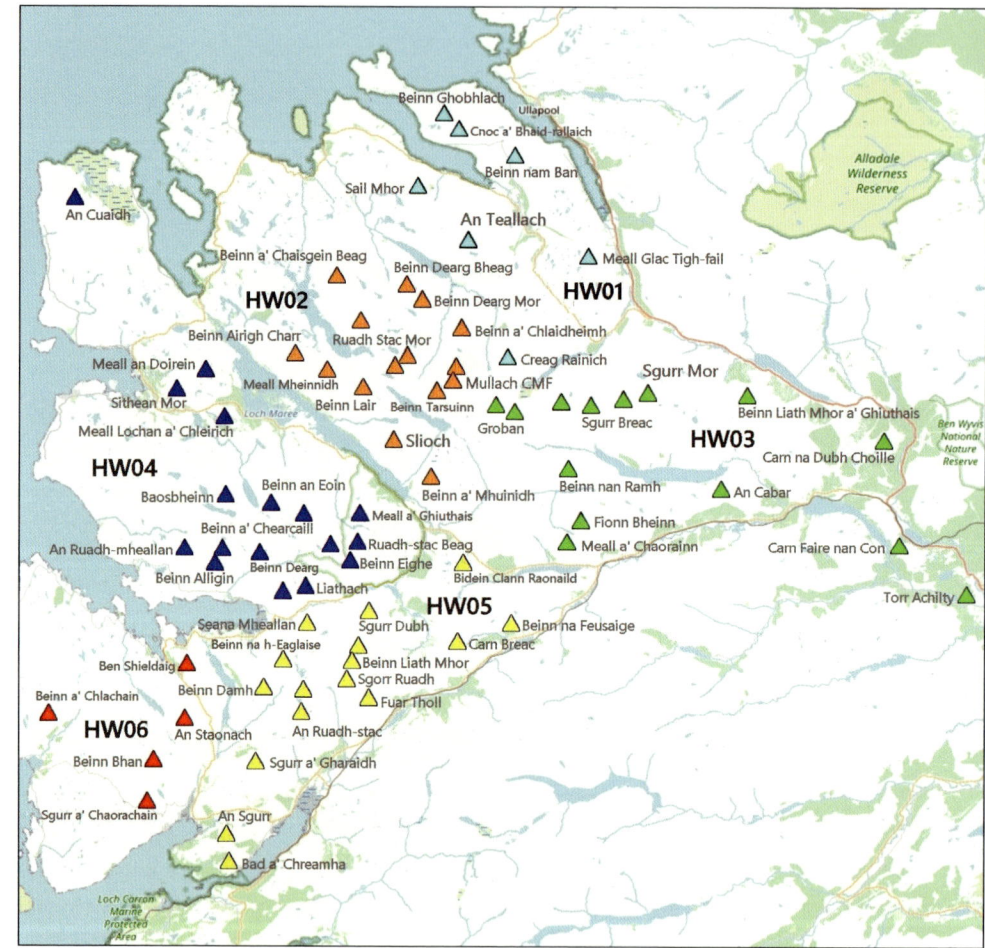

HW01 Teallach-ghobhlach

Number		Height	Name	Drop	Location	Summit
1003	A	1062.6	An Teallach - Bidein a' Ghlas Thuill	757	NH 0689 8436	Rock
1004	A	1058.7	Sgurr Fiona	141.7	NH 0640 8368	Cairn
1031		767	Sail Mhor	322	NH 0330 8869	Cairn
1029	A	807.9	Creag Rainich	450	NH 0960 7515	Rock
1035	A	634.9	Beinn Ghobhlach	400.7	NH 0555 9434	Outcrop
1036		580	Beinn nam Ban	243	NH 1089 9081	Cairn
1037	A	543.2	Cnoc a' Bhaid-rallaich	164.7	NH 0660 9304	Boulder by cairn
1038		521	Meall Glac Tigh-fail	177	NH 1613 8277	Rock

An Teallach

DAVID STALLARD, JANUARY 2011

An Teallach probably takes the number one spot for me, because of its beautiful rock architecture, the walking and exciting scrambling, the wonderful views, and that north-west Highland quality of a distinct, rugged hill surrounded by sea and lochs. I climbed it on a day of temperature inversion, with the tops of the whole of the north of Scotland sticking out of a sea of cloud in bright sunshine. I do not think I will ever forget it.

Beinn Ghobhlach and Cnoc a' Bhaid-rallaich

DANIEL PATRICK QUINN, JUNE 2016

It was not long before the shortest night of the year. I was living on Lewis and my Bohemian existence was beginning to lead to mental health issues. Having run out of new nearby Marilyns I decided I would head to Beinn Ghobhlach for my 700th. This involved walking into Stornoway, getting the ferry to Ullapool, strolling along the busy A835 south to the Letters junction, round the other side of Loch Broom to Blarnalearoch – around fifteen miles, with soles very sore from all the tarmac – then up onto the hillside overlooking Ullapool. I made it to the sharp bend on the minor road to Badrallach just before the sky darkened to navy blue at around 11pm, with great views directly across Loch Broom to Ullapool just a couple of miles away – so close yet so far. I opened my bottle of vodka and pitched the little tent for a few hours of rest.

Metallic clanging down on the loch announced the arrival of the freight ferry from Stornoway at some point in the early hours of the morning. The summer night sky was light enough that I could see this. I had another swig of vodka, got back into the tent and drifted off again. Not long after, the brightness of car headlights woke me up. The driver pulled over nearby. Very odd. A drunk driver? Something strange going on? I put on my head lamp and clambered out of the tent to have a look.

The driver was as shocked to see me as I was to see him. He was a Hungarian tourist who had arrived in Edinburgh the previous evening, hired a car from the airport and driven north until he could drive no more, then he had picked the very same isolated spot as me to get some rest in the back of the car.

The sky was already beginning to lighten further so I set off over the heather towards Beinn Ghobhlach, which was as great an experience as I had hoped for, with its lovely sandstone ridge. Then back over Cnoc a' Bhaid-rallaich and all the way back down and around and then along the road to Ullapool. Curry sauce and chips. Then the ferry back to Stornoway and the two-mile walk home.

HW02 Mullach-slioch

Number		Height	Name	Drop	Location	Summit
1007	A	1015.2	Mullach Coire Mhic Fhearchair	591	NH 0520 7351	Cairn
1009		989	Sgurr Ban	165	NH 0558 7454	Cairn
1014	A	965.8	A' Mhaighdean	443.0	NH 0077 7491	Boulder
1019	A	933.8	Beinn Tarsuinn	207.1	NH 0396 7279	Cairn on rock
1023	GA	918.7	Ruadh Stac Mor	169.8	NH 0185 7565	Rock near trig
1024	G	914.0	Beinn a' Chlaidheimh	271	NH 0613 7756	Rock by cairn
1010	A	981.2	Slioch	626	NH 0046 6907	Cairn
1033	A	689.9	Beinn a' Mhuinidh	380	NH 0320 6604	Cairn
1025	G	906.3	Beinn Dearg Mor	564	NH 0322 7992	Cairn
1027	A	856.1	Beinn a' Chaisgein Mor	346	NG 9825 7855	Rock
1028		820	Beinn Dearg Bheag	227	NH 0199 8112	Cairn
1034	A	682.3	Beinn a' Chaisgein Beag	173.8	NG 9660 8214	Outcrop
1026	A	859	Beinn Lair	456	NG 9816 7327	Cairn
1030	A	791.7	Beinn Airigh Charr	475	NG 9303 7618	Cairn
1032	A	721.8	Meall Mheinnidh	233.1	NG 9549 7484	Outcrop by cairn

Beinn Dearg Mor and Beinn Dearg Bheag

DAVID HUGHES, 2006

Beinn Dearg Mor must be one of the best summits on the mainland – a fantastic twin top with unsurpassed views, but it had taken me five hours to get there and I still had a job to do. Buoyed on by the imminent prospect of finishing the Corbetts, I was soon back at the col between the two summits, but as I started to make my way uphill tiredness hit me. My legs felt like lead as I approached the cairn on Beinn Dearg Bheag. I spent another half an hour drinking in the view before heading along the north-west ridge. This consisted of fantastic turrets of sandstone shining pink in the afternoon sunshine – a miniature An Teallach but with no trace of a path. It was brilliant but I was too tired to fully appreciate its splendid situation.

I managed to take in as much simple scrambling as I could and soon the ridge began to drop steeply away. The descent proved tricky in places and there were two heart-stopping moments before I found a way through breaks in the crags. After that I think my brain just switched off. I reached the car eleven hours after setting off, to conclude three days of solo walking to some of the finest hills in the country. It was an unforgettable experience and a fitting way to finish off a list of hills.

Beinn a' Chaisgein Mor

RON BELL, MAY 2015

I started from where the A832 crosses the Gruinard River. It involved 16 km of cycling plus 18 km of walking. Even taking account of my serious slowness, that should not really have taken longer than twelve hours, but it took me over seventeen. Reasons included the cycle route being rough and crossing the Allt Loch Ghiubhsachain on the way back. It was dark and my lights were insufficient to cycle.

I had foreseen these problems and had told the hotel staff and my wife not to expect me back until morning. I was prepared to wait until dawn, so getting back to the hotel at about 11.15pm was just fine. I slept well. The views from near the summit, across to the Fisherfield mountains, were quite stunning.

Beinn Dearg Bheag

Beinn Lair

ALAN DAWSON, SEPTEMBER 2023

In 2005 I had reached Beinn Lair the easy way, in a boat across Loch Maree after leaving a car in Poolewe. This made it feasible to continue over Meall a' Mheinnidh and the three main summits of Beinn Airigh Charr. In 2023 I made do with a bike from Poolewe to the edge of the trees past Kernsary. The good path made progress easy until I branched off right to skirt around the southern slopes of Meall a' Mheinnidh. This had the attraction of being a new route and worked pretty well. The good weather helped Beinn Lair seem reasonably accessible and benign. A summit survey was of doubtful value in view of the huge cairn but I was ready to rest and enjoy the views for a while, with a shaggy mountain goat for company. Then came the main reason for my revisit as I descended north-east toward a prominent rocky summit (Sgurr Dubh North Top), on the edge of the cliffs not easily seen from the main summit. Then over Sgurr Dubh and its South Top before heading down toward Loch Maree to check the height of Leth Creag, shown as 598m on the map. A traverse across the southern slopes of Beinn Lair completed the circuit, allowing me to rejoin the ascent route. The diversions to three new summits had made Beinn Lair seem much more interesting, and the bike helped me to reach the car without having to use a torch. Two days later I was joined by Alan Whatley for a ride and walk to Meall a' Choire Ghlais (an outlier of Beinn Airigh Charr), my final 600m summit in the Highlands (with 20m drop), 34 years after I had moved from Liverpool to Scotland. It turned out that Marilyns alone had not been enough to last a lifetime.

HW03 Sgurrmor-fannaich

RHB sections 12A, 14B

Number		Height	Name	Drop	Location	Summit
1040	A	1108.9	Sgurr Mor	913	NH 2032 7181	Cairn
1052	A	924.0	An Coileachan	148.3	NH 2417 6802	Rock
1041	T	1093.1	Sgurr nan Clach Geala	229	NH 1843 7146	Cairn
1054		766	Beinn Liath Mhor a' Ghiuthais	284	NH 2808 7130	Shelter cairn
1042	A	999.6	Sgurr Breac	450.8	NH 1584 7110	Slab
1043	A	998.6	A' Chailleach	182.9	NH 1362 7141	Cairn on outcrop
1058	A	697.8	Meallan Chuaich	146.4	NH 1154 6980	Rock
1055	A	750.2	Groban	309.8	NH 0998 7088	Boulder
1059	A	668.4	Beinn Bheag	198.5	NH 0851 7140	Rock
1050	AT	933.4	Fionn Bheinn	658	NH 1475 6214	Trig
1057	JA	705.1	Meall a' Chaorainn	189.1	NH 1360 6040	Cairn
1060	TL	558.3	An Cabar	253	NH 2573 6410	Rock by trig
1056	A	711.4	Beinn nan Ramh	387	NH 1396 6615	Cairn
1061	T	479.7	Carn na Dubh Choille	159	NH 3870 6734	Boulder by trig
924		370	Carn Faire nan Con	239	NH 3956 5917	Cairn on outcrop
925	L	256	Torr Achilty	216	NH 4476 5507	Cairn by bush

Sgurr Mor

Meall a' Chaorainn and Fionn Bheinn

Alan Dawson, June 2023

For the first time in my life, a fortnight in holiday cottages in the Highlands co-incided with high pressure and fine dry weather. After the first week I had only one Simm left to climb in Scotland, so I had to decide what to do next. My motivation for repeat summits was lower than for new hills, but I was only four short of a second set of Grahams, I had only been up Fionn Bheinn once and it had been 32 years since I set foot on this pair.

A fairly new track from Achnasheen provided a useful start, winding steeply up to a small dam, before I plunged off into the peat hags. I headed for a prominent rock to rest and assess the morass ahead, trying to pick a good line through the hags toward the gentle grassy slopes of Meall a' Chaorainn. I gradually got into a rhythm and before long was relaxing in the sun on the summit. This felt good. No rushing, no hassles, no midges, no rain, no black clouds on the horizon. Fionn Bheinn looked good and so did everything else. Not crystal clear but pretty damned fine. Too good to last? Of course.

I chose a steep and direct line down damp slopes to the broad and heathery col. Finding the right survey point was not easy but I had done hundreds of cols like this and was soon settling down to a relaxing lunch in the sun. How quickly a mood can change. For some reason I patted my pockets to feel the reassuring lump of my car key. No, must have put it in the other pocket. No, must have put it in the top rucksack pocket. The truth did not take long to sink in. The hole in my trouser pocket must have grown.

Other than serious injury or hypothermia, losing a car key is one of the worst things that can happen in a mass of heathery peat hags. I had little chance of finding it if it was more than five metres away. I checked again and found I had also lost my watch, a rather nice metal one I had had for over twenty years. Time for a few self-directed expletives.

The ascent of Fionn Bheinn was a weary one. Nothing wrong with the hill, and the views were good, but it was hard to enjoy them when I could not stop cursing my stupidity and thinking how to resolve the problem. I had already had to buy one new key for £254 but I was more concerned with the short term. My phone and money were locked in the car, along with the key to the cottage in Strathpeffer, so how could I contact the rescue service? And how would they manage to break in? And what then?

What I needed was a plan. Instead of taking a more direct line from Fionn Bheinn to the road, I would try to reverse my route of ascent. That would give me focus and a little hope. I left the path and headed through the vegetation toward the prominent rock where I had rested earlier. A wriggle in my GPS track made the rock easy to find, and within seconds I spotted a metallic gleam. It was the watch. Better than nothing, but only a consolation prize. I decided it was pointless to search the heathery peat, but as soon as I reached the track I kept my head down every step of the way.

The track was splattered with small dark blobs. I had never really studied sheep droppings before, but now I realised how remarkably similar they can look to a rounded black car key. There were also plenty of rocks and a key could easily have slipped beneath one of them, but I could not look under them all. As I neared Achnasheen and the moment of truth, the track became flatter and there were fewer black blobs. Within 400 metres of the road I noticed a black blob of promising shape, and that was the key to the rest of my holiday. My reaction was muted. I felt relief and disbelief rather than elation. I tried to find joy in the moment but my carelessness barely deserved any reward. The hills had been fine and the weather great, yet I would remember little of them. At least I had learned a lesson. I must never, ever again, put my car key in a pocket with a hole in.

Three weeks later I was on my way to Scourie in the far north-west for a week with friends. I did not have much of a hill agenda so was free to choose short walks to suit the persistently dull and damp weather. Beinn an Fhuarain seemed a suitable choice for an easy half day. Its drop was only about 140m but it was shown as 502m on some maps and 499m on others, so it was my task to survey it and resolve that uncertainty.

The path to the bone caves at Inchnadamph was good and I enjoyed heading steeply up a grassy gully toward the stony, breezy summit plateau. Breabag looked tempting but I stuck to my task and surveyed the col as well, to be sure of the drop. The walk seemed a little short so I cut across the steep-sided glen to the steep rugged slopes of Beinn nan Cnaimhseag. I reached the summit just as wind and rain started to blow in from the west, but I was in a good mood as I sped off northward and then strolled down the path. I had made the most of the day and might just reach the road before the rain became heavy.

All this had nothing to do with Fionn Bheinn until I patted my pockets and once again failed to feel the reassuring bulge of the car key. No no no, not again, please. Anyone could be careless but it would take rare stupidity to make the same mistake again so soon. Same key, same trousers, same pocket, same hole but perhaps slightly bigger.

I carried on to the car in disbelieving despair. This time I had a spare key inside the car but no way to access it. I tried all the handles and cursed but it didn't help. I had a phone to contact the rescue service but no signal, so I stashed my rucksack by the car and headed back up the path in the rain to try to get a signal. There was little chance of finding the black key on the dark wet rocks of the path. I spent a forlorn and miserable half hour going uphill until I realised I was not likely to get a signal unless I went all the way back up Beinn an Fhuarain, so I gave up and trudged back down in the damp greyness.

This time I took a good look around the car park in case someone had found a key on the path and placed it somewhere obvious. Nothing. I returned to the car and finally thought to look at the windscreen. Someone had tucked a note under a wiper blade to say where they had hidden the key. A little hut selling coffees was closed but near it was a plastic bag containing the same key that had now spent several hours lying on the lower slopes of two hills over a hundred km apart, connected by carelessness. I opened the car, wrote a thank you note and put it in the same place along with a large handful of pound coins for the absent coffee maker. I felt humbled by the kindness of strangers and a rare warmth toward humanity in general.

When I got home I sewed up the hole in the pocket and resolved never to use that pocket again, but I could not fix the hole in my head where my brain cells were escaping.

Torr Achilty

PAUL RICHARDSON, JUNE 2003

The hill looks scenic as we drive over from Strathpeffer, but from the dam it looks so steep and vegetated that we almost chicken out. After a reconnoitre we set off across the dam. The vegetation is so dense that it is quite hard to find a place to leave the track, but we eventually find a helpful outcrop of rock. The lower slopes are quite a struggle, with heather, whin, bracken and a hundred other species thickly cloaking the ground. The density of the shrubbery gradually reduces, giving slightly easier going higher up. The summit comes as something of a relief. The view isn't too exciting, but the top is a pleasant spot and the hill a suitable one for Ali's 300th Marilyn. We don't stop for a celebration, but tumble down the tangled slopes back to the car.

While showering later, I discover another lump similar to the cancerous one recently excised from my neck. Death takes a step nearer.

RHB section 13A   OS maps 19, 24, 25

Number		Height	Name	Drop	Location	Summit
953	A	1054.8	Liathach – Spidean a' Choire Leith	957	NG 9293 5796	Cairn
954	A	1023.9	Mullach an Rathain	152.1	NG 9118 5769	Outcrop by cairn
955		1010	Beinn Eighe - Ruadh-stac Mor	632	NG 9514 6114	Cairn
956		993	Spidean Coire nan Clach	172	NG 9661 5977	Cairn
971		896	Ruadh-stac Beag	185	NG 9728 6133	Cairn
972		887	Meall a' Ghiuthais	418	NG 9761 6341	Cairn
975	AJ	725.4	Beinn a' Chearcaill	367	NG 9310 6376	Rock
957	A	986.0	Beinn Alligin - Sgurr Mor	602	NG 8656 6127	Cairn
968	A	921.8	Tom na Gruagaich	154.2	NG 8595 6015	Trig
970	GA	913.7	Beinn Dearg	470	NG 8953 6082	Cliff edge
976	JA	671.7	An Ruadh-mheallan	202	NG 8361 6146	Boulder
973		875	Baosbheinn	444	NG 8703 6541	Rock near cairn
974		855	Beinn an Eoin	434	NG 9051 6462	Rock by cairn
977	A	422.7	Meall an Doirein	297	NG 8590 7541	Rock
978		403	Meall Lochan a' Chleirich	215	NG 8721 7161	Cairn
979	A	383.0	Sithean Mor ***	150.8	NG 8359 7401	Cairn
980	T	296.5	An Cuaidh	161	NG 7650 8912	Trig

Sithean Mor

Looking at the tightly-packed contours on OS maps, it seemed likely that there might be another Marilyn in this complex, undulating area between Gairloch and Loch Maree. The survey in 2015 confirmed that Sithean Mor qualifies, with 80cm to spare. The trig point on nearby An Groban is slightly higher but this is not relevant because the col connecting it to Meall an Doirein is 295m, which is much higher than the key col for Sithean Mor.

Baosbheinn

ROWLAND BOWKER, 2015

I met Ann in June 1964 on a Ramblers holiday in Glen Coe, when she agreed to leave the party to ascend Bidean nam Bian with me by a more exciting route. I decided she was worth pursuing. From then onwards, collecting countries had to be combined with climbing mountains. In June 1992 I climbed Baosbheinn with Ann. My first words on reaching the summit were 'I have never been here before', so it became my last Corbett. Next day it rained and we visited Inverewe Gardens where we bought the RHB book. This took us to climbing Marilyns and a wonderful new era. I had sunk low. I had been collecting waterfalls. At home, I found I had done over 600 Marilyns. Next date 1000, March 1995. Next was 1500, July 1998. I really intended to stop at 1500. St Kilda was good. I would like to regard Conachair as my last Marilyn, on 6 May 2003.

Ruadh-stac Beag

JONATHAN APPLEBY, 2012

This was the toughest hill of the year. The walking route is rough, scrambly and loose underfoot. It also has a feeling of isolation to it, surrounded as it is by higher peaks and feeling rather cut off from civilisation. I loved it.

Mullach an Rathain, Liathach

ALAN DAWSON, MARCH 1976

Four years after a solo ascent of Snowdon I climbed my second hill over 900 metres and only my third over 600m. It was not exactly my choice as I had never heard of Liathach or Torridon. I was only there because Lancaster University Hiking Club was looking for students over 21 to drive a minibus for their Easter excursion. My five years between school and university turned out to be useful so I offered my services, though I was not a member or a hiker and I had no relevant equipment or experience. Inevitably I got into difficulties. My cheap suede boots had no grip on the soles and were hopeless for climbing up the snow-filled stone chute that rose behind the youth hostel. I kept going upward by veering off to the right onto more rocky ground with snow-covered ledges and somehow I reached the top. In hindsight I was lucky to survive. In 1985 I learned about Munros and found that Mullach an Rathain was not classed as a separate peak (until 1997). In 2018 I confirmed that it does qualify as a Marilyn. It was my fifth ascent and one of my most satisfying survey results as well as a superb day's walking along the full length of ridge.

CHARLES EVERETT, APRIL 2012

I stayed a week at Torridon youth hostel with my son Jamie and our pet dog Ben-Ji, and we had a great week on nearby mountains. On the Friday we set off in glorious weather to climb Liathach via its Northern Pinnacles. This area is steep rock and was tricky with snow on the ledges. We were trying to avoid the most difficult section when it started to get more seriously challenging, then a short storm deposited some fresh damp snow. We were on a ledge a couple of feet wide in a precarious position.

It looked too risky to go up the five-metre pitch above us and too dodgy to retreat on the steep ground below. I decided to call the mountain rescue service for advice. About an hour and a half later, a helicopter arrived to take us off the crags. Unfortunately, and tragically, the strong downdraught of the helicopter blew Ben-Ji off the ledge. Neither Jamie nor I saw it happen as we were braced face against the rock. We only realised what had happened when we were in the helicopter. They were running low on fuel and not able to winch someone down to the bottom of the crags to see if there was an alive but injured dog.

The mountain rescue guy saw it happen and said Ben-Ji had been flung out into mid air, then fell twenty metres before he hit rock again and fell further out of sight. He was sure the dog would not have survived the fall but he joined me for a search the next day, when we went up the mountain by different routes and met close to the summit. I went round the rim of the corrie to look down, but the terrain was too difficult and the weather was too wintry to risk going down to get a better look.

An Cuaidh

The concept sometimes known as the effort-to-reward ratio can not be quantified but its meaning is easy to grasp. Some hills require a lot of effort to reach an undistinguished summit with little or no view. They can provide satisfaction but little enjoyment. At the other end of the scale are hills that are easy to climb but deliver rewards that seem out of proportion to the minimal effort involved. An Cuaidh is one of these. Some hill baggers have nominated it as having the best view of all, with a view encompassing hills in Harris, Trotternish, the Cuillin, Torridon, Fisherfield, Coigach, Assynt and as far north as Quinag and Foinaven, with a foreground of sea, lochs and islands. Not one to be climbed in mist.

Ruadh-stac Mor, Beinn Eighe

Ruadh-stac Beag

Sithean Mor near Gairloch on the day it was discovered to be a Marilyn

Number		Height	Name	Drop	Location	Summit
981	A	960.7	Sgorr Ruadh	723	NG 9590 5050	Rock by cairn
983	A	926.0	Beinn Liath Mhor	270	NG 9641 5197	Cairn
984	A	907.0	Fuar Tholl	243	NG 9754 4894	Shelter cairn
989	A	871.3	Sgorr nan Lochan Uaine	206.8	NG 9691 5315	Shelter
991		782	Sgurr Dubh	215	NG 9791 5577	Shelter cairn
1000		437	Seana Mheallan	243	NG 9288 5510	Cairn on outcrop
982		933	Maol Chean-dearg	514	NG 9241 4990	Cairn
988	A	890.4	An Ruadh-stac	328	NG 9214 4806	Cairn
993	A	732.3	Sgurr a' Gharaidh	333	NG 8840 4437	Cairn
986	A	902.4	Beinn Damh	517	NG 8926 5020	Cairn
992	A	735.1	Beinn na h-Eaglaise	305.4	NG 9087 5236	Rock by cairn
994	A	677.8	Carn Breac	392.1	NH 0463 5310	Outcrop
996	A	626.8	Beinn na Feusaige *	227.9	NH 0900 5424	Outcrop
999		466	Bidein Clann Raonaild	231	NH 0537 5918	Cairn
1001	T	395.1	Bad a' Chreamha	255	NG 8576 3664	Trig
1002		391	An Sgurr	202	NG 8570 3873	Cairn

An Ruadh-stac

ALAN DAWSON, JULY 1990

I reckoned that this hill provided one of the most enjoyable ascents of all, with huge easy rock slabs all the way up from the col. It felt as good as it looked, in contrast to Maol Chean-dearg which had felt hot and tiring with lots of clegs. Returning in 2019 from the south via the long rocky ridge of Carn Cadha an Eididh was not quite as exhilarating but still pretty good. It seemed a great pity that the summit of such a fine hill was spoiled by the usual huge litter of loose rocks and rubble deposited by hill walkers.

Sgurr a' Gharaidh

SUE AND TREVOR LITTLEWOOD, JUNE 2006

Sgurr a' Gharaidh was surprising for its extensive limestone exposures and one of the best floral displays we had ever had on a British mountain. On that one day we saw more flowers of mountain avens than in all other sightings ever.

Beinn na Feusaige and Carn Breac

ALAN DAWSON, JULY 2017

The summit of Beinn na Feusaige was relocated by around 300 metres from the first edition of RHB, when it was listed as 625m at NH093543. In 2017, a survey confirmed that the new OS spot height of 627m was correct. More surprisingly, I found a new summit location for Carn Breac, a notable outcrop 150 metres north-east from the trig pillar. On a clear day, the views over to the Coulin hills from this pair were magnificent and made me think that the whole group were undervalued, probably because they are not quite as striking as the sprawling giants across the other side of Glen Torridon.

HW06 Beinnbhan-shieldaig

Number		Height	Name	Drop	Location	Summit
987	A	895.7	Beinn Bhan	850	NG 8036 4503	Trig
990	A	793.0	Sgurr a' Chaorachain	209.9	NG 7965 4175	Cairn
998		516	An Staonach	229	NG 8300 4808	Outcrop by cairn
995	A	625.8	Beinn a' Chlachain #	375	NG 7241 4904	Outcrop by trig
997		534	Ben Shieldaig	403	NG 8336 5239	Rock by cairn

Ben Shieldaig

ALAN DAWSON, MARCH 1976

My seventh Marilyn and my first in Scotland. I had never heard of it before and only decided to climb it a few minutes before I set off up it. It was the second day of my first and only trip with Lancaster University Hiking Club. The first day we had got a thorough drenching on a walk to the Falls of Glomach and back, with no summits along the way. I burned holes in my soaking socks by trying to dry them on top of a stove in Ratagan youth hostel, not realising that the socks contained nylon.

We set off in the minibus for Torridon the next day. The weather was again awful until the mist cleared and I saw a hill loom out of the murk. Filled with rare youthful enthusiasm, I told the driver that I would like to get off and would walk to Torridon youth hostel over this hill. One of the party was also enthused and decided to join me. The hill is steep-sided and well vegetated but any horrors were soon forgotten. The next day I almost fell to my death from the direct route up Mullach an Rathain.

In 2008 I had a more relaxed return to Ben Shieldaig, via a more civilised route from the north-east. It was still obscure at the time but it became more widely known in 2023 when the Woodland Trust Scotland was awarded a grant of one million pounds over five years to help preserve and expand the pine and birch forests on the flanks of the hill. The plan included planting over half a million native trees such as Scots pine, birch, oak, willow, aspen, alder, hazel and juniper. This all sounds fine and laudable, but in many places tree planting causes barriers for hill walkers, as the planters fail to consider that walkers might want to reach the top of a hill without having to climb over fences and wade through ditches, mounds and saplings. It would not take much of the funding to include stiles or gates and keep a narrow tree-free route to the top. A circular route would be even better. It is great to hear about native woodlands thriving and explanding, but it is better to be able to see them close-up without the usual plantation problems that are likely to deter most casual walkers. Hill baggers will always find a way, but lots of hills could be made more accessible for other walkers with a little more consideration.

An Staonach

SUE AND TREVOR LITTLEWOOD, MAY 2010

During a week based at Kishorn we had a surprisingly good day on An Staonach, walking directly from Couldoran Lodge. A dreary trudge over moorland had been expected but we had an easy approach by an estate road followed by a fine time picking a way to the summit past small crags and over sandstone slabs. With sunshine and views eastwards to Beinn Damh and Maol Chean-dearg sprinkled with late spring snow, the experience was wonderful.

——— Western Highlands: Central ———

Land south of Glen Carron and Strath Bran, north of Glen Shiel and Glen Moriston

Marilyns:	75
Highest:	Carn Eighe, 1182.8m
Lowest:	Mount Eagle, 256m
Most prominent:	Carn Eighe, drop 1145m
Least prominent:	Mullach Fraoch-choire, drop 151.3m

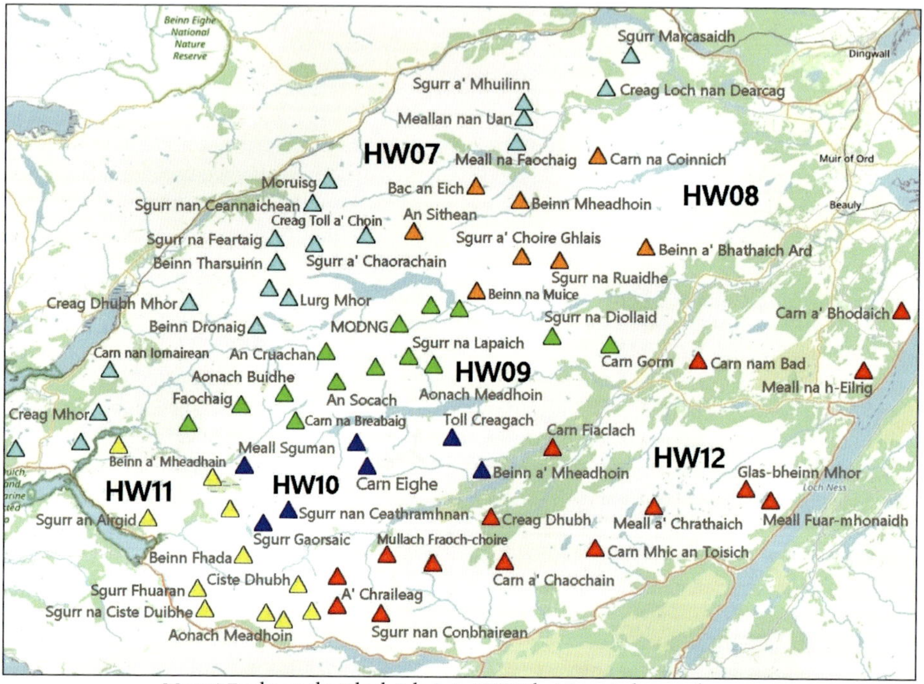

Mount Eagle on the Black Isle is in HW08 but is not shown above

The Maoile Lunndaidh plateau, before it was superseded by Creag Toll a' Choin

Number		Height	Name	Drop	Location	Summit
885	T	1053.1	Sgurr a' Chaorachain	570	NH 0875 4473	Trig
891	A	1005.3	Creag Toll a' Choin **	402	NH 1308 4532	Rock
896	A	987.5	Lurg Mhor	445	NH 0648 4045	Cairn on outcrop
898	A	945.0	Bidein a' Choire Sheasgaich	208.2	NH 0490 4126	Cairn
904	A	861.2	Beinn Tharsuinn	224	NH 0552 4334	Cairn
911	A	796.8	Beinn Dronaig	434	NH 0370 3818	Outcrop near trig
899	A	925.7	Moruisg	593	NH 1011 4994	Cairn
900	G	913.4	Sgurr nan Ceannaichean	185	NH 0872 4805	Cairn on rock
903	A	878.8	Sgurr a' Mhuilinn	579	NH 2646 5574	Cairn
909	A	838.3	Meallan nan Uan	156.4	NH 2636 5447	Rock by cairn
913	A	680.6	Meall na Faochaig	273	NH 2575 5250	Cairn
906		862	Sgurr na Feartaig	266	NH 0551 4538	Cairn
916	AG	611.0	Creag Dhubh Mhor	168	NG 9828 4047	Rock
917	T	580.2	Sgurr Marcasaidh	294	NH 3540 5927	Rock by trig
918		537	Creag Loch nan Dearcag	231	NH 3334 5672	Cairn
919		485	Carn nan Iomairean	227	NG 9142 3519	Cairn
920		453	Beinn Conchra	204	NG 8872 2916	Cairn
923		407	Creag Mhor	159	NG 9030 3159	Cairn
921	A	452.6	Auchtertyre Hill	244	NG 8325 2895	Rock near trig
922	A	447.7	Beinn Raimh	147.6	NG 8477 3119	Cairn

Creag Toll a' Choin

ALAN DAWSON, MAY AND JULY 2014

This hill became a Marilyn after my survey found it to be half a metre higher than Maoile Lunndaidh. This was a surprise, as the OS map showed it to be two metres lower. The summit area of Maoile Lunndaidh is very flat apart from a large cairn. I first surveyed it in poor visibility so I went back two months later to resurvey the pair and make sure that I found the highest point of each. I found an extra 15cm on Maoile Lunndaidh but the height of Creag Toll a' Choin was exactly the same, so it was confirmed as a Marilyn, unless the cairn on Maoile Lunndaidh conceals an embedded rock over 35cm high.

Bidein a' Choire Sheasgaich and Lurg Mhor

PAUL RICHARDSON, JUNE 1987

It was my turn to drive. After 240 miles Gordon and I arrived at Lair, near Achnashellach, at about 3pm and we set about trying to find the path to the River Carron. We soon climbed above the trees and enjoyed good views of the hills to the north and west. There was just one man in residence at Bearnais bothy, a rather surly individual who was reading ancient history. We ate and had a cup of coffee, then decided to take advantage of the good weather, though it was by now 7pm. We had gone only about a mile when another shower enveloped us. The rain got heavier and visibility worse. Several times we considered turning back, but persisted until a steep pull brought us up to the ridge.

The rain stopped and visibility slowly improved until peak after peak was revealed by the rays of the sinking sun shining between the clouds. It was a magnificent sight which more than repaid the effort of the climb. It was after 9pm when we reached the summit of Bidein a' Choire Sheasgaich. A fast descent took us to the col beneath Lurg Mhor and we began to toil up as fast as we could. We arrived breathless at the summit and almost immediately left it again as it was nearly 10pm and the light was fading. We raced down to the col and back up the ridge, passing well south of the summit. We bounded down the wet corrie and across peaty moors back to the bothy, arriving at about 11:30pm. After a drink and banana cake we retired for the night but were disturbed by a noisy mouse.

Beinn Tharsuinn

PAUL RICHARDSON, JUNE 1987

Showers battered on the bothy roof on and off all night. In the morning we exchanged plans with the new occupant, who was also planning to climb the Sgurr a' Chaorachain group. The showers continued as we plodded up through the boggy and trackless glen towards the Bealach Bhearnais. It was tough going and Gordon, who was carrying our only map, wanted to take a short-cut up the hillside to our right toward Sgurr Choinnich. I then led the way steeply up the hillside until a small gully gave access almost directly to the summit. I visited the cairn then returned to the shelter of some nearby rocks to wait for Gordon. The wind had became quite fierce. I was mentally ticking off another Munro when Gordon arrived, took out the map and announced that we were not, as he put it, on the hill we thought we were on. Because of the way he had the map folded, he had mis-read the ground. His short-cut to Sgurr Choinnich had in fact brought us to the summit of Beinn Tharsuinn. I mentally un-ticked a Munro and ticked a Corbett.

Down we went to the Bealach Bhearnais toward the real Sgurr Choinnich. The ridge towered above us, very long and very steep. We began slowly up it but the wind soon had us staggering about and clinging to rocks for support. We struggled on a bit further but soon knew it was time to give up. To go on was unwise and dangerous in this wind. We returned to the bealach and trudged back down the glen to the bothy. Gordon tried to get a fire going to dry out our wet socks but his prolonged efforts were rewarded only by a short-lived smouldering. Outside, the rain became continuous and the wind howled.

Bidein a' Choire Sheasgaich and Lurg Mhor from Sail Riabhach

Number		Height	Name	Drop	Location	Summit
884	A	1083.7	Sgurr a' Choire Ghlais	819	NH 2588 4300	Rock
886	A	1049.2	Sgurr Fhuar-thuill	148.1	NH 2358 4375	Rock by cairn
894		993	Sgurr na Ruaidhe	226	NH 2890 4260	Cairn
905	A	861.7	Beinn a' Bhathaich Ard	241	NH 3605 4348	Trig
912	A	693.8	Beinn na Muice	160.6	NH 2188 4023	Cairn
907	A	849.9	Bac an Eich	336.5	NH 2221 4895	Rock by trig
910	A	812.1	An Sithean	268	NH 1710 4539	Cairn
914	A	673.4	Carn na Coinnich	265	NH 3245 5105	Trig
915	A	664.2	Beinn Mheadhoin	221.8	NH 2588 4776	Rock rib
1110	T	256.4	Mount Eagle	221.2	NH 6485 5901	Trig

Carn na Coinnich

This is the highest of a sprawling range of hills between Strathconon and the Orrin Reservoir. There are thirteen hills in this group over 600m (with over 20m drop) but only one Marilyn, easily reached by a track from the north. For several years Carn na Coinnich was reduced to the status of a twin peak with Meall nan Damh, an undulating 4km to the east. This was the result of inaccurate mapping by OS, which showed Meall nan Damh as 673m, whereas GNSS surveys showed it to be 3.1m lower than Carn na Coinnich.

Mount Eagle

This is the highest point on the peninsula between the Beauly Firth and the Cromarty Firth that is misleadingly known as the Black Isle. Mount Eagle sounds magnificent but the reality is a mundane plod along lifeless forest tracks to reach a trig pillar half-hidden amongst gloomy conifers and gorse bushes. It was included with section 15 in RHB but is clearly connected topographically with the Western Highlands rather than the Northern Highlands, despite being so close to the east coast.

An Sithean

ALAN DAWSON, MAY 2023

The snow was soft and deep when I first climbed this hill in October 2002. Walking was hard work and so I had bypassed the distinctive summit of Meall Innis na Sine. I rectified that omission in 2023 and naturally continued to the main summit of An Sithean. The terrain was the usual mixture of heather, grass and bog, with one enormous peaty col to cross, but I was not paying much attention because I kept looking at my phone to see if there was a signal. It was the last day of the football season and Everton needed to beat Bournemouth to avoid relegation for the first time since before I was born.

I tried to forget about it and enjoy the walk, but I failed. By the time I reached the summit cairn the match had ended. There was a faint signal and the relevant page on the BBC website started to appear, but then it stalled. I couldn't wait another three hours to find out the result but I could wait on the top a while. Every few seconds I threw the phone in the air, caught it and checked the site. Eventually a photo appeared of players celebrating. They were wearing blue shirts and big grins and had won 1-0. The goal scorer shared my initials. The walk back was rough going in places but utterly wonderful.

Number		Height	Name	Drop	Location	Summit
926	A	1151.9	Sgurr na Lapaich	841	NH 1610 3512	Boulder
927	A	1127.7	An Riabhachan	301.8	NH 1336 3448	Rock by cairn
931	A	1069.6	An Socach	207.4	NH 1006 3327	Trig
936	A	992.3	Carn nan Gobhar	197.5	NH 1818 3436	Cairn
944	A	706.2	An Cruachan	239.1	NH 0938 3587	Cairn
945	A	679.2	Carn na Breabaig	179.4	NH 0666 3016	Outcrop
940	A	900.3	Aonach Buidhe	477	NH 0576 3246	Rock by cairn
941		879	Sguman Coinntich	415	NG 9770 3035	Cairn near trig
942	A	868.9	Faochaig	231	NH 0218 3171	Outcrop by cairn
943	A	817.9	Sgorr na Diollaid	308	NH 2818 3626	Tor
946	A	677.3	Carn Gorm	194	NH 3286 3551	Cairn
947	A	598.8	Meallan Odhar Doire nan Gillean	177	NH 1562 3778	Boulder
948		591	Beinn Dubh an Iaruinn	240	NH 1823 321	Outcrop
952		390	Meall Innis an Loichel	172	NH 2042 3894	Cairn on rock

Sgurr na Lapaich

This is the 17th highest Marilyn and the 20th most prominent, but only five hills are both higher and more prominent – Ben Nevis, Ben Macdui, Ben Lawers, Carn Eighe and Ben More. Its topographic significance is similar to that of Bidean nam Bian, Creag Meagaidh and Ben Lui, but it is less easily accessible and much less popular than those three. Of the sixteen hills over 1000m high with over 800m prominence, Sgurr na Ciche was the only one with fewer ascents recorded on the Hill Bagging site by the end of 2024.

Aonach Buidhe

This hill is shown as 899m on OS maps and is one of only three Marilyns to be promoted to a new metric tier as a result of a GNSS survey. In 2010 G&J Surveys discovered Glyder Fawr to be 1000.8m, and I found An Cliseam on Harris to be 800m (just) in 2021. I had hopes for Sgurr Ban in the Mamores but found it to be 999.6m, and Sgurr Breac in the Fannich group reached only 999.7m. Both could be rounded to 1000m on OS maps but that would be misleading as they don't quite make it. Cir Mhor on Arran is 799m on the map but is only 798.1m. Going the other way, The Coyles of Muick and Meallan Odhar Doire nan Gillean are both mapped at 601m but are only 599 metres. Worse was The Sow of Atholl, which shrank by 4.1m from 803m to 798.9m after my survey. It still qualifies as a Marilyn, with 10.8m to spare.

An Cruachan

This was mentioned in the first edition as one of the four most remote Marilyns, along with Creag Mhor (HN04), Carn Ban (HN07) and Beinn Bhreac (HE08), but remoteness is relative. An Cruachan is over 16km from a public road in a direct line and nearer 25km on a track or private road, yet it can be climbed fairly comfortably in a day walk from west or east by using a bike up Glen Elchaig or the private road along Glen Strathfarrar. From the west it can be combined with Carn na Breabaig and possibly An Socach, while from the east it can be combined with Beinn Dubh an Iaruinn, Meallan Odhar Doire nan Gillean and possibly little Meall Innis an Locheil to complete a fine and productive outing.

The summit of Sgurr na Diollaid

The northern slopes of Faochaig

Meall Innis an Loichel (right) and Loch Monar

Number		Height	Name	Drop	Location	Summit
803	A	1182.8	Carn Eighe	1145	NH 1235 2619	Trig
810	A	1112.7	Tom a' Choinnich	149.8	NH 1640 2733	Cairn
826	A	1004.8	Beinn Fhionnlaidh	173	NH 1155 2827	Cairn
805	A	1149.7	Sgurr nan Ceathramhnan	433	NH 0569 2285	Rock by cairn
833	A	980.6	Mullach na Dheiragain	142	NH 0806 2593	Rock near cairn
854	A	838.3	Sgurr Gaorsaic	169.2	NH 0360 2193	Vrock
860		544	Meall Sguman	153	NH 0227 2670	Cairn
818	A	1053.7	Toll Creagach	181.4	NH 1940 2828	Rock
857	A	715.5	Carn Loch na Gobhlaig	142.9	NH 2572 3015	Outcrop
859	A	611.9	Beinn a' Mheadhoin	243.0	NH 2186 2555	Rock rib

Carn Eighe

Carn Eighe is the second most prominent hill in Britain. Its key col is at the Caledonian Canal by Laggan Locks, along the Great Glen that separates the Northern and Western Highlands from the rest of the mainland. Carn Eighe therefore qualifies as one of the Relative Mountains of Earth – the Ribus – along with Ben Nevis and Snowdon. These are the only three British hills with relative height over 1000m. Sgurr Alasdair on Skye falls short by eight metres and qualifies as a Sub-Ribu. Scafell Pike may be regarded as one of the 'three peaks' politically but not topographically, as its drop is only 912m, the lowest of eleven British hills with over 900m prominence. The current total of Ribus is 7149 but this will change as more accurate data becomes available, volcanoes explode and landslides affect cols and summits. Worldwide there are only 22 peaks with over 4000m prominence, in seventeen countries. Everest, Nanga Parbat and K2 are the only three mountains over 8000m high that have prominence over 4000m.

Tom a' Choinnich

In 2016 Tom a' Choinnich was surveyed as having 149.9m drop, which was subject to uncertainty owing to the large cairn on the summit. Eight years passed before I returned to try to dismantle it, with help from Daniel Quinn, the author of the book about the Ribus (pronounced ree-boos), published in 2024. It took us over two hours to remove enough of the vast pile of rocks to be confident that there could be no natural rock embedded with the huge mess. After the survey we spent another hour trying to tidy up the rocks as there was nowhere to dispose of them. I then carried on to the col to resurvey it. After all that, I found the summit to be only 3cm higher than in the first survey. The col height figure increased slightly, perhaps owing to finding a more precise survey position, so the drop figure was revised to 149.8m and there was no new Marilyn.

Meall Sguman

Everything is relative, as Albert Einstein rather brilliantly worked out in his spare time. A 544m high hill would dominate the landscape anywhere in the central, eastern or southern areas of England, apart from Devon, but Meall Sguman is less than half the height of three of the Marilyns in this area. It is not even the main landscape feature in its own vicinity, for the Falls of Glomach is only a kilometre from the summit. Its key col is about a kilometre east of the Falls and is just low enough for it to qualify for the list.

Number		Height	Name	Drop	Location	Summit
815	A	1068.8	Sgurr Fhuaran	665	NG 9784 1668	Rock by cairn
821	A	1039.1	Sgurr a' Bhealaich Dheirg	315.6	NH 0351 1436	Rock by cairn
825		1027	Sgurr na Ciste Duibhe	177	NG 9840 1494	Cairn
828	A	1001.9	Aonach Meadhoin	172.6	NH 0488 1376	Rock near cairn
834	A	981.1	Ciste Dhubh	390.5	NH 0623 1661	Rock by cairn
855	A	798.1	Am Bathach	232.4	NH 0733 1434	Rock
823	A	1031.9	Beinn Fhada	643	NH 0185 1925	Rock by trig
846	A	917.1	A' Ghlas-bheinn	406	NH 0082 2310	Cairn on outcrop
856	A	727.8	Carnan Cruithneachd	220	NG 9944 2582	Cairn
853	A	841.2	Sgurr an Airgid	394	NG 9404 2271	Outcrop
858	A	633.3	Carn Bad a' Chreamha	146.8	NG 9257 2646	Rock
861		414	Beinn a' Mheadhain	195	NG 9185 2882	Cairn

Sgurr an Airgid

Jon Metcalf, 2003

Excellent glaciated landslip topography, spell-binding loch views to the south and a rough, intricate no-Marilyn region to the north. I departed feeling that I had seriously misallocated the day by not allowing for more exploration of this exceptional mountain.

Ciste Dhubh

Alan Dawson, August 2018

Identity politics seems to have become more socially prominent in recent years, but for those of us who were not black, female, gay, young or deprived, it was not clear which category or initial we could identify with, other than H for hill bagger and possibly N for neurodiverse, which could mean anything. I could also identify with grumpy curmudgeons but by the time I reached Ciste Dhubh on a lovely day with fabulous views, I had nothing to be grumpy about. I had already surveyed Am Bathach and its South Top, An Cnapach and Ciste Dhubh South Top, and I was confident that the last two qualified as High Hills of Britain, which were the main focus of my research in 2018. I was in such a good mood when I reached the main summit of Ciste Dhubh that I did not mind not being alone.

My fellow bagger did not move or say much because he was a stuffed bear in bright clothing. I read the note explaining his presence and learned that he was called Ben. He was on a mission to bag the Munros and could not do this alone so he needed help. I was surprised to find that my current feelings of goodwill toward all non-biting lifeforms extended as far as stuffed toys, but I was having a good day. Instead of grumpily dismissing this little bear as a twee publicity stunt, I embraced the idea, moved Ben aside so that I could survey the summit and made him comfortable. I chatted to him during the survey then packed up my equipment and found room for Ben in my heavy pack. After I got home I updated his Facebook page and then left him on top of Meall Corranaich a week later, as he needed it for his round. I never saw Ben again and soon lost track of his progress, but I was pleased to have helped him on his way. I didn't know if this was neurodiverse or normal behaviour and I didn't care, because I had enjoyed a superb day's walking in a wonderful location that yielded a most excellent set of survey data and added two metres to the height of Ciste Dhubh.

Ben supervising the survey on top of Ciste Dhubh

Sgurr nan Ceathramhnan from Stuc Bheag

Carnan Cruithneachd in evening light

Number		Height	Name	Drop	Location	Summit
862	A	1119.2	A' Chraileag	785	NH 0942 1479	Cairn
863	A	1109.1	Sgurr nan Conbhairean	382	NH 1299 1389	Cairn
864	A	1100.9	Mullach Fraoch-choire	151.3	NH 0949 1715	Rock by shelter
875		888	Aonach Shasuinn	237	NH 1733 1801	Rock by cairn
876	A	862.5	Carn a' Choire Ghairbh	198	NH 1368 1887	Cairn
877	A	706.6	Carn a' Chaochain	271	NH 2351 1779	Cairn
879	A	678.9	Meall a' Chrathaich	184	NH 3606 2208	Outcrop near trig
880	A	678.2	Carn Mhic an Toisich	176	NH 3105 1858	Cairn
878	A	698.4	Meall Fuar-mhonaidh	233	NH 4570 2221	Outcrop by cairn
881	A	650.6	Glas-bheinn Mhor	155	NH 4369 2315	Outcrop by cairn
882		539	Creag Dhubh	204	NH 2250 2164	Cairn
883		457	Carn Fiaclach	154	NH 2789 2723	Boulder
949	T	500.6	Carn a' Bhodaich	290	NH 5698 3750	Trig
950	T	465.1	Meall na h-Eilrig	187	NH 5371 3261	Trig
951	A	458.1	Carn nam Bad	210	NH 4017 3392	Outcrop near cairn

A' Chraileag

This is the 33rd most prominent peak. It is over fifty metres higher than the more popular ridge further west above Glen Shiel. Its ridiculously high but reasonably well-built summit cairn is the highest point in a varied area that stretches all the way from Loch Cluanie to the Beauly Firth and Inverness. The spelling was adjusted from A' Chralaig on OS maps several years ago, but the relentless steepness of its slopes remains unchanged.

Carn nam Bad

ALAN DAWSON, JULY 2021

Carn a' Bhodaich, Meall na h-Eilrig and Carn nam Bad are located in a large tract of land between Cannich and Loch Ness, north of Glen Urquhart. These hills were listed in region 12 in RHB but topographically they are connected to the higher hills as far west as A' Chraileag. Four kilometres east from Carn nam Bad is Carn Mor, shown as only one metre lower on OS maps. Surveying both hills in one outing would involve a very knobbly and heathery walk or a long circuit using tracks and roads. I devised a plan to avoid this effort by surveying only Carn nam Bad. If it really was 457m then I could be confident it was the higher of the pair, as Carn Mor has a trig pillar fixing the height at 456m. However, I then discovered from reports and photos that Carn Mor has a boulder about a metre higher than the trig, making it 457m and therefore a twin peak with Carn nam Bad. This meant I would have to survey both unless Carn nam Bad turned out to be about 455m, meaning demotion, or above 458m, meaning certainty.

It was a pleasant stroll along the track from the south to the easy heathery slopes of Carn nam Bad. The summit was a well-defined small outcrop, so I did not have to go rummaging in the heather looking for the highest point. It turned out to be 458.1m, confirming Carn nam Bad as the Marilyn. I had no need to survey Carn Mor unless I was going Tump bagging, which I had been successfully resisting except when I had nothing better to do. I did notice that my feet walked up 399m Meall Cluainidh without permission on the way back, but that was only because it needed a survey to find out if it was 400m.

——— Western Highlands: South ———

Land south of Glen Shiel and Glen Moriston, north of Loch Ailort, Loch Eilt, Glenfinnan and Loch Eil

Marilyns: 78
Highest: Sgurr na Ciche, 1040.2m
Lowest: Sgurr na Dubh-chreige, 197m
Most prominent: Sgurr na Ciche, drop 839m
Least prominent: Biod an Fhithich, drop 154.1m

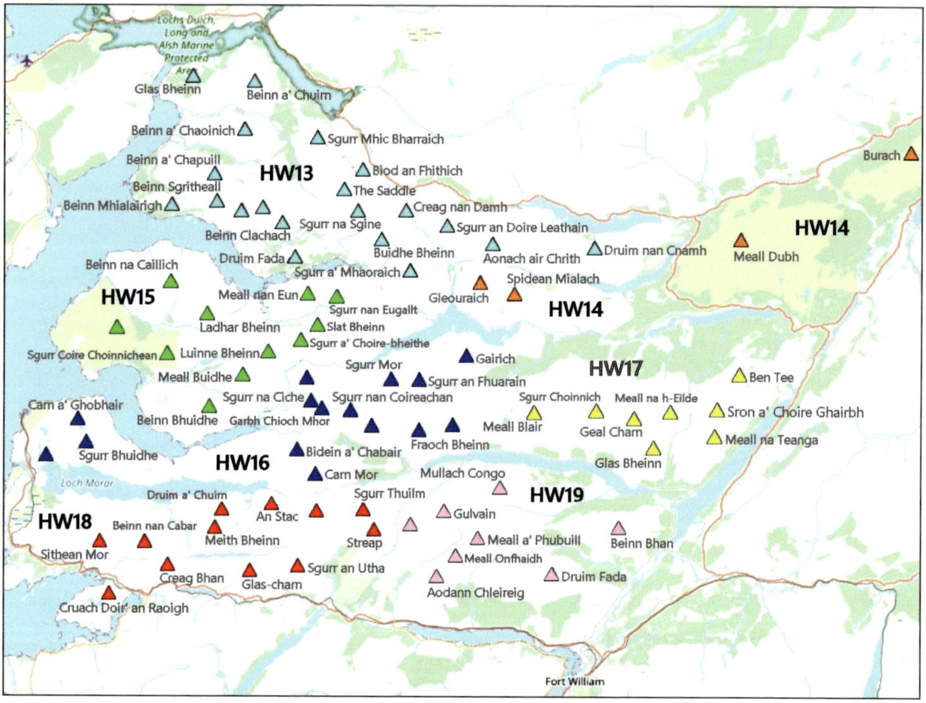

Beinn Clachach

Number		Height	Name	Drop	Location	Summit
684	A	1026.6	Sgurr a' Mhaoraich	708	NG 9839 0656	Outcrop
685	A	1019.5	Aonach air Chrith	495	NH 0510 0835	Rock
687	A	1008.4	Sgurr an Doire Leathain	187.3	NH 0152 0988	Cairn
708	A	917.2	Creag nan Damh	196	NG 9834 1120	Cairn
713	G	885.5	Buidhe Bheinn **	161.0	NG 9633 0904	Rock
719	T	789.5	Druim nan Cnamh	356	NH 1308 0768	Rock near trig
688	A	1011.5	The Saddle *	333	NG 9361 1312	Rock
701	A	945.7	Sgurr na Sgine	247	NG 9461 1136	Rock by cairn
720		779	Sgurr Mhic Bharraich	317	NG 9177 1735	Cairn
724	AG	645.9	Biod an Fhithich	154.1	NG 9508 1473	Grass
695	T	973.5	Beinn Sgritheall	500	NG 8359 1267	Cairn
718		805	Beinn na h-Eaglaise	201	NG 8543 1199	Cairn
721		774	Beinn nan Caorach	227	NG 8715 1211	Cairn
722	A	759.8	Beinn a' Chapuill	259	NG 8351 1484	Cairn on outcrop
723	A	710.7	Druim Fada	485	NG 8946 0833	Rock
725	A	642.2	Beinn Clachach	228.4	NG 8859 1091	Rock by cairn
727		548	Beinn Mhialairigh	194	NG 8001 1284	Cairn
728		410	Beinn a' Chaoinich	272	NG 8598 1839	Rock
726	A	602.6	Beinn a' Chuirn	261	NG 8700 2200	Trig
729		397	Glas Bheinn	219	NG 8216 2273	Voutcrop

The Saddle

For many years no-one was sure which was the highest point of The Saddle. When maps were the best source of data we were obliged to use map heights, so when OS changed the height of from 1010 to 1010 (1011), I duly moved the Marilyn summit back to the original point by the trig pillar, as listed in RHB. In 2014 I was able to survey both points on a calm, dry day, and found that the rock by the trig pillar was indeed 1011.2m, so the map was correct, but the other summit was 1011.5m, so the map was misleading. The result was useful and satisfying, but it caused a summit relocation for the third time.

Buidhe Bheinn

This hill was designated as a twin peak with Sgurr a' Bhac Chaolais in 1996 after Charles Everett noticed that both hills were shown as 885m on a large-scale OS map. In 2012 G&J Surveys showed Buidhe Bheinn to be 30cm higher and so it became the Marilyn on its own. The undulating ridge makes it a rugged walk to climb both hills together, with over 200m of ascent along the way and two other summits with over 50m of relative height.

Glas Bheinn

ALAN DAWSON, AUGUST 2004

It was a pleasant day by the seaside at Glenelg but there was a cloudburst halfway up Glas Bheinn. Someone had dumped an old Austin Maestro van near the top of the track, which provided shelter for half an hour. The rain did not relent but the wing mirror proved to be a useful replacement for the broken one on my tiny converted Maestro camper van.

HW14 Gleouraich-burach

Number		Height	Name	Drop	Location	Summit
683	A	1035.1	Gleouraich	767.8	NH 0394 0534	Rock by cairn
691	A	995.9	Spidean Mialach	259.5	NH 0658 0430	Rock by cairn
767	A	788.5	Meall Dubh	543	NH 2453 0784	Outcrop
771	A	606.5	Burach	236	NH 3829 1415	Cairn

A Gleouraich, a Mialach, a Burach, a Bhealaich
What a splendid array of Scottish names
Some people think that Gaelic is difficult to read
Especially those who live beside the Thames

Gleouraich

This is the 38th most prominent Marilyn though only the 78th highest. It is separated from the ridges either side of Glen Shiel by a drop of over 700 metres and therefore has to have its own hill area according to the topograpic rules applied. The only area in the Highlands with fewer Marilyns is HC07, which has the pair on Beinn a' Bheithir and the diminutive Ardsheal Hill. Sgurr na Ciche is the only hill higher than Gleouriach in the Western Highlands south of Glen Shiel. Gleouraich receives less acclaim but is much easier to access, via a finely made path from the Kinloch Hourn road.

Gleouraich

Meall Dubh

This is one of the most heavily desecrated hills in the Highlands. Although it may not have looked much, it has an extensive and complex summit area, with a steep northern face. The damage done by the wind farm extends far beyond the hill itself, as the turbines are prominent and visible over a huge area, spoiling numerous viewpoints and detracting from any sense of wildness as far away as Knoydart. The tracks do make access easier of course, particularly with a bike, and it would be perverse not to use them as that would do nothing to help matters.

Number		Height	Name	Drop	Location	Summit
731	A	1019.4	Ladhar Bheinn	796	NG 8240 0398	Cairn
750	A	848.4	Aonach Sgoilte	141.6	NG 8401 0270	Cairn on outcrop
752		796	Sgurr Coire Choinnichean	306	NG 7908 0106	Cairn
753		785	Beinn na Caillich	317	NG 79590668	Cairn
757		517	Druim na Cluain-airighe	383	NG 7516 0345	Cairn
737	A	945.5	Meall Buidhe	497.0	NM 8489 9897	Cairn
739	A	938.6	Luinne Bheinn	256.6	NG 8697 0074	Rock by cairn
749	A	855.4	Beinn Bhuidhe	308	NM 8217 9672	Outcrop by trig
742	GA	913.3	Sgurr a' Choire-bheithe	390	NG 8959 0159	Small rock
744	A	897.5	Sgurr nan Eugallt *	612	NG 9271 0486	Cairn on outcrop
755	A	700.6	Slat Bheinn	270.2	NG 9100 0274	Outcrop by cairn
756	A	666.7	Meall nan Eun	174	NG 9035 0523	Boulder

Druim na Cluain-airighe

ANN BOWKER, MAY 1999

We enjoyed a celebratory pint in Inverie after climbing our last mainland Marilyn, Druim na Cluain-airighe. We feel grateful for all the pleasure which the book has given us.

Beinn Bhuidhe

ANNE BUNN, JUNE 2014

A day trip to Beinn Bhuidhe was the objective, via a boat to Inverie from Mallaig. The first ferry was missed but we were on schedule until we descended into a dry river gorge strewn with large boulders that were difficult to climb around. When we finally escaped from the gorge, bracken above our heads made for slow progress back to the track. We missed the last ferry despite trying to run back to the jetty. Nothing for it but to pop into The Old Forge for a pint and to sort out how to get back to Mallaig. Fortunately there was an unscheduled late ferry back, so avoiding an unexpected and expensive stay in Inverie.

Slat Bheinn and Meall nan Eun

BRIAN EDRIDGE, JUNE 2013

On a blazing hot day in Knoydart, four of us reached Barrisdale from a boat anchored in Loch Hourn. The others set off for Sgurr a' Choire-bheithe but I was intent on climbing Slat Bheinn and Meall nan Eun, despite knowing my fitness and stamina were below par. I found it hard going on Slat Bheinn but felt a bit better on the descent to Glen Barrisdale, almost back to sea level again. I really started toiling on an agonisingly slow ascent of Meall nan Eun and by then my food and water had gone. As a marathon runner I once hit the wall but this was much worse. I felt utterly drained of energy and seriously doubted my ability to reach the top. Instead of feeling relief on gaining the cairn, I was further daunted by the sight of the big descent to Loch Hourn. On the nightmare descent of the rough, heathery ground I staggered constantly and fell over frequently, even being unaware of losing my glasses. The seemingly endless undulations of the loch-side track felt like individual hills but eventually I made it back, more than two hours overdue. My friends were on the point of starting search and rescue proceedings.

Ladhar Bheinn and Loch Hourn

Loch Nevis and Beinn Bhuidhe from Druim a' Ghoirtein on the west ridge of Sgurr na Ciche

Slat Bheinn

Number		Height	Name	Drop	Location	Summit
730	A	1040.2	Sgurr na Ciche	839	NM 9022 9668	Rock
732	A	1012.9	Garbh Chioch Mhor	169.5	NM 9095 9610	Outcrop
736	A	953.8	Sgurr nan Coireachan	221.7	NM 9330 9582	Grass
747	A	887.0	Beinn an Aodainn / Ben Aden	250.7	NM 8994 9862	Rock
751	A	835.2	Sgurr Cos na Breachd-laoidh	188.5	NM 9487 9467	Cairn on outcrop
733	A	1003.7	Sgurr Mor	342.4	NM 9653 9804	Cairn
746	A	889.5	Sgurr Beag	142.4	NM 9592 9709	Outcrop
741	A	918.8	Gairich	552	NN 0259 9958	Cairn
743	T	901.3	Sgurr an Fhuarain	183	NM 9874 9798	Trig
763		880	Sgurr Mhurlagain	514	NN 0126 9446	Cairn
748	A	857.3	Fraoch Bheinn	399	NM 9860 9403	Boulder
779	A	867.5	Bidein a' Chabair	553	NM 8890 9306	Cairn
780	A	830.0	Carn Mor	614	NM 9030 9094	Cairn on outcrop
796		548	Carn a' Ghobhair	470	NM 7168 9641	Cairn on outcrop
799		440	Sgurr Bhuidhe	178	NM 7227 9457	Rock
802		197	Sgurr na Dubh-chreige	164	NM 6906 9377	Vrock

Beinn an Aodainn

This hill has been known as Ben Aden for many years, but OS has converted its maps to Beinn an Aodainn and dropped Ben Aden entirely, so the table gives the Gaelic name first.

DAVID HUGHES, 2005

Ben Aden was the best hill of the year. A perfect summer's day started with a boat from Inverie to the jetty near Camusrory, then alongside a placid River Carnach and up the south-west face of the hill. The boat was a one-way trip so I had to walk back to Inverie, which meant 500 metres of re-ascent over Mam Meadail, but the beautifully constructed stalkers' path made the climb delightfully easy, and I was in The Old Forge by 7pm.

Sgurr Bhuidhe and Carn a' Ghobhair

PAUL RICHARDSON, JUNE 2001

The group which assembled at the roadside comprised seventeen plus a toddler (carried in a backpack by his parents, Jonathan and Lynda) and two dogs. I would normally be averse to walking in such a large group, but the Marilyn baggers surrounding Alan Dawson were a most pleasant bunch of people, not least the man himself. The group was swelled in part because Lynda Woods was about to bag her 600th Marilyn and thus qualify for the Marilyn Hall of Fame.

Cloud was low and a light rain was falling when we set off along the boggy path towards Loch an Nostarie. We sloshed along and then on up the hillside towards Loch Eireagoraidh. This brought us to the north-west ridge of Sgurr Bhuidhe, but first we had to cross An Leth-allt. Most waded, but I followed a few who went further upstream to an easier crossing. I was soon cast in the unaccustomed role of supporter when I fell in with Jennifer, a slow walker. We were in a dense mist and threading a way between plentiful outcrops on a complex of knolls and hillocks when the inevitable happened and we found ourselves isolated, with no sign of the others. Jennifer became anxious.

I had been following, not navigating, but I had the GPS so was not too concerned. After a few minutes we caught sight of the main party. More steep bumps were climbed, then we were at the top as there was a small cairn. Malt whisky and cake were produced to celebrate Lynda's 600th. A daft little ceremony was conducted and enjoyed by all.

Descent looked problematic, the map showing the summit ringed by crags. I'm not sure who took responsibility for the navigation, but an inspired bit of route-finding took us down the north-east face of the hill, through copious crag symbols on the map. Soon Loch Eireagoraidh appeared.

Carn a' Ghobhair was less complex than Sgurr Bhuidhe and the crags gave us no problems. There was no doubt about the top of this hill, nor was there any hope of a view. Descent west from here seemed even more problematic. Down we went through the crags and all went well until we came to a very steep drop which turned even the boldest back. Prospecting further northwards, we came across a steep, grassy gully and dropped down out of the mist. The sea views gave a hint of the grand vistas that must be available on a clear day. We returned to the cars and back to the Morar Hotel, where the somewhat ironically designated AGM was held. The evening was fun, with a good meal, an amusing meeting and a slide show on St Kilda followed by an excess of wine.

Sgurr na Dubh-chreige

PHIL DANT, 2004

This was a rest day in between Beinn Sgulaird and Ben Starav. It was a delightful little hill which enthralled my three children, who saw lizards, toads, frogs and deer en route. The view as we gained the north end of the ridge was just breathtaking.

Sgurr Cos na Breachd-laoidh

ALAN DAWSON, JULY 2024

My legs felt very heavy when I climbed this hill in 2005, probably because I had already been up Carn Mor and had not eaten much. I was tempted back by a rare fine day in the dreary summer of 2024. This time it was literally a warm-up, as I was on my way to Sgurr Mor. I surveyed the lovely rock summit, descended steeply to its col below An Eag and rested while I surveyed that too. The traverse to the Sgurr Mor col was over steep and rough ground, weaving a way between boulders and across little gullies. I stopped to rest and noticed that the top zip pocket on my rucksack was open. My phone was missing and could be anywhere in the thick vegetation of the past half hour. I rated my chance of finding it as negligible, so I gave it up and carried on. At least I still had GPS and car key.

Sgurr Beag should have been enjoyable as it had a good path up at a steady angle, but I was still cursing my carelessness. I plodded miserably up Sgurr Mor, set up the survey and plotted my descent route to the River Kingie. The views were theoretically stunning but did little to cheer me up. It had taken me almost seven hours to get there but I had been moving for only four and a half. It was 6:45pm. I realised that if I returned the same way then I could reach the track by around 11:30. Late but feasible. It meant going back over Sgurr Beag and some tough terrain, then over Sgurr Cos na Breachd-laoidh again.

I thought it worth a try so I set out to retrace my route. On the col-to-col traverse I magnified my GPS track and tried to follow it precisely past boulders, gullies and holes, looking down all the way. About fifty metres before the final col I found the phone, over five hours after I had lost it. It was hard work going back up the 188 metres but my mood was buoyant. I reached the summit around 9:30, took care going down in the dark and got to the car just before midnight, after 26km with 1900m ascent. Home at 3am, great day.

RHB section 10C   OS maps 33, 34

Number		Height	Name	Drop	Location	Summit
758	A	936.2	Sron a' Choire Ghairbh	620	NN 2224 9456	Cairn
759	A	916.8	Meall na Teanga	305.5	NN 2202 9247	Rock
761	A	901.6	Ben Tee	353	NN 2406 9719	Cairn on outcrop
764	A	837.2	Meall na h-Eilde	450	NN 1855 9463	Cairn
766	A	804.5	Geal Charn	156.9	NN 1561 9426	Outcrop by trig
768	A	747.4	Sgurr Choinnich	277.5	NN 1277 9496	Rock near cairn
769	A	731.5	Glas Bheinn	291.6	NN 1715 9189	Cairn
770	A	656.5	Meall Blair	213	NN 0774 9504	Trig

Ben Tee

Lots of hills don't look much but turn out to be full of interest. By contrast, Ben Tee looks impressive but offers little variety or stimulation. When I returned to survey it, by a new route from the north-east, it was not much better. Apart from the poor terrain, large cairn and wind farm, my mood was not helped when my survey equipment failed. I had little enthusiasm for a third ascent so it seemed astonishing to me that anyone would make the effort to climb Ben Tee over 1000 times. When the remarkable Richard Wood was living near Invergarry he also climbed Sron a' Choire Ghairbh and Meall na Teanga over 1000 times each. After moving to Cannich he climbed Sgorr na Diollaid over 1600 times. He is the only person to have climbed four Marilyns over 1000 times.

Eventually I did make the effort to go back but lost the path and ended up in a deep gorge. I got to see the waterfall on the Kilfinnan Burn but it was a struggle to escape. The higher ground was fine and the descent simple by following the path. It was no surprise that the 901m height on older OS maps was more accurate than the more recent 904m one.

Looking toward Meall Dubh and Meall na Teanga from the slopes of Sron a' Choire Ghairbh

Number		Height	Name	Drop	Location	Summit
774		963	Sgurr Thuilm	614	NM 9391 8797	Cairn
776	A	956.3	Sgurr nan Coireachan	231.8	NM 9029 8801	Trig
778	A	895.3	Beinn Gharbh	149.6	NM 8820 8766	Cairn
788	A	717.8	An Stac	226	NM 8667 8890	Outcrop
777		909	Streap	438	NM 9466 8637	Cairn
781	A	812.7	Beinn an Tuim	147.3	NM 9293 8354	Outcrop
782		796	Sgurr an Utha	499	NM 8850 8396	Cairn
792	A	633.3	Glas-charn	329.0	NM 8464 8374	Cairn
789	A	710.0	Meith Bheinn	323	NM 8214 8725	Outcrop by cairn
794		584	Druim a' Chuirn	183	NM 8272 8871	Cairn on rock
793	A	601.5	Sithean Mor	325	NM 7294 8662	Boulder
795		574	Beinn nan Cabar	198	NM 7653 8655	Rock by cairn
797		510	Creag Bhan	224	NM 7824 8466	Rock
801		292	Cruach Doir' an Raoigh	247	NM 7347 8261	Rock by cairn

Beinn Gharbh

This is one of hundreds of Highland hills that highlight the huge gaps left by popular hill categories, where lovers of landscape and fine walking can enjoy solitude and splendour. It falls 40cm short of Marilyn qualification but its combined height and drop of 1045m is the highest of any non-Marilyn under 900m and is greater than that of nineteen Munros.

Druim a' Chuirn, An Stac and Meith Bheinn

BERT BARNETT, JUNE 1998

It was a short drive to park at the path end near Arieniskill at the west end of Loch Eilt. After a mile or so up by the Allt na Criche, the path forked and I took the eastern option to see if I could find Prince Charlie's cave. I think I found it.

I found no trace of path on the descent to the sluice at the west end of Loch Beoraid, which gave a crossing to the track to Meoble. I met the keeper and we had a long chat, probably because he would meet few people in this quiet spot. The path above Meoble did not go far, so I took a rising line up the featureless slopes in the general direction of Druim a' Chuirn, which gave splendid views of sea lochs and rugged hills.

After dropping into Gleann Cul an Staca, I thought it wise to have a brew up before the climb ahead. On a later stop at this same juncture I spotted a lone figure coming off the hill and, as it was an unlikely place to meet anyone, we had a chat. Predictably he was a Marilyn bagger, Paul Caban, who at the time had collected over a thousand Marilyns.

I found the climb up An Stac somewhat wearying, perhaps because it was 'only a Graham' so ought to be easier than a Corbett, but that of course is all in the head. The day was totally dry, and with excellent clarity there was little need for the map. On the return to the glen, the way ahead up Meith Bheinn resolved itself with the reasonably well-defined ridge offering a series of steps which seemed to go on and on. The walking was pleasant and rewarding as it was the last serious climb of the day. Views were classic west coast, with hills down to sea level and acres of bare rock.

There was a long stretch of high ground before the plunge down to the sluice. Tiredness was beginning to show, but once back at the track the alternative path above looked a better option than the way in. Reaching the higher path my thoughts turned to Creag Bhan, which lay barely a kilometre to the west and not a lot higher. This was too close to ignore, so after a chocolate boost I put my head down and picked my way up the hill. I recollect there was a wee pool enclosed in the rocky summit.

It was satisfying to return to the path having bagged another unplanned hill and I was back at the van by 9pm after a thirteen-hour day. I returned to my parking spot on the Loch Ailort shore, where a ringed plover kindly pottered around nearby for a photo.

DAVID BATTY, APRIL 2014

It was hard to choose the best day of the year but the trip to Oban bothy to climb An Stac, Meith Bheinn and Druim a' Chuirn took some beating. Taking the boat up Loch Morar to the bothy, which we had to ourselves, gave plenty of time to enjoy the hills and soak up the marvellous, remote, unspoilt country. The weather was kind and I topped and tailed the trip with other ascents.

Beinn nan Cabar

DOROTHY WILSON, 2007

Perhaps the best hill of the year was Beinn nan Cabar south of Loch Morar – a wild and lonely area with stupendous views including Loch Nevis, Loch Beoraid, the hills of Knoydart, Ben Nevis, the Cuillins of both Rum and Skye, and the Corbetts to the south.

ALAN DAWSON, SEPTEMBER 2010

At 574m, Beinn nan Cabar is not exactly a roadside quickie, but after arriving back from Canna I thought I could squeeze it in before dark. I parked near Glen Mama farm (between Arisaig and Lochailort) just after 6pm and it was horrible. I could have simply driven home but I thought it would save me a long drive another time, and a lot of diesel, if I just got on with it. Once again I was rushing as I headed along the Gleann Mama path to Loch Mama, through dense clouds of tiny insects. It was still and it was hot and I just could not walk quickly enough to escape the little bleeders. Mamma mia, it was hard work. Potentially good hill I thought, but by the time I finally made it to the summit I couldn't see it too clearly through the rivers of sweat, the approaching dusk and the clouds of midges that had followed me all the way.

And so it was that, at about 20:10 on 1 September 2010, I reached 1550 Marilyns. It was not one of my more enjoyable ascents, but satisfying in a kind of dig-deep-keep-going-you-can-do-it sort of way. I had recently read Nando Parrado's book 'Miracle in the Andes' about living in a crashed plane for ten weeks with nothing to eat except a chocolate peanut and the dead bodies of his friends and family, followed by a ten-day trek across the mountains and icefields of the high Andes, wearing rugby boots, eating only rotting human flesh and surviving the freezing nights in a sleeping bag made from plane seat covers, so I wasn't going to let a few billion midges stop me. The descent was relatively easy, apart from the boulders and the tussocks and the aerial assault and the missed path and the river crossing in the dark. Then it was a simple three-hour drive home. After the first hour the car was midge-free and I was able to shut the windows.

That left four months to climb my final mainland Marilyn, Ben Aigan near Rothes, by the end of the year. I didn't manage it, as I left it until December and then found that Perthshire and much of Scotland were buried under snow for the whole month.

An Stac

The rocky summit ridge of Sithean Mor, with the highest rock next to the distant cairn

Braigh nan Uamhachan

Number		Height	Name	Drop	Location	Summit
773	A	983.2	Gulvain	840	NN 0027 8758	Cairn
785		765	Braigh nan Uamhachan	273	NM 9754 8671	Cairn
787	A	724.2	Mullach Coire nan Geur-oirean	188	NN 0491 8928	Cairn
783	A	795.9	Beinn Bhan	495	NN 1405 8571	Trig
784	A	772.7	Meall a' Phubuill	467	NN 0293 8541	Cairn
790	A	679.3	Meall Onfhaidh	297	NN 0104 8407	Rock
791	A	662.6	Aodann Chleireig	314.2	NM 9946 8255	Outcrop
786	A	742.9	Druim Fada	516.4	NN 0870 8240	Moss
800	A	326.7	Meall Bhanbhaidh	147.1	NN 1157 7895	Grass

Gulvain

The huge summit cairn seems to have been included in the height shown on OS maps. It was listed as 3224 feet (982.7m) in the 1921 edition of Munro's Tables but 987m from 1974 onward. The cairn is not 4m high but seems the most likely reason for the discrepancy. The base of the cairn has now been surveyed using GNSS and it is 3.8m lower then the OS map height. The change means that Gulvain drops out of the top twenty most prominent peaks in Britain, with Sgurr na Lapaich taking 20th place. The drop from the South Top is 99.8 metres, so it is more prominent than 26 summits classified as separate Munros.

Gaor Bheinn has always been listed as an alternative name for the hill, but all hill walkers seem to refer to it as Gulvain, which is evidently easier to pronounce and does not seem to be confused with the prosperous town of Gullane in East Lothian. Even the Scottish Mountaineering Club is sensible enough to give priority to Gulvain, though it gives the meaning, derived from gaorr or gaoir, as filth or noise. Neither word seem particularly applicable. The Gaelic word gul translates as cry, which seems far more appropriate when slogging up those steep slopes on a hot day. A linguistic compromise would be gul-ghàir (loud lamentation) or gul-ghàireach (weeping aloud).

Mullach Coire nan Geur-oirean

JOHN WARD, JUNE 2005

Not having a bicycle with me, I did not fancy the long walk in from the east end of Loch Arkaig in the hot weather. Instead I decided on an approach from Glen Loy. I parked at the entrance to a small plantation at NN107845. From here I headed north-west, passing between the crags on Am Mam and a plantation, to reach the bealach between Beinn Bhan and Meall a' Phubuill. This was a climb of about 220m. On the other side of the bealach I made out the traces of a path before dropping down through the remains of an old Caledonian forest to the River Mallie. This was easily fordable in June, though potentially a problem after wet weather. From here the route crossed the track in from Loch Arkaig and ascended the hill by the long grassy eastern ridge. The summit view was outstanding, with Gulvain ahead, the Glenfinnan hills to the south and Knoydart to the north-west. It might have been possible to combine the hill with Meall a' Phubuill but I decided to return the way I had come. I estimated that this route saved at least 45 minutes each way compared to the Loch Arkaig route.

Western Highlands: Ardnamurchan and Ardgour

Land south of Loch Ailort, Loch Eilt, Glenfinnan and Loch Eil

Marilyns: 45
Highest and most prominent: Sgurr Dhomhnuill, 888.4m
Lowest: Beinn Bhreac, 240m
Least prominent: Glas Bheinn 635, drop 151.4m

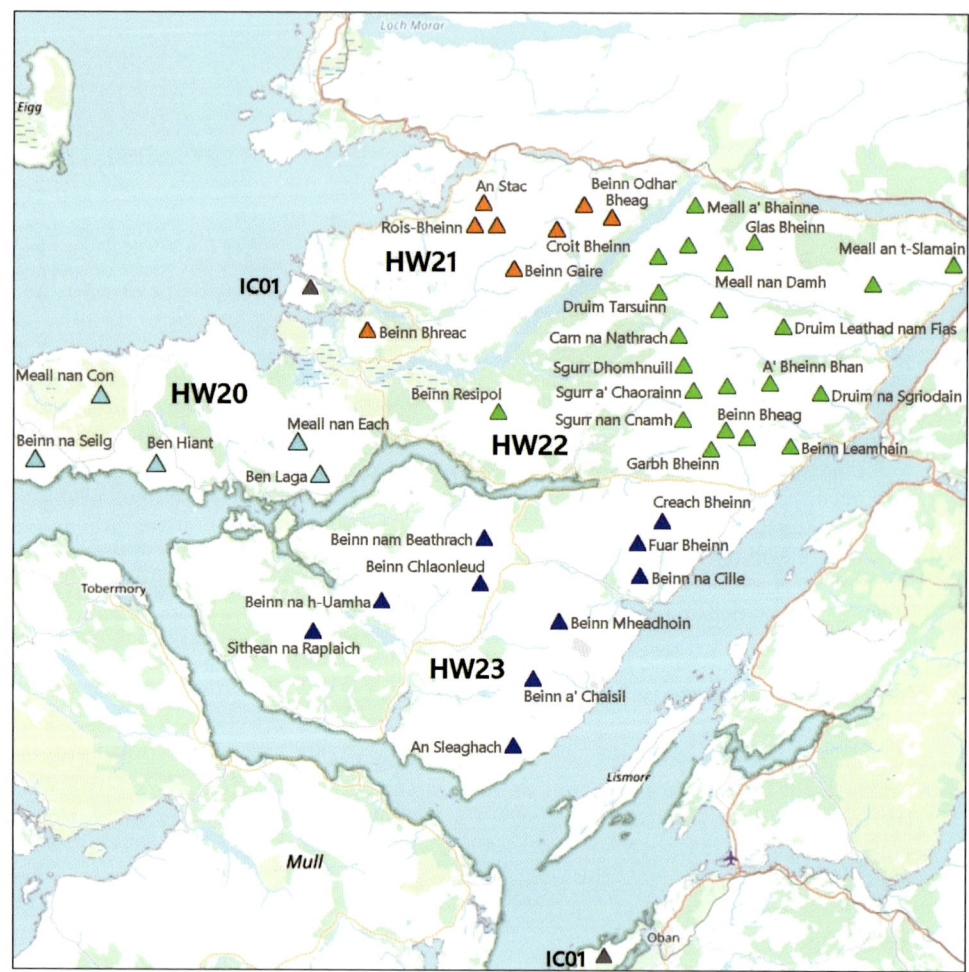

Number	Height	Name	Drop	Location	Summit
1341	528	Ben Hiant	462	NM 5377 6325	Cairn by trig
1342	512	Ben Laga	355	NM 6455 6209	Cairn on outcrop
1343	490	Meall nan Each	214	NM 6320 6430	Trig on outcrop
1344	437	Meall nan Con	289	NM 5038 6813	Trig
1346	344	Beinn na Seilg	279	NM 4583 6417	Cairn

Ben Hiant

PAUL RICHARDSON, AUGUST 2001

Ben Hiant epitomises relativity. An imposing hill, dominating the landscape for miles around, yet well beneath qualifying height for other lists. We found a path all the way up the north-east ridge, which made me chuckle. Making the obvious start from the high point of the road, the variation of paths eased all route-finding problems, then the final steep slope appeared ahead, with no sign of the path. We took a broad zigzag across the face to the foot of the slope and found the tourist path around the back, winding up easily to the top. Made me smile. And what a view.

Ben Laga and Meall nan Each

ALAN DAWSON, MARCH 1993

It took several years for Marilyn bagging to take root, which meant that I knew nothing about most hills before I climbed them. Ben Laga was a superb surprise, being complex, interesting, rocky and apparently volcanic. Meall nan Each was not quite as good but was an excellent natural extension to a satisfying circuit. The next recorded ascent on the Hill Bagging site was over five years later, though the Bowkers would also have been there.

Beinn Gaire

ERIC YOUNG, MAY 2002

Parking at Glen Moidart en route to Beinn Gaire, I was surprised to see another walker heading hill-wards. I eventually caught up and we spent a companionable time on the way to Croit Bheinn before I discovered that it was Brian Ewing, who lived within a kilometre of my house in Dumbarton. He was completing his Grahams. 'What next, Brian', I asked. And so his answer, 'Marilyns', became part of my hill walking vocabulary.

Beinn na Seilg

PAUL RICHARDSON, AUGUST 2001

Due to the clammy weather and extravagant flora, I will forever associate this fine little hill with bog, rank heather, sweat, midges, flies and flying ants. From the roadside, we toiled up very rough ground to the rocky summit ridge, dripping with sweat, attacked by midges whenever we paused and plagued by flies whether we stopped or not. I had not thought much about flying ants when we found them covering the car after the previous walk, but now they were a considerable menace as they had chosen the summit cairn of Beinn na Seilg to swarm around. I just had time to register that there was a very fine view, encompassing more or less that from Ben Hiant as well as that hill itself. We descended as quickly as the rampant vegetation would allow. Again attacked by midges, I leapt into the car cursing, dripping and stinking, and drove off still wearing my boots.

A long weekend offered superb weather, hills and company. On the Saturday I joined Stewart Logan's party to bag his final Graham and mainland Marilyn, Beinn Gaire, and then carried on to Croit Bheinn. Sunday was a six-Marilyn day – a ridge of three Grahams between Ariundle and Glen Tarbert with an easy hitch back, followed by a drive round Ardnamurchan to take in the three small Marilyns there. The highlight was a beautiful Western Isles sunset at 10:17pm from Beinn na Seilg, a wonderful experience. The golden sun disappeared and then lit up the underside of the clouds just above the horizon in a glorious shade of pink for some brief moments. I wonder what is the latest Scottish sunset anyone has witnessed. Maybe at a later June date from the outer islands.

Ben Hiant

Meall nan Con summit, with Rum and Eigg

HW21 Beinnodhar-roisbheinn

Number		Height	Name	Drop	Location	Summit
1333	A	883.3	Beinn Odhar Bheag	774	NM 8465 7787	Cairn
1337		783	Beinn Mhic Cedidh	295	NM 8283 7881	Cairn
1334	A	882.4	Rois-Bheinn	524	NM 7560 7783	Rock by cairn
1338	A	713.7	Sgurr Dhomhuill Mor	145	NM 7403 7592	Grass
1335	A	874.1	Sgurr na Ba Glaise	172.9	NM 7703 7774	Voutcropn
1336		814	An Stac	255	NM 7631 7928	Cairn
1339	A	666.1	Beinn Gaire	319.9	NM 7811 7488	Boulder by cairn
1340	A	664.5	Croit Bheinn	227.5	NM 8108 7732	Cairn
1348		240	Beinn Bhreac	153	NM 6815 7151	Cairn

Beinn Odhar Bheag

This is the 36th most prominent Marilyn but only the 265th highest and the 770th most often climbed, according to logs on the Hill Bagging site. It seems to get little recognition for its landscape prominence. One reason for this is its rivalry with the more popular Rois-Bheinn. Both are shown as 882m on OS maps and both have over 500m drop, so they are not exactly twin peaks. When I discovered that Beinn Odhar Bheag was over 883m in 2018, it soared over 100 places up the prominence table. It is not a remote hill, as it is under 4km from the A830, but the river, railway and Loch Shiel limit access routes from the north and east. There are no higher hills to the west and none to the east before Loch Linnhe, so it is an exceptional viewpoint on a clear day.

Surveying the summit of Beinn Odhar Bheag

Beinn Bhreac

This modest little hill soon became renowned for offering an excellent walk and view for relatively little effort, comments that have been reinforced by numerous contented hill baggers, with the sandy beach and Castle Tioram offering added value and contrast.

View from the coastal path to Beinn Bhreac

Garbh Bheinn

RHB sections 18B   OS maps 40, 41

Number		Height	Name	Drop	Location	Summit
1349	A	888.4	Sgurr Dhomhnuill	873	NM 8896 6788	Shelter cairn
1353	A	803.9	Druim Garbh	143.5	NM 8818 6835	Outcrop
1354		786	Carn na Nathrach	382	NM 8863 6987	Cairn
1358	G	762.4	Beinn na h-Uamha	269.2	NM 9171 6642	Cairn
1359	GA	760.7	Sgurr a' Chaorainn	205	NM 8949 6620	Boulder by cairn
1362	A	734.6	Druim na Sgriodain	482	NM 9784 6561	Cairn
1371		477	A' Bheinn Bhan	179	NM 9458 6650	Cairn
1350		885	Garbh Bheinn	685	NM 9043 6220	Rock by cairn
1361	A	737.4	Beinn Bheag	202.0	NM 9145 6353	Outcrop near cairn
1365	A	701.8	Sgurr nan Cnamh	159.5	NM 8867 6432	Outcrop near cairn
1366	A	650.5	Sgorr Mhic Eacharna	169.1	NM 9286 6304	Outcrop near cairn
1370		508	Beinn Leamhain	331	NM 9572 6228	Cairn
1351	A	849.2	Sgurr Ghiubhsachain	616	NM 8753 7513	Outcrop
1355		775	Sgorr Craobh a' Chaorainn	187	NM 8955 7578	Rock by cairn
1369		559	Meall a' Bhainne	205	NM 9015 7850	Rock
1352		845	Beinn Resipol	502	NM 7664 6545	Cairn
1356	A	771.0	Stob Coire a' Chearcaill	576	NN 0167 7268	Outcrop near cairn
1372		467	Meall an t-Slamain	200	NN 0710 7393	Cairn
1357		770	Druim Tarsuinn	259	NM 8747 7273	Cairn on rock
1364	A	720.4	Stob Mhic Bheathain	212.7	NM 9141 7138	Rock near cairn
1368		576	Druim Leathad nam Fias	187	NM 9559 7028	Cairn on rock
1363	A	723.4	Meall nan Damh	344.4	NM 9194 7449	Cairn
1367	A	635.3	Glas Bheinn	151.4	NM 9395 7577	Rock

Sgurr Dhomhnuill

BRIAN EDRIDGE, JULY 2010

I had almost no bad weather in 2010, the significant exception being Sgurr Dhomhnuill on a day of heavy rain. The burn flowing from the western corrie, easily crossed on the ascent, soon became a wild torrent, leading in a short distance to a series of thundering waterfalls. A descent beside these to the river in the glen below confirmed that it was completely impassable, but I managed to find a stick to use as a crossing aid back up above the falls. With heart in mouth and great difficulty, I just managed to force a way across, coming perilously close to losing my footing and being swept away. It was a frightening experience that I hope never to repeat.

A' Bheinn Bhan

ERIC YOUNG, MAY 2007

It was on a forestry road on the route toward A' Bheinn Bhan that I startled a roe deer. On approaching the spot, there lay a new-born fawn, stock still and ears flat. The mother barked her distress from the nearby woodland. There's something beautiful and awesome in new life. I moved on swiftly to permit reunion and further bonding.

Druim Leathad nam Fias and Meall an t-Slamain

COLIN CRAWFORD, APRIL 2002

Ardgour in April gave a haul of superlative and unfrequented summits. My favourite was Druim Leathad nam Fias, an elegant grassy whaleback offering dramatic views to the surrounding giants. Meall an t-Slamain was another delightful grandstand, with Ben Nevis seen to advantage from an unusual angle across Loch Linnhe. This hill also had the notable feature of making Fort William appear almost attractive.

Beinn Resipol

Creach Bheinn, with Garbh Bheinn beyond

HW23 Creach-raplaich

Number		Height	Name	Drop	Location	Summit
1373	A	853.0	Creach Bheinn	754	NM 8705 5765	Shelter cairn
1374	A	766.1	Fuar Bheinn	227	NM 8534 5634	Outcrop by cairn
1376	A	653.1	Beinn na Cille	192.6	NM 8539 5422	Rock
1375	T	739.5	Beinn Mheadhoin	568	NM 7991 5144	Cairn by trig
1379	T	514.6	An Sleaghach	309	NM 7648 4340	Cairn near trig
1382		437	Beinn a' Chaisil	184	NM 7807 4769	Cairn
1377	T	582.7	Beinn nam Beathrach	314	NM 7522 5726	Outcrop by trig
1380		479	Beinn Chlaonleud	275	NM 7482 5428	Rock
1381		465	Beinn na h-Uamha	241	NM 6820 5343	Cairn
1378		551	Sithean na Raplaich	524	NM 6361 5168	Cairn

Sithean na Raplaich

This is the lowest hill with a drop of over 500m. It therefore qualifies as a Thousander, meaning hills with height plus drop over 1000m. There could be any number of such hills, as a 990m summit with 10m drop would qualify, but only 181 or 182 of them are Marilyns. Hill of Stake is lower than Sithean na Raplaich at 522m, but its drop of 486m enables it to qualify as a Thousander by eight metres. Beinn Dhubh on South Harris is 506.4m with a drop of about 493m, so it may or may not qualify as a Thousander. Its col is around 13m high somewhere beside the main road in Tarbert. I could have surveyed it during a wet week on Harris in 2021 but it never occurred to me to do so.

Beinn na h-Uamha

LESLIE BARRIE, 2002

Shown on the OS map as almost entirely surrounded by a band of crags, the way to the summit of this hill was through a chink in its armour to the west. The shortest, most direct approach is from the edge of the forestry plantation at the SE end of Loch Doire nam Mart, where a path heads in just the right direction. Had I looked further upward and also reminded myself of the hill name, I would have realised where the path was leading. The cave was similar to many others – shallow, with a dripping ceiling and wet muddy floor. However, the interesting part was the many carvings on the cave walls of initials and dates from the 19th century. The summit may be nothing out of the ordinary, but the walk along the edge of the crags was very fine indeed. As for the views, on a fine clear day you can savour the tranquility of this gem of a hill in wildest Morvern.

An Sleaghach and Beinn a' Chaisil

DAVID STALLARD, JULY 2014

In 2014 I completed one little project, which was going up all the Marilyns on the Scottish mainland north and west of the Great Glen. The final ten were all in Moidart, Morvern or Ardnamurchan. My last walk in this area gave me one of my best days of the year, over An Sleaghach and Beinn a' Chaisil from Leacraithnaich bothy, in hot and clear weather. The view from the first of these was possibly my finest of the year, looking out over Loch Linnhe to Mull and a huge sweep of the Highlands and islands.

—— Skye, Raasay and Scalpay ——

Marilyns:	51
Highest and most prominent:	Sgurr Alasdair, 992.0m
Lowest:	Beinn na h-Iolaire, Raasay, 254m
Least prominent:	Beinn na Caillich 731, drop 153.3m

Number		Height	Name	Drop	Location	Summit
1239	A	992.0	Sgurr Alasdair	992.0	NG 4500 2078	Cairn
1240	A	985.8	Inaccessible Pinnacle	187.6	NG 4440 2156	Boulder
1246	A	966.1	Sgurr nan Gillean	205	NG 4715 2529	Rock by cairn
1269		495	Sgurr na Stri	226	NG 5007 1925	Cairn
1271		461	Beinn a' Bhraghad	276	NG 4097 2540	Grass
1273	T	435.3	An Cruachan	223	NG 3817 2251	Trig
1272	A	448.0	Beinn Bhreac	293	NG 3457 2695	Cairn
1274		384	Biod Mor	192	NG 3706 2738	Cairn
1275		369	Arnaval	191	NG 3453 3166	Rock

This area includes all the land south of Glen Drynoch, between Carbost and Sligachan, and west of Glen Sligachan. Bla Bheinn has its own hill area because it has a huge drop of 862m so is topographically quite separate. The Cuillin dominate the landscape but the main range includes only three Marilyns. These peaks have been well covered in other publications, such as *The 1033 High Hills of Britain* and several less entertaining works. The fourth most prominent peak in the main range is Sgurr Thuilm, only 880m high but with a drop of 131.4m, one of thirty High Hills in the Cuillin.

Sgurr na Stri

This hill is separated from the main range by the infamous stepping stones at Coruisk. It is highly acclaimed by hill walkers, for it is often judged as providing the finest view of the Cuillin, with its contrast between the water of Loch Coruisk and the line of dark serrated peaks. Its twin summits have caused uncertainty about the highest point, with RHB having listed the west top at NG499193. Its summit has not been surveyed with GNSS, but in 2015 a surveyor with Leica levelling equipment observed the west top to be lower by more than half a metre. The drop between the two is over twenty metres.

Beinn Bhreac

This hill looks simple enough on a 1:50000 map, with a 445m trig point, but the 1:25000 map has fourteen spot heights as well as heights for eight contour rings, suggesting the cartographer was very diligent or very bored. It is also the only hill known to include an Alan and a Dan (Ben Scaalan and Skridan), though the cartographer may have invented these names. The more northerly 448m spot height is 40cm higher than the other one.

Sgurr Alasdair

ALAN DAWSON, JUNE 1984

When I set off for the summit in 1984 I simply wanted to get to the top by the easiest route. Having never been on the Cuillin before, our small group went astray in thick mist and ended up on top of Sgurr Mhic Choinnich instead. We did eventually make it to Sgurr Alasdair via Collie's Ledge and went down the way we should have gone up. It turned out to be a useful navigational error when I received a copy of *Munro's Tables* six months later and counted my meagre tally. I had been back a few times since but would never forget that moment on Sgurr Mhic Choinnich when the mist cleared for a few seconds and we saw a higher peak emerge and vanish. We realised we must have climbed the wrong summit and had to work out where we were and how to get to where we wanted to be.

Inaccessible Pinnacle

ALAN DAWSON, MAY 1993 AND MAY 1994

This is the most difficult Marilyn other than those on St Kilda. I was not a rock climber but knew I would need a rope, so I bought one and set off into Coire a' Tairneilear to practise abseiling before tackling the dreaded Pinnacle. It did not go well. On the second attempt I must have jerked the rope so that it pulled the rock anchoring the rope from vertical to horizontal. The rope slipped off the end and sent me tumbling 12-15 metres down to the base of the rocky slope. The poorly-placed anchor had been careless, the outcome painful and humbling. I was saved by my helmet, got up feeling battered and bruised, and walked slowly down to the van, with support from my partner. I drove to Carbost for food, beer and recuperation in the Old Inn, but then found I was too stiff and sore to sleep in the tiny van, so I had to find nearby B&B accommodation.

The next day I managed to see a local doctor, who was slightly horrified and told me to go to Broadford Hospital for X-rays and stitches. I spent two unhealthy nights there, sharing a room with a heavy smoker and not being properly fed, so I absconded to Broadford for take-away pizza and returned to my bed with no-one having noticed.

Broken ribs meant that I could not walk much in annoyingly lovely weather, so the In Pinn had to wait. A year later I climbed it pretty quickly, to avoid thinking, looking down or being paralysed by fear, then brought my partner up on the heavy 45-metre rope. I was greatly relieved when a chap sitting on top offered us the use of his rope that was already being used by others in his party. I still had to do the dreaded abseil but did not have to set up the rope. I felt good afterwards, but the stitches under my armpit meant that my right arm was never the same again for skimming stones in the sea or throwing a cricket ball in from the boundary.

Sgurr na Stri from the slopes of Ben Meabost

Number		Height	Name	Drop	Location	Summit
1255	A	928.8	Blabheinn	862	NG 5299 2174	Boulder by cairn
1262	A	808.3	Garbh-bheinn	181	NG 5312 2324	Cairn on rock
1264	A	737.2	Marsco	414	NG 5076 2518	Grass by cairn
1266	A	701.6	Belig	246.5	NG 5439 2405	Rock near cairn
1268		569	Glas Bheinn Mhor	188	NG 5539 2575	Rock by wall
1270		493	Ruadh Stac	156	NG 5149 2326	Cairn
1263		775	Glamaig	485	NG 5137 3000	Cairn
1265	A	733.5	Beinn Dearg Mhor	318	NG 5202 2849	Rock by cairn
1277	T	283.8	Meall a' Mhaoil	155	NG 5538 3076	Trig
1276	A	345.6	Ben Meabost	232	NG 5365 1595	Cairn

Blabheinn

The ridge walk from Blabheinn to Belig
Is difficult, some call it hellish
There are sections where you can fall off it
It's safer on green hills near Moffat

Blabheinn is one of the best viewpoints for the main Cuillin ridge, along with Sgurr na Stri and Ruadh Stac. The car park by Loch Slapin and good path to get started help to make it a popular walk but not an easy one. The usual ascent route is steep and arduous, with sections of slippery scree, so the rich rewards of the summit view are not easily attained. There are interesting variations via the lower summits of An Stac to the east and Slat Bheinn to the south, but the final 350m ascent to the main summit still has to be climbed somehow. Another approach to Blabheinn, via Clach Glas, might be described as magnificent but not pleasant, for it straddles the boundary between scrambling and moderate rock climbing. Clach Glas is not a Marilyn as its drop is only 91 metres, but it does qualify as one of the fourteen High Hills of Britain that are under 838m high. These are located on Skye, Rum, Arran, Harris, and Jura.

Owing to its separation from the rest of the Cuillin, Blabheinn is the second most prominent peak on Skye and the fifteenth most prominent anywhere in Britain. Its name is still evolving, with Blaven and Bla Bheinn both in common use. OS cartographers seem to have settled on the single-word version on some maps but not others.

Marsco

This is one of the few Marilyns to be celebrated in song, but Nightfall on Marsco, by Runrig, says little about climbing the hill. A more informative and entertaining but less musical account is given in Tales from the Grahams, published by Pedantic Press in 2022, along with stories about Belig, Beinn Dearg Mhor, The Storr and other Marilyns on Skye between 600m and 762m high.

Ben Meabost

This little hill can easily be climbed on its own or as the start of a much longer walk to Sgurr na Stri. Uncertainty about the location of its highest point was resolved with a survey in 2015 that showed the summit cairn to be slightly higher than a spot height in a larger 340m contour ring to the south.

Ruadh Stac

This hill is tucked away up Glen Sligachan between Marsco and Blabheinn, well separated from the main ridge between them over Garbh-bheinn. It can be reached fairly easily by a path from Sligachan to the north or Camasunary to the south, and offers an attractive option when the weather is too windy or misty for the higher hills on Skye..

Ruadh Stac

Marsco, with Garbh-bheinn behind

Number		Height	Name	Drop	Location	Summit
1279	A	739.1	Sgurr na Coinnich	712.5	NG 7624 2226	Rock near trig
1281	A	731.4	Beinn na Caillich 731	153.3	NG 7704 2297	Rock near cairn
1283	A	609.0	Ben Aslak	329.0	NG 7507 1912	Rock
1285		561	Beinn na Seamraig	167	NG 7290 1777	Cairn
1280	A	732.1	Beinn na Caillich 732	694	NG 6013 2329	Rock near trig
1282	A	709.3	Beinn Dearg Mhor	153.5	NG 5877 2285	Rock
1284		572	Beinn na Cro	384	NG 5693 2418	Cairn
1287		301	Beinn nan Carn	248	NG 6360 1808	Cairn
1288	T	298.8	Sgorach Breac	275	NG 6516 1320	Trig
1289	T	292.5	Sgurr na h-Iolaire	179	NG 6171 0906	Trig
1290	A	281.2	Sgurr nan Caorach *	218	NG 5937 0301	Cairn

Sgurr na Coinnich

This is the 48th most prominent hill and one of only 52 with over 700m drop, as listed on page 345. Beinn Mhor near Dunoon is the only other one under 800m high.

The peak of Sgurr na Coinnich is not far from Loch Duich
To get to Beinn na Caillich you could even go by kayak
It's safer on the ferry or the bridge to near Kyleakin
You can get up in two hours if you don't take Ben Aslak in

Sgurr nan Caorach

The summit of this hill was originally listed as 280m at NG587029, where there is a trig pillar. A GNSS survey in 2015 confirmed indications from a large-scale map that the east summit is higher, by 30cm. The drop between the two points is 29.8m, so the old summit location just misses out on qualifying as a Tump.

Beinn na Cro

LIZ AND PETER HASTIE, JANUARY 2013

A key Marilyn bagging skill must be climbing barbed wire and electric fences. Our skills in that area seemed to be developing, until an unfortunate incident on our first hill of 2013 resulted in a pair of well-worn trousers becoming well-torn trousers, on the last barbed wire fence of the day. The hill itself, Beinn na Cro, was otherwise excellent. The hill was in snow and gave great views all round. We shared the walk with twelve friends from a new year get together, also adding to the enjoyment of the hill.

Sgurr na h-Iolaire

ALAN DAWSON, DECEMBER 2006

After I started surveying I had to get used to walking in the dark, sometimes for several hours, but this was only the second time I had set off in the dark. The incentive was to help Brent reach 600 Marilyns by the end of the year. It was intimidating getting started, edging across an outflow from the loch then falling on my face in a bog soon after letting go of the fence, but otherwise it was mostly harmless despite limited vision.

Number		Height	Name	Drop	Location	Summit
1218	A	718.7	The Storr	671	NG 4953 5405	Grass by trig
1219	A	668.3	Hartaval	180	NG 4801 5511	Rock near cairn
1220	A	638.2	Baca Ruadh	145.7	NG 4748 5756	Rock
1221		552	Ben Dearg	221	NG 4784 5041	Grass near cairn
1222		543	Meall na Suiramach	282	NG 4461 6951	Rock by trig
1225		466	Bioda Buidhe	184	NG 4391 6640	Rock
1232	T	392.5	Sithean a' Bhealaich Chumhaing	235	NG 5089 4662	Grass by trig

Meall na Suiramach

The northernmost Marilyn on Skye has an unremarkable grassy summit, usually reached via a remarkable walk to one of Skye's most well-known attractions, Quiraing.

Bioda Buidhe

This hill can be reached by a simple ascent from the road to the north, but it can also be the start of one of the most fascinating hill walks in the country. The nearest Marilyn to the south, Hartaval, is 13km away in a direct line, but the switchback walk along the Trotternish ridge is much further and involves well over 800m ascent. The main problems are how to get down the steep slopes to the east and how to get back to the start. Extending the route over The Storr and Ben Dearg would turn a walk into an expedition.

The Storr

MARTYN DOUGHERTY, MAY 2010

Whilst on holiday in Skye, as a favour to a friend, my son Ben and I attempted to climb The Storr. This decision was against my better judgement as there was thick mist and persistent rain. We commenced from the car park on the A855 on a north-westerly bearing. Heading along the path towards the rock columns which include the Old Man of Storr, I led the group through the eerie environs of the rock pillars, my woolly hat and jacket hood pulled low over my head. Without warning my body and head jolted backwards, with unrepeatable utterances emanating from my mouth. Closer inspection revealed an overhanging rock. Looming down at me appeared to be the frightening face of a stone gargoyle. My trusty woolly hat spared me serious injury.

All three of us continued past signs warning us not to proceed, and climbed over a barbed wire fence into the rocky buttress area of The Storr. In the thick mist we could see no easy or reasonable route to the summit and found ourselves being forced along a cliff to the north of the summit. Approximately 50 metres below the summit I decided the route was becoming too risky and we climbed back down the same route. Soaking wet and disappointed at our lack of success, I left The Storr for a revisit in 2011.

Sithean a' Bhealaich Chumhaing

The spectacular coastal location and dramatic ridge of this hill have contributed to its nomination as some people's favourite Marilyn, with the bonus of regular eagle sightings. Its summit can be reached by an easy moorland walk and might be far more popular if its name was as easy to articulate as nearby Craig Ulatota. Enthusiasts have been known to refer to it as SBC or 'that one just north of Portree'.

Ben Dearg, south of The Storr

Ben Tianavaig

Number		Height	Name	Drop	Location	Summit
1223		489	Healabhal Bheag	462	NG 2244 4207	Mound
1224		471	Healabhal Mhor	186	NG 2197 4451	Mound
1231		409	Beinn Bhac-ghlais	155	NG 2292 4049	Mound
1226		444	Ben Lee	375	NG 5025 3361	Rock by cairn
1230	T	413	Ben Tianavaig	366	NG 5117 4098	Trig
1228	T	439.6	Roineval	330	NG 4184 3505	Grass by trig
1229	T	417	Beinn na Greine	267	NG 4596 4162	Trig
1234		329	Beinn Bhreac	239	NG 2536 5307	Cairn
1233		326	Beinn Chreagach	221	NG 2891 5342	Cairn
1237	T	283.9	Ben Geary	165	NG 2535 6147	Trig
1235	T	314	Biod an Athair	179	NG 1582 5494	Cliff edge by trig
1236		295	Cruachan-Glen Vic Askill	194	NG 3575 4604	Cairn on outcrop

This is a mixed bag of an area, encompassing the central part of Skye between the west and east coast, north of the Cuillin and south of the Trotternish peninsula. The highest hills are also the most easily recognisable – the flat-topped summits in Duirinish, the westernmost peninsula. OS maps show the names Macleod's Tables South and North in brackets, but the Gaelic names translate as small and big, not north and south. As with Aonach Beag and Aonach Mor, the higher of the pair is named as the lower.

The other main attractions for Marilyn baggers are on opposite coasts. In the east, Ben Tianavaig can offer a superb coastal walk near Portree, though the summit is well away from the sea. In the west, the walk up Biod an Athair looks and feels ordinary until the spectacular summit, with the trig pillar on the cliff edge and the sea over 300 vertical metres below.

The hills on the Waternish peninsula are less memorable, not far from a road but with plenty of tussocks. Beinn Bhreac near Dunvegan is similar in character but has a useful track halfway up, past souterrain remains. In the east, Ben Lee near Sligachan does not have the same appeal as the coastal pair either side of Portree. Away from the coast, the wind farm on Cruachan-Glen Vic Askill has not added to the appeal of the hill despite the exotic name. The identity of Mr Askill remains obcure. Is Vic there? We may never know. Yet as with all hills, something of interest might turn up along the way.

Cruachan-Glen Vic Askill

JON METCALF, 2003

For many walkers this hill is a dull lump which has little intrinsic merit. My mood was not helped by the decaying remains of several sheep and a toppled wind-speed-logging mast that the contractor hadn't bothered to remove, although a larger replacement structure had been erected. Then a magical moment transformed the mundane into the unique in my experience. A shadow shot over my shoulder with an audible whoosh of displaced air on that hot still afternoon. A large white-tailed massive-headed raptor glided down the slope. I didn't know Skye had sea eagles before this, but I tracked this one down visually for hundreds of metres.

SK06 Raasay and Scalpay

RHB sections 17A, 17C   OS maps 24, 32

Number	Height	Name	Drop	Location	Summit
1227	444	Dun Caan, Raasay	444	NG 5791 3948	Rock near trig
1238	254	Beinn na h-Iolaire, Raasay	191	NG 5998 5024	Outcrop by trig
1286	396	Mullach na Carn, Scalpay	396	NG 6058 2922	Cairn

Beinn na h-Iolaire, Raasay

HAMISH BROWN, AUGUST 2006

Dun Caan I had done one Hogmanay when the turf was so hard and frozen that the summit slope needed crampons. I had been back and had taken school parties to Raasay, but had never been to the north end. What a fantastic road – a feel of utter remoteness through granite-spotted hillsides, with a young peregrine flitting from post to post.

The last section is Calum's road, named after Calum MacLeod who, when the council refused to extend the road to his house at Arnish, did so himself, single-handed. It took him almost a decade and wore out more boots than a dozen Munro rounds. The council then surfaced the road. For effect, the road rivals the Bealach na Ba or that over Mam Ratagan. A decent path goes on to Torran then the route climbs up and below a bluff. From its highest point the summit of Beinn na h-Iolaire is soon reached.

Mullach na Carn, Scalpay

HAMISH BROWN, AUGUST 2006

It was inevitable. I had a canoe, Charles needed Scalpay. I'd bought the wood-and-canvas canoe off a broke fellow-teacher forty years earlier for £5. It ran all the major rivers in Scotland, traversed the Great Glen and explored lochs and seas in the west. Quite a few Munros were reached by the old canoe. I am more into Dawson's list these body-decaying days but longing to canoe again. My baby camper van couldn't carry the old monster, so there had been a moratorium in place for years. However, a new (old) camper van could carry a canoe inside, with a clearance of one inch, so with Charles practically commuting to the Outer Hebrides (about all he had left) I suggested his gap tick Scalpay could be picked up *en passant*. For once a plan went perfectly. We met up at Broadford in early August.

I had been in Skye over midsummer with some atrocious weather but did grab the odd hill between storms. Still possessing the wee van then, it was nearly blown to a stop on the big brae under Glamaig and it's the first time I've seen white horses on a road. August could be mobs, midges and monsoon. Was it a sane time for island ticks?

We parked and started at NG598266 – parking for several vehicles and a gate into a field leading down to the sea without any barring fences. Charles had the morning, I had the afternoon. We managed to avoid any launch at lowest ebb. The hill was 1½ hours up, one hour down, the canoeing a few minutes. A good scalp, eh?

AUDREY LITTERICK, 2009

An idyllic paddle in perfect weather in the sea kayaks around the little island of Pabay, with seals and a friendly otter swimming around my boat. Then over to Scalpay for a pleasant walk up Mullach na Carn and a long bask in the summit in the sun. Glorious – Marilyn bagging at its best.

———— Rum, Eigg and Canna ————

Marilyns:	8
Highest and most prominent:	Askival, 812m
Lowest:	Carn a' Ghaill, Canna, 211m
Least prominent:	Trollabhal, Rum, drop 190m

IR01 Rum

RHB section 17D
OS map 39

Number		Height	Name	Drop	Location	Summit
1292		812	Askival	812	NM 3931 9522	Boulder by trig
1293		781	Ainshval	326	NM 3785 9432	Cairn
1294		702	Trollabhal	190	NM 3773 9520	Rock
1295	T	570.6	Orval	410	NM 3336 9911	Trig
1298		304	Mullach Mor	219	NG 3866 0151	Outcrop by trig

Askival, Trollabhal and Ainshval

AUDREY LITTERICK, 2005

I climbed these hills in perfect weather from a small yacht chartered with pals and based in Loch Scresort, my first experience of sail-mountaineering. The best part (apart from scrambling amidst the magnificence of the Rum Cuillin) was sitting on deck in the evening sun surrounded by a total absence of midges, whilst watching pairs of frantically scratching, midge-maddened campers on the beach.

MARION MITCHELL, AUGUST 2014

August bank holiday pulled us to Rum and Trollabhal was the lure. In clear weather we enjoyed sitting on the airy summit, where in the distance we could see our friends ascending Ainshval. Little did we know that this would be our last glimpse of Peter, who suffered a fatal fall on the descent. It brought home to us that in doing the things we love we also play a dangerous game.

Mullach Mor

DENISE CLARK, OCTOBER 2003

The Marilyns encouraged me to recover fully from a broken leg on Arran in 2000. When I reached the summit of Mullach Mor on a gloriously sunny October day, it was my 600th Marilyn. I had entered the Hall of Fame at the age of 71, only the 14th woman and the 97th person to have done so, but the first to have started at 50. A chance meeting had opened the door for me to experience the beauty of the British hills.

AUDREY LITTERICK, 2005

I was calling this hill a wee shite and worse as I battled through the worst imaginable terrain, trying to move upwards through head-high bracken, brambles and tussocks, infested by midges, ticks and clegs, peppered with man-eating ditches and holes, felled trees and rotting stumps. I emerged sweaty, cursing, blistered, bitten, scratched, bleeding and limping on to the plateau, to be confronted by a truly magical 360-degree panorama of mountains, sea and sky. Views of the Rum Cuillin at close range, also Canna and Skye and many of the outer isles including Mingulay and Pabbay dotted around a sparkling blue sea. Did I see St Kilda? I think so. The views were stupendous and worth the struggle.

IR02 Eigg and Canna

RHB section 17D   OS map 39

Number	Height	Name	Drop	Location	Summit
1296	394	An Sgurr, Eigg	394	NM 4632 8470	Heather near trig
1297	340	Sgorr an Fharaidh, Eigg	263	NM 4854 8929	Cairn on rock
1300	211	Carn a' Ghaill, Canna	211	NG 2638 0644	Mound near trig

An Sgurr and Sgorr an Fharaidh

ALAN DAWSON, 31 AUGUST 2010

With only five non-Kildan Marilyns left, I kept waiting for some settled weather in the west. A good forecast finally arrived three days before I was due in Shropshire for a nephew's wedding, so I had to rush. The 11am sailing from Arisaig allowed five hours on Eigg, but it was fifteen minutes less after messing about trying to glimpse porpoises, as though we were on a pleasure cruise. I raced off the boat past the busking piper towards An Sgurr. The direct approach looked tricky so I had to follow the usual route. I was surprised to find 20 young people on the summit, where I allowed a few minutes to rest.

The direct route to Sgorr an Fharaidh looked an unappealing mix of cliff, heather and forest, so it was back down the path and then a march along the tarmac. Heading uphill again, time leaked away amongst the tussocks and the pauses for breath. At the summit I judged I was still on course to catch the boat, but I had not realised the difficulties in getting down west from the Roraima-like plateau. I jogged along the cliff edge, peering over every minute or so, while also keeping an eye open for the minibus back to the pier. I could easily see the road at Cleadale but reaching it seemed impossible.

The cliff-edge path petered out into tussock and heather as I hurried along. I could see the angle of cliff ease off further south, but the slopes below were coated in gorse and bushes that looked impenetrable. I looked down a fierce gully but thought I'd rather miss the boat than come to grief there, so carried on south, but then I saw the minibus setting off, so I raced back up and clawed my way down the gully using hands and backside, half-stumbling, half-sliding. I managed to plunge down safely and was about 50 metres from the road when the bus went past. I waved and waved, but on it went. No bus meant no boat, as I could not do 5km in 30 minutes. Not a disaster, it just meant missing either Canna or the wedding. Yet, wonder of eiggy wonders, the bus turned off down a rough track, presumably to pick up a pre-booked passenger. It had to come back the same way, which gave me an extra two minutes to pick my bedraggled way through bracken and the line of washing in someone's garden and pop out on the road. No bus stop, but I figured the bus would have to stop if I stood in the road and waved my walking pole. So instead of a bed in a shed I had a beer on the sea wall while waiting for the boat to return.

Carn a' Ghaill, Canna

ALAN DAWSON, 1 SEPTEMBER 2010

On Wednesdays the CalMac ferry left ample time for a stroll up Carn a' Ghaill, but not if the ferry leaves Mallaig 40 minutes late and then cuts the time docked at Canna from 120 to 80 minutes. So it was another lung-busting race against time. I made it back on board with five minutes to spare, resentful at having to rush again but pleased the ferry was leaving on time, as I thought I might have time for Beinn nan Cabar in the evening. Ten minutes out from Canna, the tannoy announced that we were turning back to pick up a passenger who had been strolling along admiring his navel and had missed the boat.

——— Mull, Ulva and Gometra ———

Marilyns:	27
Highest and most prominent:	Ben More, 996.9m
Lowest:	Gometra, 155m
Least prominent:	Maol Ban, drop 152.1m

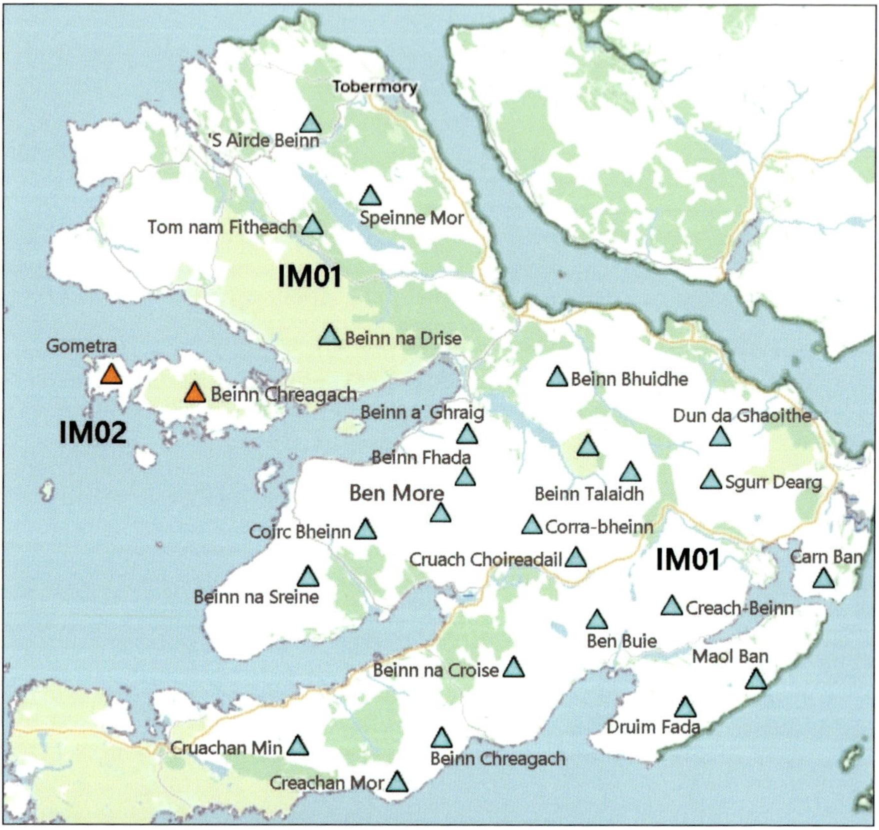

Tobermory

'S Airde Beinn

Tom nam Fitheach

Speinne Mor

IM01

Beinn na Drise

Gometra

Beinn Chreagach

IM02

Beinn Bhuidhe

Dun da Ghaoithe

Beinn a' Ghraig

Beinn Fhada

Beinn Talaidh

Sgurr Dearg

Ben More

Coirc Bheinn

Corra-bheinn

Cruach Choireadail

IM01

Carn Ban

Beinn na Sreine

Creach-Beinn

Ben Buie

Maol Ban

Beinn na Croise

Cruachan Min

Druim Fada

Beinn Chreagach

Creachan Mor

Dun da Ghaoithe

Number		Height	Name	Drop	Location	Summit
1301	A	966.9	Ben More	966.9	NM 5257 3307	Shelter
1308	A	702.9	Beinn Fhada	172.4	NM 5401 3490	Rock by cairn
1311	A	591.6	Beinn a' Ghraig	186.6	NM 5416 3727	Rock by cairn
1312		561	Coirc Bheinn	188	NM 4875 3266	Cairn
1302	A	765.5	Dun da Ghaoithe	659	NM 6724 3622	Cairn
1304	A	741.6	Sgurr Dearg	249.6	NM 6654 3399	Cairn on outcrop
1303	GA	761.6	Beinn Talaidh	430	NM 6254 3470	Outcrop near trig
1306	A	704.8	Corra-bheinn	316	NM 5732 3218	Outcrop by trig
1310	A	618.1	Cruach Choireadail	193.5	NM 5947 3048	Rock by cairn
1316		456	Beinn na Duatharach	304	NM 6047 3633	Cairn on rock
1319		413	Beinn Bhuidhe	314	NM 5901 3994	Cairn
1323	A	347.7	Cruach Torr an Lochain	148.9	NM 5640 4027	Cairn
1305	A	718.1	Ben Buie	516	NM 6041 2707	Cairn
1309	A	698.7	Creach-Beinn	553	NM 6426 2762	Rock near trig
1314		503	Beinn na Croise	252	NM 5598 2510	Rock
1313		521	Beinn na Sreine	376	NM 4564 3039	Cairn
1315	A	491.6	Creach Bheinn	145.7	NM 4194 2912	Trig
1317		446	Speinne Mor	407	NM 4994 4977	Rock
1328		295	'S Airde Beinn	153	NM 4709 5365	Cairn on rock
1318	T	424.3	Beinn na Drise	347	NM 4751 4271	Trig
1329	A	275.5	Tom nam Fitheach	177	NM 4692 4844	Grass
1320		405	Druim Fada	390	NM 6470 2255	Grass near trig
1325	G	338.3	Maol Ban	152.1	NM 6838 2387	Grass
1321	A	378.5	Beinn Chreagach *	194	NM 5198 2170	Rock
1322		376	Cruachan Min	264	NM 4458 2171	Cairn on rock
1326		331	Creachan Mor	164	NM 4962 1956	Cairn
1330	T	248	Carn Ban	233	NM 7214 2892	Ground by trig

'S Airde Beinn

PAUL RICHARDSON, AUGUST 2001

We parked beside a ruined cottage near our starting point for Speinne Mor earlier in the week. There was a stile over the fence and a boggy path leading up to the craggy little hill. Neither the distance nor the climb amounted to much, but the hill itself was very interesting and characterful. I had been on many hills of volcanic origin but none that looked so much like an extinct volcano. The crater rim, now eroded down to a circle of grassy crags, held a central lochan. The highest point was in the north but we completed the circle of the crater. Ravens croaked above. The views were superb, across to Ben Hiant on Ardnamurchan and beyond, with the hills of Rum also visible. In fact, there were many more islands in view than were identifiable. This was, mile-for-mile and climb-for-climb, the most interesting and characterful hill I can easily recall.

Carn Ban

HAMISH BROWN, 2004

Jill had been struggling, with scaffolding on her knee, disintegrating bones, missing toe and various other hindrances. She had not been so active lately but she was not giving up. We headed for the easiest hill I had not yet climbed: Carn Ban, 248m, a pleasant long dander up a green track to a finely perched trig with a view. I was so thrilled to have a view that Jill had to remind me I was on the elusive 1000 at last (I had a new camera to play with). So that was that. Bit flat really. The fun is in the approach after all. Summits only lead down. But no doubt there are other magic numbers to wind one up. Sometimes one curses Dawson. Sometimes one praises him. Thanks, mate.

Beinn Bhuidhe and Cruach Torr an Lochain

ALAN DAWSON, MAY 2009

This innocuous hill has five different names on the 1:50000 map but the 1:25000 map applies them to different knolls or features. Na Bachdanan would be a more interesting and unique name but it is south-west from the summit. Beinn nan Lus applies to the 408m trig point, Beinn na h-Uamha is a 386m Tump about 1km north-west of the highest point, and Maol na Sgreuch sounds like a painful skin complaint. On the way down from Beinn Bhuidhe toward Cruach Torr an Lochain in 2009 I was under scrutiny from a golden eagle for about twenty minutes until it concluded I was not suitable for an evening meal. When I returned to survey Cruach Torr an Lochain in 2014 I tried to force a route from the Macquarrie mausoleum but became entangled in thick rhododendrons and had to retreat, before finding a more feasible approach from nearby Gruline House.

Creachan Mor

ERIC YOUNG, FEBRUARY 2010

I approached from the main road and crossed the top of Eas Mhor waterfall, where a sign announced stalking from September to January and 'If you must walk stick to the main track and wear high-visibility clothing'. A second sign warned of a tick population capable of transmitting Lyme Disease. I survived without being shot or bitten but I was smitten. The hill has fantastic volcanic and coastal features with hidden lochans.

Beinn a' Ghraig

Number		Height	Name	Drop	Location	Summit
1327	T	313	Beinn Chreagach, Ulva	313	NM 4034 4020	Rock by trig
1331		155	Gometra	155	NM 3612 4140	Cairn by trig

Gometra

The leader of the 1933 and 1936 Everest expeditions, Hugh Ruttledge, lived on Gometra for a while. He bought the island in 1932 and is believed to have trained for Everest by climbing his local Marilyn, which he referred to as 'Gometra Island, Argyllshire' in his book about the 1933 expedition. Ruttledge moved to Dartmoor in 1950.

In recent years Gometra has probably had more visits by Marilyn baggers than by anyone else. Many of them enjoyed sampling the wines made by Iain Munro, one of only two inhabitants at the time, before getting a lift in his quad bike or boat. Iain fell from his boat and unfortunately drowned while ferrying a passenger in 2014, possibly having enjoyed too much of his own wine.

JON METCALF, MAY 2009

Ulva and Gometra's limited scheduled ferry window dictated a creative approach during a sodden week on Mull. Eric Young discovered the option of the Gometra RIB, which halved the distance to a more comfortable 12km. The first section wound through delightful woods and around scenic coves to the main track prominent on the map. Beinn Chreagach followed via gently weathered lava steps. The western descent proved steeper than anticipated, so I cut down to the north to rejoin the track.

The headland south of Gometra House sported a blow-hole that spouted fountains of water with a great thump when waves hit the caves with enough intensity. At the large natural harbour we celebrated with Gometra strawberries and rhubarb wine, courtesy of the boatman, before an exhilarating RIB ride back round Ulva to Mull.

ANNE BUNN, APRIL 2014

We arrived at the Ulva ferry only to be told by Donald the ferryman that we were a week too early. It was April Fools day. Luckily Donald agreed to take us across to Ulva, after first checking how we planned to return. Eric had already arranged with Iain Munro for help getting us back to Mull. Although Iain's main boat was out of action, a quad-bike ride followed by a short dinghy sail would see us back on mainland Mull. I was very much looking forward to meeting Iain, having heard of his home-made rhubarb wine infused with home-grown strawberries. We agreed to meet him after climbing to the high points of each island. Unknown to us it was Iain's birthday and so two vital ingredients were in place for a party. Iain invited us in, joined by his four dogs, where a jug of home-brewed carrot wine was waiting for us. Around the room there were four demijohns in various stages of fermentation.

During my fourth glass, just when I thought things could get no better, it did by way of a plate of delicious fresh crab. Luckily for me Iain forgot the dram for the road he had promised. Clinging on to the quad bike, slightly inebriated, was not fun and it got very muddy. I sobered up slightly in the dinghy, and decided that this was bagging at its best.

—— Jura, Islay and Scarba ——

Marilyns:	19
Highest and most prominent:	Beinn an Oir, Jura, 785.2m
Lowest:	Beinn Mhor, Islay, 201.7m
Least prominent:	Beinn Bhreac, Jura, drop 162m

Number		Height	Name	Drop	Location	Summit
1449		785.2	Beinn an Oir	785.2	NR 4980 7494	Trig
1450	A	757.2	Beinn Shiantaidh	303	NR 5135 7478	Cairn
1451	A	735.2	Beinn a' Chaolais	361.1	NR 4888 7345	Rock by cairn
1452		575	Corra Bheinn	208	NR 5264 7550	Cairn
1453		562	Glas Bheinn	276	NR 5003 6989	Rock
1454		508	Scrinadle	165	NR 5052 7779	Cairn
1455		485	Dubh Bheinn	468	NR 5813 8896	Rock
1456		468	Beinn Bhreac 468	162	NR 5976 9080	Cairn on rock
1458		441	Beinn Bhreac 441	189	NR 5332 7788	Cairn
1461		303	Cnoc an Ime	189	NR 5905 8016	Cairn
1459		373	Ben Garrisdale	219	NR 6406 9382	Cairn
1460		304	Cruach na Seilcheig *	181	NR 6781 9847	Cairn

Dubh Bheinn

ANN BOWKER, 1998

Dubh Bheinn looked the most inaccessible of the Jura Marilyns so we decided to do it on our first full day on the island, as it was a beautiful morning. The going low down was quite appalling – grassy tussocks interspersed with boggy holes giving some of the slowest progress imaginable. Eventually we joined a rough vehicle track which led high into the upper corrie, from which it was an easy climb onto the 477m top of Dubh Bheinn, an ascent enlivened by the sight of two beautifully marked adders. The most striking view was of the slightly lower hill Rainberg Mor, which displayed dramatically folded rock striations from this viewpoint.

The Jura Twelve

COLIN CRAWFORD, MARCH 2002

The first major event of my year was an utterly enchanting week spent on Jura in March, a north-to-south walk crossing all twelve Marilyns. The weather allowed an easy ride over the feisty mini-mountains of the north-west, before closing in to deny me any views from the Paps – an excellent excuse to return. Jura seems to me to epitomise a good reason for climbing Marilyns – summits such as Ben Garrisdale and Corra Bheinn concede no superiority of character to their higher neighbours and are far less scarred by access paths.

Scrinadle

ERIC YOUNG, JUNE 2009

The Evans path bisects the Jura trio of Corra Beinn, Scrinadle (great name) and Beinn Bhreac, to the north of the Paps. It felt remote, untroubled, fresh. I sat on Scrinadle with my thoughts running free like the deer. Juniper hangs on in the quartzite and a large brown Silverline moth hangs on a grass stem imitating a mushroom. It's good to walk on your own. It adds a lonesome quality to the space and solitude. Time for yourself and your thoughts. The west coast looked relaxingly tempting.

Number		Height	Name	Drop	Location	Summit
1463	T	491.3	Beinn Bheigier	491.3	NR 4299 5645	Rock by trig
1464		472	Glas Bheinn	207	NR 4297 5919	Rock by cairn
1466		429	Sgorr nam Faoileann	171	NR 4330 6065	Cairn
1467	T	364.3	Sgarbh Breac	289	NR 4062 7662	Trig
1468	A	317.4	Giur-bheinn	148.9	NR 3798 7286	Knoll
1470	T	231.7	Beinn Tart a' Mhill	227	NR 2105 5698	Trig
1471	T	201.7	Beinn Mhor	180	NR 2947 4046	Trig

Beinn Bheigier

Islay is the highest island under 600m and Beinn Bheigier is the ninth highest island summit, after the mainland, Skye, Mull, Arran, Rum, Lewis-Harris, Jura and South Uist.

Giur-bheinn

This hill was not in RHB but was promoted in 1995 after scrutiny of large-scale maps. It was a Marilyn for 26 years until a GNSS survey found it falls 1.1m short of qualification.

Beinn Mhor

ANN BOWKER, 1998

The trig point is not so dramatically situated as those on Noss Head and Biod an Athair, but Beinn Mhor has a similar atmosphere. There is superb cliff scenery by approaching from Mull of Oa, while Dun Athad is spectacularly connected to the mainland.

Beinn Tart a' Mhill

LINDSAY MUNRO, JUNE 2004

We decided to tackle this hill from the vicinity of the stone circle at NR197569, having been discouraged from using the obvious track up from Kelsay Farm by a sign reading 'MOD leased property. No public access'. As soon as we crossed a gate onto the open hillside a guy on a quad bike appeared. He told us abruptly, in a thick Geordie accent, that we couldn't go up the hill, as it was 'all MOD up there'. On hearing that we didn't believe this and intended to go anyway, he lost the plot completely and became extremely threatening and aggressive.

Reluctantly, we retreated and went straight to Bowmore where we reported the incident to the tourist office and the police. It turned out that the hothead was from the neighbouring farm, Coultoon, and the police warned him about his behaviour. They also contacted the farmer's wife at Kelsay, who gave permission for us to use the track from there. We just had to phone first to let her know when we were coming. Unfortunately, that wasn't the end of the matter. Three days later, on the final day of our holiday, we headed back towards the Rhinns, stopping to phone en route. The woman said that she had discussed our proposed visit with her husband and we couldn't use the track after all, as 'it wouldn't be fair on everybody else'. With our time on the island running out, I ended up making a solo ascent of the hill's rough and unpleasant east side.

Back at home, I contacted the Ministry of Defence to request clarification of the situation on Beinn Tart a' Mhill. They confirmed that access along the Kelsay track was not permitted but that the MOD has no reason to stop access by any other route.

Looking north to Scarba from Beinn Bhreac 468 on Jura

Sgarbh Breac, Islay

On the way up Beinn a' Bhaillidh on Eilean Shona

Number		Height	Name	Drop	Location	Summit
1457	T	450	Cruach Scarba	450	NM 6906 0446	Outcrop by trig

Cruach Scarba

This hill is shown as 449 metres on OS maps but it is apparent from photographs and trip reports that a nearby outcrop is around a metre higher than the base of the trig pillar. That makes it the same height as Ronas Hill on Shetland Mainland, so Scarba equals Shetland as the tenth-highest island and the joint highest under 600 metres.

PAUL RICHARDSON, JULY 2000

The main purpose of the Marilyn Hall of Fame meeting was a boat trip to the island of Scarba to climb Cruach Scarba. We formed part of the first landing party and met up with nine others, plus a baby and dog, at Crinan Harbour. There was a dense fog when we embarked. The sea was calm and the half-hour crossing without problem. Then came the news that, because the tide was lower than usual, disembarkation would consist of climbing down a ladder on the bow and jumping on to a small crag on the shore. I was to go first. In fact, except for the dog, getting off the boat was quite easy.

After a mini-scramble on a little crag, we found ourselves amongst dense bracken. Most of us followed the northward course of a burn. Amongst all these experienced old hands, mine was the only GPS. It aroused some amusement, some genuine interest and, I thought, some scorn. We climbed rough ground beside the burn in the mist, until Phil began to suggest that we should by now have reached a lochan. It was my GPS that revealed that we had in fact not been following the burn that we had supposed, but one further east. We crossed some boggy ground and continued to gain height. Lynda warned of a snake which turned out to be a slow worm. I saw my first grasshoppers of the year, and there were frogs. Jonathan occasionally asked for confirmation from the GPS, and the joint navigational effort was doing well.

We reached the top to find Rob already there with his boots off. Lynda produced a bottle of wine and a cake from a rucksack. Jonathan (to whom this was a surprise) was to celebrate his 700th Marilyn. This figure had been reached some time earlier on Orkney. Somebody else produced a bottle of malt whisky. A roar from the peat hags just below the summit announced the arrival of the Webbs – Richard had fallen in a bog. Then Jon arrived and the party was complete. There were still no views from the summit.

We returned by a marginally more direct version of the outward route. The mist broke up, we saw some sunshine and a large adder. The boat, having disembarked a second party, was waiting for us. Embarkation was much easier than the landing.

Carnan Eoin, Colonsay

This fine little hill is 143.4 metres high so it qualified as a Submarilyn when they were defined as having 140-149.9m drop. The original idea of Submarilyns was to identify hills that could potentially be Marilyns. With far more accurate data now available, there is less need for such a list. The revised definition of Submarilyns includes several hills that are very close to qualifying and others that have been Marilyns at some stage. Carnan Eoin and the summits of Tiree and Lundy are no longer classed as Submarilyns, but it is still possible to enjoy visiting these islands and climbing to their highest points.

——— Coastal Islands of Scotland ———

Marilyns:	3
Highest:	Beinn a' Bhaillidh, Eilean Shona, 266m
Lowest:	Cruachan Charna, Carna, 170m

IC01 Shona, Carna and Kerrera

RHB sections 18A, 18C, 19A   OS maps 40, 49

Number		Height	Name	Drop	Location	Summit
1347	T	266	Beinn a' Bhaillidh, Shona	266	NM 6490 7416	Outcrop by trig
1383		170	Cruachan Charna, Carna	170	NM 6183 5897	Cairn on rock
1405	T	189.6	Carn Breugach, Kerrera	189.6	NM 8150 2781	Cairn near trig

Cruachan Charna

ALAN DAWSON, AUGUST 1999

In 1999 I organised the first gathering of Marilyn baggers, with the focus on getting a boat to the uninhabited island of Carna in Loch Sunart. To make things easier, I booked a hostel in Corpach for a group. Rather to my surprise, 23 of us showed up and we enjoyed a successful weekend, including a smooth crossing to Carna. We enjoyed relaxing on the pier in the sunshine while waiting for the boat to return from Laga Bay, until I spoiled things by calling an impromptu two-minute meeting, to discuss whether anyone would like to get together again the next year. Jonathan Woods boldly offered to organise the second gathering, and so a tradition was initiated. I can't remember the location of the first chant, but I believe I was responsible for that as well.

DEE ROGERS, JUNE 2009

The Hall of Fame – is it like Grieg's 'Hall of the Mountain King', I wondered? Well, it certainly has music. I was fortunate in that I reached 600 Marilyns on the lovely island of Carna in the illustrious company of several members of the Hall of Fame, including the Chief Chanter. What a splendid welcome into the Hall, with Lindsay leading a superb, loud chant and Alison Wilson leading the choir in a song. The occasion was extra special as Charles Everett also reached the magic 600. The other discovery I made about the Hall of Fame was that it is occupied by many mad, interesting, lovely fellow baggers. Despite trying to deny it for many years, I acknowledged that weekend that 'I am a bagger'. This fact was proclaimed loudly in front of witnesses on Beinn Bhreac, near Eilean Shona.

Beinn a' Bhaillidh, Eilean Shona

AUDREY LITTERICK, 2005

This was one of my first two Marilyn-bagging sea kayak trips, with partner Andy and two pals. Cruachan Charna was an easy, pleasant short day, amidst seals, terns and an eagle, but Eilean Shona, which we circumnavigated as well as climbing to the top of Beinn a' Bhaillidh, was more than a little exciting for a novice sea-kayaker. We had to negotiate a fairly big sea, with waves coming from an awkward direction on the seaward side of the island. Amazingly, not one of the three novices capsized. Magical views from the top though, of silver sands, sparkling aquamarine seas, the wilds of Moidart and away out to Rum, Eigg, Muck and Skye.

—— Monadhliath ——

Land east of the Great Glen, north of Glen Spean and Loch Laggan and west of the River Spey

Marilyns: 40

Highest and most prominent: Creag Meagaidh, 1128.1m, drop 868m

Lowest: Burgiehill, 254m

Least prominent: Beinn Mheadhoin, drop 152.5m

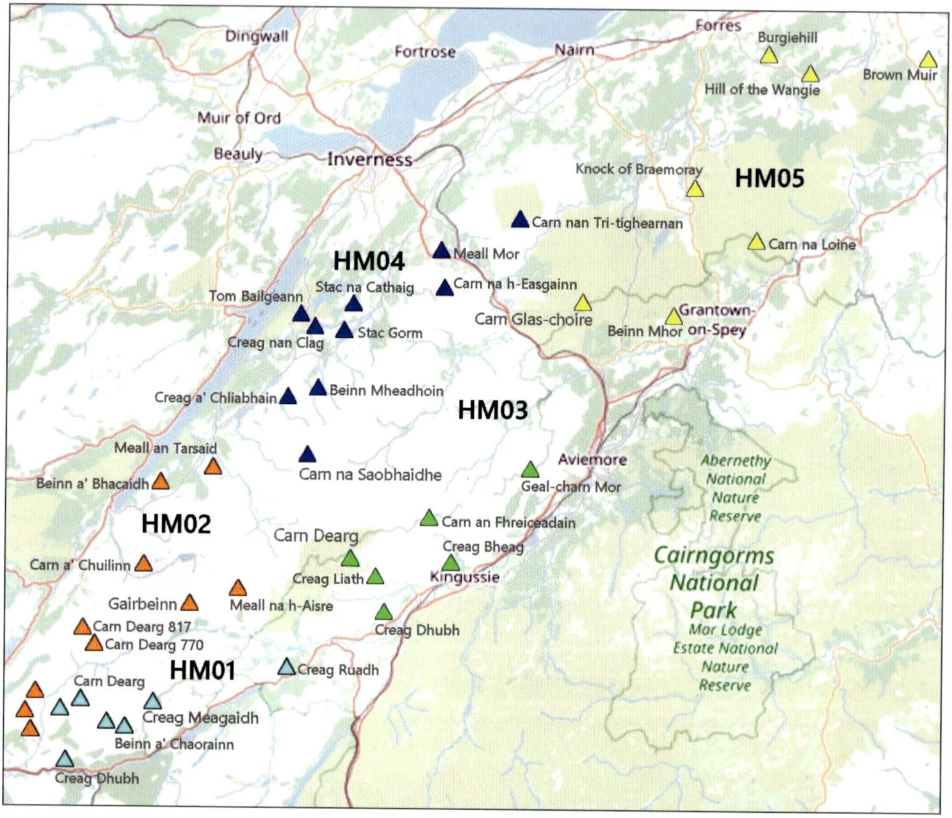

Carn na Saobhaidhe, the highest hill in area HM04, by 10cm

HM01 Meagaidh-ruadh

Number		Height	Name	Drop	Location	Summit
658	A	1128.1	Creag Meagaidh	868	NN 4183 8754	Cairn
663	A	1049.1	Beinn a' Chaorainn	228	NN 3860 8506	Rock in cairn
675	GA	914.6	Beinn Teallach	301.5	NN 3613 8597	Rock by cairn
680	A	659.6	Creag Dhubh	333	NN 3227 8245	Cairn
676	A	834.4	Carn Dearg	251	NN 3450 8870	Cairn
679	A	676.8	Leana Mhor	157.5	NN 3168 8791	Rock by cairn
681	A	622.2	Creag Ruadh	309	NN 5580 9139	Trig

Beinn a' Chaorainn

This hill is notorious for two reasons. There have been numerous mountain rescue call-outs after walkers (and dogs), have fallen through a cornice that builds up each winter along the curving ridge between the two highest summits. Secondly, the location of its highest point was unclear for several decades, with map revisions adding to the confusion. Recent OS maps show the highest, central summit as 1052m and the South Top as 1049m. In fact the summit is only 60cm higher than the South Top. The summit location has not changed but we now know precisely where it is, so it is not essential to walk along the cornice edge to be sure of reaching the highest point.

Carn Dearg and Leana Mhor

Several of the hills of the Monadhliath have identical names, similar heights and similar character, so it is useful to classify them into different topographic areas. This pair of hills in HM01 are east of Glen Roy and also south of the River Roy as it curves eastward past Brae Roy Lodge toward the source of the River Spey. They are connected to Beinn Teallach and the Creag Meagaidh group, though rarely climbed in the same walk. The other Leana Mhor, west of Glen Roy, and the other two Carn Deargs, are connected to Gairbeinn even though it is on the other side of the highest point of the Corrieyairack Pass.

Creag Ruadh

ANN BOWKER, JUNE 1995

This was a half-day hill so a good choice for our northward journey. It is gratifying for the peak bagger but rather alarming for the future prospects of the mountains that we could sleep in England and have lunch on this summit in the heart of the Highlands.

We parked close to the shore of the Spey dam reservoir. The route from here was obvious from the map, sliding between coniferous and deciduous trees. The ridge is quite steep on the north and it was more pleasant to make the effort to stay on it, although one could easily take a boggy beeline for the summit instead.

The pride of this hill is its magnificent full-length vista of Loch Laggan. Even with the western hills rather hazy, the sharp outline of Binnein Shios was particularly prominent, with the more pointed summit of its neighbour Binnein Shuas peeping over the top. We descended westwards, alongside the sizeable summit lochan, and dropped into the very flat Glen Shirra, which separates this hill from Creag Meagaidh and its satellites. After this short and easy circuit we drove a short distance east and made a quick ascent of Cruban Beag, a strategically placed hill for a panorama of the Spey valley.

Creag Meagaidh from the north

Beinn a' Chaorainn from the south

Carn a' Chuilinn

HM02 Gairbeinn-iaruinn

Number		Height	Name	Drop	Location	Summit
631	A	895.5	Gairbeinn	211	NN 4605 9852	Outcrop
641	A	779.9	Carn Easgann Bana	142.7	NH 4852 0632	Cairn
634	A	862.1	Meall na h-Aisre	155	NH 5154 0006	Rock
638	A	816.6	Carn a' Chuilinn	178	NH 4167 0340	Outcrop near cairn
637	A	816.5	Carn Dearg 817	201	NN 3500 9662	Moss near cairn
642	A	769.6	Carn Dearg 770	198	NN 3572 9488	Cairn
677	A	804.3	Beinn Iaruinn	446.8	NN 2970 9004	Cairn
678	A	683.9	Leana Mhor	174.3	NN 2847 8788	Cairn
682		567	Beinn a' Mhonicag	268	NN 2879 8548	Cairn
648		555	Beinn a' Bhacaidh	254	NH 4315 1191	Cairn
651	A	492.3	Meall an Tarsaid *	154.7	NH 4915 1306	Rock by cairn

Gairbeinn

For many years this hill was reduced in status to a twin peak along with Corrieyairack Hill, as both were shown as 896m on OS maps at the time. The original RHB listing did not bother with subtleties such as twin peaks but simply designated Gairbeinn as the Marilyn, thanks to a brilliant piece of topographic judgement, with a touch of luck. Later OS maps indicated that Gairbeinn was higher and this was confirmed by a survey in 2018 showing that Corrieyairack Hill is only 892m and 3.5m short of being a twin peak.

These two summits are merely the highest points of an extensive range of high hills over 850m, including Geal Charn, Gairbeinn North Top, Meall na h-Aisre and Carn Leac, as well as a vast number over 600m.

Meall an Tarsaid

Meall an Tarsaid is tucked in between two roads and two rivers in the north of this area. Like The Saddle, its summit has been relocated three times (Baystones also moved three times but is no longer a Marilyn). The survey to settle the matter in 2016 required the removal of one large cairn and most of another. The south top is 36cm higher than the north top, which is shown as 493m on OS large-scale mapping but is only 492m.

Surveying the summit of Meall an Tarsaid, with two sets of GNSS equipment, just to be sure

Beinn a' Mhonicag from Leana Mhor

The summit of Geal-charn Mor

Cairn on Creag Bheag, the fifth highest point surveyed

HM03 Carndearg-chailleach

Number		Height	Name	Drop	Location	Summit
621	A	945.7	Carn Dearg	591	NH 6356 0239	Cairn
635	A	833.6	Marg na Craige	149.0	NN 6206 9732	Rock
645	A	743.5	Creag Liath	190.3	NH 6637 0077	Outcrop
643	A	752.9	Creag Dhubh	387	NN 6780 9723	Cairn
633	A	877.7	Carn an Fhreiceadain	172.5	NH 7256 0713	Trig
636	A	824.1	Geal-charn Mor	227.5	NH 8363 1233	Rock by trig
644	A	745.6	Cnoc Fraing	144.2	NH 8063 1438	Rock near cairn
653	A	487.1	Creag Bheag	159	NH 7453 0165	Outcrop

Creag Bheag

ALAN DAWSON, DECEMBER 2015 AND SEPTEMBER 2024

This fine little hill can be easily reached by a pleasant signposted walk along a good path from Kingussie, but locating its highest point presented a problem. The OS map showed three 487m spot heights, making it impossible to identify the summit without a survey.

On an icy winter day my studded footwear was useful even in the car park. One of the problems with winter surveying is trying to avoid hypothermia but here I discovered another problem – it is difficult to dismantle a cairn that is frozen together. It took a lot of time and effort using thick gloves, with wellies useful for kicking rocks. I had expected that the rock under the main cairn would be confirmed as the official summit, but both the other summits were measured as over 30cm higher at 486.94m.

This result was inconvenient because I still could not be sure which was the highest point. The south summit is almost 300 metres from the central one, looks quite separate and requires a short diversion from the path, so it is easily missed. I concluded I would have to go back on a warmer day for a second survey, but then other priorities took over and I forgot about it for nine years. In 2024 I surveyed five points and found three of them to be exactly 487m. The one with the rebuilt cairn was again 30cm lower at 486.7m but this time I found a smooth outcrop north of the cairn that I had missed in 2015. This turned out to be a convincing 12cm higher than any other point. Lovely summit, lovely walk, lovely day, a triple rarity in the world of hill surveying and an excellent outcome.

Number		Height	Name	Drop	Location	Summit
639	A	811.1	Carn na Saobhaidhe	170	NH 5989 1441	Tussock
647	A	555.2	Beinn Mheadhoin	152.5	NH 6041 2146	Cairn on outcrop
650		519	Creag a' Chliabhain	209	NH 5758 2057	Cairn
646	A	617.2	Carn na h-Easgainn	172	NH 7439 3207	Heather
614		492	Meall Mor	175	NH 7373 3556	Cairn
654	T	463.9	Tom Bailgeann	242	NH 5884 2948	Trig
655		446	Stac na Cathaig	213	NH 6400 3013	Rock by cairn
656		430	Stac Gorm	183	NH 6304 2731	Outcrop
657		407	Creag nan Clag	168	NH 5975 2834	Heather
611	A	614.8	Carn nan Tri-tighearnan	333	NH 8231 3903	Trig

Carn na Saobhaidhe

This hill does not win any awards for popularity but it is the highest point in a vast hill area. It is possible to walk north-east from its summit for about 12km without dropping below 600m or crossing a road, or about 7km south-west. It is no longer a wild area, as tracks and turbines snake high on to the hillsides, but it does contain pockets of wildness as well as plenty of wildlife. Hill walkers have reason to be grateful to OS for showing the height of Carn na Laraiche Maoile as 809m on recent maps. In fact its surveyed height is 810.97m, just 10cm lower than Carn na Saobhaidhe, give or take a clump of heather. Both can now be reached easily via a turbine track from the west and combined in a satisfying circuit, but that 10cm difference means few walkers will feel the desire to do so.

Creag nan Clag

ANN BOWKER, JUNE 1992

This was the first hill we climbed specifically because it was in the book, on 19 June 1992. We don't know any other Marilyn baggers. All our friends think we are completely mad.

Carn nan Tri-tighearnan

ANN BOWKER, JUNE 1993

This is a real peak-bagger's hill, the summit being a tiny cone of drier heather in a vast expanse of boggy moorland. The vehicle track we used from Ruthven had matured into a pleasant path and a herd of goats added to the interest as the track wound up through rough territory. When the track gave out it left a very rough climb to the trig point. The distant views from the top were superb, south to the Cairngorms and west to a glorious array of unidentified mountains, ridge upon ridge, a classic scene with each one a slightly paler shade of purplish blue fading into the far distance. The nearer landscape was the sweep of empty moorland. Such a summit is hard to come to but the wildness and solitude is reward enough for the toil. One's experience of the mountains would be incomplete if one chose only dramatic or crowded hills like An Teallach or Snowdon.

Tom Bailgeann

MARTIN RICHARDSON, FEBRUARY 2011

I climbed this hill three times in two days. On the third descent I found, in deep heather, the motorhome keys that I had lost on the first ascent the day before and hence I was able to cancel the tow home to Yorkshire by the AA that I had already booked.

HM05 Glaschoire-wangie

Number		Height	Name	Drop	Location	Summit
610	A	659.4	Carn Glas-choire	254	NH 8914 2916	Cairn
612	T	548.4	Carn na Loine	233	NJ 0700 3609	Trig
616	T	471.0	Beinn Mhor	192	NH 9937 2810	Trig
617		456	Knock of Braemoray	173	NJ 0118 4172	Heather
618		339	Brown Muir	201	NJ 2584 5486	Heather
619		319	Hill of the Wangie	158	NJ 1366 5374	Trig
620		254	Burgiehill	167	NJ 0972 5590	Mound near trig

Beinn Mhor

HAMISH BROWN, OCTOBER 2002

This was another serendipity viewpoint, coinciding with a big end-of-October snowfall. I parked at the tarmac end in Glen Beg. No driving further anyway, as the bridge had collapsed in a recent spate. Non-conifer woodlands were a pleasant change. The view to the Cairngorms was astonishing. A circuit from Granton would be worthwhile, or some fiddling with two cars. Easy hill, big reward. Always, the discovery element is the delight.

Brown Muir

AUDREY LITTERICK, 2007

I went up from Millbuies Country Park along a set of tracks and some heather. The tracks were full of gorse bushes, deep muddy holes, rain-drenched, waist-deep grass and frisky bullocks. It rained steadily all the way while thunder rumbled unnervingly close. The burns had transformed into barely crossable raging torrents. The limited view was of a flat, boggy, heathery summit. I got the route wrong on the way down and had a violent tussle with a dense and seemingly endless thicket of head-high gorse.

Hill of the Wangie

The summit of this hill has become easy to reach in an era of GPS, digital mapping, online reports and forest felling, but things were not always so simple.

ALAN DAWSON, AUGUST 1999

After a pleasant ascent through open woodland, I spent over half an hour searching and still could not find the trig pillar. Shortly after getting home I discovered detailed instructions that Jon Metcalf had sent me several months earlier. I returned in 2010 to tidy up one of the loose ends before my final mainland Marilyn and found the trig pillar easily, assisted by a printed extract from a large-scale map.

CHRIS UPSON, 2002

On a revisit to the dreaded Hill of the Wangie in search of that most elusive of trig points, I found the summit area just as hopelessly confusing as last time and was on the verge of giving up again, in a state of utter despondency, when lo, a beautiful pillar of concrete appeared as if by magic in a little clearing in a narrow forest break. It was an emotional moment, snatching a result when all seemed lost. Seemed so simple once you'd found it.

——— Eastern Highlands: North ———

Land east of the River Spey and River Feshie and north of the River Dee

Marilyns:	61
Highest and most prominent:	Ben Macdui, 1309.3m
Lowest:	Waughton Hill, 234m
Least prominent:	Millstone Hill, drop 154m

Brimmond Hill, on the western fringe of Aberdeen (HE04), and Waughton Hill near Fraserburgh (HE06) are not shown above

HE01 Braeriach-bhrotain

Number		Height	Name	Drop	Location	Summit
519	A	1295.5	Braeriach	460	NN 9532 9991	Rock
521	A	1292.4	Cairn Toul	166	NN 9633 9722	Rock by cairn
538	A	1157.1	Beinn Bhrotain	258	NN 9541 9229	Rock near trig
549	A	1113.4	Monadh Mor	138.8	NN 9386 9421	Rock near cairn
548	A	1116.0	Sgor Gaoith	242.8	NN 9030 9896	Cliff edge
609		429	Ord Ban	167	NH 8916 0853	Boulder by trig

Beinn Bhrotain and Braeriach

PAUL RICHARDSON, MAY 1984

It was with even more dejection than usual that I tramped along Glen Dee towards White Bridge in a mournful drizzle, but it soon ceased. Reaching a conifer plantation I paused by a rock stained into a beautiful mosaic of browns and blacks by some form of lichen. When I eventually reached Carn Cloich-mhuilinn, Beinn Bhrotain had become clear. Gradually my route transformed itself, with snow, boulder-fields, and then the summit. By the time I had reached the summit of Monadh Mor, an increasing temptation became a fully-fledged plan. Braeriach didn't seem all that far away. Seeing that the mighty hill was now clear of cloud and I had time in hand, I set off.

The going was good, over short, crisp vegetation and gravel. Nearing the col, there were more boulders and snow-fields to negotiate. I drove myself hard up a snow-field, then more slowly up drier ground until I emerged on the rim of the Garbh Choire. Admiring the view into this dramatic complex of corries, I headed round towards the summit of Braeriach, making a detour to Carn na Criche. The cairn was buried under the snow. The views were spectacular, near and far. Ben Macdui was now clear, Cairn Gorm also visible and the broken crags of Coire Bhrocain were tremendous.

The massive plateau of Braeriach dwarfs that of Monadh Mor and even Ben Macdui. As I headed back towards Carn na Criche I had a cursory look for the Wells of Dee but the area was covered by snow. I was rather disappointed in Glen Geusachan, all heather and bog, though the cliffs on either side were very fine. The biggest lift was provided by a review of a great day.

Cairn Toul and Braeriach

MICHAEL CURTIS, MAY 2013

Even by cycling in to Derry Lodge, it is a long way to Cairn Toul. The walk is a slow burner, for it is not until you are 8km from Linn of Dee, where the path starts to turn towards the Lairig Ghru, that the scenery changes from pleasant to dramatic. About halfway up Stob Coire an t-Saighdeir I made my way to a small promontory for the view I hoped it would offer. My breath was taken from me by what was revealed. Cairn Toul was now close at hand across the snowy wastes of the corrie. The view was majestic and I felt honoured to see it. Does that sound like a romantic Victorian description of being in the mountains? If so, no apologies made. We crossed the snow line with magnificent scenery ever present, then over the plateau to Braeriach. Ours were the only footprints in the summit snows. We were able to sit in the shelter of the summit cairn for some time, enjoying the experience. I know in my walking life there will be a limited number of times to enjoy such occasions, so I tried my best to imprint the view into my memory.

Number		Height	Name	Drop	Location	Summit
518	A	1309.3	Ben Macdui	950	NN 9890 9894	Rock near trig
525	A	1244.8	Cairn Gorm	145.8	NJ 0051 0406	Cairn
539	A	1155.8	Derry Cairngorm	142.5	NO 0173 9803	Cairn on outcrop
531	A	1182.9	Beinn Mheadhoin	254	NJ 0246 0169	Rock
567		1037	Carn a' Mhaim	230	NN 9946 9519	Cairn
557	A	1090.4	Bynack More	283	NJ 0418 0637	Rock
594	A	895.1	Creag Mhor	167	NJ 0574 0478	Tor
598	A	820.6	Geal Charn	173	NJ 0905 1269	Rock near cairn
605	A	686.3	Carn na Farraidh	143.7	NJ 1144 1475	Cairn
600	A	813.8	Sgor Mor	236	NO 0072 9142	Outcrop
601		810	Meall a' Bhuachaille	436	NH 9908 1153	Cairn
604	A	713.1	Cnap Chaochan Aitinn	157	NJ 1457 0996	Mound near cairn
1494	A	722.1	Creagan a' Chaise	330	NJ 1042 2417	Trig
1496	A	710.2	Carn a' Ghille Chearr	179	NJ 1396 2985	Trig

Beinn Mheadhoin

PAUL RICHARDSON, JUNE 1983

The clag was down to the tree-line as I went up Glen Lui. We flogged up to Loch Etchachan and went steeply up to the south-west top. The gravelly plateau gave easy walking, though superb views were lost. It was a fine walk around the tors, each of which loomed out of the mist just on schedule. The best tor was a huge ribbed monolith just south-west of the summit. The summit tor was the largest and most difficult to climb, but presented no real problems. A bearing took us steeply down to the Lairig an Laoigh. The clag hung grey and oppressive. Over the years I had come to equate desolation with drabness, and it had largely lost its power to impress, but today I was transfixed by the awesome bleakness of the Lairig an Laoigh. It appeared like a tunnel, the sides formed by the steep slope I had descended and the steep flanks of Beinn a' Chaorainn opposite. The heavy, low cloud formed the roof. Down this narrow passage, I could see the black pools of the Dubh Lochan. It was a scene as bleak and elemental as anything I had ever seen or could imagine, a fantastic landscape of strangely compelling beauty. A little adversity in this setting would make the many miles to the nearest habitation a fearsome prospect.

Geal Charn

ALAN DAWSON, JULY 2005

Heading south-west off Geal Charn near Nethy Bridge, I came across a long, waist-high electric fence, with no way over. We had to change our route, following the fence west for 800 metres until we found a low section of fence with a thin plastic sleeve, where we could jump or step over. After another half hour of rough ground I had just started to enjoy the walk again when we came across the same damned fence, barring the way to the summit of Carn na h-Ailig. There was no sign of any way across without dropping well down from the ridge, so we spent several minutes trying to figure out a way over. Eventually I got down on my hands and knees so that Rhona could stand on my back then step on the post and jump over. It felt as though she was standing on my back for ages.

She eventually made the leap but then I found I couldn't get over, as it was a bit too high and slightly uphill. In the end I took off my waterproof trousers to give me a bit more spring in my legs, took a run-up and a big backswing, and just managed to vault it. I would have given up the summit but it was the direct route back, and the short heather on the ridge was far more pleasant than the spongy tussocks and wet grass lower down.

Perhaps the fence was meant to encourage natural regeneration, but it did not fit with the access code of the Cairngorms National Park Authority: 'Respect the interests of other people, act with courtesy, consideration and awareness'. I sent details to the local access officer and received an acknowledgement, but never heard any more about it.

Creagan a' Chaise

Lindsay Munro, May 2003

This was the most welcoming summit of the year. A cubby-hole in the massive cairn contained a tin of cigars and a hip flask bearing the words 'have a cigar' and 'have a dram'. The novelty of smoking Tom Thumbs at the top was denied us by the dampness of the matches provided, but the flask was passed round eagerly.

Bynack More

Ben Avon

Number		Height	Name	Drop	Location	Summit
529	A	1196.0	Beinn a' Bhuird	456.2	NJ 0923 0061	Rock near cairn
536	A	1172.0	Ben Avon	202	NJ 1319 0184	Tor
559	A	1083.3	Beinn a' Chaorainn	246	NJ 0452 0135	Cairn
593	A	900.1	Culardoch	312	NO 1934 9882	Trig
596	A	863.0	Creag an Dail Bheag **	211	NO 1573 9815	Rock
607	A	634.8	Craig Leek	143.7	NO 1853 9306	Cairn
599		818	Carn na Drochaide	221	NO 1274 9383	Cairn
603	A	743.2	Geallaig Hill	312	NO 2979 9818	Trig
606	A	668.2	Creag Bhalg	160.4	NO 0917 9123	Rock by cairn
608	L	560.3	Meall Alvie	209.6	NO 2034 9191	Woods

Ben Avon

BERT BARNETT, JUNE 2021

Late June held good weather and it seemed suitable for a biggish day which I had been hoping for since reading Alan Dawson's new book, The 1033 High Hills of Britain. Having traversed Ben Avon a number of times collecting Munros and Munro Tops, I had cast an eye over the tors which lay off my routes. Although the tors had not been listed before, they now appeared in Alan's book and presented a reason for visiting them.

The starting point was clearly from the north, by bike from Tomintoul to Inchrory. I had cycled this way many times for the summits around Loch Builg. The light tail-wind and a bit of electric help made for an easy start to a perfect morning run, with fields of rock rose opening on the verges. After parking the bike under the bridge over the Builg Burn, the track and path up towards Clach Fiaclach was a welcome start for my old legs and lungs. For once I had taken the precaution of noting the grid references of the seven summits which were on my agenda in case it was a misty day. The last time I was on this part of the hill it had been wild, wet and misty and the rolling nature of the hills did not make for easy navigation. Even on a clear day it can be confusing to figure out which tor is which. The book listing gives eight-figure grid references but I took the precaution of expanding those to ten figures from the Hill Bagging website.

The first tor was Clach Ban, which was a few minutes from the path. What a joy to gain an easy new tick after years of seeking out tough Marilyns, Grahams and Corbetts. I had my first ptarmigan encounter, with chicks scurrying in one direction and parents doing the 'broken wing' escape in the other direction.

On to East Meur Gorm Craig North Top, which I was sure I had visited previously as I had photos of the trailing azalea which survives somehow amongst the bare granite on the ridge. The ground was good, dry and not a peat hag in sight. I left the path to venture over Big Brae, as Munro had it on his original list. The path had evaporated by this stage, but the gentle angle and dry ground made for a pleasurable ascent. It was a fair stretch to Ben Avon North Tor, where my grid reference confirmed I was on the correct summit.

From there it was an easy decision to take in the South Top, as the ground was so good and the day perfectly clear. It made sense to go over the main summit, Leabaidh an Daimh Bhuidhe. I could see a figure standing on the top, the only person I saw on the hill.

The swoop down to Ben Avon South Top was excellent and the view over to Beinn a' Bhuird was surprisingly clear. This spot reminded me of the day I was coming down over Carn Eas, when I could see a mass of smoke above the Luibeg or Derry Lodge. I learned later that a major fire had destroyed a large part of the pine wood, started by a camp fire. I returned east towards Mullach Lochan nan Gabhar, contouring under the top, which was most impressive from that angle. There was a good burn coming down from the plateau with crystal-clear water, before the gradual rise to the next top. Not far below was the next objective, Clach Choutsaich. I approached it with trepidation as it looked quite daunting, with rounded holdless granite. I scrambled up and down the left-hand crack, got so far then had a look at the central mossy option. I then went further up the right-hand boot-sized cracks but did not fancy coming down that way.

After twenty minutes I chickened out and headed for Stuc Gharbh Mhor, an easy top, then decided to go back over West Meur Gorm Craig, which I had recorded three times previously, but at least once in mist with no GPS, so a confirming visit was a bonus. The trailing azalea in this traverse appeared in large patches, with one small patch of marsh marigold in a wet flush under one of the few remaining snow patches. I was accompanied here by a hen ptarmigan that ran parallel to me for 100 metres, though I saw no chicks.

The return down the path was a treat and I reached my bike to find a young family enjoying the burn and about to set up a camp. A light head-wind back to Tomintoul was not a problem, but I succumbed to the luxury of the electric bike's wee help. Why not?

The 1033 High Hills of Britain is certainly more than just a hill listing, as it is well supplemented with Alan's accounts of his many surveying expeditions, where he used his professionally capable equipment to measure summits and cols. Many of the heights vary considerably from those on the maps.

Creag an Dail Bheag

This hill superseded Carn Liath in 2013. I reported my survey results to the Scottish Mountaineering Club and Ordnance Survey. The initial response from OS was predictably dismissive, but after polite persistence the customer services department referred the matter to the OS technical team. They requested further information and so I sent them a survey report with details of the methodology. OS then offered to process the survey data themselves, so the satellite data for this pair of hills was processed three times, by different software and personnel each time, with the following results:

Carn Liath:	Creag an Dail Bheag:
861.49m by AD	863.03m by AD
861.48m by G&J Surveys	863.04m by G&J Surveys
861.47m by OS	863.02m by OS

The consistency of these results helped to confirm my confidence in the accuracy of the survey process, assuming I had identified the highest point of Carn Liath, which I had not found easy to do. The OS reported the height accuracy of the survey to be in the region of +-5cm. They also reported that they would be changing their maps to show Creag an Dail Bheag as 863m and Carn Liath as 861m (861.47m rounded down).

Craig Leek

This hill is easily reached from Invercauld and just qualifies as a Submarilyn with 4cm to spare. A hill 600m high would need 144m drop, a 650m hill would need 143.5m and a 635m hill requires 143.65m drop. The simple formula can generate complex results.

RHB sections 8, 21A, 21B   OS maps 36, 37, 38

Number		Height	Name	Drop	Location	Summit
1488		872	Morven	387	NJ 3768 0399	Cairn
1493	A	749.0	Mona Gowan	194	NJ 3360 0579	Boundary stone
597	A	828.8	Brown Cow Hill	295	NJ 2210 0445	Cairn
1513	J	619.1	Pressendye	253	NJ 4903 0897	Cairn
1514		533	Coiliochbhar Hill	211	NJ 5035 1633	Cairn
1517	T	494.4	Benaquhallie	212	NJ 6064 0870	Wall by trig
1518	T	476.5	Craiglich	167.8	NJ 5330 0543	Trig
1519		471	Hill of Fare	217	NJ 6718 0292	Cairn on rock
1521	T	447.7	Cairn William	258	NJ 6561 1681	Rock by trig
1508	L	401.6	Craigendarroch	158.9	NO 3655 9652	Viewpoint
1524		266	Brimmond Hill	159	NJ 8561 0915	Memorial

Brown Cow Hill

AUDREY LITTERICK, 2011

How many people could claim that they had spent one of their best days of the year on Brown Cow Hill? We had warm, gentle sunshine and perfect peace and quiet other than the calls of abundant moorland birds. We met a lovely chap who had borrowed the key to Corndavon Lodge for the day and he invited us to join him and his grandson to see the amazing wall-paintings inside. Quite a place and quite a story behind them. The summit was calm, with some of the clearest views I had seen for a long time of the Cairngorms and beyond. No pinnacles or precipices, no wild adventures, just a very peaceful and beautiful place to be on that warm, spring day.

Benaquhallie

Anyone looking for useful information about this hill might as well look at a map, as this paragraph is all about its unique name. Benaquhallie is the only Marilyn with a Q in the middle of its name. The only others with a Q are Queensberry and Quinag, which is one name but usually applied to three Marilyns. There are several Marilyns near Balquhidder but none share its name. Q is not the rarest letter, as Saxa Vord has the only X and Ben Chonzie has the only Z, but the rarest letter is J as there are none at all in any Marilyn name in Britain, though Djouce in Wicklow is the 37th highest Marilyn in Ireland. The most prominent British hills with a J are Milljoan Hill and Mull of Milljoan. Both have 96m drop, three more than Ben John. All three are in south-west Scotland. The best J name is Stack of Junamarka, a 50-metre high stack in Ronas Voe, not far from Ronas Hill on Shetland Mainland. It has no recorded ascents. A more well-known J name is Rig of the Jarkness, a rugged, undulating ridge north-west from 531m Craiglee in Galloway. It is also the title of a rugged, undulating track by One More Grain on the 2022 album Beans on Toast with Pythagoras. The meanings of Jarkness, Junamarka and Benaquallie are currently unclear and therefore open to creative speculation and poetic licence.

Brimmond Hill

AUDREY LITTERICK, 2005

A return trip from my desk at work in my lunch hour, on cross-country skis in perfect snow with sunny blue skies. Felt smug all day after that one.

Number		Height	Name	Drop	Location	Summit
1489	A	840.9	Ben Rinnes	513	NJ 2549 3545	Tor
1498		571	Meikle Conval	246	NJ 2911 3711	Heather near cairn
1502		553	Little Conval	165	NJ 2941 3924	Cairn
1490	T	804.4	Carn Mor	351	NJ 2657 1834	Trig
1503	A	491.2	The Bochel ***	154.9	NJ 2325 2325	Cairn
602	A	792.7	Carn Ealasaid	158	NJ 2277 1177	Heather near cairn
1491	A	781.3	Corryhabbie Hill	280.3	NJ 2809 2886	Rock by trig
1492	A	755.9	Cook's Cairn	212.9	NJ 3022 2783	Cairn
1495	A	721.7	The Buck	257.2	NJ 4121 2339	Tor by trig
1497	AG	609.1	Ladylea Hill	200.7	NJ 3430 1680	Cairn
1500	T	566	Ben Newe	182	NJ 3817 1431	Rock by trig
1499		570	Carn Daimh	194	NJ 1815 2496	Viewpoint
1501	L	564.3	Tap o' Noth	248	NJ 4840 2932	Wall
1504		471	Ben Aigan	289	NJ 3097 4814	Heather
1506	T	430.6	Knock Hill	303	NJ 5370 5514	Cairn
1509		372	Knockan	179	NJ 3510 4647	Cairn
1510		366	Meikle Balloch Hill	193	NJ 4711 4950	Heather by track
1512		320	Bin of Cullen	164	NJ 4799 6426	Viewfinder

The Bochel

This was one of fifteen hills added to the list of Marilyns in 1995, the first major revision. Its status was confirmed by a summit and col survey in October 2015.

Tap o' Noth

This is the name of the hill fort on top well as the hill itself. Lidar data has been used for archaeological research, which has revealed the height of the vitrified rock at the summit.

Tap o' Noth

Carn Mor

Paul Richardson, October 1995

The urge to bag Marilyns since the purchase of the new book continued. We parked at the Well of the Lecht and set off up the short glen. The ridge turned and climbed boggily to join the main ridge of the Ladder Hills. Most of the mountain hares were getting their winter coat and one was pure white. The walking, north from Monadh an t-Stuichd Leith to Carn Mor, was superb. The sun shone, the going was easy and the views were grand. As well as the Cairngorms, I could distinguish Mount Keen, Lochnagar, Tap o' Noth, The Buck and distant Bennachie. I was keen to see more of the range as I was walking fast and fluently, having lost a stone in weight, but on Letterach I could find no discernible summit to this strange, flat, soggy, flabby off-shoot of the main ridge.

Beinn Aigan

Alan Dawson, April 2011

My final mainland Marilyn at the time, though more were discovered later. The end of a long quest is often a bittersweet occasion as journey meets destination, and this proved to be literally true after Ben Aigan. I had such a good time lazing around for a couple of hours on the sunny summit with all manner of food and drink and friends, and then outside the pub by the river, that I overdosed on cake and was somewhat ill later. Beer and cake, bitter and sweeties, did not seem to mix well, but it was worth it.

I thought that I might retire from hill bagging and perhaps take up golf again, enjoy more cinema, theatre and concerts, do more reading, a bit of piano practice, anything to save me from getting hooked on Humps and Tumps. I even moved to Edinburgh for two years to increase my range of lifestyle and cultural options, but the idea didn't really work as I had recently invented Simms and then bought survey equipment, so there were too many hills that needed bagging or surveying. I set a modest target of 50 new Simms a year and so a new quest rescued me from inertia with possible obesity and depression.

Ladylea Hill and Ben Rinnes

Alan Castle, July 2012

As I enjoy a long tramp over the hills, I decided that I would finish both Corbetts and Grahams on the same day, in one long walk. I chose these two hills because:
- Neither is difficult to climb, and even in poor weather I could struggle up both.
- They are far enough apart to provide a long and moderately tough day.
- Except for a section of unavoidable road walking, the route is a good one, traversing the Ladder Hills on an ancient hill track.
- I am able to pronounce both of them correctly, unlike many others in the Highlands.

High white clouds with a touch of sunshine, warm but not hot, gave perfect conditions. I was amused to discover that near the start of my walk there was a signpost to Lost, but this did not turn out to be a bad omen. Beryl set off from Strathdon with me and we climbed Clashenteple and then Ladylea Hill together. She returned to the camper van to take our 12-year-old niece on a sightseeing day in the region, before meeting me near Ben Rinnes. We carried up a celebratory bottle of Laphroaig, not a local whisky but my favourite single malt. We parted again on the summit, leaving me to continue down the main Ben Rinnes path to Dufftown. A long but memorable day – 31.5 miles in 14.5 hours.

HE06 Bennachie-fourman

RHB sections 21A, 21B   OS maps 29, 30, 37, 38

Number		Height	Name	Drop	Location	Summit
1515		529	Bennachie	315	NJ 6628 2259	Rock by viewfinder
1522	L	408.8	Millstone Hill	154	NJ 6767 2024	Rock
1511	T	344	Fourman Hill	228	NJ 5709 4581	Trig
1516	T	518	Lord Arthur's Hill	265	NJ 5134 1980	Trig
1520	T	466.7	Hill of Foudland	286	NJ 6031 3323	Trig
1523	G	380.8	Hill of Tillymorgan	153.2	NJ 6523 3480	Trig
1525		234	Waughton Hill	182	NJ 9635 5723	Cairn

Bennachie

VERNON MILES, 2010

During the autumn I was working at Aberdeen prison so I took the opportunity to pick up a few Marilyns in the area. There are some real gems. Millstone Hill by the River Don was good, and Craigendarroch by Ballater was a great wee hill, in weather which showed Lochnagar at its best. However, the best was Bennachie, with some great paths over the hill. Not everyone's cup of tea I know, but personally I think it enhances the experience.

Hill of Foudland

PAUL RICHARDSON, FEBRUARY 2002

A lane sign-posted to Jericho branched off towards the north-eastern nose of Hill of Foudland. Visibility was again poor but all I had to do was take the right turning from this track up the one that served the masts at the top of the hill. I could hear the wind whining eerily in the masts long before I could see them. The trig pillar lay a few yards south of the track. Nothing could be seen except a few heathery hummocks fading into the mist. I did not know until I got home later about a well-documented story of an attack by a 'big cat' on a woman living beneath this hill. In the darkness and rain, the A920 seemed to present more danger than a big cat, but I reached the car unscathed.

Hill of Tillymorgan

Tilly Morgan is an actress who played a 'battling fairy' in 'Tooth', released in 2004. The film was not very successful despite featuring several famous names and voices. She was one of 66 battling fairies so it was not much of a role. There is no evidence that Tilly ever climbed her eponymous hill or even knew of its existence, which is a pity as she could have used the publicity to help expand her limited acting career. Google reveals various Tilly Morgans in England so it seems about time they took a break from consultancy and horsey things and so on to get together for a change of scene in Aberdeenshire.

AUDREY LITTERICK, 2004

After a long day's teaching, this was a brilliant wee hill, with amazing old slate workings on top and a cracking view all round. No way I'd have had the energy for a bigger hill.

Waughton Hill

This hill between Peterhead and Fraserburgh is over 40km from the nearest Marilyn (Hill of Tillymorgan), but unlike many isolated hills it does not offer a popular or attractive walk. A track runs within 500 metres of the summit, but hill baggers are more likely to encounter fences, tractors, cows or gorse bushes than recreational walkers.

—— Eastern Highlands: South ——

Land south of the River Dee and Feshie, east of the Truim, Garry and Tay, and north of the Firth of Tay

Marilyns:	61
Highest and most prominent:	Lochnagar, 1155.7m
Lowest:	Turin Hill, 252m
Least prominent:	Cairn-mon-earn, drop 151.7m

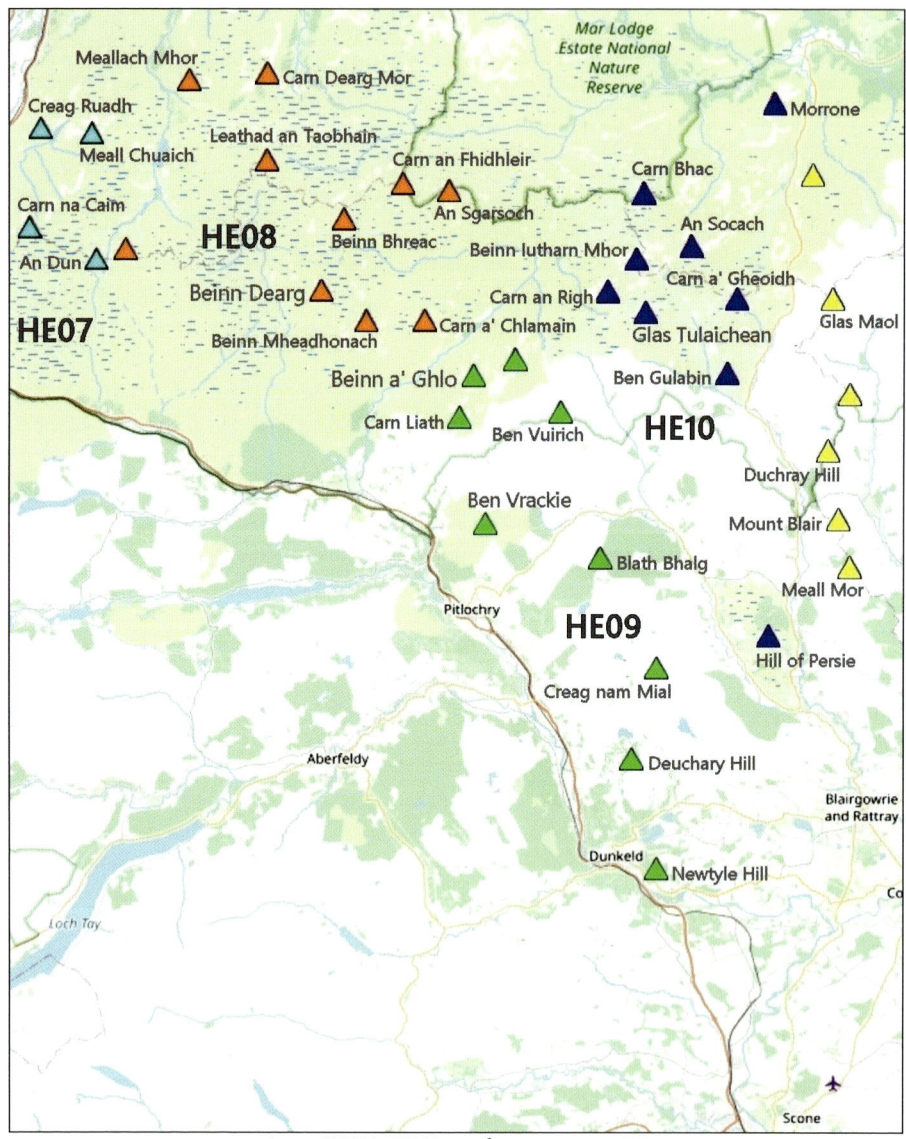

Areas HE11 to HE15 are shown on page 153

Number		Height	Name	Drop	Location	Summit
388	A	950.8	Meall Chuaich	463	NN 7164 8782	Cairn
403	A	658.8	Creag Ruadh	198	NN 6850 8818	Outcrop
389	A	940.8	Carn na Caim	328.1	NN 6769 8215	Cairn
400	A	827.4	An Dun	237	NN 7164 8014	Cairn

This well-defined area covers all the ground in the southern half of the Eastern Highlands region west of Glen Tromie, the Gaick Pass and the Edendon Water. Between the two highest Marilyns there are eight other summits over 800m high. Some of them are perched near the edge of steep eastern slopes above the Gaick Pass, such as 801m Sgor Dearg which towers above lonely Gaick Lodge. The highest hill in this group, 897.4m Bogha-cloiche, is one of the 635 Thousanders with over 100m drop. It is nowhere near being a Marilyn but it does qualify as a Simm, a Hump and one of the High Hills of Britain.

An Dun

JOHN BARNARD, MARCH 2012

A problem that had bugged us for some time was An Dun. This has two tops and there had never been a definitive measurement to identify the higher. Over the years the summit had swapped back and forth. We tried several years ago with Abney levels to resolve the issue but these instruments did not have sufficient resolution to do the job. We carried the survey gear from the main road to the south, identified the highest points on the north and south tops and then line-surveyed back and forth between them. The result was most disappointing as we cannot be sure. We measured a height difference of 0.03m, with the two measurements agreeing to within 0.005m. However, the variation in ground height around the cairns was at least as great as the measured height difference, so we felt it incorrect to make a statement that one top was clearly higher than the other. The OS accepted the result and 827m appears as a spot height on each top.

ALAN DAWSON, AUGUST 2016

My surveys found the north summit to be 827.38m and the south summit to be 827. 39m. The light vegetation and small cairns did not interfere with the survey, so I estimated the margin for error on the ground as only about 3cm at each point. G&J Surveys had found the south summit to be higher by a mere 3cm, so my finding supported theirs. I therefore nominated the south summit as the official Marilyn, but it was impossible to be certain.

Surveying the north summit of An Dun

Number		Height	Name	Drop	Location	Summit
406	A	1008.7	Beinn Dearg	473	NN 8529 7780	Rock
415	A	900.9	Beinn Mheadhonach	164.7	NN 8800 7580	Rock
407	A	1006.5	An Sgarsoch	320	NN 9333 8368	Cairn
408	A	994.1	Carn an Fhidhleir	285.7	NN 9046 8417	Cairn
414	AG	912.4	Beinn Bhreac	171	NN 8683 8207	Rock
409	A	963.5	Carn a' Chlamain	318	NN 9159 7580	Cairn
413	G	911.7	Leathad an Taobhain	155	NN 8217 8582	Grass by trig
418	A	848.6	Carn an Fhidhleir Lorgaidh	142.1	NN 8562 8748	Cairn
419	A	835.0	Meall Odhar a' Chire	144	NN 7967 7859	Cairn
416	A	875.7	A' Chaoirnich #	213.8	NN 7352 8072	Heather
417	A	857.4	Carn Dearg Mor	290.0	NN 8232 9118	Cairn
420	A	769.0	Meallach Mhor	234.1	NN 7765 9087	Rock by cairn

Nine of the ten Marilyns in this vast area of high moorland are over 838m high and qualify as High Hills of Britain, along with 22 other summits. In total there are 64 hills over 600m high with at least 30m drop. There is some superb walking available on short heather on the higher ground, where no paths are needed, and useful tracks over the lower ground.

Beinn Dearg

PAUL RICHARDSON, JUNE 1992

The long walk in was like a nature trail. We saw numerous species of flower, including many orchids, some huge dragonflies, at least two species of butterfly, caterpillars, tiger beetles and crickets. We stopped at Allt Sheicheachan bothy, which became quite busy. The path beside the burn had been bulldozed since our map was printed and a new branch created. Alert to such navigational traps, I managed to stay on the correct course.

Short, crisp vegetation led to a small boulder-field and the summit. Given the relative remoteness of the hill it was busy, as eight people visited the trig point whilst we were there. Partly to avoid the congestion, we went west down the boulder slope and dried-out bogs to the Allt Beinn Losgarnich, then followed the path down its right bank. The path between Bruar Lodge (which had been occupied on my previous visit in 1984) and the bothy was so sketchy in places that we lost track of it.

Leathad an Taobhain

ALAN DAWSON, SEPTEMBER 1993

This was a short detour from a linear 50km walk from Blair Atholl to Kingussie through the Minigaig Pass, which was subject to some access dispute at the time. For once public transport worked reasonably smoothly and I reached Kingussie station in time to get the train to Blair Atholl. It was much quicker to reach the summit by the more usual route from the north nineteen years later, with a road, a track and a bike to help, but that was just the start of another long walk, over some rarely climbed outlying summits.

A' Chaoirnich

This was listed as Creag an Loch until 2002, when the name A' Chaoirnich appeared on the map. Some sources refer to it as Maol Creag an Loch, though this is not on any OS map.

An Dun

Deuchary Hill

Ben Vrackie from Tulach Hill

Number		Height	Name	Drop	Location	Summit
421	A	1121.9	Beinn a' Ghlo – Carn nan Gabhar	658	NN 9711 7331	Cairn
422	A	1070.0	Braigh Coire Chruinn-bhalgain	222.4	NN 9456 7240	Rock
429	A	975.8	Carn Liath	207.1	NN 9360 6982	Cairn
441	A	903.1	Ben Vuirich	345.9	NN 9972 7001	Rock
449	G	634.4	Creag an t-Sithein	148.3	NO 0318 6582	Heather
445	A	842.2	Ben Vrackie	405.6	NN 9507 6324	Rock by viewfinder
448	A	640.4	Blath Bhalg	266.0	NO 0193 6112	Cairn
450	A	561.8	Creag nam Mial	208	NO 0538 5411	Outcrop
453		511	Deuchary Hill	219	NO 0373 4850	Rock
456	A	317.8	Newtyle Hill	186	NO 0500 4188	Cairn on outcrop

There lives a man who has recorded six hundred visits to Ben Vrackie
His behaviour is remarkable, colloquially wacky
And yet it makes some kind of sense for he has not far to go
It's considerably further from his house to the hills of Beinn a' Ghlo

Beinn a' Ghlo shares the distinction with Quinag of being the only names that are applied to a group of three Marilyns. The highest summit was listed as 1129m in 1992, though it was obvious to anyone on the top that it could not be nine metres higher than the 1120m trig point. OS later fixed the map error, though the height is nearer 1122m than 1121m.

Creag nam Mial

DAVID STALLARD, MAY 2015

After a long day near Dunkeld, going over Deuchary Hill, Benachally and Creag nam Mial, I confirmed that getting to Creag nam Mial is hard work. A map-reading mistake meant the last 3km were over trackless, tussocky ground. On reaching a prominent cairn on a sharp little top, I found that the summit was 500 metres away over several ups and downs and some awkward walls and fences. It was a rewarding summit when I did get there, with wide views over a big empty quarter, but it had taken some getting to. The trackless 2km westwards to the track to Loch Ordie felt at least twice that distance, and I was very pleased when I finally reached the car after a ten-hour walk. I met no-one all day.

Deuchary Hill

BILL FAIRMANER, FEBRUARY 2003

A grand little hill for a hazy winter day. The approach from the north, all bracken and crags, was reminiscent of the Lake District. The mapped path existed, through trees low and well spaced. The summit boasted a fine fin of bare rock. What more could you want?

Newtyle Hill

This hill acquired a well-deserved reputation for thick, tough vegetation but the summit has become easier to reach in recent years thanks to numerous ascents and trip reports on the optimum route. Its ascent became so benign that Newtyle Hill was chosen for a summit celebration when one couple climbed it as their 600th Marilyn in 2018. This event had been foreseen in a song written several years earlier that charted the progress of a female partner from denial to acceptance.

Fairytale of Newtyle Hill

Can you believe this, a fairy story, that someone told to me a long long time ago
It's now become a song, a little strange but true, and here's two people to sing that song for you

Kirsty: He was rugged and brave, he knew how to behave
It was seventeen years since he last had a shave
When he first took my hand in that bar in Dundee
He promised me mountains were waiting for me
He was friendly and witty, nice flat in the city
When the band finished playing we started to talk
He took me to dinner, he made me feel thinner
We had a few dates then we met for a walk
The first hill was quick, just a trivial tick
So I didn't object when we drove to the next
But I hadn't quite reckoned that after the second
He wanted a third and a fourth, fifth and sixth
I knew he was a bagger then and I know he's bagging still
When he told me of his route up Newtyle Hill

Shane: You softie you moaner, you grunter and groaner
You went in a sulk just because you got wet
You missed out the fourth top to go to a tea shop
If your total is low you deserve all you get

Kirsty: You scumbag you bagger, you filthy peat hagger
You'd bag every day and all night if you could
You lister you ticker, I don't like to bicker
But you promised me mountains not a bootful of mud

Shane: You're always complaining if it's snowing or raining
It's hardly my fault if the forecast was wrong
Your whingeing and nagging is spoiling the bagging
So learn to dig deep and stay mentally strong

Kirsty: I knew he was a bagger when he first confessed to me
That his favourite bedtime book was RHB

Shane: For richer for poorer, I took her to Jura
I'd done all the Paps so the going got rough
The ground was appalling, the Deuchars was calling
And I had to accept even I'd had enough

Kirsty: The hags made me tearful, I gave him an earful
The lumps and the tussocks were worse than the trees
The pace didn't slacken through ten-foot high bracken
But I couldn't keep up when we crawled on our knees

Shane: We could have done that top, there's hardly any drop
You took a tick from me, I'm not sure I forgive you

Kirsty: We'll come another day, maybe next Saturday
So just relax, slow down and look around you

Kirsty: The next day was better even though we got wetter
When we got to the summit there was even a view
My clothes were still wringing but my spirit was singing
Something had changed, I'd become more like you

Shane: I knew she was a bagger when, of her very own free will,
She joined me for the walk up Newtyle Hill

Together: Some members of the Upper Hall were calling out our name
As they welcomed us to join the Hall of Fame

Number		Height	Name	Drop	Location	Summit
424	A	1051.4	Glas Tulaichean	383.8	NO 0510 7601	Trig
443	A	868.3	Meall a' Choire Bhuidhe	143.5	NO 0618 7104	Rock by cairn
447	A	794.0	Meall Uaine	147.3	NO 1106 6741	Heather
425	A	1043.5	Beinn Iutharn Mhor	245.4	NO 0455 7927	Rock by cairn
426	A	1029.6	Carn an Righ	259.6	NO 0286 7726	Rock by cairn
432	A	945.1	Carn Bhac	186.9	NO 0510 8322	Cairn
428	A	976.1	Carn a' Gheoidh	299	NO 1070 7670	Cairn
446		806	Ben Gulabin	204	NO 1004 7220	Rock by cairn
433	A	942.8	An Socach	187	NO 0798 7998	Shelter cairn
444	A	859.5	Morrone	157.6	NO 1321 8865	Rock by cairn
454	A	445.7	Hill of Persie	168	NO 1224 5605	Rock

Carn Bhac

PAUL RICHARDSON, MARCH 1983

It was one of those days when it is hard to justify hill walking, even to oneself. The weather was foul, as predicted. Cagoule and over-trousers stayed on for the whole day.

It was a long, hard slog up beside Allt Connie and Allt Cristie. The wind hammered down the glen as I struggled westwards. I was resigned to the fact that I was going to have to give up. I even began to plan what I would do with the rest of the day. A couple of hares hopped about in the arctic conditions. It seemed to take an eternity to climb up through the cloud to the ridge, where I found that the wind was from the north. As it would be behind me for most of the way, I decided to carry on. I headed west until I could see the ground sloping away again. The wind blew me over the first bump on the ridge.

The next ascent, up to Geal Charn, was more marked. I reached the cairn and was suddenly battered by a wind of incredible ferocity. The ground had a covering of ice and I could not get a secure enough footing to walk. I crouched and tried to brace myself. The snow was driving horizontally. I struggled off as nearly east as I could but it was hard to walk in the right direction. Near the col I took off the rucksack and found a layer of ice had formed on its inside. I took out a solid chocolate bar, which nearly broke my teeth.

I made wind-assisted progress up to Carn Bhac and found a small cairn. I crouched behind it and got a little shelter but the wind swirled spindrift into my face. I closed my eyes and believe I could actually have slept, even in the storm on the summit. However, I doubt that I would ever have awoken. I took a compass bearing and staggered off into the clag, south-east. White-out. I was rolling snowballs ahead of me to make sure I was not stepping out into a void. The snow was knee deep and often more, and sapped my strength every time I had to pull myself out of it. Eventually I came across a burn. I was not sure it was the right one, but all the water in that area drained into the Ey Burn, so any stream would do. I began to feel really exhausted. The wind was unremitting.

At last, the cloud lifted and the plantation surrounding the ruins of Altanour Lodge appeared. I was shattered. I ate rolls and soup. Now I had to walk the length of Glen Ey with the wind in my face. The strongest gusts could be seen coming up the glen, driving the spindrift in front like a dust-storm, only colder. Upper Glen Ey is broad and beautiful. It is the only place I have ever had to stop for a breather while walking on the flat. The miles rolled slowly by. As I returned to Inverey, the snow came on again, heavily.

Summit of Hill of Persie

Creag Ghiubhais
Ballater
Glen Tanar National Nature Reserve
Banchory
Cairn-mon-earn
HE12
The Coyles of Muick
Fetteresso Forest
HE14
Kerloch
Conachraig
Mount Keen
Lochnagar
Creag nan Gabhar
Mount Battock
Drumtochty Forest
Hunt Hill
Strathfinella Hill
Glas Maol
Ben Tirran
Hill of Wirren
Laurencekirk
Monamenach
HE13
Hill of Garvock
Badandun Hill
Mount Blair
Crock
Corwharn
Hare Cairn
Brechin
Montrose
Meall Mor
Creigh Hill
Cat Law
HE11
Mile Hill
Kirriemuir
Turin Hill
Forfar
HE15
Alyth
Blairgowrie and Rattray
Coupar Angus
Arbroath
Craigowl Hill
Carnoustie
King's Seat
Monifieth
Dundee
Newport-on-Tay

Number		Height	Name	Drop	Location	Summit
461	A	1067.7	Glas Maol	195.2	NO 1670 7657	Trig
493	A	847.5	Hill of Strone	141.5	NO 2878 7292	Rock
495	A	807.0	Monamenach	199.8	NO 1760 7067	Heather
500	A	703.1	Duchray Hill	265	NO 1615 6725	Wall
498	A	740.3	Badandun Hill	155.4	NO 2074 6788	Trig
505	A	554.0	Crock	154.3	NO 2262 6325	Cairn
508	T	516	Hare Cairn	180	NO 2421 6234	Heather near trig
494		834	Creag nan Gabhar	178	NO 1546 8410	Cairn
497	A	744.4	Mount Blair	401	NO 1674 6297	Cairn
506		551	Meall Mor	176	NO 1733 6023	Cairn
502	A	670.4	Cat Law	296.5	NO 3188 6107	Cairn
503	AG	609.1	Corwharn	152.5	NO 2886 6510	Heather
509	A	498.2	Creigh Hill	168.2	NO 2707 5936	Heather
513		410	Mile Hill	186	NO 3113 5713	Cairn

Corwharn

PAUL RICHARDSON, OCTOBER 1995

The stimulus to explore this area came from the newly-acquired book The Relative Hills of Britain. The first couple of miles up Glen Quharity were on a surfaced track, but the sighting of a stoat was compensation for this. It raced around in circles, turned a couple of somersaults and then dashed off across the hillside. It was not clear if it was hunting, playing, or something else. There were also large flocks of partridges.

The glen was small and bare, sheep country. Corwharn cleared of cloud as we approached. A track took us from the glen right to the summit. Our choice from the list of Marilyns had been fortuitous, as a hill any higher would have been in cloud.

We began a traverse of the hills to the south as an alternative to going back down the glen. Tracks made for easy going. As we walked back along the road, a stoat raced across it ahead of us and was quickly followed by another, which may have been chasing it. The sighting of a couple of redpolls was the last excitement of our walk.

Crock

ALAN DAWSON

Three ascents of this hill resulted in three contrasting experiences. In July 2001 I tried to bash my way up through the trees via the shortest route, got severely entangled and lost my Leki walking pole to one of the poking, thieving, branches. Eighteen months later I met Chris Crocker and Paul Richardson for a longer but far more sensible approach, via easy forest tracks, to Chris's eponymous 600th Marilyn, with fabulous wintry views and a low-key summit celebration of his entry to the Hall of Fame. Paul declined the offer of whisky as he had recently been troubled by a mild alimentary problem. I never saw him again and he died from cancer eight months later. By that time I had been reunited with my walking pole as another bagger, Jimmy White, had inadvertently followed my stupid route, found the pole in the trees and somehow worked out its owner. In 2015 I enjoyed a relaxed and sunny solo ascent in order to survey the summit and col and confirm that this apparently innocuous hill did qualify as a Marilyn, with four metres to spare.

Hare Cairn

ALAN DAWSON, JULY 2001

My 1000th Marilyn, an easy stroll and a memorable walk as I was wearing unusual attire. Not my idea but it made a change from my usual dull plumage. I was still overshadowed by my companion, who looked far more elegant than me when standing on the trig pillar.

Ben Gulabin

Lochnagar and Glas-allt-Shiel across Loch Muick

HE12 Lochnagar-mellon

Number		Height	Name	Drop	Location	Summit
457	A	1155.7	Lochnagar – Cac Carn Beag	673	NO 2437 8614	Rock by trig
492	A	862.5	Conachcraig	185	NO 2795 8652	Tor
504	A	599.2	The Coyles of Muick	234	NO 3287 9104	Cairn
510		486	Creag Ghiubhais	205	NO 3124 9545	Cairn

The Coyles of Muick

ALAN DAWSON, FEBRUARY 1994 AND APRIL 2021

When studying a map of The Coyles of Muick, several questions come to mind. Is it really over 600m high? What are Coyles? How do I get to the top? In 1994 several people joined me because they had no better options. The Glasgow Glenmore Club had booked Ballater youth hostel for the weekend and all the cars were trapped by the depth of overnight snow. Lochnagar was out of the question, we couldn't get near it, so we needed a hill we could walk to from the hostel. The Coyles of Muick was, or were, almost high enough to be deemed acceptable by hardened hill walkers who were not convinced by the radical idea of setting off for something under 762m high.

It was useful to have a group to help because ploughing through deep soft snow all the way was hard work. We managed to find a route through the trees then had to go over another hill on the way. The view from the summit was fine if you liked a lot of white and grey. By the time we got back to the hostel we all felt as though we had done a full day's hill walking. One or two club members acknowledged that these little Marilyns were not as trivial as they had assumed. The next morning was spent shovelling snow to free the cars for the drive back to Glasgow. It had been a long way to go for only one hill.

It took me 27 years to find out that both of the summit Coyles are under 600m high. The route through the trees was simple with large-scale digital mapping and aerial photos to help. This time I deliberately went over another hill on the way and then joined a useful path most of the way to the two summits.

Creag Ghiubhais

PAUL RICHARDSON, JUNE 2000

A deer fence near the start was easy to climb but my breeches, already resembling a patchwork quilt, gained another tear. How smart I had been to wear underpants to match. Thereafter, it was rank heather all the way up the east ridge, interrupted only by a broken craggy outcrop. As the gradient eased, there were boulders among the heather. The cairn was partially hidden by a group of trees. Within it, I found a plastic ice-cream box containing records of ascents by vast hordes of people. They seemed to be parties from the Boys' Brigade. About 150 metres further on was another cairn, where I found that my wind-shirt had disappeared from its perch upon my bum-bag, where I had trusted it to remain. Convinced that it must have bailed out whilst I was dancing with the deer fence, I went back down by roughly my upward route, but I didn't find the shirt.

KLAUS SCHWARTZ, 2007

I struggled through thigh-deep heather, with the steep slabs of its east ridge the only relief. The top was a jungle of heather, birches and small pines, but all this did make it special as it was my 800th Marilyn. An easy ascent would have felt less of an achievement.

HE13 Tirran-wirren

Number		Height	Name	Drop	Location	Summit
491	A	897.0	Ben Tirran	246	NO 3734 7461	Trig
499	A	705.4	Hunt Hill	181.0	NO 3800 8053	Rock
501	A	677.9	Hill of Wirren	311	NO 5228 7393	Heather by trig

Ben Tirran

The summit of this hill has the name The Goet on OS maps, but this does not seem to be used by anyone. The summit is 896m on OS maps, based on the trig figure of 896.7m, but the trig is a little sunken, so the highest point is on the grass beside the trig.

Hill of Wirren

The summit is in a boggy mess of tussocks, but it can be reached via a remarkable warren of tracks leading up from Glen Esk to the north or east. Trig fanciers can delight in bagging three easy trig points along the way, on Hill of Crannel, West Wirren and the main summit.

Hunt Hill

Ann Bowker, August 1993

This unusual hill is untypical of the peaks in Dawson's tables, for most of them are the highest top in a substantial block of high ground or else totally isolated hills. Hunt Hill however is surrounded by higher summits and gains its place in the list only because it is almost moated by the twin Waters of Lee and Unich, both of which flow through deep valleys. Thus it is steep on every side yet fails to present a dramatic profile on any.

We rode the bicycles alongside Loch Lee to the meeting of these two waters and followed the delightful path past the Falls of Unich into the steep-sided glen above. The sun shining on the rocks and freshly blooming deep purple heather made this a most attractive and friendly place, yet the crags towering above suggested that a more menacing aspect might be felt on days of mist and storm. The higher Falls of Damff twist through an angle halfway down and are not really seen to advantage from the west bank of the burn. After teetering on the edge of the rocks above the falls in a vain attempt to encompass their full drop, we cut back through deep heather to the col and so up to the unmarked summit amongst short, cropped heather.

Despite the hemmed-in nature of the hill the view was fairly extensive, although mainly of undistinguished rolling heathery ridges. There is a remarkable expanse of high ground hereabouts, dominated by the inconspicuous Ben Tirran, with no other summit having the 150 metres drop to enter the tables. The most striking feature of the view was Mount Keen, with the scar of a path up its south ridge. We descended north-east and soon found a pleasantly sheltered clump of heather for refreshment before tackling the steep and rough descent to the bicycles. We rode them up to the old stables in Glen Lee, a pleasant little bothy showing signs of recent occupation by both man and horse.

Gerry Cummins, 2007

Hunt Hill is a gem of hill, with the well-defined path up the side of the Falls of Unich thoroughly recommended. On a misty day with lots of water around it was a highly atmospheric and tranquil place to spend some time.

HE14 Keen-battock

Number		Height	Name	Drop	Location	Summit
485	A	939.4	Mount Keen	310	NO 4090 8692	Rock by trig
516	A	337.2	Hill of Goauch	148.7	NO 6630 9418	Heather
496	T	778.5	Mount Battock	288	NO 5496 8446	Trig
507	T	534.6	Kerloch	182	NO 6965 8788	Trig
512	T	414	Strathfinella Hill	239	NO 6930 7873	Trig
515	A	378.5	Cairn-mon-earn	151.7	NO 7826 9192	Trig
517		277	Hill of Garvock	219	NO 7266 6917	Tower

This is another area with a vast number of rolling heathery hills but only two Marilyns over 600m high. It would be possible to walk east from Glen Muick for 35km without crossing a road, via Mount Keen, Mount Battock and other hills. An extensive network of tracks would make progress easy in places but the lower terrain could well be arduous.

Hill of Garvock

PAUL RICHARDSON, JULY 1981

I followed farm roads to the ridge of the Hill of Garvock. The path led through moorland teeming with rabbits towards the Tower of Johnston. The heavy wooden door of the tower was ajar, and a spiral staircase thick with bird droppings led towards the top, but one step near the top was almost completely missing. The staircase could probably have been negotiated to the top but the view was not sufficient to entice me. The tower is built on a large cairn, from which the views were outstanding for such a low elevation – the sea, Montrose and the Basin, Strathmore, the Howe of the Mearns, Strathfinella Hill and the Mounth. It was a pleasant walk onwards, to a dip through which the B9120 passes.

Strathfinella Hill

If you should suffer a fiendish headache from lugging a rucksack up Mount Battock
Why not request a keenish young medic to knock it back with a Scottish haddock
Or if you feel a little unweller while lolling around on Strathfinella
Swallow a smallish yellow pill or two from some other similar fella

Gleaming trig pillar on top of King's Seat

Number		Height	Name	Drop	Location	Summit
1665	T	455	Craigowl Hill	393	NO 3769 3999	Trig
1670	T	376.8	King's Seat	222.7	NO 2306 3300	Trig
1674	L	252.0	Turin Hill	177.7	NO 5146 5354	Fence

This area is not part of the Highlands, as the Highland boundary fault passes to the north of it. However, the key col for Craigowl Hill is to the north, near Forfar, which means that the area is more closely connected topographically to the Highlands to the north than to the hills of Central Scotland to the west, so it has been included in the HE region.

Craigowl Hill

ALAN DAWSON, MAY 2015

My longest walk of the year incorporated 32 summits in the Sidlaw Hills, starting on 275m Bandirran Hill and finishing on 266m Hatton Hill 27 hours later, after 92km and about 3000m of ascent. It had been Lindsay's idea to try to climb 30 new Tumps in under 30 hours. I encouraged him and somehow got sucked into participating after looking at maps and possible routes. We decided to add another two summits in case we failed on any of them.

It turned out to be a thoroughly enjoyable walk on the whole, rather than the tough endurance test I had been expecting. Conditions were good overhead and underfoot, feet and knees proved resilient, and the walk gave a new perspective on quiet and attractive areas of rolling hillsides and pleasant villages. Rod Munro provided extra supplies at the halfway stage and brought my boots so I could change from wellies after the first 50km.

Craigowl Hill was the 19th summit of the walk. On the top I made time for a little preventive foot maintenance and a gamble on the sock exchange. We had reached the summit via paths from Balkello Hill, a far more interesting route than my previous ascent fifteen years earlier, when I had driven up the road after a day working in Dundee. On that occasion the highlight had been a phone call made from the summit. This was a new experience as I had recently been given my first mobile phone for a new job.

The long walk provided plenty of practice in the key skill of climbing over gates and fences. As well as climbing 32 hills, we had to find our way through 29 screechers, 21 clangers, 15 clunkers, 12 rattlers, 11 janglers and 23 other types of gate. Something like that anyway, we didn't actually keep count, though I almost wished we had. Most of the gates were also classed as scrapers. It seemed to be a feature of all wide rural gates that they dropped on their hinges and had to be lifted up to unfasten and drag them open. We became connoisseurs of the complexity of gate designs, sonics and fastenings, from frayed rope-ends to finger-slicing mini-guillotines. Screechers were the worst, causing teeth to vibrate and ears to bleed as well as dogs to attack. We learned to avoid trying to open these gates but climbed over them as silently as possible.

Fences were less of an issue in this area because there were so many gates between the fields, but there were some fencing problems to be solved, such as flimsy strands of barbed wire arrayed on top of an unstable wall. We improved our hitherto neglected ballet skills by balancing gently on unconvincing stones and leaping over the wires, with extra points for landing on two feet rather than full length in the mud. It was good fun for a while but became tiresome once we had passed the 24-hour mark and wanted to plod along as quietly and smoothly as possible. Good idea, good company, good walk.

—— Central Highlands: North ——

Land south of Glen Spean, west of Glen Garry, north of Glen Coe and Lochs Laidon, Rannoch and Tummel

Marilyns: 61
Highest and most prominent: Ben Nevis, 1344.7m
Lowest: Druim na h-Earba, 287.9m
Least prominent: An Gearanach, drop 151.7m

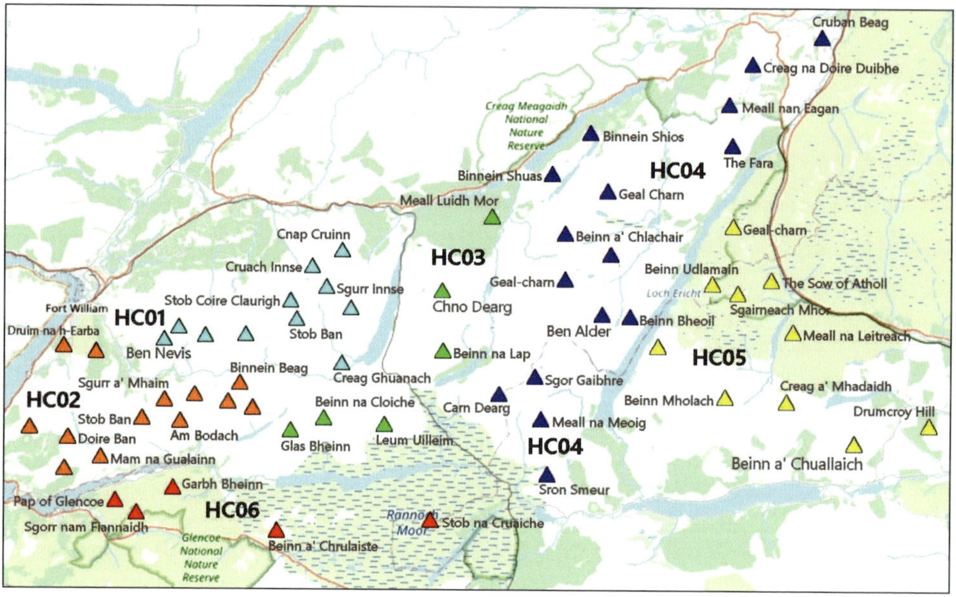

Upper part of Ben Nevis from the south

Number		Height	Name	Drop	Location	Summit
278	OA	1344.7	Ben Nevis	1344.7	NN 1668 7128	Rock near trig
334	A	712.4	Meall an t-Suidhe	149.0	NN 1394 7299	Cairn on outcrop
279	A	1234.2	Aonach Beag	404	NN 1970 7149	Rock near cairn
344	A	231.1	Cruim Leacainn	149.4	NN 1666 8074	Tussock
282	A	1221.1	Carn Mor Dearg	164.1	NN 1774 7217	Cairn on outcrop
285	A	1178.3	Stob Choire Claurigh	447	NN 2620 7387	Cairn
296	A	1094.6	Sgurr Choinnich Mor	160	NN 2277 7142	Cairn on cliff edge
314		977	Stob Ban	172	NN 2667 7239	Cairn
333	A	722.6	Meall Mor	144.6	NN 2805 7055	Cairn
337	A	620.7	Creag Ghuanach	212.1	NN 2999 6900	Cairn
290	A	1116.2	Stob Coire Easain	612	NN 3080 7306	Cairn
292	A	1106.6	Stob a' Choire Mheadhoin	144.1	NN 3164 7364	Rock by cairn
328		857	Cruach Innse	306	NN 2799 7636	Rock
329		809	Sgurr Innse	216	NN 2902 7481	Rock
332	A	741.9	Cnap Cruinn	247	NN 3028 7748	Cairn on outcrop

Creag Ghuanach

DONALD IRVINE, 2007

Passengers on board the 12:02 out of Fort William would have been treated to a comic farce as they approached Corrour station one summer Saturday. They would have seen an overweight, balding, middle-aged man in shorts running through a stretch of mud between the track from Loch Treig and the station. A foot got stuck in the glaur and he fell and rolled over, then staggered upright again, but this time without his clothes and rucksack showing their bright summer colours. He then disappeared behind a mound to retrieve a black poly bag and continued his race with the train only to fall once again, this time on stony ground, which added several streaks of a bright red colour. The train won the race, but his friends who had climbed Leum Uilleim that morning managed to delay its departure sufficiently for the unfortunate chap to catch up. The train manager looked disgusted and considered whether to allow him to board in such a filthy and bloodied state. He kindly relented, but it took time to catch breath, clean up and thank him. This hill is clearly the finest of all that can be reached from Corrour station.

AUDREY LITTERICK, 2007

This walk almost ended in disaster when Andy won the route choice argument and we set off up the craggy east face of Creag Ghuanach in pursuit of some rock. Rock there was, amidst vertical bog, slimy dripping tussocks, lichenous loose blocks and tenuously anchored rowan trees. We'd taken a long sling but not a rope. Cursing with regret, we slithered on the slime and debated whether retreat was safer than ascent. Eventually, tenacity and a determination to survive paid off and we emerged, sweating, puffing, traumatised and smeared in bog on to the summit. What a peak and what a view!

Cruim Leacainn

This little hill was added as a Marilyn in 1995 but demoted in 2014 after an easy summit survey but a difficult col survey amongst thick roadside vegetation.

Number		Height	Name	Drop	Location	Summit
287	A	1129.4	Binnein Mor	759	NN 2121 6635	Rock
295		1099	Sgurr a' Mhaim	317	NN 1647 6672	Cairn
303	A	1031.8	Am Bodach	152.8	NN 1763 6509	Cairn
305	A	1008.1	Sgurr Eilde Mor	269.2	NN 2305 6578	Cairn
309	A	999.7	Stob Ban	237.1	NN 1477 6544	Cairn
312	A	981.5	An Gearanach	151.7	NN 1877 6699	Cairn
320	A	941.5	Binnein Beag	196.6	NN 2217 6771	Cairn on rock
330	A	796.5	Mam na Gualainn	464	NN 1150 6254	Outcrop
338	A	621.8	Tom Meadhoin	156.2	NN 0873 6210	Rock
339	A	616.5	Beinn na Gucaig	453	NN 0629 6533	Trig
341		566	Doire Ban	161	NN 0905 6437	Cairn
342		528	Bidean Bad na h-Iolaire	261	NN 1149 7079	Cairn
343	A	287.9	Druim na h-Earba	155	NN 0903 7131	Tussock near trig

Some of the finest hills and hill walking in the country barely get a mention here as they are well-covered elsewhere. A survey of Stob Ban found that it fell 30cm short of 1000m, the same height as nearby Sgurr an Iubhair, which OS maps showed to be 1001m. More significant were the surveys of Am Bodach and An Gearanach, two superb hills that both had their status as Marilyns confirmed. Am Bodach later featured in *Songs from the High Hills*, the soundtrack album to the book The 1033 High Hills of Britain.

Bidean Bad na h-Iolaire

Ann Bowker, 24 December 1995

We woke on Christmas Eve to find the world completely white. Fearful of hazardous road conditions, we decided to abandon our plan to drive round the west coast. Instead we retreated across the Corran ferry, drove to Fort William and parked in the safety of the town car park. From there we walked up Glen Nevis in continuous snow and took the peat road which crosses the shoulder of Bidean Bad na h-Iolaire. At the col we stopped for lunch, having mentally written off any attempt on the summit, which was veiled in mist. Just as we set off again the mist rolled away, the sun came out and a glance at the time suggested that we might just make it in the available daylight. The fresh soft snow and deep heather made this 528m hill quite a struggle but the summit was reward enough, with glorious westward views of snowy mountains, although Ben Nevis, closer at hand, retained its cover of ominous black cloud.

Richard Wood, 2010

This is a fine wee hill in the backwaters of Fort William. There is a good way up from Blarmachfoldach above Lundavra, off the West Highland Way. There are two ancient footpaths, part of the crofting system pre-1820s. These paths were marked on early OS one-inch maps but not on more recent maps. One of these tracks, like a raised grassy dyke, reaches a small lochan, from which you can make your way to the summit.

Stob Choire Claurigh and the main Grey Corries ridge

Bidean Bad na h-Iolaire

Beinn Bheoil and Loch Ericht

HC03 Chno-uilleim

Number		Height	Name	Drop	Location	Summit
351	A	1047.5	Chno Dearg	645	NN 3774 7412	Rock by cairn
364		935	Beinn na Lap	406	NN 3762 6957	Cairn
381		514	Meall Luidh Mor	153	NN 4169 7971	Cairn on outcrop
327	A	906.5	Leum Uilleim	496	NN 3305 6413	Rock
331	A	789.8	Glas Bheinn	387.2	NN 2589 6411	Rock by cairn
340	A	571.4	Meall na Duibhe	149.1	NN 2265 6232	Cairn
335	A	645.1	Beinn na Cloiche	195	NN 2846 6486	Cairn on outcrop
336	A	631.6	Meall a' Bhainne	148.0	NN 3063 6636	Cairn on outcrop

Leum Uilleim

ALAN DAWSON, MARCH 2016

Arranging a summit celebration well in advance is a gamble. Leum Uilleim seemed a bold choice because getting a train to the base of the hill meant timetables, uncertainty and complications. Martin had chosen it because it had appeared in Trainspotting, an intensely raw, harrowing and entertainingly vivid film that had little to do with trains or hills.

To further reduce the chances of fair weather, he had picked a date in the middle of March, which was still officially winter. It seemed ambitious and daunting but I had to turn up, partly because Martin was a friend and partly because it was a unique occasion, the first time that anyone had climbed a mainland hill as their final Marilyn. Parties to celebrate having climbed 282 hills were commonplace, but this rare achievement was on a different scale. I booked accommodation at Roybridge, located my neglected ice axe and crampons in a musty cupboard and prepared myself for a chilly but necessary ordeal.

The day turned out to be as close to perfection as one could wish for, featuring blue sky, light wind, crunchy snow-fields, cloud inversions, a panorama of snowy peaks and an affable bunch of hill baggers. It seemed that nothing could go wrong. When I found that I had lost my new winter gloves on the way up, I looked down the hill to see another party coming up and they duly produced the gloves. I had to stop to retrieve my survey equipment from Beinn a' Bhric on the way down, but I managed to catch up with the stragglers and make sure that I was back at Corrour in time for the train. We all were.

It had been an amazingly successful and enjoyable day. Sometimes a gamble pays off, everything falls into place, and occasionally the world seems a wonderful place. And it had all been thanks to Irvine Welsh, Danny Boyle, Robert Carlyle, Ewen Macgregor and the rest of the Trainspotters, not forgetting Martin for his original way of thinking. As for William, whose long-forgotten leap had provided the name Leum Uilleim, none of us knew anything about him and no-one cared. History, nomenclature, past and future were irrelevant on the day. What had mattered was being there to enjoy the present, on the hill, on the train and in the hotel bar later. Days like that were to be treasured for, like trains to Corrour and brilliantly original films, they did not come along very often.

Beinn na Cloiche

Staoineag bothy sits by Abhainn Rath at the foot of the long northern slope of Beinn na Cloiche. Ken Smith lived there for several winter months in 1985 before he left to start building his own log cabin in the trees above nearby Loch Treig. His remarkable story of hardship, hermitage and persistence is told in his book The Way of the Hermit.

Number		Height	Name	Drop	Location	Summit
345	A	1147.7	Ben Alder	783	NN 4962 7186	Rock near trig
346		1132	Geal-charn	410	NN 4699 7462	Cairn
352		1034	Carn Dearg 1034	158	NN 5042 7643	Cairn
354	A	1019.5	Beinn Bheoil	186.9	NN 5170 7171	Rock near cairn
349	A	1087.8	Beinn a' Chlachair	540	NN 4712 7816	Rock by cairn
350	A	1049.7	Geal Charn	310	NN 5043 8118	Outcrop by cairn
361	A	954.7	Sgor Gaibhre	300	NN 4447 6744	Rock in cairn
372	A	901.9	Beinn a' Chumhainn	145.3	NN 4626 7103	Rock
363		941	Carn Dearg 941	221	NN 4178 6614	Cairn
374	A	867.3	Meall na Meoig #	192.4	NN 4481 6421	Outcrop
382	A	512.7	Sron Smeur	163.3	NN 4517 6017	Boulder
370	GA	911.4	The Fara	475	NN 5982 8425	Rock
376	A	674.0	Beinn Eilde	147.3	NN 5635 8504	Rock
378	A	657.9	Meall nan Eagan	166.2	NN 5967 8746	Rock
380		571	Creag na Doire Duibhe	166	NN 6150 9057	Rock by cairn
379	T	590	Cruban Beag	216	NN 6685 9245	Rock by trig
375	A	747.2	Binnein Shuas	391.4	NN 4629 8267	Cairn on rock
377	A	667.1	Binnein Shios	283	NN 4925 8572	Cairn

Beinn a' Chlachair

I would like to ask a factor if he would drive a tractor
To the top of Beinn a' Chlachair with a bunch of burly men
It would take a ton of trouble to remove those tons of rubble
But the summit could look wonderful, for ptarmigan again

Meall na Meoig

This was named as Beinn Pharlagain - Meall na Meoig in 1992, but OS maps show the name Beinn Pharlagain on an undulating 807m high ridge over 1km to the south. Another summit in between them – Garbh Mheall Mor – is also higher than Beinn Pharlagain.

Sron Smeur

GRAHAM BUNN, APRIL 2006

On a backpacking trip from near Rannoch Station we encountered an unusual hill hazard – fire. We had climbed over Sron Smeur, dropped down to Lochan Sron Smeur and pitched our tent by a small stream. With a lighter load we then went up Beinn Pharlagain and Meall na Meoig. As we descended we noticed smoke billowing across the moor below, and then flames across the hillside. The fire had not reached the tent but it blocked any easy escape. We moved the tent to the beach of the lochan, as far as we could get from the fire without having to retreat over the hill. We watched the fire spread and retired to the tent for a fitful night's sleep, constantly watching the fire's progress. During the night it started to rain so we slept a little sounder, and by morning the fire was out. On our walk out we found that the fire had stopped less than two metres from where the tent had been pitched. Still, the fire had made the terrain easier for the walk out.

Beinn Eilde and Meall nan Eagan

ANN BOWKER, MAY 1994

Approaching from the south, I crossed the col in a little snowstorm to a vast patch of old snow which was very icy indeed. Fortunately a previous walker had left steps big enough to make the descent safe without an ice axe. I pressed on past Loch Pattack and up by Allt Beinn Eilde. The hill for which this stream is named looked down reproachfully on my left-hand side. According to my map, its height was 673m and its col 525m and it seemed to be saying *'it's a lovely afternoon and yet for the sake of two measly metres you are passing me by'*. At a small cairn I suddenly heeded it and went straight up. It greeted my arrival on the ridge with a sudden burst of sunshine, but it was soon spitting snow again. From the summit I could see my next hill and the beautiful lochan which lies below it.

Lochan na Doire-Uaine is one of those places that one hesitates to write about, lest people should go there and spoil its fragile beauty. Fortunately its remoteness, both from the road and from high hills, makes it unlikely it will ever become a popular destination. The easy way up Meall nan Eagan would have been to plod up the heather over its west top. However, the narrow eastern end of the lochan looked too good to miss so I went that way and through the bealach behind, no easy task as it was choked with huge boulders swathed in luxurious vegetation. It was a place where one had the feeling of treading where none had trod before, and where a lone walker had to take particular care. Eventually I made my way through to the col between Meall nan Eagan and its craggy little west top. After my exciting approach the summit was a bit of an anti-climax and not a place to linger in the bitterly cold east wind. I made my way down the steep east ridge and was lucky to get a bed in the transport cafe in Dalwhinnie.

Binnein Shuas and Binnein Shios

ANN BOWKER, OCTOBER 1995

Binnein Shuas, like Beinn a' Chaisgein Beag, is a mountain for the connoisseur. True, the lower slopes consist of bog and tussocky grass, but these unprepossessing slopes lead up to a craggy ridge and a superb airy summit of naked rock. The eastern side of the hill has impressive cliffs and care was needed to find a way down. We did not take the best route and had a hair-raising descent, alternately sliding gingerly down nearly vertical grass and scrabbling around in a loose and slippery stream bed. Higher up, the ridge became better defined and led over two false tops to the summit of Binnein Shios. Its eastern slopes are also rough and craggy, here with the extra hazard of trees. We took the easy option and retraced our steps down the west ridge, with the outline of Binnein Shuas silhouetted against a splendid panorama of lochs and distant snow-flecked mountains. The loch was totally calm, reflecting the autumn colours and a line of pines silhouetted against the setting sun, a lovely end to an exciting eight-hour circuit.

Creag na Doire Duibhe

ANN BOWKER, OCTOBER 1995

Before driving home we climbed this hill by its east ridge. The sudden unfolding of the western vista revealed a remarkably craggy little hill, conspicuous amongst other more rounded summits. The continuation northwards was a series of rounded hummocks like a string of pearls – not a comparison that would have sprung to mind had we not been celebrating our pearl anniversary. A wedding night in the tent in the Duddon valley had been an appropriate prelude to thirty years of walking together in the mountains.

HC05 Udlamain-chuallaich

Number		Height	Name	Drop	Location	Summit
383	A	1010.2	Beinn Udlamain	556	NN 5794 7397	Shelter
384	A	991.4	Sgairneach Mhor	181.7	NN 5986 7312	Mound near trig
392	GA	917.1	Geal-charn	178	NN 5964 7826	Rock
401	A	798.9	The Sow of Atholl	160.8	NN 6251 7411	Cairn on rock
395	A	892.2	Beinn a' Chuallaich	527	NN 6845 6177	Cairn
405		512	Drumcroy Hill	189	NN 7416 6295	Wall
396	A	855.6	Stob an Aonaich Mhoir	231.8	NN 5374 6942	Outcrop
397	A	841.8	Beinn Mholach	197	NN 5874 6549	Cairn
398	A	829.3	Glas Mheall Mor	146.7	NN 5633 6730	Rock
402	A	777.1	Meall na Leitreach	331	NN 6405 7027	Cairn
404	A	611.4	Creag a' Mhadaidh	154.8	NN 6346 6502	Rock by cairn

The Sow of Atholl

OS maps show this hill as 803m but it is over four metres lower. The summit is obvious and rounded so there seems no reason for this unusually large error on OS mapping. It has two names on the map but hardly any hill walkers refer to Meall an Dobharchain as most of them prefer the novelty of being able to pronounce the name of a Highland hill with reasonable confidence.

Drumcroy Hill

This is the lowest Marilyn in the HC05 area and the only one that has not been surveyed, as the tree cover would make it difficult to receive accurate satellite signals. OS maps give a misleading impression as the ascent can be pleasant and easy, with the trees well spread, similar in some respects to Drummond Hill in HC15 though less undulating. At 512m it is not a small hill and would be regarded as a giant in most of central or southern England, yet only twelve of the 160 Marilyns in the whole of the Central Highlands are lower.

Creag a' Mhadaidh

ANN BOWKER, JUNE 1995

Those who like their mountains steep and dramatic will not venture anywhere near Creag a' Mhadaidh, which lies in an area of rolling heathery moorland. The crags which feature in its name are merely outcrops, more likely to be visited by foxes than climbers.

The closest approach would be from the shores of Loch Rannoch, but since we were driving south on the A9 we rode in from Dalnaspidal, reaching the south end of Loch Garry at full speed, courtesy of a strong north wind. From here it was only a short crossing of the bog to an elaborate bridge across the Allt Shallainn and another track, which ran up to the col below the western slopes of the hill.

The view was not dramatic, all the nearer hills being of a similarly rolling nature, but it had a wonderful spaciousness with higher, unidentified, mountains glimpsed far away to the south and west. We returned the same way, the pleasant Duinish bothy providing a welcome lunch halt before struggling back against the bitterly cold north wind.

Sgorr nam Fiannaidh

Beinn a' Chrulaiste

Summit of Stob na Cruaiche, looking west

Number		Height	Name	Drop	Location	Summit
178	A	967.7	Aonach Eagach – Sgorr nam Fiannaidh	620	NN 1404 5830	Shelter
185		867	Garbh Bheinn	332	NN 1693 6008	Cairn
187	A	742.4	Pap of Glencoe	155.8	NN 1251 5942	Rock
186	A	857.0	Beinn a' Chrulaiste	464	NN 2462 5668	Rock near trig
188	A	740.0	Stob na Cruaiche	351	NN 3635 5710	Rock

Sgorr nam Fiannaidh

If you wish to traverse the arete
It's best not to go when it's wet
With mist the outlook is rosier
You don't see the extent of exposure

The good news for Marilyn baggers who are wary of Aonach Eagach ridge is that they can ignore it by climbing Sgorr nam Fiannaidh on its own or in combination with the Pap of Glencoe. The highest hill at the east end of the ridge, Meall Dearg, has a drop of only 120m, though there is a lot more ascent than that by the time you have been up and down all the other peaks along the ridge. Some might think that avoiding the ridge between the two main summits misses all the fun, but one person's fun can be another's nightmare. There is no doubt that the ridge can be scary and potentially dangerous. Seven people died on it from 2014 to 2023, including a man whose body was not found for a year after he fell into a gully.

It has become more common for hill walkers to get help from friends, use a rope or hire a guide, but even these tactics can not guarantee safety. In August 2023, three people died in the same incident after falling from the ridge. All three were roped together, one of them a guide, in a very unusual incident. A stumble, slip or brief loss of concentration can lead to a fatal fall, and if three people are roped together then all three can fall if none of them are securely roped to a rock. Similarly, one serious error by a vehicle driver can cause multiple fatalities. Every year thousands of people walk and scramble safely along Aonach Eagach, just as millions of people drive tens of thousands of miles every year without being involved in any road traffic accidents. Solo hill walking is not generally recommended on mountain safety grounds, but it does mean that you are responsible for your own safety and for getting out of any difficulties that may arise.

Stob na Cruaiche

This isolated hill feels a world apart from Glen Coe but it is topogaphically connected to the Aonach Eagach ridge because that has such steep drops to north, south and west, while the ground between Rannoch Moor and Blackwater Reservoir never drops below a col at 389m. Stob na Cruaiche has probably the best view over Rannoch Moor, which gives it a great atmosphere of spaciousness, though its relative height of 351m is nothing unusual. It is only two metres lower than the Pap of Glencoe but is very different in character. The Pap is a prominent and popular pimple on the side of a much higher peak, offering spectacular views westward over Loch Leven, but it only squeezes into the Marilyn list with under six metres to spare. A rare walk between the two would offer a challenging study in contrasts.

—— Central Highlands: South ——

Land south of Glen Coe and Lochs Laidon, Rannoch and Tummel, north of Glen Lochy and Loch Tay

Marilyns:	99
Highest and most prominent:	Ben Lawers, 1214.3m
Lowest:	Airds Hill, 181m
Least prominent:	Beinn Molurgainn, drop 150.3m

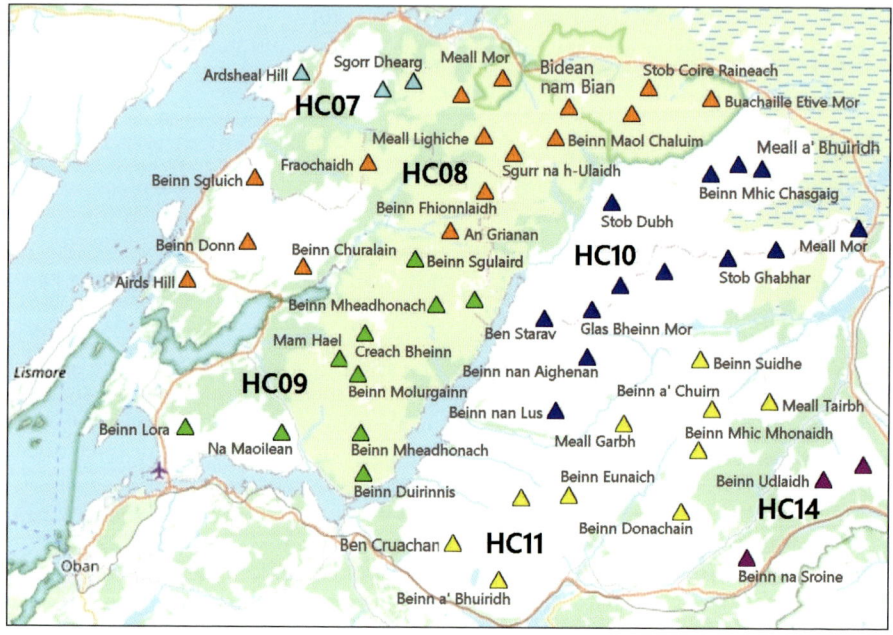

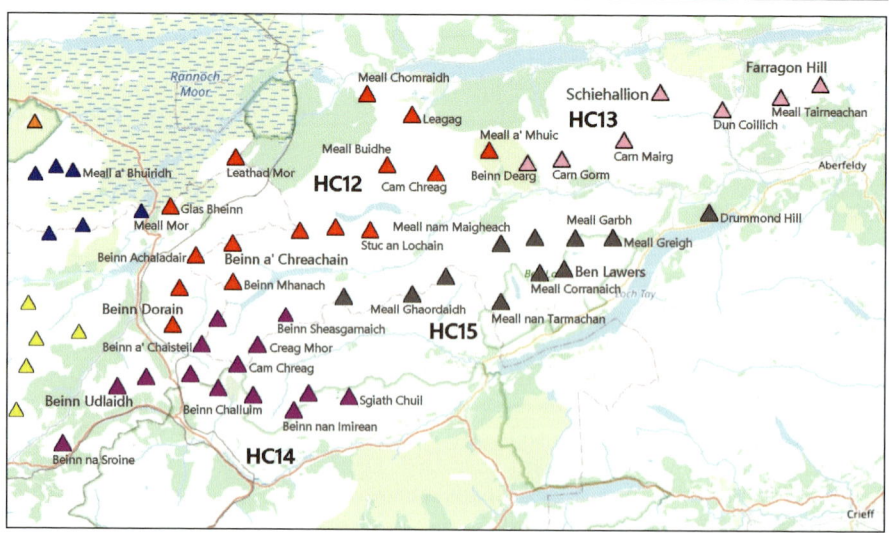

HC07 Dhearg-dhonuill

Number		Height	Name	Drop	Location	Summit
195	A	1024.2	Beinn a' Bheithir – Sgorr Dhearg	729	NN 0568 5584	Cairn
198	A	1002.1	Sgorr Dhonuill	245.1	NN 0405 5554	Rock
230	T	263.4	Ardsheal Hill	231	NM 9951 5685	Trig

Sgorr Dhearg is the 43rd most prominent peak in Britain, one of 52 with a drop of over 700 metres. It therefore has its own hill area but it is a tiny one. It is more topographically prominent than Buachaille Etive Mor and Schiehallion but less visually dominant. This is partly because it is near to a hill of similar height and partly because there is a higher range nearby. Only two pairs of P700 peaks are closer together than Bidean nam Bian and Sgorr Dhearg – Sgurr a' Mhaoraich and Gleouraich plus Ben Nevis and Binnein Mor.

Sgorr Dhonuill and Sgorr Dhearg

ALAN DAWSON, JULY 2016

I aimed to climb all seven summits of Beinn a' Bheithir in one walk by starting from South Ballachulish and heading toward the long, curving western arm of Sgorr Dhonuill. I wasted time messing about on some precarious ledges and ended up well south of Creag Ghorm, my first target. The going was good on the undulating rocky ridge, but surveying the first four summits and cols consumed most of the afternoon. The walking got even better on Sgorr Dhonuill but there was then a big drop and a climb of 267m up to Sgorr Dhearg. Sgorr Bhan looked appealing in the low evening light, but that diversion meant it was 10pm by the time I returned to Sgorr Dhearg. The north ridge looked an obvious way down but I could not see any path, so I used GPS to aim for a point where the end of the forest track ought to be. Most of the trees had been felled but the ground was steep and I stumbled down in the dark over stumps and lumps and roots, through high grass and unstable piles of loose branches. It was one of my worst descents ever, until at last I found the lovely forest track. By the time I reached the car at midnight, I had almost convinced myself that it had been a great day. Excellent hills, shame about the forestry.

Evening view from Sgorr Dhearg over Sgorr Bhan toward Loch Leven

RHB section 3B

OS maps 41, 49, ,50

Number		Height	Name	Drop	Location	Summit
191	A	1149.4	Bidean nam Bian	844	NN 1434 5421	Cairn
211	A	906.3	Beinn Maol Chaluim	197	NN 1349 5258	Cairn
196	A	1021.4	Buachaille Etive Mor – Stob Dearg	532	NN 2226 5425	Rock
197	A	1010.5	Stob na Doire	144.0	NN 2075 5327	Grass
202	A	956.7	Buachaille Etive Beag – Stob Dubh	468	NN 1790 5353	Rock by cairn
209	A	924.5	Stob Coire Raineach	177.7	NN 1914 5479	Outcrop by cairn
199	A	994.0	Sgurr na h-Ulaidh	415	NN 1111 5179	Rock by cairn
215		772	Meall Lighiche	244	NN 0948 5282	Cairn
201	A	959.4	Beinn Fhionnlaidh	510	NN 0950 4976	Outcrop near trig
224		549	An Grianan	180	NN 0751 4782	Cairn
212		879	Fraochaidh	550	NN 0290 5170	Cairn
221	A	654.9	Meall Ban	147.9	NM 9965 4987	Vcairn
219	A	676.0	Meall Mor	304.8	NN 1060 5596	Cairn
220	A	661.8	Sgorr a' Choise	288.6	NN 0846 5514	Cairn
225		549	Beinn Churalain	176	NM 9904 4612	Cairn
226		473	Beinn Donn	204	NM 9612 4770	Rock
227	T	466.7	Beinn Sgluich	216	NM 9666 5124	Trig
231		181	Airds Hill	154	NM 9262 4586	Tussock

Buachaille Etive Mor

The large ugly cairn on Stob Dearg made it impossible to tell if there was any natural rock beneath it, but a survey showed that a small cairn on the ridge above was 24cm higher than an embedded rock next to the monstrosity. The summit of Stob na Doire was far more enjoyable and satisfactory. After the 1997 revision of the SMC version of Hugh Munro's list, it became the only hill over 3000 feet with drop over 130m that had not been awarded the dubious accolade of Munro status. Stob na Broige at the end of the same ridge is less prominent and 57 metres lower. It was deemed to be a Munro in 1997.

AUDREY LITTERICK, DECEMBER 2008

A stunning end to the year. On 31 December, three of us panted up the corrie from Lagangarbh in dense, calm, low cloud, and struggled with extensive swathes of hard water ice and verglassed rocks in the upper corrie. We passed several parties coming down who had not gone for the top, since the ice was making things difficult and there was nothing to see up there. We persevered and then, very suddenly, we burst out into blue, sunny skies with a shifting, fluffy cloud sea all around. Only the tops of the higher peaks were visible, along with brocken spectres and glories.

At the summit were two incredulous, grinning young climbers from south of the border who had barely climbed a mountain before and never seen anything remotely like it. The five of us stood together, sharing the silence, the sun and the unforgettable prize for perseverance on what had felt like a dull and forgettable day. Then we shook hands, celebrating the near end of 2008 as we readied ourselves to welcome in the new year, and descended slowly into the freezing darkness of the misty corrie.

However, the celebrations were to be delayed. Just after I took off my crampons, when descending a steep and rocky section, I slipped on an unseen patch of water ice and tumbled down a few metres, landing in a pile of boulders. I was lucky not to break any bones, but I did dislocate my knee. I managed to hobble down the required 600 metres with considerable assistance from Tony and Andy. I was being extremely careful at the time and did not learn anything that might prevent a similar thing happening in future. I often walk alone (though rarely in serious winter conditions) and it made me think what might have happened had I not had my trusty companions with me. The accident happened in the precise spot where three people lost their lives a few weeks later.

Airds Hill

ANN BOWKER, 25 DECEMBER 1995

With further blizzards forecast we had decided to take the coastal route rather than cross Rannoch Moor. The main reason we ended up on this hill was that we found a lay-by free from snow and usable. An approach from the east was not really sensible, but eventually we crossed all the bumps and depressions which separate hill and road on this side. Then the real problems began. Christmas Day should have Christmas trees, so this hill was an appropriate choice. There were hundreds of them, each with its branches picturesquely loaded with snow, ready for deposition down the neck of the careless walker. The trig point was quite pleasantly situated in an open area, giving good views over Loch Linnhe. It had not escaped our notice that the highest point of the hill was further east from the trig – a mound amongst yet more hostile conifers. As we struggled back through the trees and out onto the road via Glaceriska we wondered, not for the first time, whether Alan Dawson had entered some of these hills into his tables with a quiet sadistic smile.

HAMISH BROWN, JULY 2000

The path seemed to start in a house's garden and I funked going in, instead crossing a couple of field fences. Usually with height the going eases, but here it became diabolical tussock which made every step a gamble. In the end I teetered along a decaying wall to the forest change in direction. Then it was wobbly fence, ditches, tussock, savage low branches and thrutchy, crutchy heather. One ditch I fell into took the heather over head height. When I reached the trig I actually wrung out my sweaty shirt. The indeterminate summit gained, and no other way out appearing, I returned to the trig and followed the handfuls of deer grass I had draped on every tree like some lost explorer. Airds Hill is a hill I would recommend to all my best enemies. What one will do for a tick in a daft book.

Beinn Churalain and Beinn Donn

HAMISH BROWN, JULY 2000

When anyone snorts at the idea of the Relative Hills as being bumps for old men, I'd send them to this pair, in a heatwave, in July, when the ticks are hungry for tickers and the bracken is chest high. Having a camper van I had to find a lay-by in the shade, and that led to a 'just go straight up' decision. I had no machete and my specs constantly glissaded off my sweaty nose. The summit is about 1km from the start but 549m up. That equals a sweaty, steep slope. You can rather go off grass that the sheep haven't mown properly, especially with such a yoyo down-and-up for Beinn Donn, on which I ran out of film in two cameras. Thank god for gravity, and the long slope down went in a free-wheel. At the Creagan Inn I realised my money was in the van. When I reached it, red and radiating heat, a large tin of peaches disappeared in two minutes, followed by five cups of tea.

Sgorr a' Choise and Sgorr Dhearg

View from Bidean nam Bian

Stob Coire Raineach

HC09 Sgulaird-lora

Number		Height	Name	Drop	Location	Summit
207	A	935.0	Beinn Sgulaird	661	NN 0530 4608	Cairn
213	A	839.4	Beinn Trilleachan	477	NN 0864 4390	Cairn
222		589	Beinn Mheadhonach	191	NN 0641 4348	Boulder
214	A	809.9	Creach Bheinn	249.2	NN 0237 4224	Boulder
216	A	723.8	Mam Hael	157	NN 0086 4089	Rock
218	A	688.3	Beinn Molurgainn	150.3	NN 0195 4006	Boulder
217	A	716.5	Beinn Mheadhonach	255	NN 0198 3689	Rock near cairn
223		555	Beinn Duirinnis	249	NN 0210 3475	Rock by cairn
228	A	352.6	Na Maoilean *	193	NM 9753 3721	Rock
229	T	307.8	Beinn Lora	170	NM 9193 3774	Trig

Beinn Molurgainn

This is one of the most marginal Marilyns, qualifying by only 30cm. Its status is dependent on a fine solid summit boulder and a narrow boggy col. The hill would be much the same if the col was half a metre higher but it would have been very disappointing if it had failed to qualify. The only less prominent Marilyns are Kirriereoch Hill (150.2m drop) and the two that just about qualify with nothing to spare: See Morris Hill and Mynydd y Cwm.

Beinn Duirinnis

This hill challenges any preconceptions about the distinction between mountains and hills. It is under 600m high but steep and rugged on all sides. The summit is little more than a kilometre from the shore of Loch Etive, so it has the potential for outstanding views of loch, sea and higher hills, such as nearby Ben Cruachan. There are several granite outcrops near the summit, with scrambling options to confirm the mountainous impression. It could be the main objective for a short winter day or the start of a much longer walk over higher hills to the north. Beinn Mheadhonach is not quite as rugged, as it has a more gentle approach from the west, but the 250-metre descent from Beinn Duirinnis to its col is at least as steep as the ascent.

Beinn Lora

Only five of the 160 Marilyns in the Central Highlands are under 450m high. Beinn Lora is one of the few lower hills with a path to the summit. It also has (or had) a noticeboard describing the walk and the fact that Beinn Lora qualifies as a Marilyn, a distinction shared with Kit Hill in Cornwall. Its popularity is possibly due more to its superb coastal view and simple name than its relative height and status.

Na Maoilean

ALAN DAWSON, MARCH 2015

This modest hill near the western end of Loch Etive provided quite a challenge. Climbing it from the B845 was easy enough, but identifying the highest point took a few hours as it has four separate 350-metre contour rings shown on the 1:25000 map, as well as a 350m trig point. After surveys of three of the summit candidates the final result was clear, with the highest point over half a metre higher than the other bumps. Good viewpoint.

Number		Height	Name	Drop	Location	Summit
233	A	1107.9	Meall a' Bhuiridh	795	NN 2506 5034	Cairn
235	A	1099.8	Creise	169.4	NN 2385 5064	Cairn
264		864	Beinn Mhic Chasgaig	166	NN 2215 5022	Boulder
237	A	1089.2	Stob Ghabhar	392	NN 2301 4551	Cairn
255	A	945.0	Stob a' Choire Odhair	279.4	NN 2573 4598	Cairn
277	A	492.5	Meall Mor	162	NN 3031 4712	Outcrop
238	A	1079.5	Ben Starav	448.8	NN 1257 4271	Rock by cairn
245	A	997.7	Glas Bheinn Mhor	231.3	NN 1532 4298	Cairn
254	A	959.0	Beinn nan Aighenan	343.4	NN 1485 4054	Boulder
268	A	709.7	Beinn nan Lus	241	NN 1307 3757	Cairn on outcrop
241	A	1044.9	Stob Coire an Albannaich	307	NN 1695 4430	Cairn
258	A	928.1	Meall nan Eun	174.5	NN 1924 4490	Cairn
263	A	884.2	Stob Dubh	522	NN 1664 4883	Vrock near cairn

Meall a' Bhuiridh

This hill does not seem to arouse much enthusiasm from walkers, perhaps because of its rounded shape or the ski equipment high up its slopes, but it is higher than Stob Ghabhar and Ben Starav and far more prominent than either of them. It is one of only nineteen summits with height and prominence over 1900, putting it above Scafell Pike, Sgurr na Ciche, Ben More Assynt, An Teallach, Carnedd Llewellyn, Schiehallion and Ben Lomond on this esoteric indicator of landscape significance. The top ten in this tenuous table, with height plus prominence over 2000, are Ben Nevis, Carn Eighe, Ben Macdui, Ben More, Ben Lawers, Snowdon, Sgurr Mor (Fannich), Liathach, Ben Cruachan and Ben Lui.

Beinn nan Lus

DONALD SHIACH, 2010

After much humming and hawing about the best route into Beinn nan Lus, I ended up canoeing in from the head of Loch Etive and camping overnight at Inverghiusachan Point. Kayakers will tell you Loch Etive is barely tidal, but that's not true. They will also tell you that for Loch Etive in a head-wind, kayaking is a better option than an open canoe, and that is true. It is a big brute of a hill from anywhere, but this approach at least reduced the walk-in.

ALAN DAWSON, APRIL 2021

In 1997 I reached this hill via Ben Starav and its outlying tops. It was after 8pm by the time I got to the summit, leaving a long and dark walk back along the shore of Loch Etive. The revisit in 2021 was much easier thanks to the assistance of an electric bike, which made light work of 14km along the track from a forest car park near Taynuilt, with over 300m of ascent before reaching the foot of the hill. Excessive crag symbols on the OS map made the route from Narrachan bothy look fearsome, but in practice the numerous rock ribs made the approach from the west a highly enjoyable walk. Not all walkers or cyclists are keen on this method of approach, but as we get older it can ease the strain on limbs, lungs and soles, as well as saving a lot of time and making some summits more feasible.

Beinn Fhionnlaidh

Beinn Duirinnis across Loch Etive

Loch Etive, Ben Starav and the western slopes of Beinn nan Lus

Number		Height	Name	Drop	Location	Summit
232	A	1127.0	Ben Cruachan	880	NN 0696 3047	Rock
262	A	898.4	Beinn a' Bhuiridh	172.2	NN 0943 2838	Rock
249	A	990.3	Beinn Eunaich	425.9	NN 1356 3279	Cairn
251	A	981.3	Beinn a' Chochuill	251.8	NN 1097 3285	Cairn on rock
269	A	700.3	Meall Garbh	258.7	NN 1679 3672	Rock
267	A	794.8	Beinn Mhic Mhonaidh	419	NN 2087 3501	Rock
272	A	651.4	Beinn Donachain	376	NN 1989 3165	Rock
270	A	676.3	Beinn Suidhe	280	NN 2117 4005	Outcrop by cairn
271	A	664.4	Meall Tairbh	255	NN 2509 3758	Cairn on outcrop
273	A	637.5	Ben Inverveigh	146.4	NN 2712 3820	Rock
276	A	569.4	Beinn a' Chuirn	159.2	NN 2171 3731	Rock

Beinn a' Bhuiridh

RICHARD WOOD, OCTOBER 2010

Quite often October can bring surprises, such as days warmer than in August. There was a misty dawn start from Inveraray hostel, but just before coming in sight of Loch Awe, the mist parted and a magical scene unfolded, with Kilchurn Castle and Beinn a' Bhuiridh reflected in blue water. The higher we went on Beinn a' Bhuiridh the warmer it got. The day was to end even better than it started, on an easy summit south of Oban, where we were just in time to see the sun drift toward the horizon. A perfect day.

Beinn Donachain

RICHARD MCLELLAN, DECEMBER 2012

At 15:15 Glen Orchy is deep in shadow, the iron-hard ground white with frost as I cross the bridge over the dark waters of the river and set off for Beinn Donachain. Brown oak leaves glisten with frost, the oaks give way to conifers and soon I am climbing the open hillside. The sun sets into a pale orange glow and the valleys darken. Snow-topped peaks rise ghostly into night skies. It is a superb night to be out alone under the star-filled skies, in absolute calmness, with only the gentle squeak of snow underfoot. A steep ascent then the gradient lessens and I arrive at the tiny summit cairn. Lights twinkle in distant villages. It feels so very late though it is only 17:00. After a few moments in total silence, I retrace my footprints back through the snow to Glen Orchy and the warmth of the tent.

Meall Tairbh, Beinn a' Chuirn and Beinn Suidhe

RICHARD MCLELLAN, DECEMBER 2012

Snow glistens in the brilliant sunshine, -3C and not a breath of wind. Sitting on the summit of Meall Tairbh, all around stretch high snow-covered mountains, a jigsaw puzzle of peaks. It takes a few moments of thought to name at least some of them. The horseshoe continuing over Beinn a' Chuirn and Beinn Suidhe is a very fine walk. With the sun sinking into golden skies I make a fast descent down a snowy gully on the east of Beinn Suidhe, pick my way along Glen Curra and back through the forest, strangely eerie in the silence, clouds of breath lingering in the stillness and reflecting in the head-torch beam. I enjoy a superb week among snow-covered peaks, with hardly any wind, blue skies streaked by cirrus and bands of altocumulus. The days never feel cold in the blinding sunshine.

Stob Ghabhar

Beinn Mhic Mhonaidh

The upper slopes of Leagag

179

Number		Height	Name	Drop	Location	Summit
104	A	1080.6	Beinn a' Chreachain	650	NN 3738 4407	Cairn
105	A	1074.5	Beinn Dorain	330.1	NN 3255 3785	Cairn on outcrop
108	A	1038.6	Beinn Achaladair	226	NN 3446 4324	Rock
112	A	1002.3	Beinn an Dothaidh	245	NN 3317 4087	Cairn
122	A	952.5	Beinn Mhanach	315	NN 3737 4114	Cairn
120	A	959.5	Stuc an Lochain	482	NN 4830 4484	Outcrop by cairn
130	A	908.4	Meall Buidhe 908	258	NN 4269 4496	Cairn
133	A	835.0	Sron a' Choire Chnapanaich	205.8	NN 4560 4530	Cairn
123	A	932.1	Meall Buidhe 932	321.1	NN 4983 4994	Cairn
132	A	861.7	Cam Chreag	166.2	NN 5368 4912	Cairn
137	A	745.9	Meall a' Mhuic	236.0	NN 5793 5080	Rock by cairn
138	A	601.0	Leagag	218	NN 5188 5391	Cairn
140	A	466.3	**Meall Chomraidh *****	150.9	NN 4839 5567	Cairn
189		547	Leathad Mor	210	NN 3784 5101	Cairn
190	A	502.1	Glas Bheinn	182	NN 3268 4731	Outcrop by cairn

Meall Chomraidh

This hill was promoted to Marilyn status in 2005 after a visual inspection of the summit, which seemed to be about a metre higher than the 465m trig pillar. In 2013 a rare joint survey effort proved that the promotion had been justified. G&J Surveys had the more difficult task in identifying the critical survey point in the broad, flat col. The summit survey was easy by comparison, in pretty good weather for November.

PETER MALONE, JANUARY 2006

In January I had a short trip to Rannoch in the camper van and bagged Drummond Hill, Dun Coillich and Leagag to finish region 2, so I thought. I later discovered the addition of Meall Chomraidh. To make matters worse, when climbing Leagag I had looked at this hill, and thought 'what a nice hill, that should be a Marilyn'.

Meall Buidhe 932

ALAN DAWSON, OCTOBER 2014

In the summer of 2014 the weather in Scotland was often strangely superb. Best days of the year involved long routes on undulating ridges, sometimes reaching familiar summits via unfamiliar routes. Most of my walking was solo and unhurried, with no schedules, deadlines or boats to catch. Perhaps the best day of all was 12 October, when Glen Lyon looked as lovely as ever in autumn colours. From the summits of Meall Buidhe and Garbh Mheall, shifting shafts of light played across the fabulous views toward Glen Coe, Rannoch Moor and Ben Alder. On the dusky descent, Stuc an Lochain slowly turned orange in the setting sun. Meall Buidhe and nearby tops are unassuming grassy summits, but I felt very much at home and at peace in these surroundings. I was aware at the time that I could have been on Lewis ready for an attempt on the St Kilda stacks, but I was happy with my choice of rolling hills rather than rolling waves. Perhaps I had learned to give more priority to enjoyment and less to achievement. The next day the stacks were finally climbed. Eddie Dealtry described the top of Stac Lee as a 'guano nightmare'.

Number		Height	Name	Drop	Location	Summit
103	A	1083.3	Schiehallion	714	NN 7138 5476	Rock
139	A	570.7	Dun Coillich	186	NN 7624 5364	Heather by cairn
107	A	1043.0	Carn Mairg	467.0	NN 6848 5125	Cairn
109	A	1029.5	Carn Gorm	188.5	NN 6351 5007	Outcrop by cairn
134	A	829.5	Beinn Dearg	200	NN 6087 4975	Rock
135	T	787.3	Meall Tairneachan	419	NN 8074 5437	Trig
136	A	782.4	Farragon Hill	185.6	NN 8403 5530	Cairn

Schiehallion

RODERICK MANSON, 2005-2006

I saw in the new year on the top of Schiehallion again, with my inspirational reading of Norman MacCaig's 'Landscape and I' to a totally absent audience. I went a little too far south in descending the west ridge for a full traverse, and eventually found the estate track on the west side of the Tempar Burn. I had overlooked the fact that the road at the west end was 300 feet lower than the car park. By the time I arrived back at my car it was 04:27. I decided to forgo another walk that day on the grounds of physical incapacity.

Dun Coillich

This hill has heather moorland with boggy areas and limestone outcrops, a small Scots pine plantation and two burns. Those words could apply to hundreds of hills, but they are taken from the website of the Highland Perthshire Communities Land Trust, which bought Dun Coillich in 2002. It was the first community-led land purchase in Perthshire. There has been some sensitive tree planting but most of the land has not changed much. The hill now benefits from a good path from car park to summit, with signs welcoming walkers and pointing the way. A direct route would be only 1km from the car park but it is worth walking twice that distance at a gentler gradient on the path, with no tussocks and no heather bashing needed. The key path junction to the summit is at NN 7605 5308.

Beinn a' Chaisteil

HC14 Sheasgarnaich-udlaidh

Number		Height	Name	Drop	Location	Summit
145	A	1077.4	Beinn Sheasgarnaich	579.0	NN 4138 3833	Cairn
148	A	1046.8	Creag Mhor	394.0	NN 3915 3611	Cairn
169	A	900.8	Beinn Odhar	457	NN 3373 3388	Cairn
171	A	883.6	Cam Chreag	158.3	NN 3754 3467	Vrock
173	A	818.5	Beinn Chaorach	180	NN 3588 3282	Rock near trig
152	A	1025.0	Beinn Challuim	450	NN 3868 3224	Cairn
158	A	959.3	Meall Glas	554	NN 4314 3219	Outcrop
165	A	920.1	Sgiath Chuil	311	NN 4629 3179	Rock
172	A	848.3	Beinn nan Imirean	189.1	NN 4192 3095	Boulder
170	A	885.2	Beinn a' Chaisteil	466	NN 3471 3640	Cairn
174	A	804.2	Beinn nam Fuaran	259.3	NN 3609 3816	Rock
265	A	840.4	Beinn Udlaidh	525	NN 2802 3326	Cairn on outcrop
266	A	802.0	Beinn Bhreac-liath	214.9	NN 3027 3391	Cairn
274	A	635.8	Beinn na Sroine	222	NN 2339 2894	Trig

Sgiath Chuil

ALAN DAWSON

If we think of the summit of a hill as being the highest point of a territory, like the highest point of a county or country, then everyone in Britain lives on the slopes of a Marilyn, unless their home is on an island under 150m high. It is not always easy to work out which one though, and it can change. The Wirral peninsula was part of the Raw Head territory when I lived there, but after Raw Head was found to have only 148m drop, its Marilyn territory was ceded to Cadair Berwyn. Raw Head still has its own Hump territory but that is much smaller. Living in Crieff made it easy to stroll up the Knock of Crieff from home, but most of Killin lies on the lower slopes of Sgiath Chuil. Its summit is only 11km from the village but there are numerous less prominent summits on the way and it would be an arduous walk over them all, before working out how to get back home.

I had lived in several other territories too. Edinburgh was obvious as I could see Allermuir Hill from the house. Glasgow was less easy as the canal complicated things, but the answer was Duncolm not Earl's Seat. Lancaster must be on Ward's Stone but where was Arnside before Arnside Knott was promoted? Liverpool was presumably on Billinge Hill and Southampton on Butser Hill, but what about Bath and Leicester, and Thickwood in Wiltshire, where I spent a few months? Maybe it wasn't all that important to know.

Beinn Odhar

ALAN DAWSON, MARCH 2010 AND MAY 2016

I climbed this hill on successive days in 2010 as I lost a camera and went back to look for it. It wasn't there but I found it three days later on nearby Meall Buidhe. In 2016 I spent almost two hours on top removing a huge and ugly cairn in order to survey the summit.

Beinn Challuim

ALAN DAWSON, APRIL 2017

I climbed this hill on successive days in 2017 as I had lost a camera. I found it the next day by the remains of a huge ugly cairn that I had reduced but failed to remove entirely.

Number		Height	Name	Drop	Location	Summit
141	A	1214.3	Ben Lawers	915	NN 6355 4143	Outcrop by cairn
143	A	1123.1	Meall Garbh	198	NN 6443 4375	Cairn
146	A	1067.2	Meall Corranaich	201.2	NN 6153 4104	Cairn
154	A	1000.7	Meall Greigh	167	NN 6740 4380	Cairn
163	A	925.6	Meall a' Choire Leith	150.5	NN 6124 4388	Stone
176	A	778.9	Meall nam Maigheach	176	NN 5859 4360	Rock
149	A	1043.6	Meall nan Tarmachan	494.4	NN 5851 3899	Cairn
150	A	1039.8	Meall Ghaordaidh	492	NN 5144 3970	Trig
168	A	909.6	Beinn nan Oighreag	272	NN 5416 4120	Rock
175	A	806.3	Meall nan Subh	214	NN 4608 3975	Rock
177		460	Drummond Hill	312	NN 7496 4548	Wall

Meall nan Tarmachan

ALAN DAWSON, MARCH 1986

The village of Killin played a notable role in my early attempts at climbing mountains in Scotland. Three months after receiving a copy of *Munro's Tables* as a Christmas present, I spent a few days in Killin with two friends. Our first walk was over the Tarmachan ridge from east to west and back down the middle. These were the first summits I climbed knowing they were Munros and Tops. Ben Lawers and others followed the next day.

After studying the Tables I was left puzzled by the absence of an explanation of qualifying criteria other than height. The following month I had the idea for the list of hills that would turn out to be called Marilyns. This in turn helped provide motivation to move from Liverpool to Scotland, and I managed to get a job in Glasgow three years later.

Not knowing anyone in Scotland apart from my new colleagues, I joined a club for the first time. The first outdoor meeting I attended was a day trip to Killin, and I was able to reach the top of Beinn Ghlas without having to crawl through wind and snow, though by then I knew it was not prominent enough to qualify as one of the Relative Hills.

I was 33 on my first visit to Killin and 33 years later I ended up living there. The urge to climb these peaks again did not seem very strong after I could see them from my bedroom window, possibly because I spent so much time somewhere else seeking out new summits. Pity really. Maybe being able to see them on a daily basis was enough, maybe I needed the satisfaction of new hills, or maybe I was just getting old.

Drummond Hill

AUDREY LITTERICK, 2012

Since moving house to Perthshire in 2011, I have been able to enjoy a life on the far southern slopes of Schiehallion, with lots of other fine peaks, high and low, within cycling distance. I was unsure whether it is an advantage or a disadvantage to live right beside Drummond Hill. So far I have managed an unsuccessful ascent and three successful ascents but have not yet enjoyed a completely struggle-free ascent. I have encountered vertical, slime-covered rocks, dense, dripping, prickly sitka, wind-thrown mature trees, thigh-deep snow, knee-deep mud, vegetatious hidden holes, an angry stag, an irritable male capercaillie and a grumpy husband, who had lost heart for the battle. I am sure Drummond Hill will have some jewels, so I will keep trying to find them.

Southern Highlands: West

South of the Pass of Brander and Glen Lochy, west of Strath Fillan, Glen Falloch and Loch Lomond

Marilyns: 82
Highest and most prominent: Ben Lui, 1131.4m, drop 874m
Lowest: Beinn Mhor, 194.2m
Least prominent: Sgreadan Hill, drop 155m

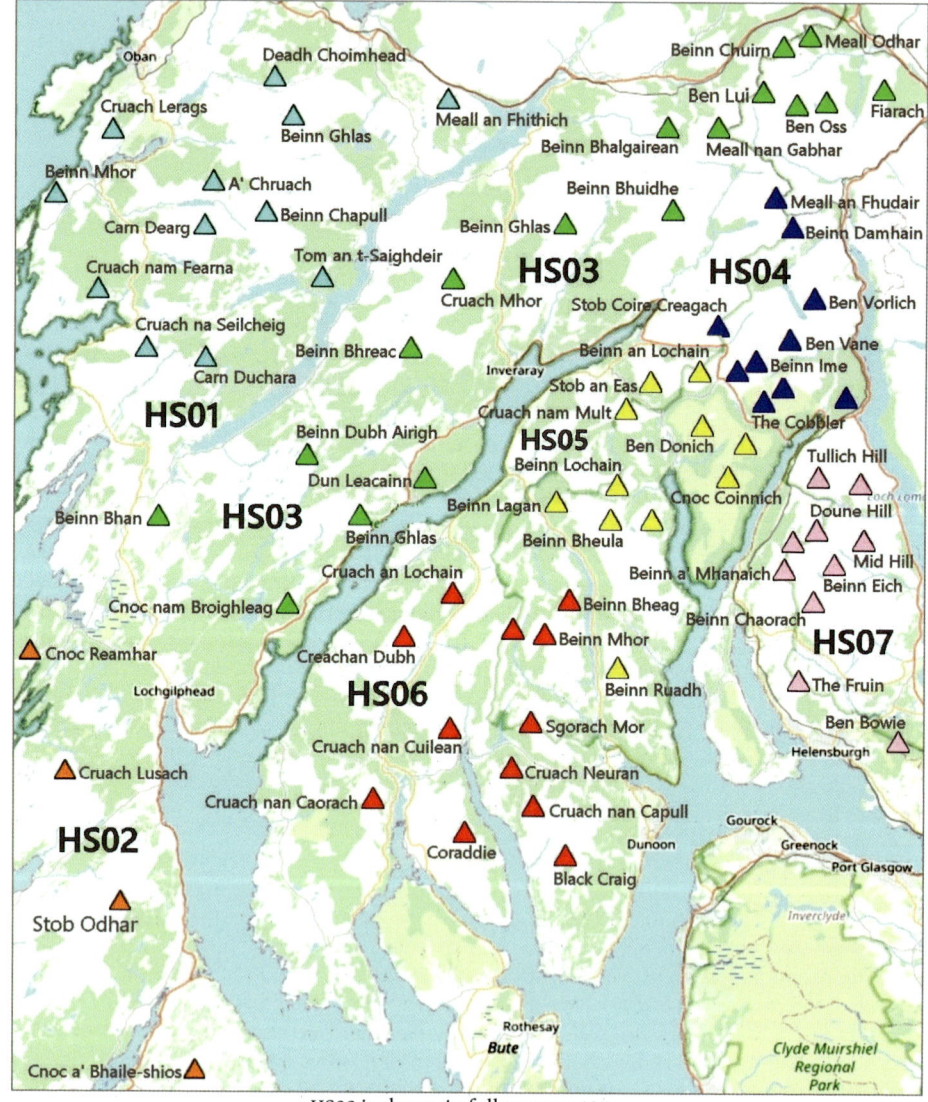

HS02 is shown in full on page 187

RHB section 19A   OS maps 49, 50, 55

Number		Height	Name	Drop	Location	Summit
1386	A	516.4	Beinn Ghlas	471	NM 9574 2596	Rock by cairn
1393	T	383.1	Deadh Choimhead	283	NM 9468 2864	Cairn
1387	T	515.1	Beinn Chapull	268	NM 9373 1960	Trig
1391		437	Carn Dearg	174	NM 8961 1897	Cairn
1395		366	A' Chruach	202	NM 9036 2189	Moss
1388	T	491.1	Carn Duchara	338	NM 8927 1027	Rock by trig
1394		380	Cruach na Seilcheig	207	NM 8544 1104	Grass by cairn
1398	T	332.3	Cruach nam Fearna	204	NM 8232 1511	Trig
1401	T	302.8	Tom an t-Saighdeir	174	NM 9719 1523	Trig
1402		294	Meall an Fhithich	169	NN 0594 2674	Grass
1403		252	Cruach Lerags	217	NM 8381 2573	Tussock
1404	T	194.2	Beinn Mhor	162	NM 7983 2158	Trig

Beinn Ghlas

This hill was listed as 515m in RHB but it is 512m on most current maps. However, the maps are wrong as it is over a metre higher than Beinn Chapull. Its ascent has become easy via a track from Glen Lonan that avoids the wind farm and leads up to a mast on a knoll at 450m. From there a faint path carries on to the 503m East Top. The main summit has extensive views of coastline, islands, lochs, trees and mountains.

Carn Duchara

DAVID RAFFE, FEBRUARY 2012

Carn Duchara was my favourite Marilyn of the year. It is my local hill and has many different qualities, including the masochistic challenge of forestry plantations lower down, a rugged character higher up and fantastic views back inland. Most striking of all, however, are the views to the west including Jura and Scarba.

JIM FOTHERGILL, SEPTEMBER 2012

I was heading up a forest fire-break en route to Carn Duchara when I noticed something shiny in the trees. It turned out to be a deflated balloon with a message from a five-year-old lad with a request to post it back to him. His address was only ten miles from my home. As I often did the forty-mile bike route from home round the Preston Guild Wheel and back, on my next outing I posted it through his door. His mum rang me later to say that he had released it several months before from Arran.

Deadh Choimhead

COLIN CRAWFORD, AUGUST 2002

I expected little from this modest eminence other than a toil through the trees, yet it really is a star, and straightforward to ascend. The map showed a track heading north from Glen Lonan. Just after entering the conifers, a right fork, though very overgrown, offered a pleasant and firm stairway for a few hundred metres. A vague path continued uphill, marked occasionally by orange ties on trees. Once clear of the forest, a thin trod wound up to the summit with an all-round view. To the west one looks over low coastal land to Kerrera and Mull, while to the east Ben Cruachan looked truly awe-inspiring.

PHIL COOPER, 2005

Glen Lonan provided a beautifully peaceful camping spot prior to an ascent of Deadh Choimhead, an ideal miniature mountain, perfectly suited for a family outing and just an hour's return walk from the glen. The forest path was easy, followed by avoidable scree and a rougher upper section, with a path to the trig point, which lay smashed to pieces.

Tom an t-Saighdeir

JON METCALF, JULY 2000

Following a failure the day before, I finally got up Tom an t-Saighdeir by Loch Awe. Both ends of the loop path mapped from the road were almost undetectable. The southern one seemed completely choked with brambles, bracken and holly, with no easy way off the road into the undergrowth. The northern one started in mature woodland, then above a line of crags was a post with a green disk to confirm I was on the right route. I managed to force a way above this through head-high bracken, via assorted bog and thorns, and many rotten wind-felled trees and self-seeded new sitkas. I gave this up as unsafe, since I just stepped through some of the rotten logs. The black flies were hellish.

The successful way up was from a quarry at NM986162. From here forest roads and fire-breaks led to a dry stream and a very steep grass bank. There were even more trees, but only five or six deep. After 800 metres of clambering over tussocks and peat grikes, there was the trig point with great views of Loch Awe and Ben Cruachan. On the top near there were five posts, each with a green disk, which led to the top of the marked northern path, which from the tree-line springs into existence steeply down on a lush carpet of grass with a good aggregate base. After the struggle this was a joyful release. It was head-high bracken and more self-sewn trees, but at least the track under all the herbage was sound. Very satisfying to beat the little swine after the earlier frustration.

Cruach Lerags

JOHN BARNARD, 2004

Sometimes there are hills that test your sanity. I had a 1984 map which indicated the summit was at the edge of a wood. Not any more, it was in a wood. The ascent took an amazing amount of crawling underneath pine trees to arrive at two insignificant bumps, looking like a scratched porcupine. Can anyone tell me how pine needles get inside your underpants when you are wearing over-trousers and a long cagoule with the hood up?

KEN FALCONER, JULY 2006

By far the worst hill of the year was what I thought would be a gentle evening stroll up 252m Cruach Lerags, south of Oban. I got attacked by a pig going through the farm at Gallanachbeg, then stuck in a bog sprouting head-high bracken and stinging nettles whilst skirting the loch, then I ended up scaling a near-vertical crag full of loose rock and heather. There must be an easier way. To crown it all, what had seemed quite a nice evening turned into heavy rain. It was a relief to get back to the youth hostel in time for the last few minutes of the World Cup Final.

Beinn Mhor

AUDREY LITTERICK, 2007

What a magic wee hill. An easy (if rather muddy in places) track to the top and then stunning wide-open views over the Firth of Lorn to Mull, Kerrera, Scarba and away out to Colonsay and Islay in the far distance, over fifty miles away.

HS02 Stobodhar-slate

RHB section 19B   OS maps 55, 62, 68

Number		Height	Name		Drop	Location	Summit
1407		562	Stob Odhar		542	NR 8188 7422	Rock by trig
1408	A	466.8	Cruach Lusach		281	NR 7860 8321	Rock
1410	T	454.2	Beinn an Tuirc		439	NR 7522 3617	Rock by trig
1411	T	446.6	Cnoc Moy		433	NR 6115 1522	Tussock near trig
1415		384	The Slate		160	NR 6338 1652	Heather
1412		428	Beinn na Lice		221	NR 6027 0854	Cairn by trig
1413	T	421.6	Cnoc a' Bhaile-shios		319	NR 8635 6286	Trig
1414		397	Sgreadan Hill		155	NR 7411 2956	Tussock by trig
1416		354	Beinn Ghuilean		276	NR 7293 1707	Tussock
1417		266	Cnoc Reamhar		217	NR 7664 9124	Grass near trig

Cruach Lusach

Two OS maps showed two different points as 466m, so it was impossible to know which was the summit until 2015, when a survey showed the original grid reference given in RHB to be correct. The western top is 1.1m higher than the eastern one.

COLIN PHILLIP, 1890

There is a most astounding view to be had from this hill... The land and sea are superbly mixed up. I think it is about the finest view I know, and that is saying a good deal.

Sgreadan Hill

ANN BOWKER, MAY 1996

This was probably the most baffling RHB of all. Here is our experience, which may be totally useless now, as trees have a habit of growing thicker or being felled, which is often worse. We cycled in from the east (a 16m trig point on Kildonald Point). We found no chink in the massed conifers until the pipeline at NR730273, where some felling was taking place, and vehicle track marks led upwards, to leave only a short amount of excess density before reaching the eerie 'island' of moorland at the top. Fortunately we realised that on the way back we should be faced with millions of identical looking sitkas and had the foresight to tie a plastic bag to the crucial one which marked the line of weakness. I recollect sunshine and a leisurely lunch at the top, enjoyed with a satisfaction akin to that on reaching the top of the In Pinn. I also remember thinking that this was the most unlikely spot in Britain to encounter another walker, but perhaps now that Marilyns are becoming more popular it could get crowded up there?

ALAN DAWSON, AUGUST 2002

Slipping and stumbling are inevitable at times, but this is the only hill that had me flat on my face twice after low tackles around the ankles. One was due to a hidden tree root and the cause of the other was erased from memory when trying to forget the trauma.

Beinn na Lice

JANET CLARK, DECEMBER 2005

I loved the Corbetts for their isolation and separate identities, and was thrilled to discover the existence of Marilyns for more of the same – isolated hills, some hard to get at, sometimes being turned back without success. Right up my street. I found out that you needed 600 of these to get into the Hall of Fame. Well, they're only small so they must be easy. Not so. They're everywhere, so the totals will soon add up. Again, not so. They can sometimes be found on an orienteering map, and cryptic conversations can be heard in the car park: 'there's one on this map' ... 'if my course goes anywhere near the summit I'm going to go for it' ... 'what's your current total?' Sometimes you can do one on the way home.

I discovered that two orienteering fanatics were both collecting Marilyns, and to my surprise I found that Alison, my friend of 45 years, was way ahead of both of them. It's an esoteric obsession. Alison introduced me to the concept of 'par' being two Marilyns per day, and we had a weekend at Oban practising that. We had considered Kintyre but it was too far for a weekend. Then in December 2005 four of us found ourselves in Tarbert, with short days and several miles away from the southern tip of Kintyre but raring to go. Start before dawn. Drive many miles. Work out a way to cover three in one day. First a pair then the single outpost of Beinn na Lice, in low cloud, rain and gathering darkness. YES! Back to Tarbert late, wet and exhausted. This is the life.

Beinn an Tuirc

Alan Dawson, August 2002

I struggled over some appalling terrain in heavy rain until I neared the summit and encountered a coach parked on the wind farm track, which I knew nothing about. Ignorance was not bliss, it was very annoying, but sometimes you have to laugh.

The Slate

Alan Dawson, August 2002

It started deceptively easily when I drove in along the rough track to Glenahanty. This made the ascent of Cnoc Moy quick and easy, with a series of grassy runs through the tussocks enabling me to reach the top in 45 minutes. I enjoyed the views from this pleasant hill and prepared myself to dig deep for the traumas ahead.

The descent to the col was a routine variety of heather, grass and tussock, and the col itself was not so bad, with deep heather, holes, lumps, tussocks and a stream. Standard narrow col really. Just over the stream I noticed a small wooden stile over an electric fence. So, someone had been this way before. I didn't use it but started upwards, crossing another fence a few minutes later. The terrain was harder than on Cnoc Moy but not too intimidating, so I was able to maintain upward progress through a series of mini-hazards: an armpit-level grass ramp, a tough tussock traverse, then the heather walls. As I tackled the first heather wall I veered left where the angle seemed to ease and felt a sharp pain in my knee. I looked down and saw a red smear. The route had drawn first blood.

For a while things looked up with some short stretches of easy grass, but these led to the next hazard. I stood on a small lump and looked down into the black depths of an oozy peat pit. The only way across was to grasp the top of the fence for support and hope it wasn't electric. I grabbed for it. No shock. A few seconds later I had leapt across the black depths.

After a few more good pull-ups on long heather and grass clumps I reached the top of Creag nan Cuilean, from where I could survey the long traverse out to the well-guarded summit cone of The Slate itself. I was almost ready for a summit push, but I paused to recall the stories of others who hadn't made it. The route looked within my capabilities if I had the will to keep going. I tightened my rucksack belt, took a deep breath, and began to weave my way east through the tussocks, expertly picking out short lines of level ground through the lumps and hollows. Time passed, distance was gained, and I became lost in the intense concentration required for the micro-navigation. It wasn't exactly a rhythm, but it was a routine.

Suddenly there was a loud bang from the north, then another and another. I looked up and realised I had been in something of a reverie, paying such close attention to the terrain that I had forgotten where I was, so it took me a few seconds to understand what I was seeing. Waves. Breaking on the sandy beach of Machrihanish. I had been so focused on my feet that all thoughts had gone and I had not noticed a view opening up. Slowly my mind creaked back into gear. I remembered my name, where I lived and where I was. Oh yes, I was on The Slate.

The spell was broken, so everything became harder work. I had been breezing across awkward, lumpy, boggy terrain by not noticing it. Or rather, by concentrating so hard I had lost awareness of how hard it was. With my mind back in control I plodded on toward the tree-line, aware now of other sounds – pipits, skylarks, grouse, jackdaws.

As I neared the tree-line I realised I had made a major error – I didn't know where I was going. I had got too close to the trees without stopping to pick out a viable line. I had covered the awkward ground too quickly by not noticing where I was. I couldn't face going back so I decided to have a guess at the route. When I reached the forest fence I veered left as the terrain became much lumpier and more awkward, as it so often does around the tree-line. This must be the wood-schrund.

I climbed the fence and traversed left around the edge of the trees for about 100 metres, aiming for a break I thought I'd seen. Light rain began, and I looked back to see Cnoc Moy disappearing into mist. As I entered the forest and saw the gap in the trees close behind me, I was aware of the route feeling more serious. The rain got harder, the mist a little thicker. I stopped for a drink and got some protection in place – over-trousers covering shorts and skin. I looked around a full 360 degrees and couldn't see quite how I had got where I was. This was ridiculous. I had only been inside the forest a few minutes and already I had that familiar and uncomfortable sensation of being trapped. Ahead there was a ride of maybe 30 metres of grass and heather and then just a blank wall of trees. As I reached them I turned right, then left, and was soon in trouble. I could sense this route wasn't going to go. Time for retreat. But which way? There were few clues about how to get out, and there seemed little point in wasting time trying to work out exactly how I had reached this impasse.

I rested a minute to regain composure, then set off on a compass bearing directly westward, pulling back the nearest branch and ducking under it. A ditch immediately opened up beneath my feet, making progress awkward. I managed to swing a leg across to the far side, regained my balance, and continued for several metres straddling the ditch and hoping it wouldn't get any wider. Eventually I managed to get my legs back together but then the branches edged closer to each other, making movement harder and choking potential exit routes. My back was getting sore from ducking and bending, my legs weary of bridging and straddling. Knowing that I needed to change my technique, I pulled my hood up, turned around and backed my way out. After a few minutes in reverse gear my backside popped clear of the last spruce and I was free.

I retraced my steps along the forest edge back to the fence junction, continued a few metres further south, and before long I caught sight of an easy ride opening up to the left. At last, I had found the key to the summit. It was trivial really, requiring no crawling or thrashing, merely a stroll up through a gap that was wide enough for two. I laughed at how simple it was. The forest had been fun in a way, but it was poor route finding. I should have spotted this line from way back on the tussock terrace. Soon the trees ended and the summit clearing was in sight. It wasn't quite a simple stroll, as there was a peat wall which might have been awkward in very wet conditions but was easily bypassed in the drizzle. I looked back to check the exit route, keen not to make another mistake, and felt stupidly happy as I mounted the final few heathery lumps to the summit.

In a way I was glad it had been a struggle, as it made reaching the top more satisfying. The mist lifted a little to give snatched views of open country, then closed up again within seconds. There was little reason to linger, so I turned and was quickly back at the peat wall, through the ride and back out below the forest, retracing the traverse of tussock terrace. The Slate hadn't been easy, but it had been tamed. Or so I thought, but really I ought to have known better. It hadn't gained its evil reputation for nothing, and sure enough I wasn't going to get down unscathed.

I relaxed too soon, and either impatience or over-confidence made me cut a corner on the descent rather than return over Creag nan Cuilean. Bad move. Another little trap had been set and I had fallen right into it. The angle steepened, trees started to appear all around me, the lumps underfoot got bigger, and suddenly both hands were busy as I needed to use my skill and experience to slow the descent. I clung on to clumps of grass to check my momentum and ease the strain on my knees, then suddenly I felt my teeth jam together as I slammed to a halt. My foot was stuck in a hole, a deep one, hidden in the long grass. I realised I was in a heavily crevassed area and that meant the ground had been prepared for more planting. I had blundered into the middle of a series of awkward trenches and hidden runnels.

Now that I understood the type of terrain I knew the best bet was to get out of there fast, so I forgot about descending and traversed further west, over lumps and ditches toward the final trench, until I was nearer the line of the ascent route. I found that the heather walls were easier going down than up, somehow I missed the black peat pit altogether, and soon I was back to the armpit-level grass just above the col.

I looked across at Cnoc Moy, which had begun to look rather impressive from below, and decided I wouldn't be climbing it again even though its terrain was relatively placid, so I turned left and began the long wallow back along the forest edge. The grass was deep in places, with foot placements uncertain, but soon I reached an old ruin and gained a bit of height just beyond it, hoping to avoid the deepest vegetation. It had looked better but the going soon deteriorated, with patches of brutal, hard-core vegetation – bottomless grass, with every step unseen and uncertain, and no way of knowing whether each foot placement would land on a wet slithery lump or in a hidden trench. This was bad, very bad. I had done all the hard work, this wasn't fair. The breeze had gone, sweat started dripping, flies and midges swarmed over my face and in despair I resorted to swearing. Bloody ground, bloody flies, this was crazy, why were there no breaths of wind, no sheep to cull the grass, no birds to cull the flies. If the start had been like this I would never have made it. August was clearly the wrong time of year to be on this ruthless terrain. The only thing to do was try to keep moving, slowly one step at a time, gain a little height, and surely there must be some friendlier heather and tussock soon.

It felt as though I was stuck in that stuff for hours. Eventually I reached a low stone wall, climbed over it, and on the other side I could see the ground dropping away and a beautiful view opening up – scattered old farm buildings, a flourish of gorse bushes and a little blue van. It was downhill all the way to safety.

The Slate had thrown down challenge after challenge. Some I had biffed aside with ease, others I had fluffed at first but passed in the end. It had been hard, even desperate at times, but I had kept my nerve and done all right.

As I drove slowly back down the rutted track I felt the warm glow of accomplishment in the face of adversity, and judged that I was ready to move up a grade. Back at the road I turned the van northwards and set off toward Sgreadan Hill.

MARTIN RICHARDSON, APRIL 2009

I struggled to find a route off The Slate, having lost my map earlier. To escape a ravine I had to get over a rusty old barbed-wire fence that did not take my weight. I ended up with my leg impaled on the spikes and a visit to Campbeltown hospital for a tetanus jab.

Near the summit of Cruach Lusach

Beinn Bhuidhe from Beinn Ghlas 551

Dun Leacainn

HS03 Lui-bhuidhe

Number		Height	Name	Drop	Location	Summit
65	A	1131.4	Ben Lui	874	NN 2663 2629	Boulder by cairn
67	A	1029.8	Ben Oss	341.2	NN 2877 2532	Rock
69	A	978.6	Beinn Dubhchraig	198.9	NN 3076 2549	Cairn
80	A	881.9	Beinn Chuirn	448	NN 2802 2923	Cairn on outcrop
87	A	656.9	Meall Odhar	184	NN 2979 2985	Outcrop by cairn
88	A	652.2	Fiarach	181	NN 3448 2615	Rock
70	A	948.5	Beinn Bhuidhe	592	NN 2036 1871	Cairn
84	A	744.0	Meall nan Gabhar *	265	NN 2357 2402	Rock
89	A	636.8	Beinn Bhalgairean	210	NN 2026 2410	Rock
90	A	551.2	Beinn Ghlas 551	255	NN 1315 1808	Rock
1384	A	590.2	Cruach Mhor	383	NN 0572 1474	Cairn
1385	T	526.1	Beinn Bhreac	160	NN 0277 1026	Trig
1389	A	483.3	Beinn Dearg	145.5	NN 0242 0501	Rock
1390	T	459.4	Beinn Dubh Airigh	180	NM 9585 0353	Rock by trig
1392	T	420.1	Beinn Ghlas 420	197	NR 9892 9928	Trig
1396		360	Dun Leacainn *	271	NN 0336 0161	Mound
1399	T	319.5	Beinn Bhan	244	NR 8568 9980	Trig
1400	T	314.5	Cnoc nam Broighleag	160	NR 9400 9373	Trig

Meall nan Gabhar

This hill has three distinct knolls. The summit grid reference was updated in 1995, when an OS 1:10000 map correctly showed the 744m height, but thirty years later the 1:50000 map continued to omit this, giving only 743m for the northern summit and 739m for the southern one (Meall nan Tighearn). In fact the difference between the two is only 80cm, not four metres. The middle summit is 60cm higher than the northern one.

Beinn Ghlas 551

Visual observations from hill baggers indicated that the 550m trig pillar might not be the highest point of this isolated hill between Dalmally and Inveraray. These observations were confirmed to be correct by a survey in March 2021. The rock on top of the relocated summit was found to be 84cm higher than a rock next to the trig pillar.

Beinn Dubh Airigh and Beinn Bhreac

ALAN DAWSON, JUNE 2001

A satisfying if unlikely combination from the shores of Loch Awe, sniffing out viable routes though the forests guarding both summits. A long track plod through fine rain and mist was assisted by some obscure post-punk rock music on the MP3 player, helping me to get into a speedy rhythm with synchronised feet and beat.

The sight of a surprisingly large Beinn Bhreac looming above the gloom was rather uplifting. The return along the Kames River brought even greater reward, as it turned into a tremendous steep-sided gorge, with the only feasible descent route veering wildly from one side to the other, then clinging uncertainly to the steep vegetation way above the torrent, with tightly-packed trees masking potential escape routes.

Number		Height	Name	Drop	Location	Summit
68	A	1012.2	Beinn Ime	713	NN 2549 0848	Cairn
74	A	926.8	Beinn Narnain	290	NN 2716 0665	Outcrop by trig
76	GA	915.8	Ben Vane	426	NN 2775 0984	Outcrop
79	A	886.7	The Cobbler	259	NN 2595 0581	Tor
81	A	859.7	Beinn Luibhean	181.0	NN 2428 0792	Outcrop
71	A	942.8	Ben Vorlich	632	NN 2950 1247	Rock
82	A	817.8	Stob Coire Creagach #	505	NN 2306 1091	Rock by cairn
83	A	764.9	Meall an Fhudair	383	NN 2706 1924	Rock by cairn
86	A	684.2	Beinn Damhain	220	NN 2821 1729	Rock by cairn
91	T	415.3	Cruach Tairbeirt	279	NN 3126 0586	Rock by trig

Beinn Ime

There used to be a trig pillar on top of this hill. Its height was recorded as 1011.94m. Some of its remains were discovered during an archaeological dig that attempted to locate the natural summit of the hill. Heavy rain during the dig may have loosened some of the rubble that obliterated the pieces of pillar. Some rocks at the base of the shelter cairn on top had become embedded and vegetated, making it impossible to distinguish the natural from the unnatural. The survey point was a large rock that may have been moved by human hand many years earlier but looked plausibly natural and could not be shifted. The height of Beinn Ime may have been nudged above 1012m by the cairn construction.

The Cobbler

Reaching the fabulous and unique summit of this popular peak is not particularly difficult in dry weather but it takes confidence at any time and can be intimidating if wet or icy. It is shown as 884m on OS maps, suggesting that aerial surveying failed to identify the summit tor. May 2020 seemed a good time for a summit survey as outdoor recreation was bizarrely judged to increase the risk of Covid infection and was either banned or severely discouraged. There were several people on the main path up the hill but the summit was clear by the time the survey was set up, so data collection could proceed undisturbed.

Stob Coire Creagach

This steep-sided hill was listed as Binnein an Fhidhleir in 1992 as its summit was not named on OS maps at the time, so a name was adopted from the peak with a trig pillar further west along the summit ridge. By 2024 the summit was still unnamed on OS 1:50000 maps, though Stob Coire Creagach did appear on larger-scale mapping.

Cruach Tairbeirt

AUDREY LITTERICK, 2011

A totally foul day. Heavy rain, low cloud and gales, but special nonetheless because I was there with five of my best friends to climb my 1000th Marilyn. We might just have made it to a rain-free summit if the tardier pair in our party had made it to the start at the appointed time. Conditions at the top were sufficiently awful that it was all we could do to claim the summit briefly with a few photos and then stagger back down to the cover of the trees to celebrate in more traditional style. It was not quite as I had imagined it would be, but I will not forget my 1000th Marilyn.

RHB section 19C   OS map 56

Number		Height	Name	Drop	Location	Summit
1419	A	901.7	Beinn an Lochain	640.0	NN 2180 0789	Grass
1425	A	732.6	Stob an Eas	249	NN 1853 0739	Outcrop near trig
1420	A	846.5	Ben Donich	557	NN 2183 0430	Trig
1421	A	787.5	The Brack	403	NN 2456 0306	Trig
1423	GA	763.5	Cnoc Coinnich	273.6	NN 2335 0075	Cairn on rock
1422	A	779.4	Beinn Bheula	557	NS 1547 9832	Trig
1435	A	606.6	Cruach nam Miseag	206	NS 1829 9812	Cairn
1444	T	465.2	Beinn Lagan	243	NS 1199 9966	Trig
1426	A	702.9	Beinn Lochain	375.4	NN 1601 0062	Rock
1428	AG	658.4	Stob na Boine Druim-fhinn ¬	149.5	NN 1688 0253	Trig
1433	AG	611.2	Cruach nam Mult	282	NN 1681 0563	Knoll
1427	A	664.6	Beinn Ruadh	502.1	NS 1556 8844	Rock

Cruach nam Miseag

HAMISH BROWN, 1944

I had reached the UK a few weeks earlier, having been marooned in South Africa after escaping the fall of Singapore. We had a family holiday in Carrick Castle and my new big brother, his friend Margaret and I went up Cruach nam Miseag. I recall us running down. Margaret paused to warn us of a dirty big hole, turned and went in up to her waist.

Stob na Boine Druim-fhinn

This hill was listed in 1992 but demoted in 2015 after a survey showed it to fall short of qualification by around half a metre. Another survey in 2016 confirmed the result.

Beinn Lochain

AUDREY LITTERICK

Lowlight of the year was a horrific struggle in pouring rain through a wind-thrown forest in an attempt to reach Beinn Lochain. This was hill walking at its worst. After crossing the Lettermay burn we were lured into a gap that might have been a fire-break once, but it had degenerated into a mess of collapsed mature sitka spruce that got darker and wetter as we battled upwards. We climbed up through a confused muddle of branches, under and over trunks, and squeezed through holes too small for a rucksacked person. We shoved the sacks through first then struggled after them, grunting and gasping, filthy and wet, trying to avoid being poked in the eye by numerous branches. I swore a lot. To my surprise Andy, who dislikes long, traumatic hill walks, seemed to enjoy the experience and kept up a cheerful banter throughout. To him, apparently, it was so completely awful that it held a sort of horror-laden challenge.

When we emerged from the forest, a shocking two hours after we had entered it, we were muddy, lichenous, thoroughly soaked and picking spruce needles from every orifice. The hill and its neighbour, Stob na Boine Druim-fhinn, are very fine, and we did eventually get some good views from them, but I could remember nothing about my ascent other than those two hours spent in the forest.

The Brack

Cnoc Coinnich

Number		Height	Name	Drop	Location	Summit
1424	A	741.5	Beinn Mhor	700.2	NS 1078 9081	Trig
1431	A	619.8	Beinn Bheag	302	NS 1257 9315	Cairn
1437	A	568.4	Cruach Bhuidhe ¬	149.2	NN 1252 9470	Trig
1429	A	644.5	Creag Tharsuinn	399	NS 0880 9132	Tussock
1446		432	Cruach nan Cuilean	211	NS 0435 8479	Tussock
1432	GA	612.0	Cruach nan Capull	488.3	NS 0958 7955	Outcrop near cairn
1434	A	607.3	Cruach Neuran	294.2	NS 0839 8204	Grass by trig
1439		522	Black Craig	197	NS 1159 7605	Cairn
1436	A	602.2	Sgorach Mor	429	NS 0968 8499	Rock
1440		519	Coraddie **	371	NS 0500 7786	Rock
1441	T	508	Cruach an Lochain	258	NS 0494 9385	Trig
1443	T	470.2	Creachan Dubh	177	NS 0157 9106	Grass near trig
1445	T	458.2	Cruach nan Caorach	210	NR 9913 8043	Rock by trig

Beinn Mhor

CRAIG WELDON, JUNE 1998

Halfway down ribbon-like Loch Eck on a foul summer's day, Billy and I saw a small stand of boats outside the Whistlefield Inn and had a Plan. We were heading for Beinn Mhor directly above the opposite shores, but if we hired a rowing boat for the day we could save ourselves a considerable walk halfway up the length of Loch Eck and back. On other days I had seen people out fishing in boats on Loch Eck, and an idyllic scene it makes, with the trees of Argyll Forest Park swathing the steep shores and the deep waters of Loch Eck lying still and reflecting a liquid sun. This, however, was a different day.

After arranging boat hire with the dubious owner, we rowed out. Halfway across the narrow, funnel-like loch, the wind and waves became so strong that we had to turn the boat 90 degrees to face into the wind to reduce the rocking, which was threatening to capsize us. At this point we spotted a crowd by the shore, enticed out of the bar to bet on our chances of making it across the loch. This did not inspire confidence but it did lend us some bravado. Eventually we made it across, dragged the boat well out of the water, tied it to a tree and started on up the hill. This is possibly a good walk, and could be continued to Clach Bheinn. Today though the weather was so foul, the wind so strong, the rain so cold and cutting, that we headed straight back downhill. We had to bale out the rain-filled boat before setting off again across the loch. Knowing about the severity of the waves, we managed to cautiously navigate our way back across. But wet as we were, we were grinning. We had had a Plan, and it had led to an Adventure. A pint next to the open fire in the Whistlefield Inn before heading back home was well justified.

ANDY HYAMS, SEPTEMBER 2009

I do not recognise bad days on the hill – just good ones, great ones and notables ones, such as taking a bus from Benmore Gardens to Glenbranter to walk back over Beinn Bheag and Beinn Mhor, only for it to collide with another bus from the same company, prompting the two drivers to stand in the middle of the main road arguing furiously. The day after Bus Wars, I was marooned in Cowal when a landslip closed the Rest and Be Thankful road, with my B&B owner stuck on the Arrochar side.

Coraddie

This hill replaced Beinn Bhreac as a Marilyn in 1995.

JON METCALF, 2007

I was chilled to hear, on local evening television news, that a walker had gone missing, fearing it likely to be a Marilyn bagger due to the area mentioned. Sinking confirmation of the worst followed from Alan on the Monday. He phoned to see if I had heard from Jennifer Thomson, as she was booked to join a party I had organised to go to Islay and Jura the following week. No joy. Jennifer had set out from the Colintraive Hotel to climb Beinn Bhreac. Conditions deteriorated rapidly into gale-force blizzards. It is not known if she knew of the higher nearby Coraddie, promoted since Alan's book was published.

Dozens of Marilyn baggers and more friends from the Perth Hillwalking Club pitched in to support the emergency services in the unsuccessful searches. No-one can doubt the strong bond this terrible event illuminated between those who share what can sometimes seem the most individual of pastimes. Over 1500 hours were spent over many following weeks and weekends combing rough hill, dense forest, awkward coast and treacherous ravine. Many dropped their own agendas to try to help a friend in trouble and her family, sadly to be frustrated by the astonishingly rough, inaccessible, overgrown and hazardous ground that makes up this seemingly innocuous bump on the map.

JON FOOTE, 2007

There's a hill, all alone, called Coraddie
That between two grey lochs can be found
Where the rough ground lifts up from the shorelines
With the burns falling raggedly down

You could head from Beinn Bhreac to Coraddie
Past peat hags and green bog and moss
When the weather turns foul and confusing
All sense of direction soon lost

Many friends and acquaintances searched there
And rescue teams long combed the land
For Jennifer Thomson was missing
But never a sign did they find

Did she turn from the wind and the blizzard
And head down for more sheltered ground
Did she hide from the storm in the forest
Where it's likely she'd never be found

We'll remember the hill of Coraddie
And the one who is missing there still
In wind and in rain and in sunshine
We must leave her alone on the hill

ALAN DAWSON, 2011

I had first met Jennifer at a gathering of hill baggers and she had once been to a small party at my house. She had set out to climb a hill, a severe snowstorm had blown in and she never returned. Her remains were found four years later by some canoeists, near the shore of Loch Striven. She had managed to get down the hill but not back to safety. Jennifer's presence in the Marilyn Hall of Fame was of little interest to the family she left behind, but it kept her alive in the memories of her hill walking friends.

HS07 Doune-fruin

RHB section 1E   OS map 56

Number		Height	Name	Drop	Location	Summit
93	A	734.5	Doune Hill	695	NS 2905 9709	Cairn
94	A	713.1	Beinn Chaorach	381	NS 2874 9237	Grass by trig
95	A	708.8	Beinn a' Mhanaich	358.9	NS 2691 9460	Cairn
96	A	701.5	Beinn Eich	157.3	NS 3020 9468	Grass by cairn
97	A	683.6	Cruach an t-Sidhein	169.3	NS 2751 9648	Cairn
99	A	656.9	Mid Hill	430	NS 3214 9626	Cairn
98	A	680.8	Beinn Bhreac	528	NN 3215 0007	Trig
100	A	633.1	Tullich Hill	274	NN 2935 0064	Rock by cairn
101		361	The Fruin	169	NS 2762 8722	Cairn
102	A	313.5	Ben Bowie	219	NS 3399 8288	Grass

Doune Hill

The trig pillar was assumed to be the highest point of this hill until April 2017, when a routine survey unexpectedly found a higher point about fifty metres further south.

ANDY HYAMS, SEPTEMBER 2005

Alone in the mist on Doune Hill, I was deafened by a public address announcement requesting Euan MacDonald to report to the main gate at Faslane. A visit to Glen Douglas the next day for Tullich Hill and Beinn Bhreac produced the explanation – the extensive array of weapons bunkers and associated security apparatus.

The Fruin

This hill is unnamed on current OS maps. Its name was the result of local consultation and was proposed by staff in the Helensburgh tourist office. The name Tom na h-Airidh shown on OS maps is applied to a south-eastern top seven metres lower than The Fruin.

JOHN BARNARD, 2004

Some hills clear of trees can test one's resolve. I found The Fruin particularly tedious. The heather was energy-sapping and I was pleased the ground was partially frozen, otherwise continuous bog would have added to the drudgery. Despite this, I have really enjoyed the challenge of the variety of hills that Marilyn bagging has posed.

Ben Bowie

This low hill is an oddity, the only Ben in an area with four Beinns over twice as high. Trees are no longer a barrier, as the hill can be easily reached via the John Muir Way from the north-west. There seems to be no evidence that John or David ever walked this way, but you can pretend to be walking in the footsteps of heroes.

No-one would describe the hill as a pretty thing, for an extensive plantation mars the lower slopes, which on the surface shows little sign of life. A path through a fire-break offers a fairly direct line to the summit through a felled area, but a more ziggy route round to the north provides the insurance of avoiding trunks, trips and slips. Above the tree stumps the terrain changes and all is hunky dory up to the grassy summit, which has extensive views over lochs and lowlands. There is no sense of doubt about the highest point, as the more northerly 313m spot height is almost a metre lower than the summit. All the madmen go up the hill backwards but it ain't easy.

――― Southern Highlands: East ―――

East of Loch Lomond and Glen Falloch, South of Glen Dochart, Loch Tay, River Tay, north of Strath Allan

Marilyns:	55
Highest and most prominent:	Ben More, 1173.9m, drop 986m
Lowest:	Moncreiffe Hill, 223m
Least prominent:	Creag Gharbh and Creag na Criche, drop 150.8m

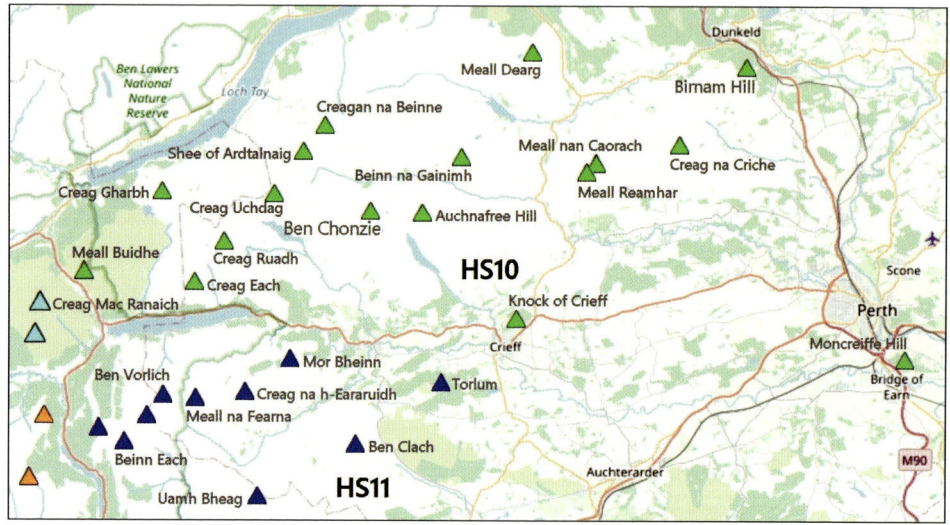

Moncreiffe Hill is east of the M90 but between the River Tay and the River Earn, so it is part of HS10

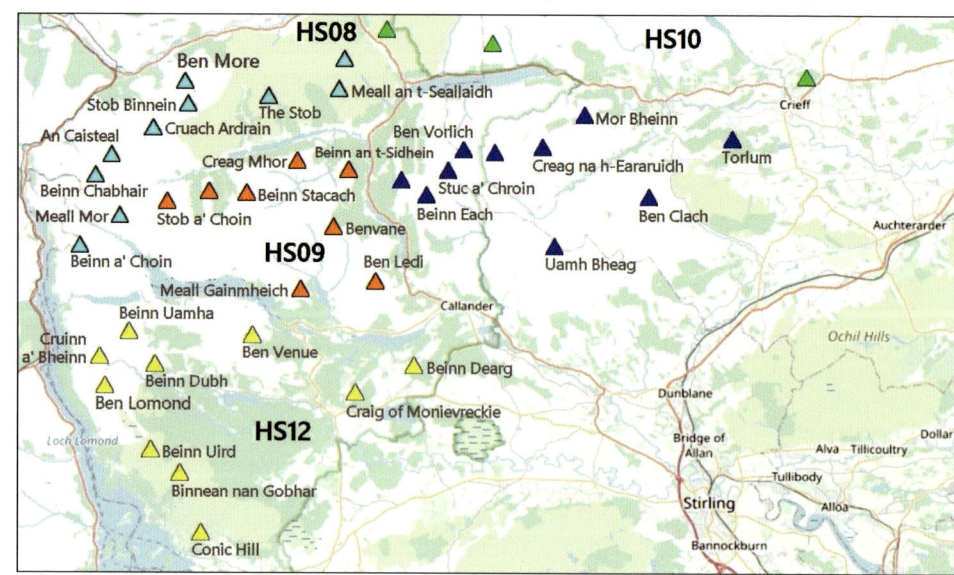

Number		Height	Name	Drop	Location	Summit
26	A	1173.9	Ben More	986	NN 4327 2441	Trig
27	A	1164.8	Stob Binnein	304.4	NN 4347 2270	Cairn
30	A	1045.9	Cruach Ardrain	549	NN 4092 2121	Cairn
31	A	995.9	An Caisteal	474	NN 3787 1934	Cairn
38	A	932.2	Beinn Chabhair	313	NN 3676 1795	Cairn
44	A	852.7	Meall an t-Seallaidh	426	NN 5421 2341	Outcrop by trig
46	A	808.6	Creag Mac Ranaich	213	NN 5456 2556	Rock
49	A	753.6	The Stob	228	NN 4913 2318	Cairn
48	A	768.7	Beinn a' Choin	345	NN 3542 1302	Cairn
50	A	746.0	Meall Mor	264.4	NN 3837 1514	Cairn

Ben More

This is the fifth most prominent hill and one of only ten with height and drop together totalling over 2000 metres. Its ascent is straightforward but arduous, entailing a climb of over 1000 metres in about 2.5km. Most hill walkers carry on down and up another 304.4 metres to its big twin, which looks as high from most view points but has a flatter top.

Stob Binnein

Every hill on the mainland apart from Ben Nevis has a topographic parent, but working out which one it is can take time. Snowdon is the highest hill south of the Southern Highlands and its key col is near Cumbernauld. Ben Lomond is the southernmost hill in Scotland over 900 metres but it is lower than Snowdon so can not be its parent, whereas Stob Binnein is 80 metres higher. Proximity and height are not the only considerations, as the line of parentage must also follow any intervening key cols, such as that for Earl's Seat in the Campsie Fells. In this case the outcome is that Stob Binnein is the topographic parent of Snowdon. It would be a long walk to climb them both together.

I set off to climb Stob Binnein, I did not want to stay in again
And by the time I got to the top I felt aware, alive, fit and thin again
Then I climbed Beinn nan Aighenan, had to abandon a long lie again
Told myself I would not be back and so I said my goodbye again
I went up to climb Sgurr na Sgine again, the ridge made me feel rather keen again
On the top I looked all around and I saw that wonderful scene again
Up and down and up again, reaching the top again
Ah but it's not a bad life, don't want to stop again
So I went back up Stob Binnein...

The full version of these lyrics appears on the album *Songs from the High Hills*.

Beinn a' Choin

BARBARA JONES, 2005

I'm very partial to a Bounty bar when on the hill, but I didn't have one with me for my 1000th Marilyn celebration on Beinn a' Choin. Yet, surprise surprise, there by the summit cairn was a carrier bag containing an Aero bar and a milk chocolate Bounty. I prefer dark ones but could hardly complain. They were rather too runny from the sun for immediate consumption but it was a strange coincidence. I camped down by the Corriearklet Burn.

Number		Height	Name	Drop	Location	Summit
42	A	878.6	Ben Ledi	528	NN 5623 0977	Trig
45	A	820.5	Benvane	215	NN 5351 1372	Cairn on outcrop
59	A	572.1	Beinn an t-Sidhein	285	NN 5469 1785	Tussock by cairn
43	A	867.2	Stob a' Choin	478	NN 4172 1597	Cairn on outcrop
52	A	686.4	Stob Breac	247.8	NN 4472 1661	Cairn
47	A	771.8	Beinn Stacach #	364	NN 4743 1632	Trig
53	G	674.0	Meall Cala	149.0	NN 5083 1277	Rock
54	A	659.8	Creag Mhor	292.9	NN 5103 1851	Outcrop
60	A	567.7	Meall Gainmheich	225	NN 5096 0951	Rock

Beinn Stacach

This hill was originally listed as Ceann na Baintighearna, though that name refers to a lower summit 2km to the north. The new name was derived from nearby Bealach Stacach.

Beinn an t-Sidhein

This hill is usually easy to climb, on a pretty good path from Strathyre, but it has been a nuisance to survey, as it has two tussocky summits of equal height. In March 2016 it was very windy on top so the data quality was poor and the result could not be trusted. In March 2023 the weather was better but not the result, which showed both summits to be precisely 572.11m. The one with a cairn has been declared the official summit.

PAUL RICHARDSON, OCTOBER 2002

After climbing Dumyat I indulged in one of the greatest debacles of my walking career to date. A new path up Beinn an t-Sidhein was being built but work had been postponed due to bad weather. I walked fast on the older path and made good progress until I spotted a track deviating more directly towards the ridge. My progress soon slowed on the steeper and rougher ground. When I climbed clear of the trees I took a gentler, less direct line towards the craggy top, where I met a man with a dog who had come up the main path.

Ben Ledi and Benvane dominated the view, along with Sgiath a' Chaise on the other side of the glen. We chatted for a while before parting and heading in slightly different directions. I opted for the easier way down via the proper path and got back to the car without incident. Consideration of climbing Sgiath a' Chaise was quickly dismissed and I drove home. I did not realise my fatuous mistake until many hours later. Back home, I even edited the patchy GPS track without noticing. Then, at last, as I looked at my route on the computer. I saw that the top I had been to was not the summit of the hill. In fact, it was not even near. The summit lay about half a mile to the south and was a hundred feet higher, a fact I had failed to notice in conditions of perfect visibility.

GARY JONES, 2014

We probably all occasionally muse on the silliness of the numbers game. My 2014 epiphany resulted from a snap decision to climb Beinn an t-Sidhein above Strathyre on my way home, purely because I had noticed I was on 1299 Marilyns. I went up from Glen Buckie as it gave a higher starting point, but the going was dreadful and the rain poured down. I returned soaked to the skin and drove home to discover that a summit in southern Scotland had been demoted and I was still on 1299. There may be a moral somewhere.

Cruach Ardrain

Creag Mac Ranaich

Beinn an t-Sidhein from Benvane

Number		Height	Name	Drop	Location	Summit
1	A	930.4	Ben Chonzie	647.0	NN 7731 3086	Rock
3	A	878.8	Creag Uchdag	276.4	NN 7082 3232	Trig
4	A	787.4	Auchnafree Hill	211.7	NN 8086 3081	Cairn
2	A	889.1	Creagan na Beinne	460.7	NN 7444 3685	Cairn
5	A	758.2	Shee of Ardtalnaig #	225.6	NN 7295 3517	Cairn
6	A	729.3	Beinn na Gainimh	287	NN 8371 3446	Heather
7	A	719.2	Meall Buidhe	273	NN 5768 2759	Rock
11	A	637.4	Creag Gharbh	150.8	NN 6323 3272	Trig
8	A	712.3	Creag Ruadh	199.1	NN 6739 2925	Cliff edge
10	A	673.7	Creag Each	217	NN 6525 2637	Rock
9	A	690.3	Meall Dearg	172.1	NN 8866 4149	Trig
12	A	623.7	Meall nan Caorach	323	NN 9286 3389	Rock near trig
13	A	617.8	Meall Reamhar	154	NN 9220 3326	Cairn
14	G	456.8	Creag na Criche ***	150.8	NN 9857 3507	Rock
15	A	403.8	Birnam Hill	171	NO 0320 4017	Cairn
16	A	279.2	Knock of Crieff	162.6	NN 8730 2340	Mound near cairn
1676		223	Moncreiffe Hill	185	NO 1357 1997	Cairn

Creag na Criche

JANET MUNRO, JUNE 2009

I was on 597 Marilyns and had been considering plans for my 600th. I needed a fairly local hill that could be done in an evening so that Lindsay and Rod could both be there, yet my two nearest options were proving difficult to get to quickly from Pitlochry. If only there was something closer. I scoured the book but there was nothing suitable for an evening walk. Then a new Marilyn was announced – Creag na Criche. I didn't realise the relevance until Lindsay explained that it was only about five miles from home. A date was set and so eighteen of us set off from Little Glenshee. Celebrations at the summit were something else, with champagne and strawberries amongst other goodies. I was presented with a black silky scarf by Alan (not the usual fleecy version) and an RHB 600+ badge. I was also given a black t-shirt by Lindsay and Rod with a pink 'Creag na Criche' on it. Various other gifts were received and I was serenaded with a song by Ali Wilson.

Birnam Hill

This historic hill is half a metre higher than nearby Craig Obney. It can be reached easily via a choice of pleasant paths, a walk enjoyable enough to be worth repeating. By the time of publication, Lindsay Munro had climbed Birnam Hill over 1750 times.

Knock of Crieff

ALAN DAWSON, JANUARY 2024

I lived in Crieff for fifteen years but only climbed this hill about 36 times even though it was an easy walk from my house, with a choice of good paths and routes. I had never had a view from the summit until 2024, on my first ascent for eight years and first visit since the trees on top had been felled. I went back a few weeks later to survey it.

Number		Height	Name	Drop	Location	Summit
17	A	985.3	Ben Vorlich	834.3	NN 6291 1891	Trig
18	A	973.0	Stuc a' Chroin	252.1	NN 6174 1746	Rock near cairn
19	A	811.2	Beinn Each	157.1	NN 6016 1580	Cairn
20	A	810.0	Meall na Fearna	233	NN 6507 1868	Cairn
22	A	644.2	Sgiath a' Chaise	303	NN 5836 1694	Tussock
3937	AG	708.3	Creag na h-Eararuidh **	353	NN 6851 1900	Grass
23	A	640.3	Mor Bheinn	327	NN 7162 2117	Trig
24	A	533.1	Ben Clach	230	NN 7593 1523	Tussock
25	A	393.7	Torlum	232.8	NN 8190 1923	Trig
1644	AG	665.8	Uamh Bheag	325	NN 6911 1185	Cairn

Creag na h-Eararuidh

This hill superseded Beinn Dearg as a Marilyn in 2014, when a survey found it to be higher by over 1.6m. The story of its name, discovery and pronunication is told in track 5 on the *Songs from the Grahams* album, the soundtrack to the *Tales from the Grahams* book.

Uamh Bheag

For anyone heading north on the M9 past Stirling, the first sight of the southern Highlands is likely to be a huge array of turbines sprawled across the southern slopes of Uamh Bheag and Beinn Odhar. It offers a suitable warning of what is to come over much of the landscape further north. Uamh Bheag straddles the boundary between Highlands and lowlands, being slightly to the south of the Highland Boundary Fault but connected topographically to hills further north. There is some sense of wildness to be found on its northern slopes above Glen Artney or western slopes above Callander, and the summit offers extensive views in all directions as some compensation for the turbine turmoil.

Ben Clach

BRENT LYNAM, AUGUST 2006

A late summer bag for me and Alison, and we parked my car due east of the summit. Alan was meeting us after the walk and it was agreed we would see him on the farm track to the north-east. The descent in the dark wasn't helped by bracken eight feet high, and I took a few falls just to make Alison feel better. We finally arrived at the track only to be met by a deranged farmer, supposedly worried about someone attempting to steal his quad-bike. Alan had already told him that he was waiting for a couple of walking friends, but the man raved at us and shouted that we were entitled to be on the hill, but not at night. Much threatening and finger-wagging in our faces. Despite our attempts at reason, he demanded our names and addresses, before I told him he wouldn't be getting any details and we left the yard. The fun had only just started though, as his headlights came down the track and we realised that he was hot on our trail. We ran for the car and he attempted to chase us to Braco, little realising that the owner of the Mazda estate was in fact a grand prix driver in a bad mood. Well, my nose was up against the window as we sailed past my own car at ooh, 80mph? We eventually lost the mad farmer, and he wasn't waiting for me when I got dropped back at my car about an hour later than anticipated.

Number		Height	Name	Drop	Location	Summit
32	A	973.7	Ben Lomond	820	NN 3670 0286	Outcrop by trig
55	A	632.5	Cruinn a' Bheinn	175	NN 3653 0514	Cairn
51	A	729.5	Ben Venue	543	NN 4745 0633	Outcrop
56	A	596.8	Beinn Uamha	265	NN 3864 0690	Outcrop
61		508	Beinn Dubh	193	NN 4044 0450	Cairn
57	A	596.6	Beinn Uird	213	NS 3995 9851	Cairn
58	A	584.8	Binnean nan Gobhar	152.2	NS 4190 9675	Cairn on outcrop
64		361	Conic Hill	153	NS 4328 9239	Cairn
62	A	427.0	Beinn Dearg	213	NN 5887 0379	Grass by fence
63	A	400.1	Craig of Monievreckie	175	NN 5465 0199	Heather

Beinn Dubh, Beinn Uamha, Cruinn a' Bheinn and Ben Lomond

HUGH BARRON, MARCH 2005

A memorable trip from Loch Dhu near Aberfoyle. The contrast between the solitude of the lower hills, with their woodpecker, snipe and skylark song, and the throngs on the main Ben Lomond path, highlighted one of the real pleasures of the relative hills.

Beinn Uird and Binnean nan Gobhar

This pair of hills look innocuous on the map but much of the terrain is tussocky, heathery and uneven, providing a far tougher walk than a stroll up the path to Ben Lomond or Conic Hill. Forestry and parking restrictions limit possible routes but none offer easy going. An average overall speed of 3km per hour would represent good progress.

Beinn Dearg

This is the higher of two Marilyns in the Menteith Hills. From the map it looks obvious and straightforward to climb the pair in a single circuit, but the terrain between the two is tussocky and tiresome. Beinn Dearg can however be easily reached by a track up to the masts on Ben Gullipen and a reasonable undulating path on to the main summit.

Craig of Monievreckie

URSULA STUBBINGS, OCTOBER 2004

The ground had steepened again, but the safe, flat land at the edge of the forest was just visible in the darkness. The dead bracken had given way to sharp, shiny conglomerate approaching the vertical. I contoured right and left, looking for a way down, but the crags seemed to be continuous. To the left was a wide easy gully leading down to the forest, but there was no way into it. I would have to go back up the little rushy stream I had slid down, which had been fine until one finger had suddenly received the full weight of my body when I slipped faster than intended. At the base of this gully was a mast with a solar panel and a small platform. By clambering up the mast I managed to get some way up the gully, but then I couldn't make it past the vertical section. I was stuck!

I had a tiny torch. By flashing it on to the solar panel, I thought to make its impact larger. Six flashes and six blasts on the whistle then rest and repeat, rest and repeat. In the rests I howled like a wolf. The howls reverberated round the surrounding hills and across the lonely forest to the twinkling lights, where people sat warm and dry indoors, having their suppers by cosy fires. So near and yet so far...

Suddenly I saw a moving torch beam in the forest beneath me. Could there really be someone down there at 10pm on a cloudy, damp night in late October? The beam was coming towards me. My feet were wet and cold, my broken finger shouting for attention. Twenty minutes passed and then again a light, much nearer now. There were voices at the edge of the forest, and the yapping of a dog. Someone was shouting. Then a voice:

'*Stay where you are*'.

Good, that's what I wanted to do. After more incomprehensible shouting back and forth, I became aware of a man approaching from above.

'*Are you the mountain rescue?*'

'*No, I work in the forest.*'

He was great, this Jim, dragged from his TV, still in his indoor shoes. He led me down an invisible crack containing the cable to the mast, joking all the time, straight to the wide gully and to the safe flat ground which had seemed so unattainable for a long two hours. I was so thrilled to be on safe ground I could have kissed him, and the dog as well.

Ben Lomond from the east

Ben Vorlich

——— Central Scotland ———

North of the River Clyde and Forth-Clyde Canal, south of Flanders Moss, Strath Allan and River Earn

Marilyns:	19
Highest and most prominent:	Ben Cleuch, 720.8m
Lowest:	Mount Hill, 222m
Least prominent:	Cairnie Hill, drop 150.4m

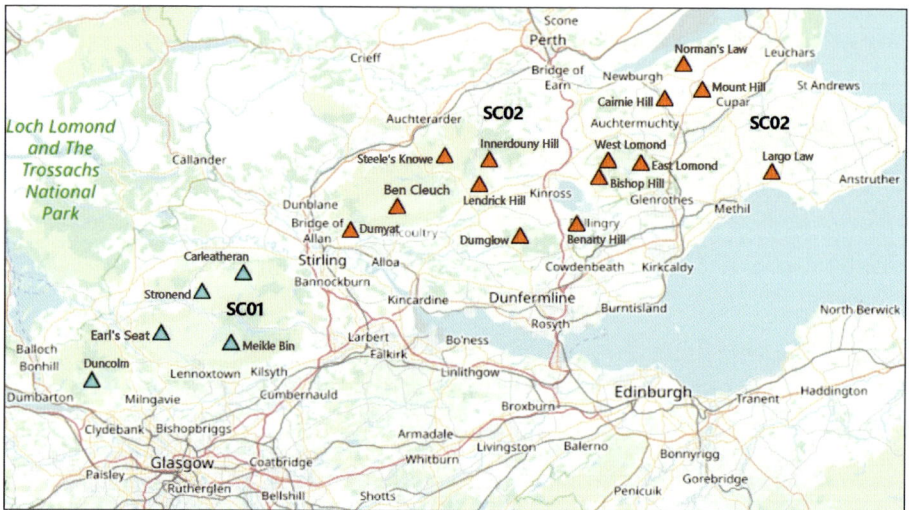

The boundaries of this regions are defined by topography not geology and plate tectonics, so it resolves some anomalies in the old region 26. Craigowl Hill, King's Seat and Turin Hill are now in hill area HE15. They are not Highland hills but fit better in the Eastern Highlands than Central Scotland. Moncreiffe Hill is included in the Southern Highlands East region as it is north of the River Earn.

Innerdouny Hill from White Creich Hill

Number		Height	Name	Drop	Location	Summit
1656	T	578.2	Earl's Seat	510	NS 5698 8380	Trig
1657		570	Meikle Bin	237	NS 6672 8217	Trig
1659	T	511.6	Stronend	286	NS 6292 8947	Trig
1661	T	485.3	Carleatheran	168	NS 6879 9187	Trig
1668	LT	401.1	Duncolm	305.4	NS 4708 7748	Trig

Earl's Seat

Three km west of Earl's Seat is the popular pimple of Dumgoyne, which people have been known to climb over 1000 times, but few of those ascents have involved carrying on to the highest point of the Campsie Fells, where the terrain could be politely described as disappointing. There is a reasonably interesting approach from the north, via Corrie of Balglass, and a reasonably easy approach from Ballagan farm to the south, but the best feature is Clachertyfarlie Knowes, an ordinary lump worth visiting for its fabulous name.

Duncolm

ALAN DAWSON, JULY 1994

I took part in one of my rare media appearances while climbing this hill, as I was being interviewed by James Shaw of BBC Radio as we walked up. It was publicity for a Summit Sweep organised by the John Muir Trust. I had suggested this event although it's not clear why, as hardly any Marilyns had a litter problem, possibly because not many people were climbing them at the time. We did pick up some rubbish but it had been dumped near the roadside at the start and had not been dropped by walkers. I doubt if we got halfway up the hill during the interview. Four months later I returned and made it all the way to the summit, but I didn't notice any litter on the way. Duncolm was my nearest Marilyn when I lived in Glasgow but I only bothered to climb it once, in contrast to Colin Crawford who made his 100th ascent in 2024.

Stronend

CRAIG WELDON, FEBRUARY 1998

We had all been up Earl's Seat before, so Stronend was chosen as the half-day's objective. With little expectation except a short workout and some fresh air, we parked up a couple miles east of Fintry and headed up steepening grassy slopes to a line of cliffs.

There is a line of weakness in the cliffs, so we go and investigate and climb higher into a tiny hidden, broken corrie, made of friable volcanic rock. An unexpected treat. We are all standing at different levels when Brian, off to one side, makes a discovery. A cave. He wanders in and we follow him. I am last. Above me, I see his head pop over the line of the cliffs. The cave turns out not to be a cave at all, but a steep-floored chimney, the rock of the cliff face flaking away from the bedrock to create a fissure. I pull on tough heather roots in this dark, claustrophobic space to get to the top and have to be hauled up the last step by my more nimble friends. And then my head pops up through the heather, and I am on top of the cliff edge with the others. Covered in dirt, we laugh, and head uneventfully for the summit of Stronend, with a fine wide view of the edge of the Highlands across the Carse of Forth this February day.

SC02 Cleuch-largo

Number		Height	Name	Drop	Location	Summit
1642	A	720.8	Ben Cleuch	595	NN 9027 0064	Trig
1667		419	Dumyat	192	NS 8354 9769	Rock
1658		522	West Lomond	405	NO 1973 0663	Trig
1663		461	Bishop Hill	179	NO 1854 0437	Cairn
1666		448	East Lomond	155	NO 2441 0618	Grass by viewfinder
1660		497	Innerdouny Hill	228	NO 0321 0732	Trig
1664		456	Lendrick Hill	222	NO 0191 0370	Cairn
1662	A	485.6	Steele's Knowe	178	NN 9694 0799	Trig
1669		379	Dumglow	252	NT 0759 9650	Cairn
1671		356	Benarty Hill	228	NT 1537 9788	Trig
1672	T	290.3	Largo Law	196	NO 4270 0497	Trig
1673		285	Norman's Law	210	NO 3050 2021	Shelter
1675	GA	228.9	Cairnie Hill	150.4	NO 2793 1548	Grass
1677	A	222.1	Mount Hill	162.6	NO 3308 1648	Grass near tower

Benarty Hill

This fine hill near the edge of Loch Leven is well-known for the bird reserve and cafe at its foot. The area south of the hill has a long history as a communist enclave. The West Fife constituency elected Britain's last Communist MP, Willie Gallacher, between 1935 and 1950, and the communists won twelve seats on the Lochgelly and Cowdenbeath council in 1973. In 2015 a communist councillor, Willie Clarke, was still active in the area.

Innerdouny Hill

ROWLAND BOWKER, 1995

I do not consider there is as such a thing as the 'worst hill' (at least not encountered so far). There are a number of hills I have climbed more than once, and on different ascents I have disliked them or thought they were superb. Much depends on weather conditions, mood, foot problems or company (solitude is often best). However, I think my worst memory is Innerdouny Hill, for two reasons – foul underfoot conditions and failure to get to the top, partly due to time shortage as we had a dinner engagement in Stirling.

Mount Hill

BILL FAIRMANER, 2008

A highlight of the year was a revisit to Mount Hill, for as we wandered round the base of the monument, a visitor emerged from the doorway and asked if we would like to go up. Torches would have been useful for finding our way up the staircase, for the blackness was oppressive at times. There was a panoramic view from the top, with Norman's Law looking particularly fine.

Norman's Law

ALAN DAWSON, MAY 2009

This modest hill offers an easy walk via woodlands or Whirly Kips, with views over a diverse landscape, villages and distant mountains. It was an ideal choice for a stroll with a small group to celebrate Val Hamilton's 600th Marilyn and entry to the Hall of Fame.

Norman's Law

John Barnard surveying the Cairnie Hill col in 2012. The railway cutting helped it to qualify by 40cm.

A rare game of trig cricket on Lendrick Hill in 2005

—— Arran, Bute and Ailsa Craig ——

Marilyns:	14
Highest and most prominent:	Goat Fell, Arran, 875.1m
Lowest:	Windy Hill, Bute, 278.7m
Least prominent:	Sail Chalmadale, Arran, 150.5m

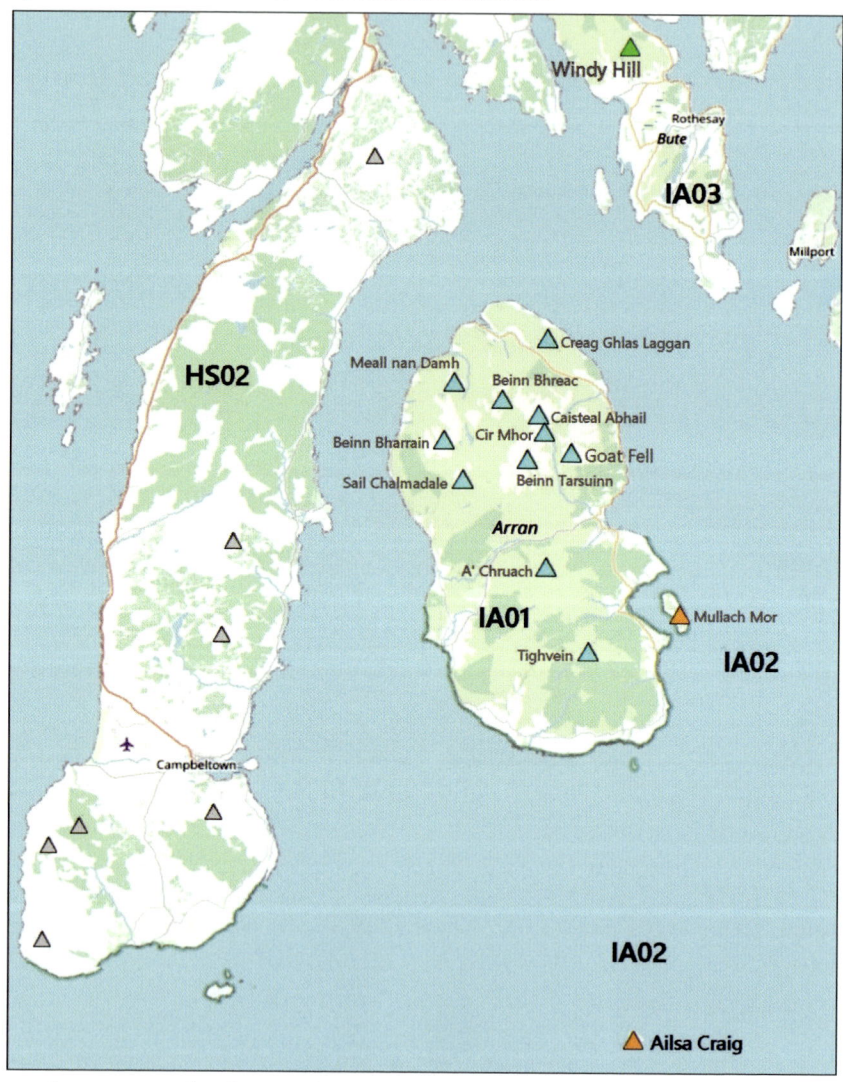

On the western side of Arran the highest hill is Bharrain
It's a pleasure not a duty to appreciate its beauty
For Ailsa the boat sails from Girvan, but the ocean is never a servant
The landing can often be tricky, the crossing sometimes sicky

IA01 Arran

Number		Height	Name	Drop	Location	Summit
1472	A	875.1	Goat Fell	875.1	NR 9914 4153	Boulder near trig
1473	A	859.0	Caisteal Abhail	428.6	NR 9690 4432	Outcrop
1474	A	826.0	Beinn Tarsuinn	236.9	NR 9595 4120	Outcrop
1475	A	798.1	Cir Mhor	176.6	NR 9727 4311	Rock
1476	A	721.4	Beinn Bharrain	387.2	NR 9019 4277	Trig
1478	L	570.2	Meall nan Damh	178.6	NR 9109 4689	Cairn
1482	G	479.7	Sail Chalmadale ***	150.5	NR 9143 4009	Rock by cairn
1477	L	574.1	Beinn Bhreac	215	NR 9433 4554	Rock
1479	G	555.9	Beinn Tarsuinn	148.5	NR 9307 4517	Rock
1484	LT	443.5	Creag Ghlas Laggan	241.2	NR 9771 4973	Trig
1480	AJ	512.5	A' Chruach	278.4	NR 9697 3355	Cairn
1483	LT	458.3	Tighvein	183.1	NR 9977 2741	Rock by trig

IA02 Holy Island and Ailsa Craig

Number		Height	Name	Drop	Location	Summit
1485		314	Mullach Mor, Holy Island	314	NS 0631 2974	Rock by trig
1731	T	338.7	Ailsa Craig	338.7	NX 0190 9983	Outcrop near trig

IA03 Bute

Number		Height	Name	Drop	Location	Summit
1447	T	278.7	Windy Hill	278.7	NS 0435 6985	Grass near trig

Goat Fell

OS maps showed the height as 874m but Lidar data showed an 875m point at the summit, for a boulder half a metre higher than the OS trig figure. In 2023 a GNSS survey confirmed this to be correct. Lidar had got the height of Caisteal Abhail wildly wrong, showing it as only 850m, so the Goat Fell survey result was reassuring confirmation of Lidar accuracy.

Sail Chalmadale

In 2008 this was the first Marilyn to be discovered by a GNSS survey, thanks to the work of John Barnard and Graham Jackson of G&J Surveys. They also surveyed the lower Beinn Tarsuinn but found it to be 1.5m short of qualification.

Cir Mhor

DENISE CLARK, SEPTEMBER 2000

We were nearly at the top of Cir Mhor when I slipped on a gravelly slab on the path, snapping my femur six inches above the knee. Two hours later I was in a helicopter heading for hospital at Kilmarnock. The assurance of the members of the Arran Mountain Rescue Team that I would soon be back on the mountains helped to get me through this traumatic experience. I had a pin inserted from the hip to the knee but the bone would not heal and the operation had be re-done in Leicester in February 2001.

Cir Mhor

The main Arran ridge from Beinn Bharrain

Meall nan Damh

Beinn Bhreac

TONY SMITH, JULY 2009

I had planned that my final Corbett, Benvane, and my 1000th Marilyn would be climbed on 22 August. The reality turned out to be rather different. On my 989th, Beinn Bhreac, about five minutes from the Lochranza road on a good path, I misplaced my footing, dislocated an ankle, and broke tibia and fibia. After excellent work by Arran Mountain Rescue Team and Ayrshire NHS, I was on the road to recovery and making plans for 2010.

A' Chruach

ALAN DAWSON, APRIL 2016

A survey confirmed this hill to be higher than nearby Ard Bheinn, by half a metre. It was one of the rare hills where I found a visitors' book on the summit, hidden within a small cairn. It was damp and musty but I made a note of some readable contributions.

Victoria Morris: Second geocache of the day. I'm actually looking for relative hills.

John Barrowman, 6 July 2014: My 887th Marilyn.

Chris Osmond, 18 Aug 2014: Great viewpoint for such a featureless hill. Another tick in the book.

David Milbank, Aberdeen, 11 Sep 2014: Please get a sharpener for this pencil. Arran is great.

Adrienne and Gordon Coventry, 30 Sep 2014: Our 1096th Marilyn.

Mullach Mor, Holy Island

JON METCALF, 2000

We were met by a member of the community, who told us a bit about the place and asked that we didn't disturb a retreat at the far end of the island, otherwise it was unrestricted access. We went over the hill (narrow at the top) and down to the far end of the island. There were large fissures near the path down to the lighthouse, which were cordoned off with plastic tape. We came back round the west coast path, which was naturally beautiful and adorned with Buddhist paintings on rocks and carvings in the caves.

Ailsa Craig

BRIAN EWING, JULY 2005

Having failed to arrange passage on a number of occasions, I received a phone call from Mark McCrindle in Girvan saying he could fit me in on a sailing to Ailsa Craig the following day. His Saturday sailing had not been able to land because the wind had been blowing from the wrong direction, so on the Sunday I was fitted in with members of Kilmarnock and Loudon Ramblers for the trip. It was sunny and the sea was calm. While we were exploring the island, Mark had been lifting his lobster creels, so I got two lovely live lobsters for my dinner that night. You certainly don't get that on a CalMac ferry.

ANDY HYAMS, APRIL 2014

Sometimes your past and your future flash before your eyes. I was on a small open boat between Girvan and Ailsa Craig, being very seasick, when the first thing to flash before my eyes was my breakfast. My fellow travellers all seemed to be coping much better than me. The boatman decided that it was too rough to land, circled the island and then headed back to Girvan, while I began to contemplate the future, in between bouts of retching. If I were to continue prioritising Marilyns it would require many more such boat trips. Absolute height was to be my new goal, which would keep me on terra firma for longer. Having already climbed every Marilyn above 560m, I decided to collect my outstanding Simms and start doing 500-metre hills.

———— Southern Scotland: West ————

Land south of the Firth of Clyde, west of the River Clyde, Clydes Burn, Evan Water and River Annan

Marilyns:	61
Highest and most prominent:	Merrick, 843m
Lowest:	Cairn Pat, 182m
Least prominent:	See Morris Hill, drop 150.0m

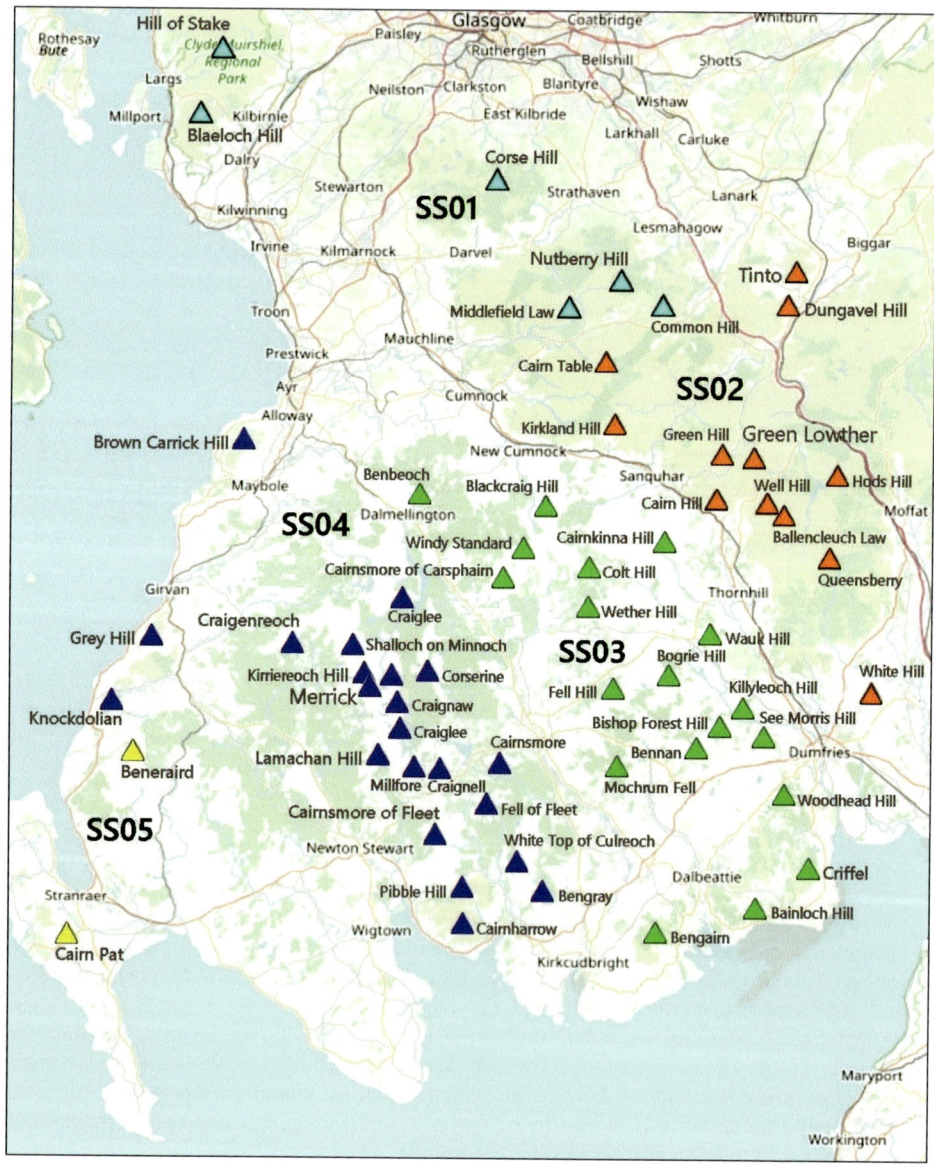

SS01 Nutberry-stake

RHB section 27A

Number		Height	Name	Drop	Location	Summit
1679	T	522.1	Hill of Stake	486	NS 2735 6300	Trig
1685		407	Blaeloch Hill	185	NS 2433 5531	Tussock
1680	T	522.6	Nutberry Hill	272	NS 7438 3382	Tussock near trig
1682		488	Common Hill	172	NS 7919 3078	Tussock near trig
1683	T	466	Middlefield Law	168	NS 6810 3072	Cairn by trig
1686	T	375.6	Corse Hill	173	NS 5983 4646	Trig

Hill of Stake

This is the lowest of the 542 Marilyns with height and prominence adding up to over 1000 (the Thousanders), but this vital information does not make the terrain any easier.

CAMPBELL SINGER, JANUARY 2009

Hill walkers often seem to be concerned about farmers and landowners being precious about access. However, there are occasions when they can be the opposite. I drove up to Muirshiel Country Park on a bleak mid-week afternoon to find the car park of the Centre surprisingly busy. Apparently there were some important European visitors who were just leaving, and a full complement of staff was on site to host the event. As I got out of the car, the Centre manager approached me from across the car park and enquired where I was off to. I told him that my objective was Hill of Stake and explained how it featured as a Marilyn. He advised me that my intended route up to the disused mine was the best, but to be careful of a recently exposed shaft. He was keen to tell me about the work of the Centre and invited me in to see a short film about hen harriers. I had a bit of time and so I went in and, without being asked, was given a large mug of tea and a biscuit. After viewing the film and asking a few questions, I was wished a pleasant afternoon and set off.

I ended up having a few navigational problems in thick mist on Queenside Muir, so when I returned to the Centre it was beginning to get dark. Another member of staff saw me opening the car, came out from the warmth of her office and asked if I would like a shower as they had excellent facilities. I didn't need to be asked twice. Warm, clean and dry, I drove back to my cousin in Perth reflecting on the kindness of certain people.

Nutberry Hill

BRENT LYNAM, NOVEMBER 2006

The forest gate was open and the sign simply said 'Please close the gate', which is what I duly did. I exercised caution and parked up when the mud started to thicken. The mountain bike got me to the summit and back, passing the timber company van on the outward ride. The van was gone on the way back, having left the forest and locked me in. I attempted an exit via the east of the forest (easily negotiating the muddy area) but another locked gate barred my way. The chap at a bungalow in Douglas West thought that the forestry man would be back in the morning, but offered his bolt-cutters to get me out. I said I would sit out the night and treated myself to a firework show over Douglas through the car windscreen. There was no sign of the wood-cutter the next morning, so it was the bolt-cutters instead. Very impressive. I offered money for the padlock but he pointed out that the timber company had cut one of his own locks, and they continued to trundle wagons past his house hours after the agreed times, so no love lost there.

Number		Height	Name	Drop	Location	Summit
1678	A	711.6	Tinto	443	NS 9532 3437	Cairn
1681		510	Dungavel Hill	222	NS 9428 3055	Rock
1740	A	732.5	Green Lowther	424	NS 9003 1203	Trig
1776	A	573.1	Steygail	144.7	NS 8886 0843	Tussock
1775	A	588.1	Green Hill	157.8	NS 8625 1254	Tussock
1785		451	Cairn Hill	159	NS 8519 0703	Cairn by fence
1745	A	697.1	Queensberry	364	NX 9890 9974	Cairn
1746	A	691.4	Ballencleuch Law	203.9	NS 9355 0496	Fence
1772	A	606.1	Well Hill	200.5	NS 9137 0646	Grass by fence
1778	A	567.1	Hods Hill	173	NT 0008 0978	Tussock by fence
1774		593	Cairn Table	323	NS 7243 2422	Trig
1783	T	511	Kirkland Hill	163	NS 7316 1628	Grass near trig
13420	A	249.7	White Hill **	164.4	NY 0383 8333	Mound

Tinto

The height of this hill was increased by unknown prehistoric hands for uncertain reasons. The ancient summit construction is partially vegetated and has merged with whatever is left of the original summit. Almost everyone who climbs the hill walks up to the viewfinder on top of the mound and most seem to ignore the trig pillar, which is over four metres lower. The surveyed height refers to an embedded rock near the base of the viewfinder.

Ballencleuch Law

For several years there was some doubt over whether this hill was higher than nearby Rodger Law, which has a 688m trig pillar, so there was only one metre difference on the map. A survey in 2018 settled the matter as it found Ballencleuch Law to be higher by a convincing 2.9 metres.

Hods Hill

The highest point of this hill was relocated in 2006, based on OS mapping which showed a 569m spot height. However, a survey in April 2024 found this point to be under 567m and the original location to be 23cm higher. Both summits have tussocky grass that impeded measurement accuracy, and the data quality was poor owing to high wind, but the 23cm difference was sufficient evidence to move the summit back to its original 567m location.

White Hill

This gentle grassy hill was promoted in November 2021, when a survey showed its summit mound to be 20cm higher than the trig pillar on Hightown Hill, though OS maps currently show White Hill to be a metre lower. Both can easily be climbed together in a simple circuit via a track from the west, though fans of unusual names may wish to extend the walk to include Tipperwhippy Wood and T Wood, which gives the impression of being a secretive minor celebrity or a cartographic error. Anyone hoping for even more excitement by detouring north to Pinnacle Wood and Pinnacle Hill may be disappointed by the absence of pinnacles.

Well Hill

Queensberry

White Hill from Hightown Hill

RHB section 27C   OS maps 77, 78, 84

Number		Height	Name	Drop	Location	Summit
1739	T	797	Cairnsmore of Carsphairn	583	NX 5944 9800	Boulder near trig
1743	A	700.9	Blackcraig Hill	236	NS 6476 0640	Rock
1749	A	681.0	Blacklorg Hill	148.1	NS 6538 0423	Grass
1744	A	697.9	Windy Standard	212	NS 6200 0147	Trig
1779	A	569.1	Enoch Hill	144.4	NS 5621 0674	Trig
1773	T	598.6	Colt Hill	246	NX 6987 9901	Tussock near trig
1782	L	533.2	Wether Hill	245.2	NX 6964 9421	Cairn
1777	T	569.4	Criffel	489.6	NX 9572 6186	Trig
1781		554	Cairnkinna Hill	161	NS 7910 0185	Tussock near trig
1784		463	Benbeoch	161	NS 4955 0829	Cairn
1786		432	Bogrie Hill	226	NX 7892 8588	Grass by trig
1787	T	417.6	Fell Hill	184	NX 7219 8447	Cairn near trig
1788		398	Bennan	186	NX 8218 7696	Monument
1789		393	Bishop Forest Hill	176	NX 8491 7963	Rock by cairn
1790	T	391.4	Bengairn	340.0	NX 7706 5451	Outcrop by trig
1792	T	357.2	Wauk Hill	220.6	NX 8412 9094	Trig
1793	T	316.7	Mochrum Fell	153	NX 7239 7503	Trig
1795		287	Bainloch Hill	189	NX 8935 5709	Cairn on rock
1796	L	259.5	Woodhead Hill	170.0	NX 9276 7130	Cairn
1798	A	240.1	See Morris Hill	150.0	NX 9029 7795	Trig
1799	A	239.7	**Killyleoch Hill *****	151.6	NX 8785 8203	Rock

Killyleoch Hill

This hill was promoted in 2013 after a survey. The summit was near the edge of high trees but there were enough satellite signals to obtain good quality data and a conclusive result.

See Morris Hill

This was chosen as an easy hill to survey on a dull November day. The summit was simple but the col was by a hedge, underneath a large tree. I had to set up the survey point across the road and measure the offset from survey point to tree. This increased the estimated margin for error on the ground to 15cm and overall uncertainty to 20cm. The drop was surveyed as 149.90m, giving a range from 149.7m to 150.1m. I decided that this was not strong enough evidence to justify demotion, so it remained a Marilyn.

I later discovered that Lidar data showed the centre of the road to be 6cm lower than my survey result, which was remarkably close. This raised the calculated drop figure to 149.96m. It is not possible to survey a col under a roadside tree to within 10cm accuracy, so See Morris Hill marginally retained its Marilyn status with 150.0m of relative height.

Bennan

Turner's Monument on the summit looks impressive but it appears to be a monument to misery: 'On earth I wandered waiting to be free / Honest and poor I trode life's thorny way / No comfort save hope in heaven for me'. Plenty of hill baggers have grumpy tendencies but there is usually some wry humour hidden beneath the gruff exterior. John Turner did not seem to look on the bright side of his life as a cutlery maker and religious fanatic.

Benbeoch

ALAN DAWSON, DECEMBER 2001

My first ascent in 1996 was quiet and untroubled, but a revisit five years later was more dramatic. On a late Sunday afternoon in December the whole hillside was a roar of trucks and a blaze of lights. The roadside was plastered with British Coal 'keep out' notices, and so it became a challenge. We climbed a fence just west of a stream, then there was a stile over a second fence. After that it was a raid on enemy territory. The trees initially gave some cover from the guards, but once on the open-cast site the tactic was to duck and run, keeping out of the worst of the grey mud and slithering over banks and trenches. Worst moment was crossing a wide truck track in full view of searchlights, before scampering for cover amongst long grass and bushes. Fine rocky hill once we got to it. Although it had become almost surrounded by mine workings, there seemed to be no immediate threat of demolition. Descending east toward Benbain seemed to risk confrontation, so it seemed safer to return the same way. As it was almost dark, most of the trucks had quietened down for the night.

JOHN BARNARD, 2003

Having not researched Benbeoch, I decided this would be a quick up-and-down in the late afternoon via a dismantled railway track from just east of south. How wrong I was! My first attempt was along a track, starting at NS513756 on the B741. It was easy to break out to the edge of the forest, follow the edge for a while and then strike west to the hill. After ignoring the 'No Admittance' signs (standard practice), I came to a scooped-out area with large vehicles hurling truck-loads of rocks over the edge. I decided to retreat.

The next attempt was to go further east to a forestry track starting at NS523086. Following this north-west from the main road, I took the first left to reach a locked gate. There was a 'No Entry' sign and a tripod on which there looked to be a microphone. This track turned out to be dangerous, as it ended with no warning and a vertical drop of about 200ft into the mine. No way here even for the most determined.

I walked back to the locked gate and tried to go north to see if I could get in behind Benbain, but there were no forest breaks to allow a chance of access. Now totally annoyed, I abandoned the attempt, realising that the time spent messing around here could have been more effectively spent on Craiglee to the south.

While debooting at the car, a guy in a four-wheel drive vehicle came out of the forest track and stopped to talk. He told me that the mining operations had been greatly extended in the past year, and that when they finished all the trees would be flattened to make way for a large wind farm. He was just off to Castle Douglas to go to a protest meeting. Before leaving, I decided to go to reception at the mine and ask what was happening. I was told that there was absolutely no access to the hill and that this had been the case for a year, since mining operations now totally encircled the hill.

ANDY HYAMS, FEBRUARY 2012

My first Marilyn of 2012 was one of the most bizarre ever – Benbeoch, the official way. Having obtained permission from the mining company, Anne Bunn and I duly reported at the appointed time to the office a few miles away for a safety briefing and the issuing of high-visibility jackets, hard hats and walkie-talkies. We followed the engineer to a car park at the foot of the hill where we had to wait ages for a guy in a Land Rover to appear and take us to within a few hundred metres of the summit, where he waited while we bagged the hill and then ferried us back to safety. The bureaucracy was so tedious that we wished we had just sneaked in and dodged the site vehicles.

Bainloch Hill

PETER MALONE, 2006

Bainloch Hill must rate as one hill I would like to forget. The first attempt involved taking my dogs on what looked to be an easy forest track, to be faced with a huge deer farm, with notice boards displaying many rules and regulations, including NO DOGS. The next day dawned with abysmal weather for my second attempt. Having entered the deer forest I found great difficulty in finding the right cairn in rain, mist and waist-deep heather. The return was worse. Trying to follow a deer track back to the main path, I fell off a small cliff, in deep bracken, to sustain knee ligament damage, putting me out of action for several weeks.

RON BELL, 2014

My least favourite Marilyn is Bainloch Hill because I failed due to a surfeit of brambles, trees and barbed wire fences. It is in my notes simply as 'Inaccessible Marilyn'.

Kirriereoch Hill

Mullwharchar and Loch Enoch

Number		Height	Name	Drop	Location	Summit
1688		843	Merrick	705	NX 4275 8554	Trig
1691	A	786.8	**Kirriereoch Hill** ***	150.2	NX 4209 8695	Rock
1692	A	774.2	Shalloch on Minnoch	193.6	NX 4076 9056	Rock
1702	A	692.9	Mullwharchar	188	NX 4541 8663	Rock
1709	A	646.0	Craignaw	151.3	NX 4592 8333	Cairn on outcrop
1719	T	531.2	Craiglee	197	NX 4616 8013	Trig
1689	T	813.5	Corserine	487	NX 4978 8706	Trig
1697	A	716.7	Lamachan Hill	452	NX 4353 7699	Boulder
1707	A	656.1	Millfore	248	NX 4781 7546	Rock by trig
1722	L	477.5	Craignell	228.0	NX 5100 7522	Vrock
1699	A	711.1	Cairnsmore of Fleet	521	NX 5011 6704	Cairn
1723		470	Fell of Fleet	247	NX 5662 7069	Cairn
1727	A	382.7	Shaw Hill	146.9	NX 5905 7186	Heather by cairn
1718	T	565.1	Craigenreoch	177	NX 3351 9108	Trig
1720	T	523.1	Craiglee	200	NX 4707 9624	Rock by trig
1721	T	493.5	Cairnsmore	295	NX 5838 7578	Trig
1724	L	456.6	Cairnharrow	305.3	NX 5333 5610	Cairn near trig
1728		383	Pibble Hill	159	NX 5338 6051	Cairn
1729	L	367.0	Bengray	236.3	NX 6308 5983	Heather near trig
1730		344	White Top of Culreoch	157	NX 6006 6337	Cairn
1733	T	297.2	Grey Hill	154	NX 1646 9279	Trig
1734	A	295.6	Troweir Hill ¬	149.3	NX 2112 9602	Cairn
1736	T	265.2	Knockdolian	202	NX 1132 8480	Trig
1687	A	287.6	Brown Carrick Hill	226.5	NS 2835 1595	Trig

Kirriereoch Hill

The promotion of Kirriereoch Hill was no surprise, as an OS map showed two 786m spot heights on a large summit plateau. The highest point turned out to be a smooth rock to the south of the summit area, more satisfactory than either of the cairns. The col was well defined with little margin for error, giving confidence in the survey and drop of 150.2m.

Knockdolian

LINDSAY MUNRO, JULY 2004

As memorable as any of the higher hills was little Knockdolian. A carpet of beautiful grasses and flowers led up to a sharp, rugged summit with a superb view to Ailsa Craig.

Cairnharrow

AUDREY LITTERICK, 2005

On Hightown Hill I persuaded six of my fifteen organic farming students on a study tour to Galloway that they really should be going out for an evening walk to gain a better appreciation of the surrounding countryside. Then I left the students studying dairy cattle and raced off up Cairnharrow, where I was amazed to see the Isle of Man so close. I was back with the students before any of them noticed I was missing.

White Top of Culreoch

Hamish Brown, September 2002

White Top of Culreoch is not a tame hill. Its nature is quite different to near neighbours Bengray or Pibble Hill or Cairnharrow, all well-behaved Relatives. I left my camping van on the delightful road from Gatehouse of Fleet over to Laurieston, setting off at 7:30 and being back at 9:00, so the hill can't have been too bad. The outing actually proved easy, a pleasant surprise, like having a dry day when the forecast was for rain. The track was a well-made forestry effort but when it dipped I turned off to contour round Craig of Grobdale. This led to very rough ground, a mix of heather and tussock, not nice at all, then I crossed a wall and thereafter all else fell into place. The steep heather slope, with bracken and gritty runnels, was full of useful sheep trods. It was worth dropping down to follow a rough track up a wee valley till due east of the summit – all easy going.

I sat to contemplate the evil potential of the forest, which I had studied all the way up. The fence had plastic sacks tied over the barbed wire, so that was the obvious crossing. Going straight up from there to keep to a due west bearing took me only a short way into the larch before there was a hopeless tangle of wind-blown trees. I skirted left and found the larch relatively open and not even demanding my going bent double. There was then an upward stretch of clearing, before wending deeper into the spruce. By feel I bore a bit left and came on a small green knoll. Could that be it? But beyond a dip there could be another rise so I pushed on and, after several wiggles, came on a further knoll with a small cairn. Eureka! There had been only the briefest nastiness, otherwise all had been easy.

Every major forest edge with wall or fence is almost certainly going to have a sheep or deer trod along its length, so I decided to follow this straight down to the forest track. Recent tracks had flattened the bracken. This line made for a fast descent and I was back at the van in half an hour from the top, almost disappointed at not having experienced evil, of any kind. This was an example of how subjective any day can be. The hill has an abundance of nasty going – deep heather, tussocky grass, bracken, etc, in which no foot can be placed with certainty. Picking a route is a craft, and the crafty usually perform best (the dividend of experience). White Top of Culreoch was highly satisfying to me because of its challenge accepted and, largely, concluded satisfactorily.

Simon Smith, May 2006

This is the kind of hill you climb solely to get a tick in the book. As we approached the top on a cold, drizzly day, I was asking myself what on earth I was doing up there when I could have been climbing a more normal hill somewhere else. Anyway, we headed for what looked like the summit and sure enough there was a pile of twigs, which at first I thought marked the top. Upon closer inspection, the twigs were an arrow pointing towards another tree-covered knoll, which was the proper summit. The fact that someone else had suffered White Top of Culreoch and taken time to make an arrow lifted my mood considerably. As I couldn't believe anyone other than Marilyn baggers would climb this hill, I felt a real sense of camaraderie with our unknown benefactor.

Fell of Fleet

Colin Crawford, June 2002

This was Galloway roughness at its most intimidating – tall tussocks surmounting deep holes, interspersed by cloying vegetation. It did not help that I was ambushed by a drenching squall as I struggled up from the forest road to the west. Loch Fleet offered a minor mitigation, and there may be an easier route, but I won't be in a hurry to return.

Cairnsmore, Shaw Hill and Fell of Fleet

There are several candidates in this area for hill with the most unpleasant terrain of all. The summit of Cairnsmore is only just over a kilometre from a track to the north, but the terrain has been described as 'an appalling mess of long grass, tussocks, rocks and holes, giving a real taste of purgatory'. There is a track to the summit of nearby Benniguinea, but some of the ground in between the two also offers very tough going. Less than 5km to the south of Cairnsmore is Shaw Hill, which falls 3.1 metres short of Marilyn status. It has a broad track to within about 800 metres of its summit, but the terrain between track and summit is the sort where about 1km an hour represents reasonable progress. Shaw Hill is connected to Fell of Fleet, about 3km away to the south-west. Anyone looking for a challenging walk might consider a circuit over Cairnsmore, Shaw Hill and Fell of Fleet, with a crossing of the River Dee as a bonus feature, plus Rig of Craig Gilbert, Nick of Orchars and Mullgibbon to make it sound oddly intriguing. If Galloway were to become a national park, perhaps this circuit could be promoted as an attraction, offering the toughest short walk in the country. Running it would be difficult.

Troweir Hill

This hill lost its Marilyn status in 2014 after a difficult and unsatisfactory survey. The summit appeared to be suspiciously unnatural and the col was broad, rough and boggy. Two possible col locations were surveyed but the difference between them was only 7cm, whereas the drop was 70cm short of 150 metres. To make things worse, Saugh Hill was found to be about the same height, but it was impossible to be sure because its summit was covered in thick vegetation that prevented an accurate reading. It was clear that neither Troweir Hill nor Saugh Hill qualify as Marilyns, but not clear which one is higher.

SS05 Beneraird-cairn

RHB section 27B · OS maps 76, 82

Number		Height	Name	Drop	Location	Summit
1725	T	438.8	Beneraird	307	NX 1354 7851	Trig
1732	A	321.8	Carlock Hill	148.4	NX 0856 7723	Wall
1737	T	181.7	Cairn Pat	163	NX 0442 5635	Trig

This area illustrates the consequences of using topographic criteria to organise lists of hills. Looking at a road map, it would seem obvious to group together hills west of the A714 between Girvan and Wigtown. However, Grey Hill and Knockdolian are in area SS04 because they are separated from Beneraird by the River Stinchar. The key col for Grey Hill is north-east from its summit, so it is connected to the higher hills of Galloway. This leaves lonely Beneraird and lowly Cairn Pat as the only Marilyns in SS05. The two areas could have been combined for Marilyn purposes, but SS05 includes a hundred Tumps so the two areas are best kept separate for the overall topographic scheme.

Cairn Pat

This is a metre higher than Airds Hill, the lowest Marilyn in mainland Scotland. It offers a simple walk up a road to a mast and trig pillar, a good viewpoint over the Irish Sea and an opportunity for nominative bagging. However, as yet there is no record of anyone called Pat or Cairns climbing it as their 600th Marilyn. Chris Crocker's 600th was Crock and Peter Drummond's 600th was Drummond Hill, but few others with suitable names have had the inclination to synchronise their own name and that of their landmark hill.

—— Southern Scotland: East ——

Land south of the Forth-Clyde canal and Firth of Forth, east of the River Clyde and River Annan

Marilyns:	54
Highest and most prominent:	Broad Law, 840.1m
Lowest:	North Berwick Law, 187m
Least prominent:	Lamberton Hill, drop 150.4m

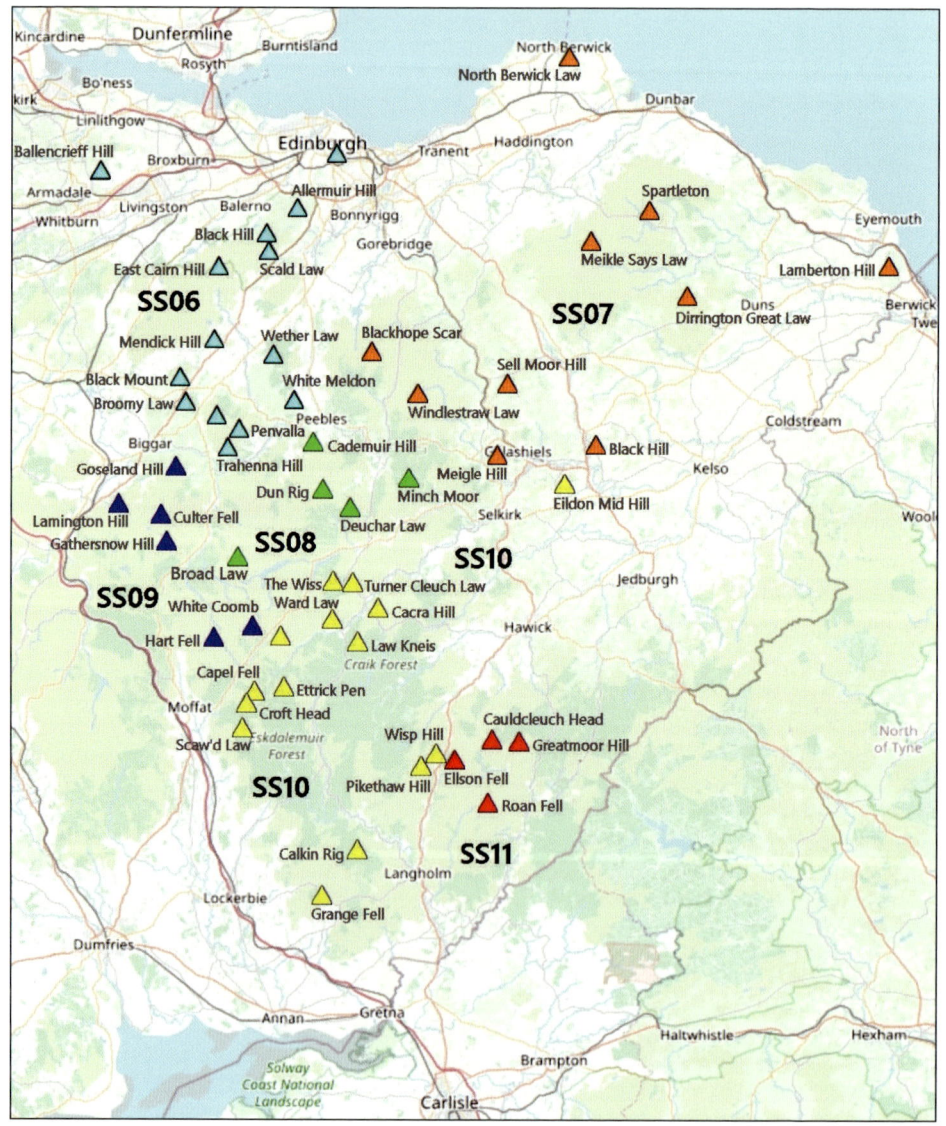

RHB section 28A   OS maps 65, 66, 72

Number		Height	Name	Drop	Location	Summit
1807	T	578.8	Scald Law	313	NT 1917 6108	Trig
1809	A	565.9	East Cairn Hill **	168	NT 1280 5931	Cairn
1815		501	Black Hill	184	NT 1882 6317	Cairn
1816	T	493.5	Allermuir Hill	236	NT 2270 6617	Trig
1808	T	570.6	Broughton Heights	347	NT 1229 4109	Trig
1811		549	Trahenna Hill	165	NT 1359 3740	Cairn
1812	L	537.5	Penvalla	188.1	NT 1505 3958	Grass
1814	T	515.7	Black Mount	258	NT 0799 4596	Trig
1822		426	Broomy Law	165	NT 0854 4287	Mast and fence
1817	T	478.6	Wether Law	209	NT 1946 4837	Trig
1820	T	451.5	Mendick Hill	165	NT 1215 5053	Grass by trig
1821	T	427.3	White Meldon	157.6	NT 2193 4284	Rock by trig
1827	L	312.0	Ballencrieff Hill #	167.9	NS 9875 7114	Grass by trig
1828	T	251	Arthur's Seat	174	NT 2753 7294	Rock by trig

East Cairn Hill

This was a significant omission from the first edition of RHB, which listed West Cairn Hill as a Marilyn, although large-scale OS maps showed it to be five metres lower than East Cairn Hill. The OS Landranger map at the time was not helpful as it showed only a 561m spot height in a contour ring west of the highest point, which is a small cairn just north of a wall that runs over the summit area. A survey later confirmed it is higher than West Cairn Hill, though by four metres, not five. It feels like a marginal hill, on the edge of the Pentlands and local authority boundaries, with extensive views over the low ground of the central belt toward the Firth of Forth. The obvious route to East Cairn Hill shown on OS maps is via a track to the north, but there is also a path from the south which may offer a more appealing circuit over East and West Cairn Hill, starting from Baddinsgill and taking in the grassy summits of Mount Maw, The Mount and Wether Law.

Broomy Law

RICHARD SPEIRS, DECEMBER 2010

Winter required much shovelling of snow, with walking restricted to hills close to a road to the south of Edinburgh. This gave rise to the amusing task of reporting an open door on an electrical cabinet belonging to Orange on the top of Broomy Law, to an operative in a Mumbai call centre. It appeared that they could not search by grid reference, but required either their own site reference number or a postcode. I tried to explain that there was not much call for delivering mail to the top of a hill, and suggested that they search online for the postcode for Biggar. Amazingly, this allowed them to identify the correct set of masts.

Ballencrieff Hill

This hill north of Bathgate was renamed in 2024. The summit is about 600 metres south of the mast and antiquity on top of Cairnpapple Hill. The name Ballencrieff Hill is shown in the OS trig point database but omitted from most OS maps.

Allermuir Hill

Broughton Heights

White Meldon

SS07 Windlestraw-lammerlaw

RHB section 28A

OS maps 66, 67, 73, 74

Number		Height	Name	Drop	Location	Summit
1800	A	659.2	Windlestraw Law	459.7	NT 3712 4309	Tussock
1802	A	651.8	Blackhope Scar	283	NT 3151 4833	Tussock near trig
1813	T	534.9	Meikle Says Law	267	NT 5812 6173	Trig
1819		468	Spartleton	156	NT 6532 6554	Cairn by trig
1823	A	423.9	Sell Moor Hill ***	150.7	NT 4803 4446	Tussock
1824	T	422.8	Meigle Hill	256	NT 4662 3600	Grass by trig
1825		399	Dirrington Great Law	157	NT 6983 5492	Cairn
1826	T	314.5	Black Hill	171	NT 5855 3701	Trig
1944	A	217.1	Lamberton Hill ***	150.4	NT 9444 5865	Grass
1829	T	187.2	North Berwick Law	168	NT 5563 8422	Outcrop by trig

Meikle Says Law

JON FOOTE, OCTOBER 2004

Meikle Says Law had the highest ratio of effort to enjoyment all year. It was bleak, the track was not as easy to follow on the ground as on the map, and a dessicated hare corpse would have made a perfect picture commentary if I had taken a camera.

Windlestraw Law

DONALD SHIACH, 2006

Highlight of the year was, surprisingly, Windlestraw Law, from Holylee in the Tweed valley. It was not a particularly exciting ascent, but the view suddenly resolved itself twenty metres from the trig point into a clear and stunning panorama over Edinburgh, North Berwick, Fife, etc. This was quite unexpected and helped me to cope with the complaints from a non-bagging brother-in-law.

North Berwick Law

MILES HUTCHINSON, SEPTEMBER 2012

Having reserved North Berwick Law to be my 1000th Marilyn, this geriatric member finally made it on 1 September 2012. I was accompanied by my granddaughter and several good friends.

ALAN CASTLE, 2014

A short detour from the John Muir Way, which I walked from east to west in spring. My excursion onto North Berwick Law was sheer joy. The view out into the Firth of Forth, dotted with its several islands, was a delight.

Meigle Hill

This hill can easily be reached via a track through a farmyard at Clovenfords, 4km from Galashiels. It offers a routine and innocuous short walk, but there have been reports that some baggers have driven to the top, either with or without permission from the farmer. Those observed doing so have been reported to the hill bagging authorities and issued with a reprimand, a fine and a warning about their future conduct. Hills referred to as 'drive-ups' are an accepted part of the game, but Meigle Hill pushes the concept beyond the bounds of acceptability, casting a shadow of shame over innocent hill baggers.

Lamberton Hill

ALAN DAWSON, JUNE 2013

This hill became the first Marilyn I discovered by GNSS surveying, though G&J Surveys had earlier found Sail Chalmadale on Arran, Mynydd y Cwm in North Wales and Creag na Criche in Perthshire. It was my first walk after a knee arthroscopy to remove some torn cartilage that had been troubling me for over a year. As I hobbled up, I met a man in a caravan and asked him about the name of the hill he was living on, which I had been referring to as Ayton Hill. It was a useful start. The grassy walk was easy but climbing over a fence was awkward. Cows in the summit field did not bother me but one of them kicked over the Leica controller while I was waiting by the field edge. The antenna was undisturbed and carried on recording data, so I did not have to start again.

Surveying a summit is usually relatively straightforward compared to a col. With a summit you tend to know roughly what to expect, and most summits have something positive to offer. With a col you never know what it is going to be like until you get there, and that uncertainty can be part of the appeal, in theory if not always in practice. Maps may offer clues but they do not tell you whether you are going to find grass, heather, peat bog or something else. This variety can enhance the enjoyment of col surveying.

The map of the col area for Lamberton Hill showed a small area of water near a gap between two burns. This turned out to be a reclaimed quarry that appeared to be a rural boating lake, with a hut, a dinghy, a jetty and even a narrow beach. It all looked idyllic on a sunny June day. The col itself had a small unmapped pond that looked like an unofficial bird reserve, with a row of hides overlooking the water and flourishing vegetation. It was not feasible to set up a survey point inside the fenced-off pond area, but readings were taken in the flat fields either side, and both of them showed the col to be over 150m lower than the summit. The successful leg rehabilitation had a satisfying outcome.

Sell Moor Hill

ALAN DAWSON, JULY 2013

This hill was promoted to a Marilyn in 1995 based on map research, but it was a marginal judgement and a survey was required to check its status. Even if maps are accurate and up-to-date, they cannot identify the specific point that separates one hill from another and is the optimum point to set up a col survey. Working out which is the highest point of a hill can take some time, yet summits are easy compared to cols. Water is often the biggest clue to finding the optimum location. Observing the way water flows and where it settles can help eliminate numerous false bottoms, but there was no water visible at the col for Sell Moor Hill. The map of the col area showed nothing at all. It was an unknown quantity that turned out to be almost impossible to survey. The col contained a large area of impenetrable bushes, trees and shrubs surrounded by long lush grass that could swallow a survey pole without trace and possibly a person as well. I walked around the jungle but could not penetrate the trees or set up a survey within them. In the end I waded into a thicket and pushed in my metre-long pole until it just poked out above the vegetation. I retreated to shorter grass but there was no wind and I was pursued by all kinds of blood-sucking predators for an hour as I tried to keep moving during the survey.

In 2022, Lidar data indicated that my col survey had been in the wrong place and had recorded the wrong height, by over a metre. The drop was reduced from 152m to 150.7m, but Sell Moor Hill survived as a Marilyn and I had survived its trauma. It had been utterly unpleasant, my worst col experience ever, even after over two thousand more col surveys.

SS08 Broadlaw-minchmoor

Number		Height	Name	Drop	Location	Summit
1830	A	840.1	Broad Law	653.5	NT 1464 2353	Trig
1831	A	830.2	Cramalt Craig	147.4	NT 1684 2473	Grass
1845	A	742.7	Dun Rig	242	NT 2531 3155	Tussock
1923		543	Deuchar Law	155	NT 2850 2970	Cairn
1919	T	566.6	Minch Moor	212	NT 3586 3305	Trig
1924	A	543.9	Mountbenger Law	145.1	NT 3120 2757	Cairn
1939	L	415.1	Cademuir Hill	201.6	NT 2419 3769	Trees

Broad Law

Broad Law is the highest point of a vast area of land south of Stirling and north of Cross Fell in the Northern Pennines. The col that separates it from Merrick, the only higher hill in Southern Scotland, is between Cumnock and New Cumnock in East Ayrshire, well to the west of the M74. This mean that the territory of Broad Law is much larger than the territory of Merrick. Other than that, Broad Law is notable for having a track almost all the way to the top, where there is one of the strangest of all summit constructions. The air traffic control beacon has been there for well over forty years but it looks as though it landed from a another planet fairly recently.

MARK SMITH, JUNE 2009

Broad Law was done as a day trip from home in Surrey using Scotrail's sleeper service and the community bus that operated between Annan and Peebles once a month.

Cramalt Craig

This hill has never been a Marilyn but it was listed as a Corbett until 1981, along with Kirriereoch Hill, which is now the only Marilyn of Corbett height that is not a Corbett.

Deuchar Law

NEIL STEWART, JULY 2010

When I suffered a heart attack in 2005, in Orkney while on a business trip, I reckoned that my hill walking days were over. A week later I flew to Glasgow on a day of outstanding clarity. Looking to the west, all of the distinctive peaks of Sutherland stood out sharp and clear. I was thankful that I was still around to see them, but I did wonder if I would ever be able to stand on their summits again. While I was recuperating, I found a reference on the web to Marilyns and saw that there was a book on the subject. It was to prove an inspiration to me to keep going with my hill walking and an encouragement to walk in many new areas. I saw that reaching 600 summits entitled me to an entry in a Hall of Fame. What more encouragement could I have to get back to hill fitness?

A few months after my illness, I made my way slowly and tentatively up Dumyat from the high point on the Sherriffmuir road. The feeling when I reached the trig was almost indescribable – a mixture of relief and elation. My hill walking activities were not over. By the start of 2010, the Hall of Fame was in sight. As I did a lot of hill walking on my own and didn't like making a fuss, I decided that my 600th should be no different from any other hill. I had no definite objective in mind – it was so good reaching the Hall of Fame that I was not fussed about the doorway. In the event, it turned out to be Deuchar Law in the Borders. It was a pleasant walk, with the added attraction of a gorge and a wee loch.

Black Hill

North Berwick Law

Ettrick Pen

Number		Height	Name	Drop	Location	Summit
1832	A	821.6	White Coomb	375	NT 1632 1509	Cairn
1835	T	808.1	Hart Fell	200	NT 1136 1357	Trig
1843	A	748.4	Culter Fell	350	NT 0528 2908	Fence by trig
1870	A	689.5	Gathersnow Hill	210.6	NT 0587 2569	Cairn by fence
1931	T	492.4	Lamington Hill	161	NT 0016 3048	Grass by trig
1936		435	Goseland Hill	202.8	NT 0711 3510	Trig

Hart Fell

ALAN CASTLE, 2009

When we relocated to live in Scotland, it never entered my head that I would still be living in the southern half of Britain. On moving north of the border in 2002, Beryl and I lived in Dumfries for a year before moving to a rural location in the Moffat hills. According to one analysis, the centre point of Britain was reckoned to be close to Moffat. If this was correct, then our Dumfries abode was in southern Britain, but my present home might just be in the northern half of Britain. It would be of interest to quite a few Scots to learn that a substantial part of Scotland lies in the southern half of Britain.

I had some concern that the actual centre would lie in the middle of an impenetrable forestry plantation, but GPS showed that the magic spot lay in a small clearing in the trees. And was it worth the effort? Was it hell, but I was pleased that my local Marilyn, the very fine Hart Fell, was so close to being the most central Marilyn of Britain. It is around 610km further north than Western Rocks near St Agnes and Great Wingletang in the Isles of Scilly, and about 610km further south than Out Stack, just north of Unst.

Lamington Hill

PAUL RICHARDSON, AUGUST 2003

I had reached that point in my chemotherapy regime when I should be at my strongest. We decide on a weekend in Biggar but cannot get accommodation in Biggar and go instead to Abington. The hotel is mediocre and I feel unwell. The weekend is off to a poor start. The next morning is hot and sunny. We drive to the attractive hamlet of Lamington to climb its eponymous hill less than a thousand feet above. Surely I can manage this.

Things begin badly when we select the wrong track heading up through woods. Our track peters out and we are left floundering about in the trees. Eventually we escape over a fence to a newly-mown hay field. We try to avoid a farmer cutting another field as we climb up beside the woodland edge. I am not doing too badly but we take a rest before following a broad, grassy, unmapped track up to the trig pillar at the summit. On the one hand are the Culter Fells, merging in the distance into the Lowthers. Tinto is prominent, neighboured by a lump subsequently identified as Dunvagel Hill. It is pleasant up here, the heat moderated by a pleasant breeze. I lie down for half an hour. Another rest on the way down, after which we find the right track which leads easily through the woods. We return to the hotel, where I flop on the bed and remain there as long as possible. Later we go to Biggar, but my stomach pain and utter weariness cut the evening short. Things are no better the next morning and we are forced to go straight home after what might in better days have been considered a poor weekend. But now, everything is a bonus.

Number		Height	Name	Drop	Location	Summit
1865	A	691.8	Ettrick Pen	356.3	NT 1999 0764	Cairn
1875	A	678.3	Capel Fell	159.3	NT 1639 0690	Tussock
1876	A	677.3	Andrewhinney Hill	194	NT 1975 1387	Tussock
1894	A	636.2	Croft Head	194.0	NT 1530 0565	Grass
1922	A	549.7	Scaw'd Fell	158.2	NT 1494 0280	Heather by post
1915	T	595.4	Wisp Hill	262	NY 3864 9934	Fence by trig
1920		564	Pikethaw Hill	225	NY 3696 9777	Cairn
1916		594	Ward Law	158	NT 2623 1595	Cairn
1917	T	589.2	The Wiss	170	NT 2645 2062	Trig
1921	A	551.0	Turner Cleuch Law	179	NT 2874 2044	Tussock
1929	A	501.7	Fastheugh Hill	144.9	NT 3932 2771	Heather
1930	L	498.5	Law Kneis	186.7	NT 2927 1308	Tussock
1932	L	471.6	Cacra Hill	166.9	NT 3176 1733	Cairn
1933		451	Calkin Rig	230	NY 2889 8762	Fire-break
1942	LT	319.3	Grange Fell	152.1	NY 2440 8192	Grass near trig
1938	T	422.3	Eildon Mid Hill	172.4	NT 5482 3228	Trig and viewfinder

Law Kneis

CHRIS UPSON, 1999

I encountered a totally insane, violently abusive and threatening lunatic at the Deephope footbridge across the Ettrick Water by Law Kneis. I spent several unpleasant minutes being violently threatened and abused and physically pushed around, then spent the afternoon travelling to Selkirk police station to give a statement and file a charge for assault. I then went back and bagged Law Kneis by a different route, from the north-east.

Turner Cleuch Law

ALAN DAWSON, MARCH 1995

This hill was Rowland Bowker's 1000th Marilyn, the first Marilyn landmark celebration and my first meeting with him and Ann. I returned twenty years later to confirm that it is definitely a Marilyn, as my survey showed it to be 60cm higher than Black Knowe Head.

Fastheugh Hill

ALAN DAWSON, MARCH 2012

This was the first hill I surveyed and it qualifies as a Submarilyn by the narrowest of margins, a compiler's call. Its col was on a track and I measured it twice, on the way up and on the way down. The two height figures were found to be within one centimetre of each other, which provided great confidence in the accuracy of the survey process.

Eildon Mid Hill

DEREK SIME, SEPTEMBER 2015

Having worked on the new Borders Railway for over three years, I thought it would be appropriate once the line opened to take the train to the Borders hills. I headed for the Eildon Hills from Tweedbank station on a fine sunny day, and a week later for the somewhat nondescript Sell Moor Hill from Stow station.

Number		Height	Name	Drop	Location	Summit
1906	A	618.6	Cauldcleuch Head	256	NT 4564 0068	Tussock by fence
1914	T	599.3	Greatmoor Hill	163	NT 4898 0068	Trig
1925		537	Ellson Fell	163	NY 4103 9849	Tussock
1918		568	Roan Fell	258	NY 4517 9311	Cairn
1926	A	521.5	Arkleton Hill	147.5	NY 4052 9218	Tussock

Cauldcleuch Head

ANN BOWKER, AUGUST 1993

These Southern Upland ridges are rough and rolling, with peat hags their major hazard. This one was particularly twisted, writhing its way over Tudhope Hill, Millstone Edge and Langtae Hill to the flat summit plateau of Cauldcleuch Head. The greatest attraction was the loneliness and the spaciousness, though these were somewhat spoiled by the forest which covers the northern slopes hereabouts. Few walkers wander these empty hills.

We continued as far as Greatmoor Hill, another of Dawson's summits, then swung south-east to join the track alongside the Braidley Burn. The road walk back was not unpleasant on this very quiet lane, in fact it turned out to be the highlight of the day as we had a marvellous close-up view of a fox on the parapet of the bridge at Billhope.

GILL STEPHENS, JANUARY 2020

A squalid, filthy walk. Both legs up to the knee in bogs at different times, a fight with a gate (I lost), followed by a walk down a very muddy farm track. At least the fog cleared while I was at the top of Cauldcleuch Head. The name and appearance was reminiscent of a pimple or boil waiting to be lanced and drained. Glad I chose a circuit, as climbing and descending the same way would be a recipe for suicide. Great relief to get onto decent terrain going up Greatmoor Hill, except for a short stretch of hags about halfway up.

COLIN CRAWFORD, FEBRUARY 2020

Sixth visit. Why do I keep punishing myself on this dreary hill?

ALAN DAWSON, OCTOBER 2021

Approaching from Priesthaugh, the terrain was not too bad but the wind cranked up to another level, so I loitered in the trees a while to postpone the full onslaught. I cagily crept along through the trees until the way was blocked. The wind was getting stronger and the rain was not going away, so I had to move on up or retreat through the trees. I pulled my two hoods tight, staggered out and stepped over the fence. There was a bit of a path but landing my feet on it was not easy as the wind was coming from my left and blowing me sideways. I tried to use my pole for stability but I sometimes missed the ground with it as the pole was almost torn from my grasp.

The path deteriorated into lumpy bog but my wellies did their job and eventually a gate appeared with a pole marking the pitiful summit. I felt no elation at being there. The outlook was one of utter bleakness as I stood there for twenty minutes for a survey, but I noted a familiar feeling of grim satisfaction at having done what I set out to do.

By the time I got back to the car the rain had stopped. Before changing out of wet clothes I drove 20km east to fit in a quick survey of Belling Hill before heading home.

—— Cheviot Hills ——

Land east of Liddesdale, south of the Teviot and Tweed, north of River Irthing, Tipalt Burn, River Tyne

Marilyns:	14
Highest and most prominent:	The Cheviot, 815m, drop 556m
Lowest:	Housedon Hill, 268.3m
Least prominent:	Belling Hill, drop 151.6m

Lucy Leonelli on the way up Peel Feel

David Robinson

We guys who hills in Blighty bag might shy away from Sighty Crag
It surely is a mighty drag, enough to make the sprightly flag
When faced with forest, mire and hag, shrouded in a whity clag
But conquer and you'll rightly brag 'I found the top of Sighty Crag!'

Number		Height	Name	Drop	Location	Summit
2302		815	The Cheviot	556	NT 9090 2052	Trig
2306	A	714.4	Hedgehope Hill ¬	147.3	NT 9438 1980	Cairn
2309	A	616.2	Cushat Law ¬	148.7	NT 9282 1374	Tussock
2314	LT	501	Shillhope Law	159	NT 8731 0967	Trig
1934	T	449	Hownam Law	167	NT 7965 2192	Cairn by trig
1943	T	282.2	Linton Hill	176	NT 7873 2795	Trig
2315	LT	441.7	Tosson Hill	249.1	NZ 0048 9824	Trig
2316	LT	319.4	Long Crag	170.4	NU 0622 0693	Trig
2317	L	316.0	Ros Castle #	221.5	NU 0810 2531	Heather by wall
2318	L	268.3	Housedon Hill *	182.4	NT 9021 3270	Cairn

Hedgehope Hill and Cushat Law

These hills were removed from the Marilyn list in 1995 after letters from Clem Clements highlighted spot heights at the relevant cols and also suggested some new Marilyns in Wales. Surveys in 2014 confirmed the demotions but they both qualify as Submarilyns.

Housedon Hill

ANN BOWKER, 1995

This hill is separated from the main range of the Cheviots by road and river and lacks their wild moorland character. As the ridge flattened out we cowered behind a wall as we were struck by a ferocious west wind. As we came down, a beautiful misty light over the Cheviots reminded us of our much more satisfying climbs on these wild and open hills. Although this hill does not bear comparison with its higher neighbours to the south, it does have the distinction of being the most northerly Marilyn in England.

Shillhope Law

ANN BOWKER, 1995

With only a few of the English Marilyns left to do, we decided to leave Shillhope Law as our final summit. We felt that it would be a more satisfying finishing post than one of the insignificant hills of the south. However, shortly after polishing off our presumed penultimate summits on the Isle of Wight, we received a letter from Alan Dawson which revealed a new Marilyn, Cheriton Hill in Kent. Although our ascent of Shillhope Law did complete the task as originally envisaged, our celebrations were somewhat muted. The hill itself seemed to match this muted mood with its easy grassy going and its pleasing but undramatic outlook across the whaleback ridges of the Cheviots. We used its two west ridges to make a short horseshoe – up Inner Hill and down south-west from the ancient cairn and trig point.

Linton Hill

MIKE KNIPE, DECEMBER 2006

Linton Hill let me climb it in the middle of my cardiac rehabilitation. It was the nearest unticked Marilyn, about 75 miles from home. I was so happy about walking up this hill that it was an absolute joy. I would like to bet that very few people have been as happy on this particular hill. All hail to the NHS – they did a good job on my cardiac arteries.

Number		Height	Name	Drop	Location	Summit
2311	A	602.7	Peel Fell	194.9	NY 6259 9972	Cairn
1927	A	514.6	Fanna Hill	148.1	NT 5697 0319	Tussock
2313	L	519.6	Sighty Crag	297	NY 6013 8092	Outcrop near trig
1928	T	511.7	Larriston Fells	158.9	NY 5690 9209	Trig
1935		447	Blackwood Hill	189	NY 5317 9619	Mound
1937	T	424.6	Rubers Law	196	NT 5803 1557	Rock by trig
1941	A	354.4	Belling Hill	151.6	NT 6420 1183	Cairn

Sighty Crag

ANDY TOMKINS, AUGUST 2014

I started in sunshine and put sun cream on. An hour later I was sheltering in the forest while hailstones the size of 5p pieces pelted me and thunder rumbled. My first objective was Christianbury Crag, but when I got there I saw that in the conditions there was no way I could get to the top of the highest pinnacle. The sky was apocalyptically black as I slowly made my way over rough moorland towards Sighty Crag. Before I made it to the summit the storm broke again with a vengeance. The rain was unbelievably torrential and I saw lightning heading for earth in several directions. I crouched down for an hour while the rain hammered down and the air sizzled, but the storm showed no signs of stopping. Any sane person would have turned back but I carried on to the summit.

I stayed long enough to set foot on the summit then started the descent, terrified that I would be struck by lightning. Actually I was really scared that I was going to die. On the way back to the forest I had to cross a beck which was only a few steps across but was a raging mass of boiling white water. Putting a stick in the water at different points, I found that it was between waist and thigh deep. Heading upstream I eventually found a crossing place that was only knee deep and I went for it. The strength of the water was tremendous and without the sticks I would have been knocked off my feet. In the forest I met a forester who, in ten years of working in the area, had never seen a walker there before. When I got to the car I felt thoroughly traumatised and all I wanted to do was to go home. Instead I headed for Wooler, which was a scary two-hour drive in heavy rain along little roads that were waterlogged. By the end of the day I was thankful to be alive.

Peel Fell

ALAN DAWSON, NOVEMBER 2014

A weekend gathering enabled Hill Baggers to fill the H gap in Alphabet Britain between Goths and Intentional Communities. We were one of the curious cults of Britain, a late substitute for Hell's Angels, as their activities turned out to be too dubious for publicising. Lucy Feltham (later Lucy Leonelli) was the researcher and author. Her presence on Peel Fell enlivened and enlightened us, with tales of Larpers, Otherkin, Wiccans and Yogis, while we introduced her to the categories, ethics, subtleties and tussocks of hill bagging. It was an uplifting occasion, but I remained dutiful and surveyed the summit to check its location, height and borderline status. Lucy's book finally appeared in 2022, retitled from Alphabet Britain to 'A Year in the Life: Adventures in British Subcultures'. It was a great idea and a great read, as a brief extract from chapter H shows, reproduced with permission.

Apprehensive at the prospect of climbing hills with a nasty head cold, I booked a plane to Northumberland. *'Oh come on'*, my friend had said the night before. *'Going walking with a bunch of middle-aged men, how hard can it be?'* This made me feel marginally better. Maybe they would all be puffed-out geriatrics meeting up for a gentle stroll.

I am assigned a day's 'Tump' bagging with Rob, an outdoorsy-looking chap with unruly windswept hair and a wise face. Over the course of the day we summit Ridlees Cairn, Calf Lee, Dumbhope Hill, Crigdon and Highspoon, all as arduous and purposeless as the next. We do it with 25% gusto and 75% trudge. The final hill of the day involves a stream crossing and picking our way through waist-high heather for about twenty minutes, uphill.

After dinner we head back en masse to the cottages for a nightcap. Bottles of expensive whisky are passed around as Alan plugs his laptop into the huge flat-screen TV for the traditional baggers' singing session. A karaoke version of Daydream Believer can be heard and a photo of Stac Lee appears in the background behind cascading lyrics. The words have been changed to pay homage to those who made the climb earlier this year.

'Climbing up Stac Lee would not frighten me
I'm a daydream believer in a summiting team.'

There follows a similar rendition of Unchained Melody and Fairytale of New York. This has to be one of the most eccentric and endearing hobbies imaginable.

The following morning is the big one: a climb up Peel Fell, where Rick and Jen will be ticking off their final English Marilyn. Six of us head off at 8:30 for a drive to the England – Scotland border. I muscle my way into the car between Alan and Martin and quiz them during the hour-long drive. *'Most baggers start out collecting something'*, Alan explains in his considered and articulate baritone. *'Stamps, bus tickets, car numbers, trains.'* Much like the other communities, talk about what people do in their outside lives is rare.

We pull over, tighten our belts and begin the long trek up Peel Fell. The ascent starts on a nice gentle path, but it isn't long before we go off-piste to find a more direct way to the top, thrashing our way through a forest and crawling on all fours to avoid the more inhospitable branches. *'Put your hood up, Lucy'*, Rick warns me. After a bog crossing and a leap over a ditch, the real climbing starts. Every time we get over a ledge that I think is the summit, another appears in the distance, seemingly stretching on forever. To distract myself from the exhaustion, I talk Alan through my other letters.

'I'm starting to learn that a lot of what we think makes us different is just completely made up', I self-righteously proclaim as we near the end of my story so far.

Alan jumps on my point. *'I like that. Everything is made up isn't it. Apart from the hills – they're not made up. I think that's what I like about them.'*

When we finally make it to the summit, the feeling is euphoric. The trees on the horizon look like a herd of elephants walking trunk to tail. Rick and Jen ceremonially hold hands and ascend the highest point together to exuberant cheers from the group. This is Rick's 1200th Hump so he is now entitled to enter the 'Hump Hall of Fame'. To initiate him, the group breaks into a chant.

Cake, whisky and plastic cups appear from a backpack to mark the occasion and we manage to drink an entire bottle between six of us, keeping us warm on the blustery top as the rain starts to descend. Once his surveying is complete, Alan rushes over to the group. *'We forgot a very important toast'*, he says. He pulls another bottle of whisky from his backpack and fills us all up. *'Here's to Lucy completing another chapter of her book'*.

—— Lake District ——

Land between the Solway Firth and Morecambe Bay, west of the River Eden and River Lune

Marilyns: 55

Highest and most prominent: Scafell Pike, 978.1m, drop 912m

Lowest and least prominent: Arnside Knott, 159.1m, drop 150.8m

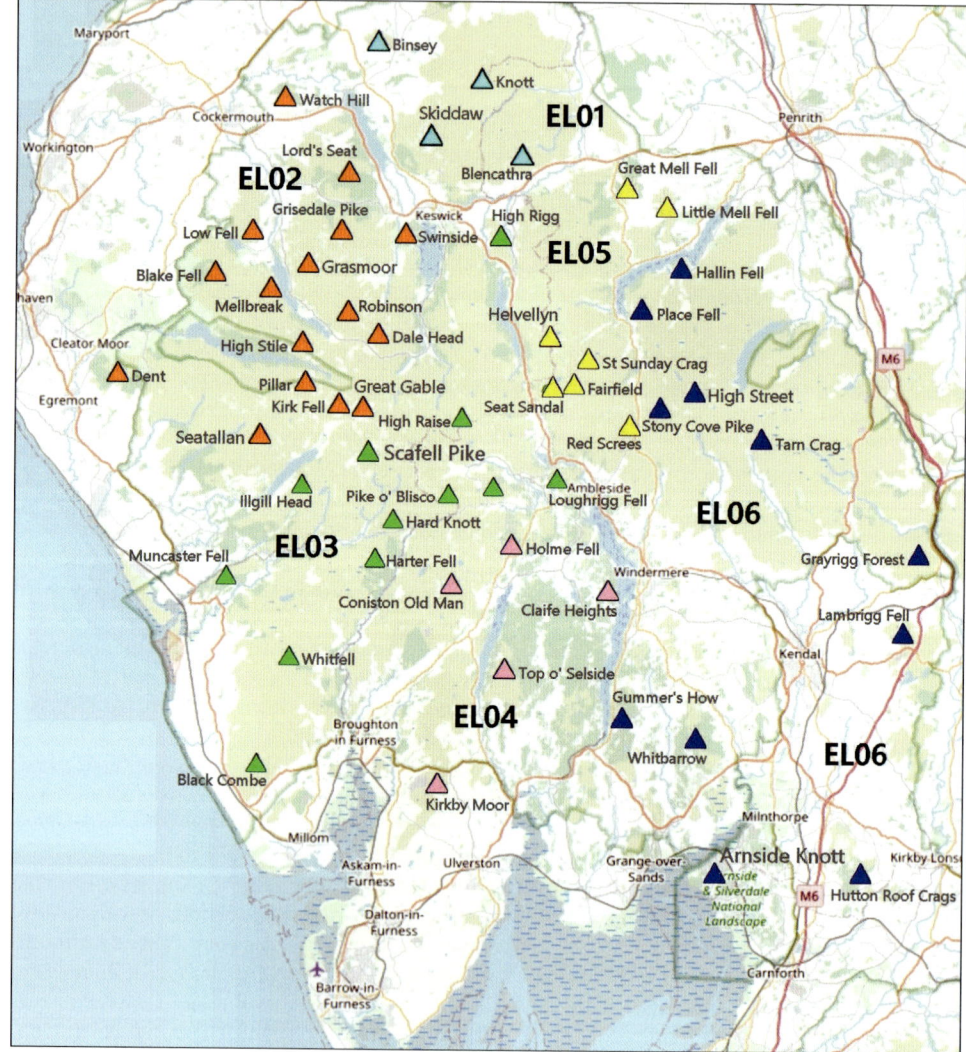

EL01 Skiddaw-knott

RHB section 34A OS maps 89, 90

Number		Height	Name	Drop	Location	Summit
2319	T	930.7	Skiddaw	706	NY 2604 2908	Rock by trig
2320	A	867.8	Blencathra	461	NY 3234 2771	Outcrop
2328	L	710.1	Knott	242.2	NY 2961 3298	Cairn
2351	LT	446.9	Binsey	242.1	NY 2251 3552	Trig

Skiddaw

ALAN DAWSON, 4 MAY 1986

This was the day my life changed, though of course I did not realise it at the time. It was to be a routine walk over what turned out to be my 50th Marilyn, via Long Side and Carl Side and on to Lonscale Fell. The reasonably linear and rational route was spoiled by a bizarre diversion to a small round lump called Sale How, which appeared in one of the lists of hills over 2000 feet in England and Wales. It was not my idea but I went along with it. It seemed odd to go all the way down to a featureless little lump on the side of a proper hill, with no apparent merit except as a tick in a list. Then we had to climb about 200 metres back up to reach Little Man and regain the reasonable route.

I was new to hill bagging but had received a copy of *Munro's Tables* for Christmas and that had triggered my brain to start analysing criteria for the inclusion of hills in lists. Sale How helped me to start thinking about alternative ways of defining hills rather than ignoring everything below 2000 feet or 3000 feet and including almost everything above. I was aware of Corbetts as they were listed in the *Munro's Tables* book, so I thought it might be worth applying a similar principle to hills of any height throughout Britain. Soon afterwards I started studying maps and contour rings in detail. I was fortunate that Liverpool University had a good map library, so I began to spend lunch hours and evenings in there to look for relatively high hills, modifying the Corbett criterion of 500 feet to 150 metres because the most recent OS maps used metric heights and contours.

I started at sheet 1 and worked my way south, so Saxa Vord was the first relative hill I found. I made an error on sheet 3 by including Cunnigill Hill but improved as I worked my way south. I became enthused by the concept but soon realised that it would be a huge amount of work and I was reluctant to waste my time going through all the maps if no-one else was likely to be interested. In February 1989 I wrote to three publishers to explain the idea and included a two-page summary of a book with the provisional title 'The Marilyns of Great Britain'. Cicerone Press wrote back within a month expressing interest, though they disliked my proposed Chapter 8 on Memorable Marilyns, which they said would be 'out of context with the practical nature of the book'.

Twenty years after leaving school, in 1989 my life somehow found a new direction and purpose. I submitted some draft chapters to Cicerone Press in July then spent three weeks in Africa in August, climbing Mount Kenya (Point Lenana) as well as Kilimanjaro. Five days after getting home I moved to Scotland and started a new job. In November I signed a contract with Cicerone Press on the same day the Berlin Wall came down. The map library at Glasgow University was even better than the one in Liverpool so my research continued, after sorting out distractions like renting a flat and then buying a house. In January 1990 I submitted the full manuscript, on floppy disk, but waited over two years for the book to appear. By the end of 2024 I had still not been back up Skiddaw.

Number		Height	Name	Drop	Location	Summit
2367	L	898.8	Great Gable	425.6	NY 2110 1032	Cairn on rock
2368	L	892.4	Pillar	348.7	NY 1712 1210	Trig
2450	A	628.7	Yewbarrow	143.9	NY 1733 0847	Rock by cairn
2383	L	802.0	Kirk Fell	182.5	NY 1949 1048	Shelter
2427	L	693.0	Seatallan	193.2	NY 1400 0844	Grass near cairn
2372	L	851.6	Grasmoor	518.2	NY 1748 2035	Shelter
2386	L	790.3	Grisedale Pike	191.0	NY 1984 2254	Cairn
2400	L	754.0	Dale Head	397.7	NY 2229 1532	Grass near cairn
2436	A	653.1	High Spy	147.8	NY 2340 1622	Cairn
2405	L	737.6	Robinson	161.9	NY 2019 1687	Rock
2345	L	552.1	Lord's Seat	237.3	NY 2043 2655	Rock near post
2381	A	806.5	High Stile	361.3	NY 1700 1481	Cairn on outcrop
2462	L	572.6	Blake Fell	163.1	NY 1105 1968	Grass by shelter
2479	L	511.1	Mellbreak	259.0	NY 1485 1861	Rock
2493	L	422.5	Low Fell	266.6	NY 1373 2261	Grass by cairn
2504	L	351.4	Dent #	174.8	NY 0415 1290	Ground by cairn
2355	L	255.4	Watch Hill	160.2	NY 1600 3182	Trees
2513	L	244.8	**Swinside *****	151.9	NY 2433 2244	Grass

Swinside

This was one of the first batch of new Marilyns added in the 1995 revision.

ANN BOWKER, 1995

We were delighted to see Swinside enter the tables. We have climbed it of course, it is our local hill. This is to admit trespass. We have an old guidebook of 1902 which actually advises the ascent as a 'pleasant stroll' from Keswick. Now it is covered in trees and surrounded by 'Private' notices. Wainwright, it seems, failed to notice it, which may be one reason why everyone else does too. Well, it's great to have a Lake District hill that does not have a badly eroded path to the top and where one can walk completely alone. Let's hope it doesn't get overrun with Marilyn baggers.

There seems to be no demand for access, leaving it as a haven for the trespasser who may find solitude on its secluded forest tracks. No path leads to the summit and indeed a direct approach encounters unpleasantly rough and overgrown terrain. My favourite circuit, for a walk of little more than one hour, enters at the first gate as one approaches from Portinscale. A couple of right forks lead one close under the north top and one can then scramble up through the trees to this exquisite viewpoint, which gives a unique view of Keswick, seen across the northern end of Derwentwater, and of Bassenthwaite Lake beyond the plain of the Vale of Keswick. From here the main summit is reached easily, without obstruction from trees, and it reveals the Vale of Newlands, perhaps the most beautiful of all the Lakeland valleys, surrounded by the ridges of the north-western fells. By back-tracking a short distance northwards, a way can be made down through the trees to a track on the eastern flank of the hill which can be followed northwards to rejoin the outward path.

Pillar

Tom Read, July 2012

My son Jimmy and I finally completed all the English Marilyns in 2012. In fact we could claim to have 182 out of 176, having also done Thorpe Fell Top, Lovely Seat, Baystones, Raw Head and Horse Head Moor when they were valid, and Black Mountain when it was half in England. We have, of course, revisited it since it emigrated to Wales.

After setting up the completion with camping tours of Devon, Cornwall, Dorset and the west country in 2010, and Northumberland in 2011, we were left with ten Lake District summits for 2012. The first six – Low Fell, Mellbreak, Hard Knott, Black Combe, Dent and Blake Fell – were climbed in a youth-hostelling trip with my two sons Jimmy and Liam. Mellbreak was found to be steep, while Blake Fell was a satisfying and beautiful route.

That left four fairly big ones, so I returned with Jimmy (aged 19 at the time) to sort them out, but one of them nearly sorted me out. Our first one was Seatallan, which was a straightforward ascent, taking in Buckbarrow on the way down. After overnighting at Ennerdale Youth Hostel, we climbed up on to Red Pike and then across to High Stile for the second one of the four we needed. We crossed High Crag and dropped steeply into Black Sail Pass, where we overnighted at the famous hostel-cum-bothy. The following morning looked rather greyer and wetter, but we pressed on with our climb up Pillar. This was a formidable mountain, not to be messed with. We sheltered from a heavy shower of rain about halfway up then pressed on to attain the summit – 175 down, one to go.

The initial descent from Pillar took us into Wind Gap, and the weather really closed in. The original plan had been to press on to Scoat Fell and take a longer descent into Ennerdale. However, with the deterioration in the weather, I suggested using an escape route down toward Wind Gap. This was a poor piece of decision making, for the steep grassy slope down Wind Gap was not suitable terrain in the wet conditions. Jimmy coped admirably with it but I slipped and discovered how much friction there was between my wet waterproof over-trousers and wet steep grass – none.

I accelerated at a terrifying speed as I overtook my son from ten minutes behind to fifteen minutes ahead in a matter of seconds. Rolling over onto my ample belly appeared to be the manoeuvre that enabled me to come to a halt. I was bumped, bruised, cut, sore and shaken, but still in one piece. I was undoubtedly lucky that I had not tumbled, only slid, and that my head had not hit a rock. Jimmy carefully picked his way down to where I was, collecting my dropped trekking poles on the way. We then carefully and slowly zigzagged our way down to safer ground, paused for a lunch of hot soup, and then completed the route to Ennerdale Youth Hostel.

A mixture of wholesome hostel food, a good night's sleep, several painkillers and our shared determination meant that I awoke the following day as keen as ever to have a crack at our last English Marilyn, Harter Fell. Although the ascent route was a rather steeper one than I would have chosen, especially after the previous day's scare, it was a relatively untroubled walk, and we had done it.

We participate in SOTA – Summits on the Air – in which we make radio transmissions from the summits we reach. We did this as usual from the top of Harter Fell, with Jimmy (M0HGY) on VHF FM chatting to local radio hams while I made contact across Europe on short wave, using Morse code. We headed towards Hard Knott pass initially, for a more graded descent, and that was it – we had achieved our aim of activating every English summit, becoming only the fourth and fifth to do so in amateur radio terms.

Kirk Fell and Great Gable

Lingmoor Fell

Harter Fell from Green Crag

Number		Height	Name	Drop	Location	Summit
2359	OA	978.1	Scafell Pike	912.2	NY 2154 0721	Cairn
2365	A	902.9	Bowfell	148.2	NY 2447 0645	Rock
2454	G	608.8	Illgill Head	312.2	NY 1689 0492	Rock
2469	L	549.6	Hard Knott	156.2	NY 2318 0237	Rock
2396	LT	762.5	High Raise	284.2	NY 2809 0952	Rock
2507	L	335.1	Loughrigg Fell	174.1	NY 3469 0513	Rock by trig
2419	L	703	Pike of Blisco	177	NY 2712 0421	Cairn
2485	L	469.9	Lingmoor Fell	247.8	NY 3027 0460	Rock by cairn
2643	L	653.2	Harter Fell	273.5	SD 2187 9971	Tor
2646	LT	600.4	Black Combe	361.8	SD 1355 8549	Trig
2647	L	573.3	Whitfell	223.1	SD 1588 9298	Cairn
2627	L	355.7	High Rigg	186.7	NY 3085 2199	Rock by cairn
19242	GA	232.1	Muncaster Fell *	193.1	SD 1155 9866	Outcrop

Muncaster Fell

In September 2016 G&J Surveys found the NE summit of this hill to be 74cm higher than the summit with the trig point (Hooker Crag). There is just over 30m drop between them. Two months later a second survey confirmed the height to within 1cm of the first survey result, though GNSS data was recorded for only 20 minutes rather than 120.

Scafell Pike

ALAN DAWSON, JUNE 1977

My ninth Marilyn and my first fiasco. After a year living on Lancaster University campus I spent two years sharing a large house in Arnside, looking through lounge windows across the Kent estuary toward the hills of the Lake District. I had been up Ward's Stone and Arnside Knott and Ingleborough but not a single Marilyn in the Lake District, despite living so close and having a car. I was as lazy as the eight other inmates. As the three years drew to a close I thought I should make an effort to stand on the highest point in England.

Hundreds of people streamed past as I struggled up Brown Tongue along with a fellow student who was equally unfit and ill-equipped. We had no map, no grip on our footwear and no idea that there were two summits. Somehow we found our way to the top of Scafell and wondered where all the people had gone, before we noticed the crowd on top of another summit not far away. Our highly educated brains eventually concluded that the other summit must be higher. We stumbled back the way we had come, via Lord's Rake, instead of taking a direct line via Broad Stand, which might have been fatal. We then struggled, slipped and scrambled our way up to join the crowd on top of Scafell Pike.

Illgill Head

ANDY TOMKINS, JANUARY 2013

The year started badly when I slipped and fractured my wrist whilst climbing Illgill Head. I was in plaster for nearly seven weeks and could not drive for three months, which meant that it was mid-April before I took to the hills again.

Number		Height	Name	Drop	Location	Summit
2634	G	802.5	The Old Man of Coniston	415	SD 2724 9781	Cairn on platform
2640	L	763.1	Wetherlam	146.2	NY 2882 0111	Cairn
2667	L	333.3	Top o' Selside	187.0	SD 3092 9193	Heather
2668	L	335.0	Kirkby Moor / Lowick High Common #	231.0	SD 2599 8391	Cairn
2673	L	315.7	Holme Fell	165.4	NY 3150 0060	Rock
2683	T	269.9	Claife Heights	176.1	SD 3820 9734	Outcrop by trig

Coniston Old Man

This hill has been more troublesome to classify than to climb, with an ambiguous name and longstanding uncertainty about whether it is higher than nearby Swirl How. It was one of the most difficult summits to survey, with a huge man-made platform on top making it difficult to identify the highest remaining natural point. John Barnard and Graham Jackson finally tackled the problem in May 2018, along with Jim Bloomer. As part of the team behind of Database of British and Irish Hills, they had a good incentive to try to resolve the matter.

The survey proved to be as awkward as expected, as the natural ground on Coniston Old Man had been obliterated by the platform and cairn, while on Swirl How the natural summit rocks were covered by a large cairn. After diligent and detailed sightings and surveys, the result after processing of GNSS data was 802.42m for the highest visible natural point on both summits. This was unhelpful, but they had measured the base of the cairn on the platform to be 802.53m and observed that there was a high probability of higher ground underneath the platform, so the balance of evidence indicated that Swirl How was likely to be lower.

Coniston Old Man therefore retained its Marilyn status, but it would be helpful if someone were to remove the cairn on Swirl How in order to be certain that it does not obscure a higher embedded rock. As for the name, OS maps continue to offer the more cumbersome variant, but both names seems to be in regular use and equally applicable.

Lowick High Common (Kirkby Moor)

ANN BOWKER, 1995

It was an appalling day. Thick mist covered the hills and torrential rain drove across them. We had driven down from Keswick in moderately promising weather with the primary purpose of climbing Whitfell. Despite the increasingly foul conditions there was no ambiguity about its summit, with its substantial cairn and trig point. It seemed daft to do another hill but equally daft to come down here again for what looked like a trivial ascent, so we drove down and climbed the oddly named hill, Lowick High Common. The quarry edges made navigation easy despite the mist. We located the top of the gash in the hill and took a bearing from there until we encountered a cairn which looked convincing enough to be the summit. Having convinced ourselves that ground was dropping away southwards, we returned to the car fairly satisfied that we had bagged our summit, although hardly satisfied with the quality of the walk. Maybe we will go there again some time.

OS map 90

Number		Height	Name	Drop	Location	Summit
2515	L	949.8	Helvellyn	713.4	NY 3424 1511	Cairn
2521	A	873.3	Fairfield	300.3	NY 3587 1175	Outcrop in cairn
2527	A	841.2	St Sunday Crag	160.6	NY 3692 1339	Rock by cairn
2545	G	736.8	Seat Sandal	151.9	NY 3442 1152	Rock
2538	L	778.8	Red Screes	260.9	NY 3966 0875	Rock by cairn
2583	L	536.7	Great Mell Fell	200.8	NY 3968 2536	Cairn
2598	LT	505.1	Little Mell Fell	224.8	NY 4232 2401	Trig

Seat Sandal

This was one of the first Marilyns to be surveyed, by John Barnard and Graham Jackson in January 2009. It proved to be easier than their previous surveys. After two promotions (Sail Chalmadale and Mynydd y Cwm) and one demotion (Raw Head), Seat Sandal became the first Marilyn to have its status confirmed by GNSS survey.

Fairfield

Fairfield and Seat Sandal are the closest pair of Marilyn summits in England, 1.47km apart, closer than Great Gable and Kirk Fell, 1.61km apart. The closest pair in Wales are Rhinog Fach and Y Llethr, 1.3km apart, then Pen Llithrig y Wrach and Creigiau Gleision, 1.48km apart. All these figures refer to direct aerial distances, not walking routes. The flat summit area of Fairfield has suffered from a proliferation of cairns that made it difficult to know which one marked the top. The highest natural rock was found to be hidden beneath one of these cairns, but since the summit survey in 2019 it has probably been buried again by those intent on obscuring natural rock summits with an ugly mess.

Little Mell Fell

ALAN DAWSON, JANUARY 2001

The name suggests this hill is an obvious pair with its Great Mell neighbour, but there are two roads and a river in between them, so climbing them separately makes sense if time is short or one of them can be squeezed in as a diversion from the M6 on the way north or south. In 2001 I had time for Place Fell after driving south from Scotland and then went looking for a parking spot big enough for a tiny camper van.

Sometime during the cold night I was woken by voices, torches and a bang on the window by local police with nothing better to do than harass a harmless hill bagger parked legally and responsibly. They claimed to be worried about my welfare but their line of questioning made it obvious that they viewed me with suspicion. They had already checked the number plate, realised that my little white van was not from the local area and concluded that I was likely to be up to no good. My explanation that I was parked by the foot of Little Mell Fell because I intended to climb it the next day was assumed to be a cover story for a day of thievery or thuggery. I had to drive further away from the hill until they stopped following me and went off to look for someone else to intimidate. I did climb the hill but did not enjoy it or remember anything about it, as my mind was still polluted by indignation as I thought of all the eloquent responses I could have given if I had not been in a semi-conscious stupor. I left Great Mell Fell for another day, another year and another diversion from the motorway in another vehicle.

Number		Height	Name	Drop	Location	Summit
2528	L	828.5	High Street	373.8	NY 4414 1111	Grass
2537	G	779.0	Harter Fell ¬	149.2	NY 4597 0932	Cairn
2540	A	763.7	Stony Cove Pike	172.1	NY 4178 1000	Rock
2607	G	486.9	Baystones ¬	147.7	NY 4031 0514	Rock
2559	L	664.0	Tarn Crag	160.4	NY 4879 0786	Rock
2561	LT	657	Place Fell	261	NY 4053 1694	Outcrop by cairn
2603	LT	493.9	Grayrigg Forest	188.8	SD 5986 9980	Trig
2623	L	387.7	Hallin Fell	161.1	NY 4330 1982	Cairn on outcrop
2665	G	339.6	Lambrigg Fell *	159	SD 5868 9418	Grass
2671	LT	321.1	Gummer's How	216.7	SD 3904 8848	Trig
2682	LT	274.3	Hutton Roof Crags	175.9	SD 5570 7750	Rock
2697	L	215.8	Whitbarrow	184.9	SD 4417 8704	Rock
3321	G	159.1	**Arnside Knott *****	150.8	SD 4561 7747	Tree near trig

Harter Fell

This hill was reclassified in 1996 after further study of large-scale OS mapping. Its fate was sealed by a GNSS survey in 2010 that confirmed the drop to be under 150m.

Baystones

This has been the most volatile hill ever listed as a Marilyn. It was included in RHB in 1992, demoted in 1996, reinstated in 2001 after information from OS and demoted again in 2010, when a GNSS survey finally settled the matter. In the end it was not very close to qualification, as there are 38 hills with a greater drop that do not qualify, 27 of which have never been classed as Marilyns. Apart from Cunnigill Hill and Scafell, which were errors, the only less prominent former Marilyn listed in 1992 is Hedgehope Hill.

Grayrigg Forest

GILL STEPHENS, AUGUST 2017

This was the fifth of seven M6 Marilyns on the same day, climbed from a huge lay-by on the A865 by Hause Bridge. After a short road walk to a gate, the lower reaches were covered in lanky, lumpy grass with few paths but easy enough. After stream-hopping up to a ridgelet then along a broad ridge to a gate in the wall, it was a stroll to the summit. A lovely hill with little noise and splendid views, if you ignore the M6.

Lambrigg Fell

ANN BOWKER, 1995

This is the highest point of an area of rough and undulating ground which is separated from the Howgills by the deep gash of the Lune valley. Any trace of drama lies on the western side, where Benson Knott and The Helm stand above Kendal, but the unimposing summit of Lambrigg Fell overtops Benson Knott by 21 metres. The area is agricultural and laced with a maze of minor roads. The M6 also slices across this area and the exit for Sedbergh and Kendal lies within a mile of a useful bridleway. This gave us a very easy ascent and it did not seem worth seeking any extension, although the little summit ridge was quite pleasant, with the hills of the Lake District and the Howgills in view.

Hutton Roof Crags

ANN BOWKER, 1995

Many years earlier we had climbed its sister hill, Farleton Fell. This is the bold hill which stands close to the M6 but it is overtopped 30 metres by its less conspicuous neighbour. We started from the village of Hutton Roof using the right of way which climbs westwards onto the hill. The route of this path became vague as various tracks appeared amongst the limestone. The top of the hill is crowned by a limestone pavement with its characteristic clints, which made progress quite a problem. After several false starts we found a fairly persistent track which seemed to be going in the correct direction. It wandered amongst trees and when we finally emerged onto a higher bump we realised that we had gone too far west. Eventually, after more struggling amongst clints, we reached the trig pillar. The highest point could have been anywhere within a radius of several hundred metres, but the immediate surroundings were far from flat, consisting mainly of a limestone pavement cracked by crevasses. We set off on a clear east-bound path but once again it petered out in the limestone. We started to drop off south-east, made our way above a wall and eventually found a path of sorts which vanished again, forcing us to climb up around the crags and rejoin our outward route. Despite, or perhaps because of, the tough going it was an enjoyable climb up a worthwhile hill.

PAUL WHEELER, 2015

I messed about happily looking at flowers and butterflies and watching climbers on limestone crags before finding the summit by trial and error. If there was not so much grazing, a lot of the limestone country could be like this – fascinating and bio-diverse, but be careful what you wish for.

Hallin Fell

JONATHAN APPLEBY, 2013

What a wee gem of a hill. It was so easy that I managed to persuade my better half to climb it too, having walked around first, so she could see it would not be too unpleasant.

Arnside Knott

ALAN DAWSON, AUGUST 1975 AND FEBRUARY 2005

I had a good reason to climb Arnside Knott in 1975, not to bag it or to look at the view but as something to do to entertain my parents during their visit to see my new student accommodation. It turned out be a pleasant and easy walk, but as I was not a hill walker I did not bother to repeat it for almost thirty years, despite living in Arnside for two years. I could not claim to have had better things to do, I was just lazy and lethargic.

When I began researching the Marilyns I did not spend much time studying the map of Arnside Knott as it looked as though its drop was under 140m. However, topographic modelling by Jonathan de Ferranti in 2004 suggested it was worth a close look. The key col is in a railway cutting, so the crucial contours were not shown on any OS map. In 2005 I spent a long time studying the railway line and checking its height with my altimeter in various places. The hill was promoted after this research but I could not be certain of its Marilyn status until 2010, when this was confirmed by G&J Surveys.

GILL STEPHENS, AUGUST 2017

An absolute gem of a hill. Lovely woods and fabulous views of Morecambe Bay, Lakes, Bowland and Yorkshire hills. Climbed from lay-by next to Arnside Tower Farm.

——— **Pennines and Moors** ———

Land south of River Eden, Irthing, South Tyne and Tyne, east of the Eden and Lune, north of the Trent

Marilyns:	49
Highest and most prominent:	Cross Fell, 893.1m, drop 649.9m
Lowest:	Billinge Hill, 179.3m
Least prominent:	Gisborough Moor, drop 150.8m

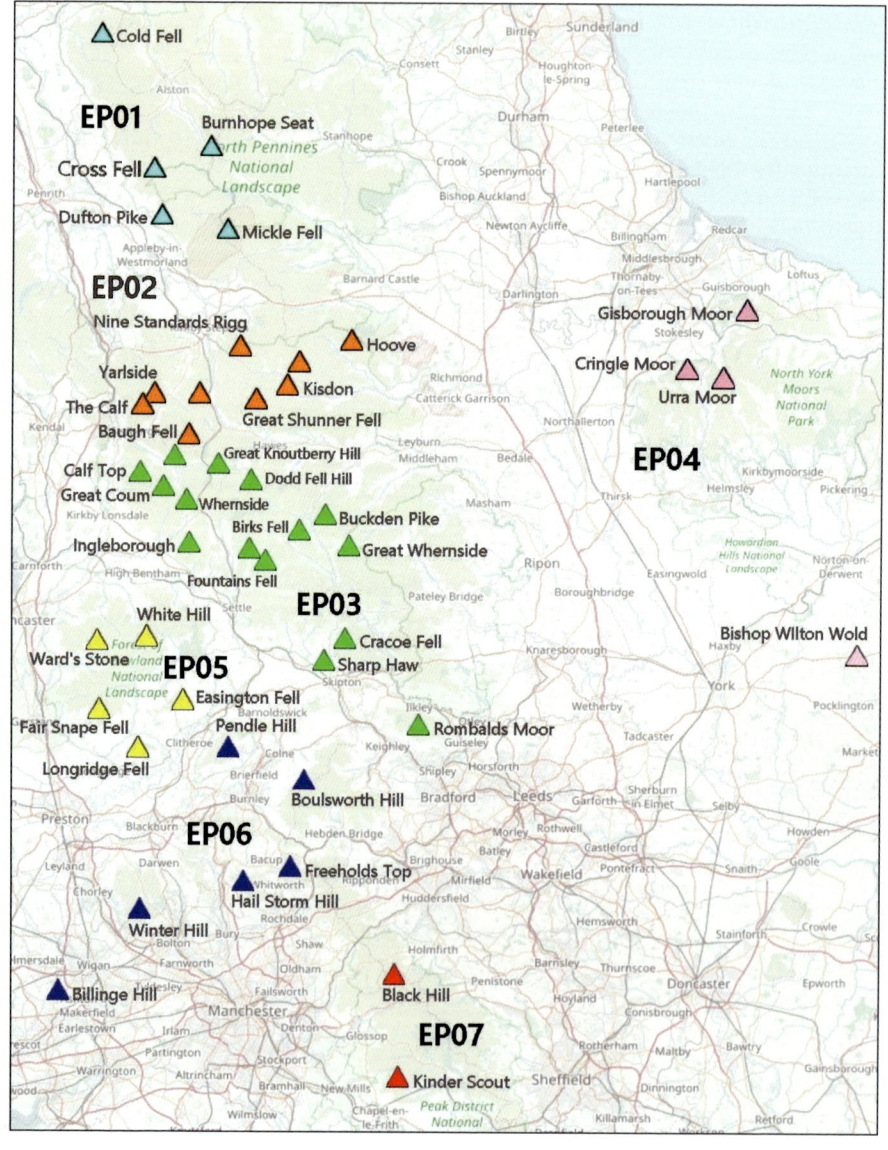

Number		Height	Name	Drop	Location	Summit
2707	LT	893.1	Cross Fell	649.9	NY 6873 3432	Trig
2711	L	790.2	Mickle Fell	212	NY 8060 2454	Rock near cairn
2714	L	747.8	Burnhope Seat	194.4	NY 7845 3755	Grass
2761		621	Cold Fell	169	NY 6057 5563	Trig on cairn
2775	L	481.2	Dufton Pike	163.4	NY 6998 2663	Grass

Mickle Fell

TED JACKSON, 2013

Mickle Fell provided electrical entertainment in the form of a thunderstorm and a deluge of rain. I had bivvied within mortar range and arose during a brief respite in the rain before the storm. On a normal hill with easy access I would have retreated. The prospect of another application for access and a return to this hill spurred me on.

HAMISH BROWN, 2014

I had a van night by Cow Green reservoir, cycled via the Spout and then went up and down the north flank to the summit. Afterwards, as I was driving along the south side of the hill, I was horrified to see a notice saying that I should have written in advance to the range officer stating the date, number in walking party and route. It also said that the officer would contact all the relevant landowners and gamekeepers before issuing a permit. What preposterous bureaucracy over going up a hill.

Burnhope Seat

GILL STEPHENS, JUNE 2017

A purgatorial Pennine plod from Burnhope reservoir in heavy rain, fog and cold wind. After the path from Stripe Head and the moor to Highwatch Currick there was a bit of path but also numerous peat bogs and hags to avoid, with wooden pallets at the most gruesome section to avoid drowning. After the trig and the top of Burnhope Bog Seat, there were more bogs to the delightfully dry and hag-free Great Stony Hill, the best summit of the day. There was a fence all the way so navigation was easy.

Dufton Pike

ANN BOWKER, JULY 1995

The great Pennine wall on the eastern side of the vale of Eden is characterised by a series of distinctive small hills lying at its foot. Murton Pike is the highest of them but Dufton Pike is the only one sufficiently separated to qualify for inclusion in Dawson's tables. The Pennine Way hereabouts zigzags erratically either side of the main ridge, perhaps making the best of its exclusion from the large area of firing ranges above Warcop to visit the two fine waterfalls, High Force and Cauldron Snout on the Tees, and then to cross to the dramatic gash of High Cup Nick and the civilisation of Dufton and its youth hostel, before heading toward Cross Fell. We set out up the bridleway which runs NE from Dufton and left it to gain access to the south-east ridge of the hill. The top was pleasantly narrow with splendid views along the Pennine edge. We continued on the ridge north-westwards until it came up against a wall with fields beyond. Here a path cut back sharply to join the public footpath alongside Great Rundale Beck, which we followed to the bridge where it joined the Pennine Way and hence back to Dufton after a pleasant short climb.

RHB section 35A   OS maps 92, 98

Number		Height	Name	Drop	Location	Summit
2716	L	715.7	Great Shunner Fell	295.3	SD 8486 9729	Shelter
2734	G	674.8	Lovely Seat	149.1	SD 8790 9504	Ground by shelter
2740	L	671.6	Rogan's Seat	193.3	NY 9192 0305	Grass by cairn
2745	L	661.9	Nine Standards Rigg	159.0	NY 8256 0609	Grass near trig
2773	L	554.6	Hoove *	176.7	NZ 0018 0691	Grass
2774	G	498.6	Kisdon	185.8	SD 8991 9985	Rocks
2720	LT	708.4	Wild Boar Fell	352.6	SD 7580 9879	Rock
2730	L	678.4	Baugh Fell	265	SD 7409 9164	Grass by wall
2732	ML	676.6	The Calf	383.2	SD 6674 9703	Cairn near trig
2755	L	639.2	Yarlside	209.0	SD 6857 9853	Cairn

Lovely Seat

This hill was added as a Marilyn in 1995 and survived for fifteen years before G&J surveys discovered it should not have been promoted, as the 675m summit height and 526m col height shown on OS maps were found to be more or less correct.

Wild Boar Fell

According to a leaflet produced by the defunct Eden District Council, Wild Boar Fell takes its name from the killing of the last wild boar in England by Richard de Musgrave in 1376. Apparently a boar's tusk was found when his tomb was later opened. Wild boar have since returned to parts of England but none have been reported on Wild Boar Fell.

Hoove

ANN BOWKER, 1995

Rowland was going cycling in Holland. I drove him to Hull, bagging Bishop Wilton Wold en route. The plan was to do Hoove on the way back, a week later. However, as I drove westwards towards Bowes it was an amazingly beautiful evening. Lovely cloud formations promised a spectacular sunset. Where better to enjoy it than from the summit of Hoove? I drove up to a point where the road emerged from the trees. A tiny path led towards the hill but it soon petered out and the going became dreadful, through tussocky grass covering deep, water-filled, ankle-twisting holes. Eventually I struggled across to the banks of Hurr Beck where a tiny path made things a lot pleasanter. So flat was the top of the hill that the views were disappointing. Even the declining sun was unspectacular since the clouds had now dispersed and the sky was an unbroken blue.

Six days later we were back and followed a track to the edge of the forest. At first the going was quite pleasant, running up a little valley past mine workings to Jinglepot Hole. Above Elsey Crag the trig point appeared but there was still some very rough ground to be crossed to reach it. We descended by Hurr Gill again and strolled back down the road, which made a more satisfying circuit than my route of six days before.

ALAN DAWSON, MARCH 2004

Maybe I had had enough, as it was my fourth hill of the day, or maybe it was the twilight, or maybe the rain, or maybe it was the flat and unsatisfying summit, but my memory is of depressing dreariness, with never a chance to walk two paces without looking to see whether my feet were landing in water or damp, spongy energy-sapping moss. Just as well it was only 1km from the road.

Number		Height	Name	Drop	Location	Summit
2779	L	736.6	Whernside	408.3	SD 7389 8154	Path north of trig
2780	L	723.3	Ingleborough	426	SD 7412 7458	Cairn
2784	A	686.4	Great Coum	221	SD 7008 8358	Cairn
2797	G	609.6	Calf Top	320.3	SD 6645 8562	Cairn
2781		704	Great Whernside	288	SE 0020 7391	Cairn
2782	L	701.6	Buckden Pike	208.6	SD 9606 7878	Grass near trig
2783	LT	694.2	Pen-y-ghent	304.7	SD 8385 7338	Rock by trig
2788	L	667.9	Fountains Fell	243	SD 8641 7158	Mound near cairn
2799	L	610.4	Birks Fell	158.2	SD 9188 7637	Cairn
2786	L	672.5	Great Knoutberry Hill	253.0	SD 7886 8716	Grass by trig
2787	LT	668.1	Dodd Fell Hill	232.5	SD 8410 8458	Trig
2802	LT	556.4	Aye Gill Pike	167.0	SD 7206 8861	Trig
3682	G	507.8	Cracoe Fell **	310	SD 9931 5883	Monument
2805	LT	356.6	Sharp Haw	168	SD 9594 5527	Trig
2804	LT	402.5	Rombalds Moor #	244.5	SE 1146 4522	Trig

Cracoe Fell

This summit was promoted in 2008 when a line survey carried out by G&J Surveys found it to be about 1.8m higher than Thorpe Fell Top.

Ingleborough

ALAN DAWSON, JANUARY 1976

My sixth Marilyn and my third as a student. The walk was something to do during a bleak weekend staying in a cold cottage in Clapham that was being used by a group of ecology students from Lancaster University who were studying albino shrimps living in one of the nearby caves. Somewhere near the summit, my friend Rod's glasses were blown off his face and dispatched high into the distance. He could see very little without them but there was little to see anyway. We went back down the same way and found the glasses lying on the path several hundred metres from the summit.

Ten years later I stupidly decided to attempt to follow the well-known three peaks route. This was not a natural hill walking route and I got fed up with traipsing along roads and flat paths. I was put out of one misery and into another when I started to jog down Whernside, stumbled and tore my ankle ligaments. I managed to hop down to the road before the worst of the pain kicked in, then sat in an empty pub for a few hours while my friends carried on over Ingleborough to collect the car and then me. The pub was not serving anything and I had nothing to read except Landranger 98, which kept me occupied until my lift arrived. I was on crutches for several weeks. Perhaps I deserved this fate, as the only time I had gone through the formality of registering to do a walk was the only time I had failed to finish it. At least I did not have to be rescued.

Rombalds Moor

This was reluctantly renamed from Ilkley Moor in 1999 after correspondence from a local hill walker.

Looking toward Wild Boar Fell from the Howgill Fells

The Cloud

Summit of Eston Nab

Number		Height	Name	Drop	Location	Summit
2830	L	454.6	Urra Moor	409.4	NZ 5943 0159	Grass by trig
2831	L	435	Cringle Moor	176	NZ 5374 0296	Cairn
2832	L	328.7	Gisborough Moor	150.8	NZ 6324 1241	Rock
2834	A	242.9	Eston Nab	148.1	NZ 5686 1831	Grass near tower
2833	L	247.9	Bishop Wilton Wold	207.2	SE 8217 5702	Tumulus

Urra Moor

This is the highest point of the North York Moors. It is one of only sixteen Marilyns in England with relative height over 400 metres, and the only one of the sixteen under 500 metres high. The nearest more prominent Marilyn is Ingleborough, over 100km away.

Cringle Moor

Lidar data shows the ground at NZ 5381 0289 to be 434.7m, almost as high as the Drake Howe antiquity, which has become so well vegetated that parts of it look like natural ground, allowing it to retain its status as the Marilyn summit.

Gisborough Moor

This is the least prominent Marilyn that has not been surveyed using GNSS. Lidar data for summit and col shows that the hill qualifies with a convincing 80cm to spare.

Eston Nab

ALAN DAWSON, FEBRUARY 2022

I had been putting off a survey of this hill for many years, but the release of Lidar data revealing the col location and height made it a more appealing prospect, as I only needed to survey the summit. It was also an opportunity to see a part of the country I rarely had reason to visit and to see a friend I had been threatening to stay with for several years in her natural habitat. Uncertainty about the summit height and position gave Eston Nab a slight chance of promotion to Marilyn status.

The approach walk was along pleasant paths with squelchy boggy patches, while the summit had a curious mixture of appealing rocky outcrops, industrial detritus, litter, brick folly and modern masts. The view north over Middlesbrough, Redcar and the coast offered a bipolar prospect of distant beauty and urban sprawl. The hill was popular with locals but none of them bothered to seek out the highest patch of grass, a few metres from the tower and trig pillar. Nearby trees all appeared to be on lower ground.

Bishop Wilton Wold

The original summit was the trig pillar next to the road, which made it one of the easiest Marilyns. Lidar data indicates that a tumulus in the nearby copse of trees is almost two metres higher. The relocated summit is still easy to reach, if not entirely natural.

PETER MALONE, JANUARY 2006

The year began in good style, without changing my shoes. After new year celebrations with friends in Yorkshire, I was driven to Bishop Wilton Wold, which involved all of ten metres walking to the trig point. However, I did eventually pull on the wellies and tramp south across a ploughed field to the coppice of trees which looked a little higher.

Number		Height	Name	Drop	Location	Summit
2811	L	562.5	Ward's Stone	400.9	SD 5919 5873	Cairn
2814	LT	544.9	White Hill	161.9	SD 6739 5879	Trig
2815	L	521.9	Fair Snape Fell	226.2	SD 5971 4726	Knoll
2822	L	396.3	Easington Fell	193.5	SD 7302 4868	Cairn
2824	L	349.9	Longridge Fell – Spire Hill	240.0	SD 6579 4106	Trig

Ward's Stone

ALAN DAWSON, 1975 AND NOVEMBER 2008

My fourth Marilyn, reached after encouraging a handful of other students out of their halls of residence to run across the M6. There was no plan in mind except to head for Clougha, but once we got started I must have felt an urge to ensure we carried on to the highest point of the Forest of Bowland. My record keeping was poor in 1975 so I don't know what month it was but it felt wintery. When we got back to the campus I remember that the cold tap water felt warm on my ice-cold hands.

On my return visit I was accompanied by my two sisters on a mission to scatter our mother's ashes on the summit area. The choice of hill was obvious once I had worked out that the name was an anagram of Dawson Rest. It was also in Lancashire, where our mother had lived for almost half her life, though Liverpool separated politically from Lancashire in 1974 and became part of the metropolitan county of Merseyside. Scattering the ashes was less sombre than expected as we had the hill to ourselves and enjoyed stunning early sunset views over the Irish Sea. We finished the walk in the dark but it was not a day for discord, so any sisterly grumbles were muted and good-natured.

Fair Snape Fell

ANN BOWKER, 1995

This is in some ways the best of the hills in the Forest of Bowland for the peak bagger because the highest point is close to the edge of the escarpment instead of being in the middle of featureless boggy moorland. By coming up over Parlick one can even enjoy an almost narrow bit of ridge, which loses its character as the steep western edge swings round to the trig point. It was less than a kilometre north-east from here to the summit, over territory which was fairly firm.

Easington Fell

The summit of this hill is less than 1.5km from a road and car park, from where it is easily reached, with an ascent of under 50 metres. The route passes near two unremarkable piles of stones that have been glorified with the names Old Ned and The Wife on the OS map large-scale map.

South-west from Easington Fell, across the B6478, is Waddington Fell, which also has a 396m spot height on OS maps. A line survey by G&J Surveys in 2008 found Easington Fell to be 70cm higher. Study of Lidar data in 2024 confirmed that Waddington Fell is 60-70cm lower than Easington Fell.

Number		Height	Name	Drop	Location	Summit
2813		557	Pendle Hill	395	SD 8046 4141	Trig
2816	L	517.7	Boulsworth Hill	335	SD 9297 3563	Rock
2817	G	476.7	Hail Storm Hill	247.8	SD 8349 1934	Cairn
2820	LT	454.1	Freeholds Top	154.8	SD 9060 2188	Trig
2819	L	456.5	Winter Hill	215.1	SD 6599 1494	Grass near trig
2829	L	179.3	Billinge Hill	151.8	SD 5255 0146	Trig

Freeholds Top

ANN BOWKER, 1995

By parking on Todmorden Moor near the highest point of the A681, we had a climb of less than 200 feet to the summit. The main feature of note was the trig point number, 4444. Rowland had calculated that this was his summit number 771 from Dawson's tables, so this was supposedly the halfway point to 1542 in the book. Later we discovered that we had previously climbed Sharp Haw, which invalidated this calculation.

Billinge Hill

ANN BOWKER, 1995

We had been invited out to lunch close by and so felt obliged to bag this minor hill while we were in the neighbourhood, although it was a miserable day. We set out on the track which ran up outside the fence, topped with barbed wire. We soon discovered that the sound of activity beyond this fence was caused by rubbish lorries dumping their load in an enormous tip which was carved into one side of the hill. The trig point gave a bird's eye view of the rubbish and the large flocks of gulls that were attracted to it. The lousy weather prevented us from getting any more distant panorama.

SUE AND TREVOR LITTLEWOOD, FEBRUARY 2003

The much-maligned Billinge Hill was a pleasant surprise, with wide views over urban and agricultural landscapes. It helped that the landfill site had been filled.

Hail Storm Hill

SUE AND TREVOR LITTLEWOOD, JANUARY 2004

We approached from the south via a tooth-loosening cobbled road. The majority of the vehicles up there seemed to have brought trail bikes with them. The rasp of engines was with us for most of the day. Taking a route east away from a pair of burnt-out cars, we first went up Hunger Hill by a rutted route caused by endless motor-cycle ascents and descents. Heading north on a fine partly-cobbled fell road, we were passed by several more noisy bikes. Passing an abandoned and wrecked car, then twenty or so dumped car wheels, we turned off the road to Hail Storm Hill itself. Big boring bog describes it perfectly. We traipsed over endless waterlogged tussocky ground to locate what could reasonably be called the highest point, then turned off south for Knowl Moor. The trail bikers and their noise were everywhere. They seemed to use the moorland freely and some doubtless saw it as a duty to churn the peat into a black porridgy morass. On the passage to Knowl Moor there were several places where small elephants could have been lost without trace in the goo generated by bike use.

RHB section 36   OS maps 110, 118

Number		Height	Name	Drop	Location	Summit
2807	G	636.3	Kinder Scout	496.6	SK 0848 8756	Mound
2810	L	581.1	Black Hill	165.2	SE 0782 0477	Tussock
2812	L	559.0	Shining Tor	235.7	SJ 9946 7375	Mound
2823	LT	385.3	Gun	168.8	SJ 9700 6151	Trig
2825	L	343.4	The Cloud	181.2	SJ 9044 6369	Rock

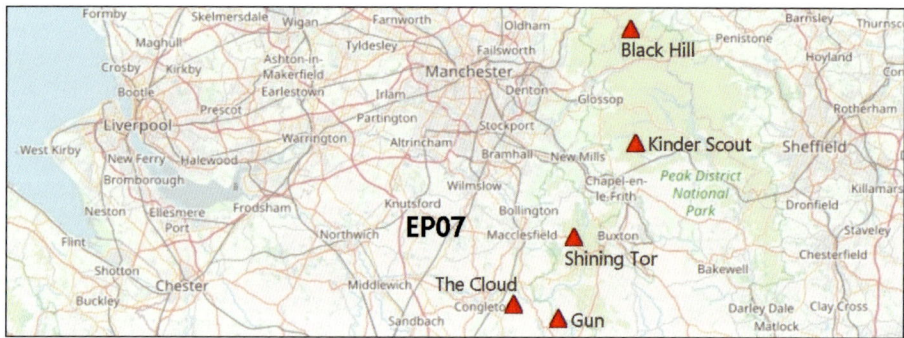

Shining Tor

ALAN DAWSON, 17 APRIL 1987

The first hill I climbed specifically because it was a Marilyn. I had been researching the list for a year and was passing by. I did not have any boots with me so walked up in trainers.

Gun

ANN BOWKER, 1995

We had been on the Roaches many times yet could not be certain we had been to the highest point. For a good long day this outlier could be incorporated into a circuit to include a traverse of the Roaches and inspection of their rocky ramparts. On this occasion we took a simple route up the north ridge and continued to the summit. To avoid road walking we returned along the pleasant ridge with a view north towards Shutlingsloe, the reverse of its aspect from Shining Tor. What a pity it fails to make the tables.

Kinder Scout

PAUL RICHARDSON, JULY 1977

This was my first time on Kinder Scout. We got lost on the way back across Kinder Low. Many subsequent visits were to provide the same experience.

PAUL RICHARDSON, SEPTEMBER 1978

This was an attempt at the Kinder Round. The rain started as I reached Jaggers Clough and never stopped. I could see mist on Kinder Scout but had come so far that to continue was the shortest way back. When Ashop Clough petered out, I was soon lost. Lost, for the first time, in the mist in mountainous terrain. I was pretty scared. I took out my compass and tried to walk due south. Then I discovered what I took to be the Pennine Way and a group of people on it. I found such reassurance to replace considerable anxiety that I tried to continue with my original route rather than follow the Pennine Way to Edale.

I was soon lost again, but I managed to regain the Pennine Way back to Edale. Safely ensconced in the Jolly Rambler, feelings were mixed. I had given myself a fright but I had survived, I had walked further than ever before and reached the dizzy height of 2000 feet.

Six days later I set out on a fine day, armed with map and compass, for a revenge trip to show Kinder Scout who was boss. Of course, I knew already who was boss. Despite good visibility, I got lost again. My route entailed a crossing of the plateau from east to west. I found the first trig pillar but none of the others. I eventually picked up a tributary of Red Brook, took it for a tributary of the River Kinder, and followed it to the edge of the plateau. I returned to Edale, this time by field paths, after another visit to the Downfall. Another victory for Kinder Scout, though perhaps I might call this one a draw?

PAUL RICHARDSON, JUNE 1979

My records were originally intended to be happy reminders of the pleasures of walking in the countryside, but they are becoming a catalogue of minor disasters and a monologue of petty frustrations. The failure of expeditions into the countryside leaves me feeling most disappointed. On this particular day of disaster the local train (to Birmingham) was late. We missed the Sheffield train and then missed the connection from Sheffield to Edale, so we took the bus to Castleton, intending to walk to Edale.

It began to rain as we travelled on the bus and the rain persisted for most of the day. We passed the succession of strangely weathered boulders at Edale Head, the Wool Packs, Pym Chair and so on, and joined the Pennine Way below Kinder Low. The intention was to go to the Downfall before returning to Edale, but time was running short and the cloud base engulfed the tops. We decided to go down immediately, past an impressive landslip at Broadlee Bank. Old Peculier from the wood eased our disappointment in the pub. We caught the train in Edale and returned via Sheffield, arriving home at 2:30am.

PAUL RICHARDSON, FEBRUARY 1981

Kinder wins again! The aim was to make a circuit of the Kinder plateau on the tops. Light snow fell as we ascended Grindsbrook, mist hung at low level and visibility was poor. Snow was thick in places up there, having formed some deep drifts, which made walking difficult. Later I removed my watch whilst washing on the train and forgot to pick it up again. As usual, I vowed to return again to Kinder Scout and do better the next time.

PAUL RICHARDSON, APRIL 1988

In my previous ramblings on Kinder Scout, the summit did not seem to have been the goal of any walk. An absence of seven years, during which summits have increasingly been sought out, left me marvelling at this omission. This time I intended to cross the desperate maze of gigantic peat hags and reach that highest point.

The short journey to the summit changed my entire outlook on Kinder Scout. Firstly, it was comparatively easy. The peat groughs of ten feet and more deep simply did not exist here. There were many boggy areas but there was much more relatively solid ground and vegetation. We reached the pole and small cairn with ease, despite their being almost moated. We headed off for the trig point on Kinder Low and experienced little difficulty. The Pennine Way proved to be harder going than the open moor. The peat often had the consistency of deep snow. Several detours had to be made to avoid large morasses. To vary our return journey we went eastwards, above Nether Tor, crossed Golden Clough and took the track skirting Ringing Roger to The Nab. Subsequent calculations suggested that our walk took us just fourteen miles, though it certainly felt more than that. Whatever the statistics, it was a grand day that I greatly enjoyed.

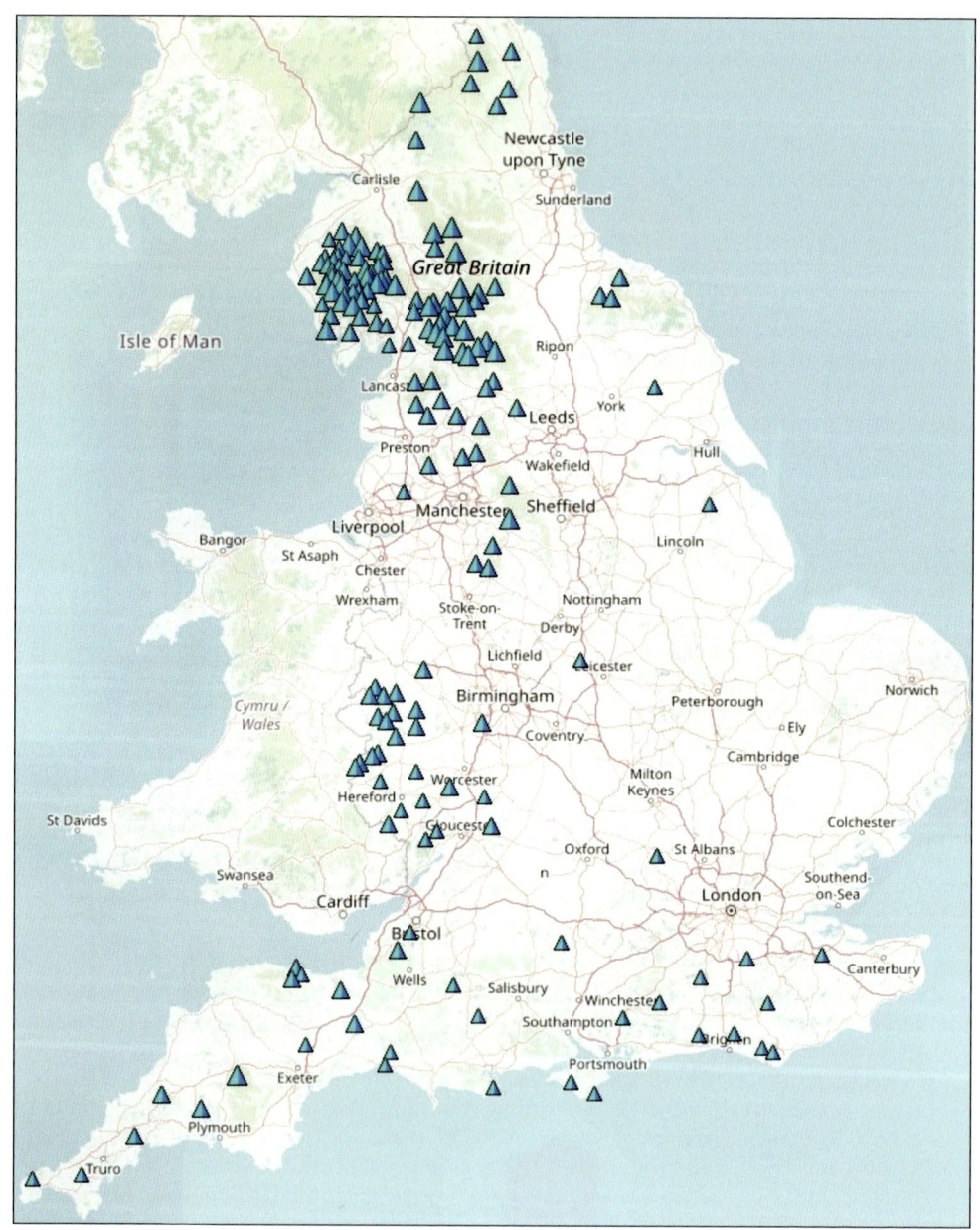

Distribution of Marilyns in England

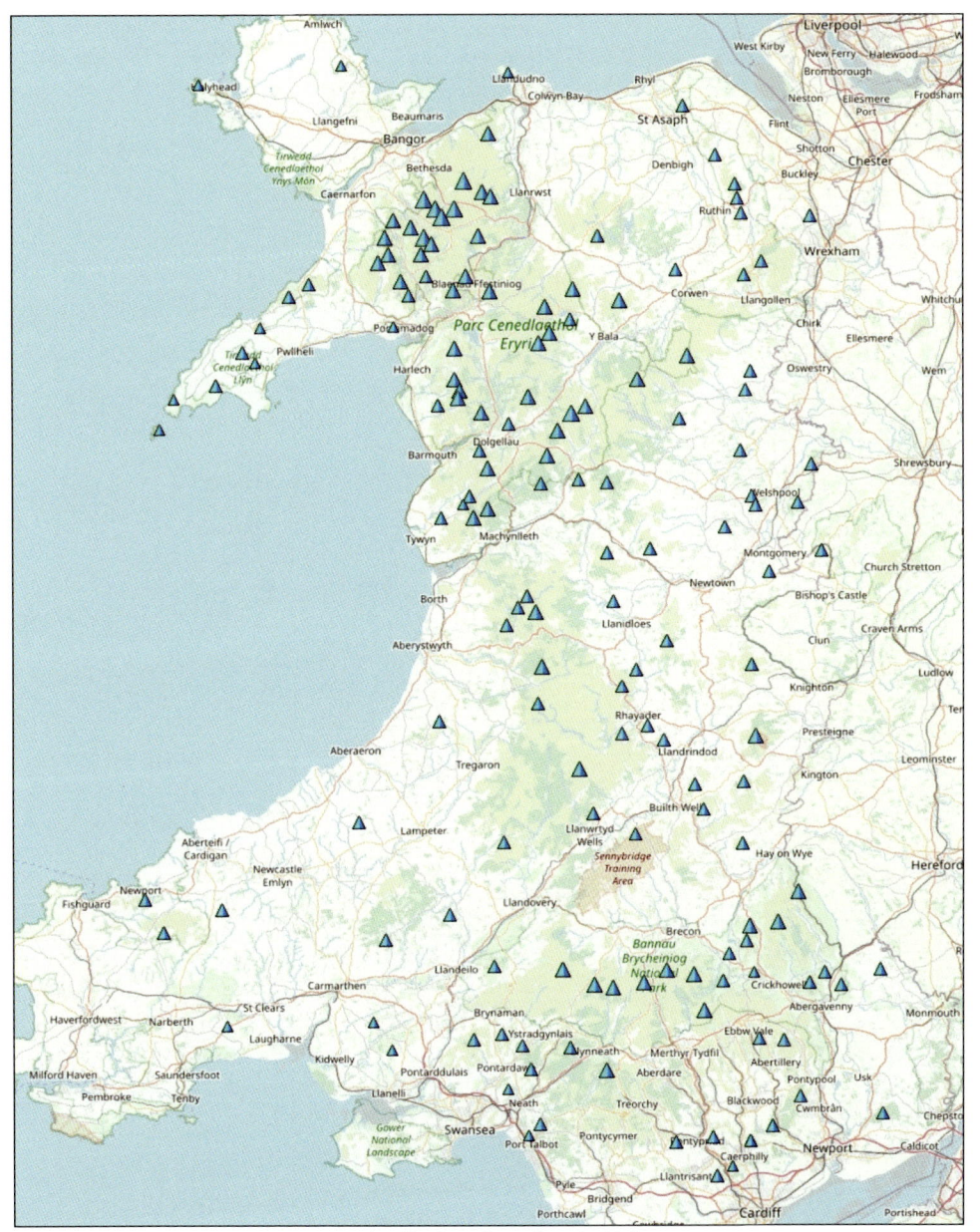

Distribution of Marilyns in Wales

North Wales, Anglesey and Bardsey

Land west of River Weaver and Tern, north of Afon Dyfi, Dugoed, Banwy, Efyrnwy and River Severn

Marilyns:	77
Highest and most prominent:	Snowdon, 1084.7m, drop 1039m
Lowest:	Mynydd Enlli, 167.9m
Least prominent:	Mynydd y Cwm, drop 150.0m

The other areas in North Wales are shown on page 272

Number		Height	Name	Drop	Location	Summit
1959	LT	220.1	Holyhead Mountain / Mynydd Twr	220.1	SH 2185 8294	Trig
1961	LM	177.5	Mynydd Bodafon / Yr Arwydd #	177.5	SH 4724 8541	Trig
1962	M	167.9	Mynydd Enlli, Bardsey	167.9	SH 1231 2193	Rock

Mynydd Bodafon

This hill was renamed from Yr Arwydd in 1997, possibly because it seemed to be a more appropriate name and possibly because it seemed easier to pronounce.

Holyhead Mountain, Anglesey

ANDY HYAMS, AUGUST 2009

It was a dreich day in North Wales. Snowdonia was out of the question. A first visit to Anglesey looked ideal. I could first bag Holyhead Mountain and afterwards Yr Arwydd.

I should have feared the worst as I turned on headlights and foglights as my car climbed out of Holyhead, following the signs for South Stack. However, from the car park, the 'Mountain' looked straightforward. I could see a track leading onto the open hillside. It disappeared into the clag after a few metres but I knew there was a trig on top. Keep ascending until you reach the trig then turn round and retrace your steps. I'll leave food, map, compass and GPS in the car and go without a pack. Back in an hour.

Finding the summit was easy. There were almost too many paths. I thought I had memorised the lie of the land but I wished I had been able to look at Landranger 114, which was in the car. Emboldened by all the paths, I decided to return slightly north of my ascent route and have a look at South Stack lighthouse. After an eternity, I emerged from the mist above a car park. It was not the one holding my car. I assumed it was closer to the lighthouse. Descending further and surprisingly steeply, I began to ponder why a vehicle leaving the car park had the sea on its left rather than its right. Slowly the horrible truth dawned. I had crossed the headland and was approaching the Soldier's Point car park, east of the hill and 180 degrees away from where I wanted to be.

I re-ascended to the misty trig and convinced myself I was continuing in a straight line back to my car. Another age passed. Vision returned and I saw a white coastguard building. South Stack lighthouse. I had given up on my plan to go there but no worries, it was only a few hundred metres from my car and my emergency box of Mars bars.

Imagine my horror when I reached the perimeter wall and saw a notice reading North Stack Signal Station. Having intended to descend south-west, my first descent had been north-east and my second due north. Pausing to gingerly inspect the caves and cliffs (which someone later told me give some of the best sea climbs in Britain), I decided I was not going to re-enter the mist and pay a third visit to the trig. Instead I stayed just below cloud level and inched my way along precipitous ground, with fearsome drops into Gogarth Bay on my right, until South Stack eventually loomed into view. Five hours after starting what I expected to be a one-hour excursion, feeling soaked, cold, tired, hungry and more frightened than I had ever been south of the Cuillin, I reached my car's Mars. Yr Arwydd would have to wait. Food and a stiff drink were required. Since then, I have banned myself from stepping onto a hill without map, compass and GPS.

Mynydd Enlli, Bardsey

CHRIS WATSON, JUNE 2005

The highlight of the weekend for most of us was the trip to Bardsey Island. It was a nervous cavalcade that drove down to Aberdaron, as the organiser had had dreadful trouble pinning down the boatman as to when he would be leaving and how much room there was. In the event it turned out to be a big boat and 30 of us embarked for Bardsey. Nobody ended up in the sea as we were transferred out to the island in a small dinghy. Sadly, the visibility was poor and it was a misty Mynydd Enlli where 28 of us gathered together to witness Welsh Marilyn completions for Alan Holmes and Dr Ian Watson. None of us twigged the Holmes and Watson scenario until the photos were developed a couple of weeks later. Lindsay Munro led the Hall of Fame chant in the absence of the Chief Chanter, who was off to bigger hills (or wouldn't pay the fare). We still had time for a stroll around the island and a look at the seal colony before the journey back to the mainland and the even longer journeys back home.

Holmes and Watson on misty Mynydd Enlli

CAMPBELL SINGER, JUNE 2007

What should have been a pleasant day-trip to Bardsey Island turned into a bit of a drama for some of the 30 passengers. Due to the low tide it was necessary for us to be ferried to the boat in a small inflatable dinghy. As the first group of passengers were transferring to the boat, the unsecured dinghy pulled away from the side and a passenger, who was in mid stride, slipped between dinghy and boat into the sea. She was a non-swimmer but had been issued with a life jacket, which kept her afloat A chivalrous crew member jumped from the dinghy into the sea in order to effect a rescue, but his sudden leap caused the dinghy to overturn and its one remaining passenger to join the two others in the water. Eventually they were all able to scramble aboard the boat but were shocked and drenched, with some minor injuries. One of them was celebrating his 60th birthday.

Number		Height	Name	Drop	Location	Summit
1992	L	783.7	Moel Hebog	585.2	SH 5652 4696	Rock near trig
2037	ML	552.4	Moel-ddu	199.4	SH 5795 4420	Cairn
1999	M	733.4	Craig Cwm Silyn	398	SH 5255 5026	Shelter
2004	L	709.7	Trum y Ddysgl	208.6	SII 5448 5164	Grass
2007		698	Mynydd Mawr	463	SH 5397 5469	Cairn
1957		263	Moel-y-Gest	236	SH 5492 3889	Boulder near trig
1951	G	560.7	Yr Eifl	430	SH 3649 4474	Trig
1952	M	522.1	Gyrn Ddu	385	SH 4011 4678	Cairn
1953	G	510.3	Bwlch Mawr	147.6	SH 4267 4785	Boulder
1954		371	Carn Fadryn	343	SH 2787 3518	Rock by trig
1958	L	235.9	Carneddol	155.9	SH 3012 3310	Wall
1955	TL	304.9	Mynydd Rhiw	239.5	SH 2285 2939	Rock by trig
1956	L	280.1	Garn Boduan	176.7	SH 3121 3935	Rock by plinth
1960	G	191.4	**Mynydd Anelog *****	151.0	SH 1519 2722	Rock

Moel-y-Gest

ALAN DAWSON, AUGUST 1967

My first Marilyn, with my uncle during a family summer holiday in a caravan. I quite liked the walk and the view but there was no revelation. I never would have guessed that I'd climb all the rest, in 1967 on the top of Moel-y-Gest. I was drawn back from Wirral to Porthmadog a few times later on but that was because of its wonderful shop, Cob Records.

JON METCALF, 2003

Probably the most mountain per metre above sea level I've found over the first half of the list. This is just a phenomenal small ridge when taken east to west.

Moel-ddu

CHRIS CROCKER, 2005

Moel-ddu had been saved for my last Welsh Marilyn and it proved to be a good choice. The outward route over the summit and return along the east side was interesting, the topography quite complex and the weather near perfect.

Yr Eifl

ANDY HYAMS, SEPTEMBER 2011

Wonderful sea views in great light. Purple heather and yellow gorse in the foreground with the added bonus of the rocky approach to the north top and a visit to the nearby Celtic hill fort of Tre'r Cairi.

Mynydd Anelog

JOHN BARNARD, JULY 2013

Mynydd Anelog had been on our radar for several years and everything went well on the day of the survey that discovered it to be a Marilyn. The farmer gave us permission to drive our cars through the field to the bwlch, having transferred his livestock out of the field. The summit was a glorious viewpoint, and while the Leica GNSS unit was collecting data, we were able to admire the Llyn peninsula in more detail while sunbathing.

Number		Height	Name	Drop	Location	Summit
1963	G	1084.7	Snowdon / Yr Wyddfa	1039	SH 6099 5437	Trig
1978	L	897.9	Y Lliwedd	153.8	SH 6224 5334	Rock
1997	G	747.2	Yr Aran	238.4	SH 6043 5152	Rock by cairn
2000		726	Moel Eilio	259	SH 5558 5771	Shelter
2015		674	Moel Cynghorion	176	SH 5861 5639	Cairn

Snowdon

In recent years there has been a drive by Welsh organisations to insist that the big one must be referred to as Yr Wyddfa, not Snowdon. In principle that makes sense. There seems no good reason for English speakers to refer to Rome or Naples when Italians call them Roma and Napoli. The big difference is that almost everyone in Italy speaks Italian and not that many speak English. In Wales the proportion of Welsh speakers was under 30% in 2022 and almost everyone can speak English, even if they choose not to. Almost all hill walkers refer to the hill as Snowdon, and probably most people in Wales outside the national park. Both names are given here as a matter of courtesy, but Snowdon remains the main Marilyn name. Most other hills in North Wales have Welsh names and need no English version. As for the height, this is taken from an old OS figure before the summit was reconstructed. It was surveyed with GNSS at the request of OS but there was a corporate reluctance to accept the result. A decimal point may not be justified.

PAUL RICHARDSON, AUGUST 1995

We climbed the Pyg track, along with scores of others, on another very hot day. Snowdon remains a noble mountain, patiently enduring the hordes and their idiot ways, as it has endured the indignities of the tourist railway, summit hotels, mining and hydro-electric schemes. It embraces all this nonsense, as it embraces its more natural friends the ravens, and its enemies the ice and wind. From Glaslyn, deep within the massif, its summit soars in a majestic pyramid. We did not disdain the summit restaurant when we got there.

BERT BARNETT, OCTOBER 2002

Fine morning at Pen y Pass at 8am. Car park £4 for day ticket, officious little squirt of a warden. Up Crib Goch, only one group of four ahead, one young guy passed us, otherwise empty. Great fun, over too quick, easy option routes usually inferior to tricky options. Wind blasting cold, hat flaps tight and hood too, gloves higher up. Some people on high but none on the actual top when we were there. Men in sleeveless shirts and no hats, red faces, red arms, grinning with determination. Mad or ill-equipped? Probably both.

ANDY TOMKINS, MAY 2015

With only three Welsh Marilyns to go, I finally got round to scaling Snowdon. For a person who hates crowds I strangely chose a bank holiday Saturday, although I chose the ridge route from Llanberis and had it all to myself until I got close to Garnedd Ugain. Standing on this summit I saw a long snake of people making for the top. I had never seen so many people on a hill. There was a queue to get to the trig pillar and a huge crowd around it. I still thought it a magnificent mountain though. The scramble on Y Lliwedd was enjoyable and much of the crowd had disappeared.

WN03 Glyder-tryfan

Number		Height	Name	Drop	Location	Summit
1967	G	1000.9	Glyder Fawr	642	SH 6424 5795	Rock
1977	G	917.5	Tryfan	190	SH 6640 5939	Rock
1972		947	Y Garn	236	SH 6309 5957	Cairn
1975	M	922.3	Elidir Fawr	210.8	SH 6117 6129	Rock

There are only thirteen Marilyns in the Snowdon group, Glyderau and Carneddau, so they could have been combined in a single topographic area. However, the three hill areas are well separated by deep valleys with major roads, they include numerous less prominent peaks and they tend to be regarded as separate groups by most hill walkers.

Glyder Fawr

Glyder Fawr is the highest point of the Glyderau range. In August 2010 John Barnard, Graham Jackson and Myrddyn Phillips carried out a summit survey of Glyder Fawr, which was shown as 999m on OS maps at the time. They knew that the highest point, a rocky outcrop, could have been missed by a cartographer examining the three-dimensional aerial photograph. After collecting four hours of GNSS data their suspicions proved to be correct and Glyder Fawr was shown to be the fifth peak in Wales over 1000m high.

Tryfan

In an opinion poll for Marhofn magazine in 2009, Tryfan was voted the best hill in Wales over 600m high, with over four times as many votes as Snowdon and Cadair idris. Some people voted it the best hill in Britain, despite its summit being notoriously tricky to stand on. Perhaps that challenge adds further appeal to a magnificent mountain.

Glyder Fawr from Llechog on the slopes of Snowdon

Number		Height	Name	Drop	Location	Summit
1965		1064	Carnedd Llewelyn	750	SH 6836 6437	Cairn
1989	M	798.6	Pen Llithrig y Wrach	180.3	SH 7162 6228	Cairn
2013	L	675.9	Creigiau Gleision	261.4	SH 7290 6154	Cairn
2031	GA	610.0	Tal y Fan	189.6	SH 7293 7264	Rock by trig

Carnedd Llewelyn

PAUL RICHARDSON, APRIL 1980

As we walked through the streets of Llanfairfechan, I pondered the words of the Gospel According to Poucher: the Carneddau 'can be difficult in mist... to make a successful traverse of the range in bad weather conditions requires expert use of map and compass, together with long experience of the group as a whole.'

A track led us all the way to the summit of Drum. It was still misty but less wet as we continued to the summit of Foel Fras, littered with huge piles of rocks. We could see nothing, but followed the fence toward Garnedd Uchaf. A short section of easy climbing brought us to the hut on Foel Grach for a brief rest. It was now as easy to go on as to turn back, so we continued along the ridge to Carnedd Llewelyn. More rocks and a grey haze everywhere. No great feat of compass work was needed to traverse the narrow ridge of Bwlch Cyfryw-Drum. The views down on either side should have been spectacular, but we saw only a grey wall of cloud in every direction.

We crossed the ridge and began to climb towards Carnedd Dafydd. Suddenly, and without warning, the cloud parted, revealing the ridges, the Nant Ffrancon valley and the lakes far below. It was like a miracle – a stunning sight so unexpected and so beautiful that it was unforgettable. I began shouting like a schoolboy and struggling to get the camera out of my rucksack. We managed a couple of photographs then the cloud rolled in again and we were back in the grey world once more. We were grateful for slightly improved visibility for the descent from Pen yr Ole Wen. We struggled and scrambled down, guided by the cottages below, sometimes sliding on the seats of our pants, never relaxed and occasionally scared half to death. Darkness was falling quite quickly, and we had only a cursory look at Ogwen Falls on our way to the youth hostel.

Pen Llithrig y Wrach

ALAN DAWSON

I was grateful to the Association of University Teachers for calling a one-day strike in January 1986 and allowing most university staff a rare mid-week day off. I had recently discovered hill lists and seized the opportunity to join some colleagues for bit of extra-curricular bagging on a cold winter day.

Pen Llithrig y Wrach is five metres lower than Beinn Iaruinn, to the west of Glen Roy. These two hills would appear to have little in common but they were linked together in the title of one of the few poems about the Iraq war to be created entirely from the names of Marilyns. The original verses from 2003 are included below, though Raw Head no long qualifies, Sotan on Berneray has been superseded by Sron an Duin, and some hills have been renamed. Names are intended to be read as if they were English words.

Y Wrach Iaruinn

Eas tor y avon eaval billinge
Faire east of aden llan ddu fawr
Ben buck bin dent a sighty belling
Sow calkin alvie ghent tor ward
Scout o scoursburgh, cocyn cobbler
Lamachan donachain trilleachan trum
Wills o wisp an windy brimmond
Loaf badandun, neuran gorm

Mam hael, mam hael, ben fourman says
An rombalds bleaval hutig horn
Yr armine ditchling keen tee shuas
How orval tirran broughton doune
Cnoc knockdolian, knockan doir
Cille bathach king, hunt oss an bin
Each raise yr loyal standard oir
Mendick conchra, watch willy win

See persie pibble seager grianan
Saddle royl fuar common corse
Balloch mhor an belig spidean
Breac da barrule, noup da law
Sell the dumglow, firle the pillar
Cook the buachaille, speinne beag lice
Smeur an smean an raw scrinadle
Button hutton, cul pressendye

Head bathach fleet bhraghad a roan
Plynlimon pendle dundry down
Great sotan armin dubh dubh dubhain
Rainich birks an blackwood brown
Streap an birnam, wrekin sgreadan
Blisco scald an mhaim an scar
Chleirich begwns, shios sguman
Scaraben the cacra corr

Nevis, west raplaich, nevis
Shalloch tal y fan abhail
Dinas hir grey rubers broomy
Teallach wirren ruardean hill
Elidir eunaich vane an callow
Hail the newtyle hallin law
Auchnafree pen gyrn cairnpapple
Mullach shiantaidh rig the sgor

Donn garrisdale gun ronas botley
Fitful innis burrow cam
Ffridd an feartaig, fitty fennli
Garn bogrie doirein uamha nam
Eighe on an dun mawr sandness cuilean
Meallan deadh an mynydd mor
Eighe on an dun achilty mountain
Meallan deadh an mynydd mor

Partial glossary:

billinge: killing spree / ben buck: USA / ben fourman: US president /
alvie: allies / ward: war / loaf badandun: sense abandoned / rombalds: Rumsfeld /
orval tirran: Saddam Hussein / bathach king: Saddam Hussein /
oss an bin: Osama Bin Laden / persie pibble: Tony Blair /
breac da barrule, noup da law: ignore legal advice and the United Nations
buachaille: books, dossier / lice: lies / raw scrinadle: spin / hutton: Hutton report /
sotan armin: US army / chleirich: clerics / shios: shias / mullach: mullahs /
rubers broomy: ugly rumours / garrisdale: garrison /
fitful, ffridd, feartaig: fearful and jittery /
garn bogrie doirein: getting bogged down / uamha nam: another Vietnam /
ruardean: road in / auchnafree pen: free press / sandness: senseless /
mynydd: many / cuilean: killing / meallan: millions /
achilty: the guilty/ mountain: mounting

Pen Llithrig y Wrach

Manod Mawr from near Blaenau Ffestiniog

WN05 Siabod-arenig

RHB sections 30B, 30D   OS maps 115, 124, 125

Number		Height	Name	Drop	Location	Summit
1980	ML	872.2	Moel Siabod	599.8	SH 7052 5463	Rock by trig
1994	T	770.1	Moelwyn Mawr	385.6	SH 6582 4486	Trig
2006	L	697.9	Allt-fawr	246.1	SH 6817 4746	Outcrop
2038	L	382.4	Moel y Dyniewyd	214.3	SH 6126 4773	Rock
2068		661	Manod Mawr	265	SH 7244 4466	Boulder
2053	T	853.5	Arenig Fawr	480.1	SH 8270 3694	Trig
2057		751	Moel Llyfnant	206	SH 8083 3518	Cairn on rock
2081	M	540.0	Mynydd Nodol	169.2	SH 8651 3934	Rock by cairn
2063	M	688.9	Arenig Fach	298.3	SH 8202 4158	Rock
2065		669	Carnedd y Filiast	317	SH 8712 4460	Trig
2043	M	522.4	Moel y Gydros	145.9	SH 9143 4538	Cairn
2059	T	734.2	Rhobell Fawr	306	SH 7868 2566	Trig
2082		405	Foel Offrwm	236	SH 7498 2099	Cairn
2079	M	611.0	Foel Goch	274.2	SH 9538 4229	Trig

Moel Siabod

Only seven summits in Wales, and four in England, have relative height over 600m (there are 82 in Scotland). The drop from Moel Siabod is close to 600m, but a survey by Myrddyn Phillips in 2018 found it to be 599.9m. This could be rounded up to 600m, but Lidar data has supported the survey finding, suggesting a slightly higher col and 599.7m drop.

Foel Offrwm

BERT BARNETT, OCTOBER 2002

From the car park at SH746213 we headed straight up Foel Offrwm through a thin line of trees, over a low fence, up through deep but surprisingly dry bracken and steep grass and heather to a pleasant viewpoint. All in the dry and good visibility, the benefits of a wee hill. The surrounding countryside was idyllic.

Memorial on the summit of Arenig Fawr for the crew of an air crash in 1943

Number		Height	Name	Drop	Location	Summit
2042	T	531.6	Mwdwl-eithin	262.8	SH 9171 5405	Trig
2049		389	**Mynydd Rhyd ddu *****	165	SJ 0545 4774	Ground by trig
2052	M	207.1	Great Orme / Y Gogarth	201.7	SH 7675 8333	Rock by trig

Number		Height	Name	Drop	Location	Summit
2039	M	576.9	Moel y Gamelin	381.2	SJ 1763 4651	Rock
2040	M	564.6	Cyrn-y-Brain	163.8	SJ 2082 4887	Knoll
2041	GM	554.9	Moel Famau	281.8	SJ 1612 6267	Wall
2045	G	510.9	Foel Fenlli	152.4	SJ 1648 6008	Cairn
2046	L	466.7	Moel Gyw	178.8	SJ 1715 5754	Cairn
2047	G	440.2	Penycloddiau	157.4	SJ 1271 6789	Cairn on mound
2050	M	330.0	Hope Mountain	187.3	SJ 2947 5689	Trig
2051	G	304.9	Mynydd y Cwm ***	150.0	SJ 0730 7673	Tussock

Moel Famau

This is the highest point of the Clwydian Range and the most popular Marilyn in Wales under 600m high. It does get very busy at times, but the good paths mean there is no problem coming down in the dark for those who enjoy a solitary summit sunset. As well as being an outstanding viewpoint, it is a landmark from much of the low-lying land to the east, being visible from the Thelwall Viaduct by Warrington, the top floor of Calday Grange Grammar School on Wirral and lots of less notable locations.

Mynydd y Cwm

This hill was promoted to Marilyn status in 2009 after surveys of summit and col by John Barnard, Graham Jackson and Myrddyn Phillips. The survey was not conclusive, with the probability for inclusion around 51%. It is one of the two most marginal Marilyns, along with See Morris Hill near Dumfries. Its relative height hovers around the 150m mark, as the soil at the col is subject to fluctuations induced by wind, rain, plough, hooves and possibly the activities of moles and worms. Mynydd y Cwm appears to have quantum status, varying according to when it is observed. Further surveys would be unlikely to alter this. The full survey report gives a flavour of the terrain at col (bwlch) and summit:

The critical bwlch is 13.4km south-east from the summit. Visually the shape of the bwlch was not obvious and we had to use the level and staff to build up a picture of the line of the bwlch between the hills. We located its position by first surveying in parallel lines about 1-2m apart in the line of the bwlch and marking the lowest points with coloured flags. Then we surveyed along the line of coloured flags, at right angles to the line of the bwlch, to locate the highest flag. This procedure was carried out independently on both survey days. Bearing in mind the local variation in ground surface height we would estimate the average value to be accurate to about +/-0.1m.

Surveying the summit was no easier:

There is a cairn but a survey with level and staff showed this not to be the highest point. The summit is about 6m away under a tree and is a few cm higher – we checked this by dismantling the cairn. The summit area is covered extensively with trees and it was not possible to set up the GPS on the summit position. Satellite reception was a problem generally and we were forced to set up the GPS in nearby clearings and then optically level to the summit position. Over the two surveys, six different positions for the GPS were chosen, but still satellite reception was limited and we were constantly vigilant of loss of satellite reception compromising our data. This factor reduced the accuracy of our results.

Number		Height	Name	Drop	Location	Summit
2087	M	832.0	Cadair Berwyn	347.3	SJ 0716 3235	Rock
2828		227.1	Raw Head ¬	148.4	SJ 5084 5484	Rock
2132	LT	522.9	Gyrn Moelfre	233.3	SJ 1844 2938	Trig
2135		341	Mynydd-y-briw	163	SJ 1740 2607	Grass

Cadair Berwyn

There are only three Marilyns in this large hill area but there is a lot of relatively high ground. Cadair Berwyn has thirteen subsidiary summits over 600 metres high (with at least 20m drop), which is more than any other hill in Wales. Carnedd Llewelyn also has thirteen and the next highest is Waun Fach with eight.

For many years the highest point in the Berwyn range was uncertain, as both Moel Sych and Cadair Berwyn were shown as 827m on OS maps. The answer turned out to be neither of them. The story of the discovery made headlines in 1988 on a rare occasion when a summit relocation was judged to be worth an article in a national newspaper:

'Bernard Wright and a band of superannuated ramblers have discovered a new mountain in Wales. The 2723ft peak in the Berwyns, south-west of Llangollen, has been confirmed by the Ordnance Survey, which had somehow managed to overlook it. Mr Wright, aged 63, a former motor oils scientist from Tarvin in Cheshire, was leading a 20-strong party from his Retired People's Club, all in their sixties and seventies, along the Berwyns last October when they found themselves staring at a peak absent from their OS map. They were standing on Cadair Berwyn, looking toward Moel Sych. The map shows these as the twin peaks of the Berwyns, both 2713ft high, but their view was blocked by another peak a quarter of a mile away.' *(The Guardian, 26 Sep 1988)*

A survey by Myrddyn Phillips in 2014 showed the summit to be five metres higher than the two 827m points, yet by 2024, 36 years after the newspaper article, OS maps still did not show any spot height for the summit, just a tiny 830m contour ring.

Raw Head

This was one of the first hills to be surveyed using GNSS equipment, in April 2009. It turned out to have one of the most complex col locations, which took a long time to identify and survey, but in the end the result was clear. Raw Head falls short of being a Marilyn by 1.6 metres. This was probably the most disappointing of all survey findings, as it had seemed to be a classic Marilyn – the highest point in a wide area, located on a distinctive ridge with good paths and a variety of pleasant walks. It illustrates the value of including Submarilyns with the main listing, as it would be unfortunate to overlook an enjoyable outing for less than two metres of prominence. Its summit is about nine km from the Welsh border but its parent hill is Cadair Berwyn, so the topographic rules mean it has to be included within the North Wales region.

ANN BOWKER, 1995

As far as I know Raw Head is unique in having a summit cave which passes through the highest outcrop so that you can crawl from one side to the other under the ground. This makes it a marvellous goal for a walk with children. Indeed it is a great walk for anyone, along the red sandstone escarpment of the Peckforton Hills. We did it as part of the Cheshire Sandstone Trail, a lovely walk throughout, and this summit is the highest point.

Number		Height	Name	Drop	Location	Summit
2056		756	Y Llethr	561	SH 6613 2577	Grass by wall
2058	G	750.4	Diffwys	147.6	SH 6613 2341	Grass by trig
2060		720	Rhinog Fawr	367	SH 6570 2901	Trig
2062	M	711.6	**Rhinog Fach *****	151.0	SH 6648 2701	Rock by cairn
2080		589	Moelfre	162	SH 6262 2459	Cairn
2074	M	624.0	Moel Ysgyfarnogod	181	SH 6584 3458	Cairn
2073		629	Y Garn	317	SH 7027 2303	Cairn

Rhinog Fach

MYRDDYN PHILLIPS, AUGUST 2021

There are many upland areas in Wales that captivate and draw me back time and again but few can compare to the quality of the northern Rhinogydd. These hills are rugged and unforgiving and form a barrier between the land to their east and the coastal plain to their west. I wanted to revisit a hill I had been up on 18 previous occasions and one that was long overdue an accurate survey. With a high pressure system centred over the country, I headed toward Coed y Brenin to park at the end of a narrow paved road that heads west from the busy A470. My favoured route of ascent for Rhinog Fach was from the west via Cwm Nantcol, giving an open view of the hills from a beautiful high valley, but the forest route has a higher start and is easier to get to when driving from the east.

After a survey of the bwlch for Rhinog Fawr, I peered up at the horrendously steep slope I had chosen as my ascent route. This route is uncompromising and just heads up through heather and rock. It looked intimidating. Eventually the steepest section of the ascent was behind me and the upper part of the hill bulged up in front. This resembles a cone of a hill seemingly plonked on top of what is already quite a substantial land mass.

The summit of Rhinog Fach consists of a small protruding rock about two metres from the base of an untidy cairn. I set up the Trimble aligned with the highest part of the rock and started to gather data. To have wanted to survey this hill for many years and now to finally be here on its summit with the Trimble quietly beeping away gathering data was both a relief and a joy. As I sat, glimmers of sunshine fed across the land toward the coast to the west. It felt like being on top of the world, perched on this boulder-strewn hill, looking out at an evolving view, with the cloud base now above the summit.

I walked part of the way down in the company of two walkers from South Wales but they still had a long day ahead whilst I concentrated on the bwlch for Rhinog Fach and a a small area of land just east of the stone wall, taking two data sets on the hill-to-hill traverse and one on the valley-to-valley traverse. I was at the bwlch for over 40 minutes.

Happy with my efforts at the bwlch, I walked back toward Rhinog Fach to connect with the path leading down to the northern shore of Llyn Hywel, which I'd heard by many to be the most beautiful mountain lake in Wales. I would not argue otherwise. All that remained was to follow paths back to the forest track, with Rhinog Fawr looking a beast of hill from this perspective, its profile a great lump of rock and heather.

The survey result gave Rhinog Fach a relative height 151.0m, making it the first entirely new Marilyn in Wales since the survey of Mynydd Anelog in 2013, and the first in Britain since Beinn Dearg in the far north-west of Scotland in 2018.

Rhinog Fach (Myrddyn Phillips)

Llyn Cau on the way up Cadair Idris

Number		Height	Name	Drop	Location	Summit
2083	A	905.6	Aran Fawddwy	672.9	SH 8627 2238	Rock by trig
2091		779	Glasgwm	215	SH 8367 1945	Cairn
2104	ML	669.7	Esgeiriau Gwynion #	170.0	SH 8892 2361	Fence
2137	A	892.7	Cadair Idris	606.0	SH 7111 1303	Rock by trig
5622	G	383.1	Pared y Cefn-hir	149.4	SH 6619 1488	Rock
2157	M	380.1	Foel Cae'rberllan	211.8	SH 6762 0820	Voutcrop
2158		321	Moel Fynydd ***	153	SH 6978 1620	Heather
2145	AM	678.5	Maesglase *	318.0	SH 8169 1500	Tussock
2154	A	544.1	Ceiswyn	144.7	SH 7453 1090	Heather
2155	M	468.3	Craig Goch / Mynydd Cwmcelli #	156	SH 8048 0995	Trig
19413	MA	667.5	Foel Cedig **	180.1	SH 9817 2833	Knoll
2148	ML	666.9	Tarren y Gesail	465.4	SH 7104 0589	Tussock near trig
2151		634	Tarrenhendre	203	SH 6828 0415	Cairn
2131	LT	540.5	Rhialgwm	220.5	SJ 0550 2117	Grass by trig
2134	LT	356.3	Allt y Main	174.6	SJ 1621 1515	Trig
2159	M	312.9	Foel Cocyn / Ffridd Cocyn #	250.4	SH 6245 0429	Cairn
2160	L	288.5	Gamallt	208.4	SH 6655 0676	Knoll

Foel Rhudd was renamed Esgeiriau Gwynion in 1997, as Foel Rhudd is a separate 659m summit. Other hills in this area have been assigned new names more recently following useful place name research by Myrddyn Phillips. Ffridd Cocyn was renamed Foel Cocyn and Mynydd Cwmcelli renamed Craig Goch. Moel Fynydd was added in the first revision in 1995 as Craig y Castell and has since been renamed.

Foel Cedig

A survey by Myrddyn Phillips in August 2018 showed this hill to be 1.2m higher than Cyrniau Nod, which it superseded. It is a more appealing summit, with a distinctive mound near a track and less heather to wade through. There were few complaints about the change. In a small poll published in 2009, Cyrniau Nod was voted the worst Welsh Marilyn over 600m, with as many votes as Waun Fach and Drygarn Fawr combined.

Aran Fawddwy

The trig pillar is listed as 906.8m by OS but this is positioned on top of a large cairn. The highest natural rock is a few metres north from the trig. Aran Fawddwy is the 61st most prominent hill in Britain and the fourth most prominent in Wales. Despite that, it does not feature in the ludicrous 'full house' concept promoted by the Scottish Mountaineering Club. This house includes Carnedd Uchaf, the 2380th most prominent summit, and several hundred other summits that are much lower and far less prominent, though not Cadair Idris, which is another one of the 93 hills in Britain with relative height over 600 metres.

Cadair Idris

MALCOLM CLARK, JANUARY 2012

Highlights of the year included a traverse of Cadair Idris from Fairbourne to Dolgellau on a perfect January day. Hard to imagine this was achievable in a day trip from the Midlands on public transport.

——— Mid Wales and English Borders ———

Land south of Dyfi, Banwy, Efyrnwy, west of Onny and Lugg, north of Tywi and upper Usk and Wye

Marilyns:	47
Highest and most prominent:	Pumlumon Fawr, 752m, drop 526m
Lowest:	Brandy Hill, 206m
Least prominent:	Garreg-hir, drop 150.7m

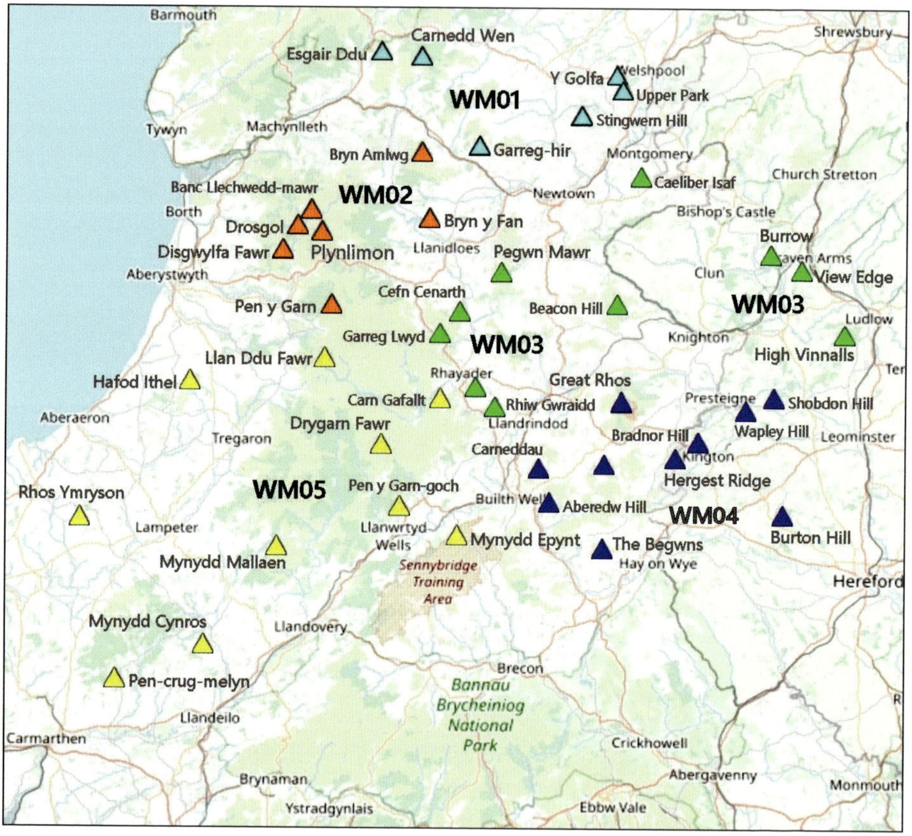

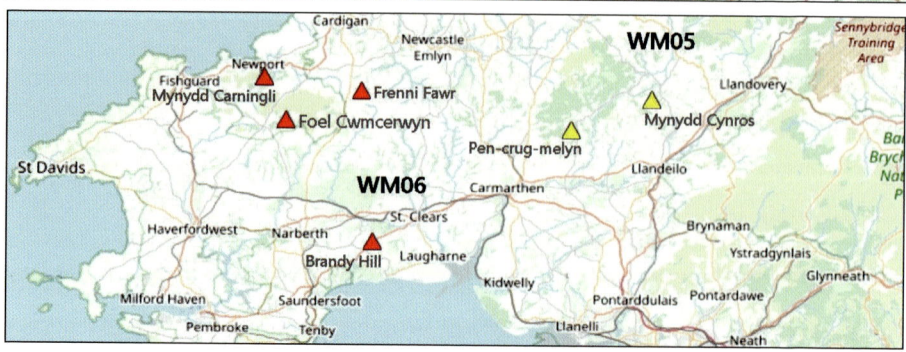

RHB section 31A   OS maps 125, 136

Number		Height	Name	Drop	Location	Summit
2168		523	Carnedd Wen	232	SH 9240 0992	Tussock near trig
2171	G	484.9	Garreg-hir	150.7	SN 9987 9792	Vrock
2173	ML	464.1	Esgair Ddu	224	SH 8732 1064	Tussock
2174	M	358.1	Stingwern Hill	180	SJ 1328 0145	Trig
2175	M	354.0	Upper Park	177.0	SJ 1898 0527	Grass by tree
2136	M	341.4	Y Golfa	165	SJ 1824 0708	Trig

Garreg-hir etc

DAVID ROBINSON, 2002

In my opinion, attractive and little-known hills in Wales are Garn Fadryn, Foel Offrwm, Garreg-hir, Carneddau, Allt yr Esgair, Tor y Foel and Mynydd Allt-y-grug. Garreg-hir was approached on a bridleway between lakes and returned via a rocky ridge, in raven country with grand views.

It was discovering RHB that inspired me to walk and climb in areas that I had never previously visited. I made my own rules. If I had been there, the hill got a tick. I didn't worry if sometimes I had not trespassed into a field to reach a trig point or convinced myself that I had actually stood on the very highest point. I was there for the hill, to look around and to enjoy the view, trees permitting. I generally tried to return from a summit by a different route, though if I analysed the true position I'd probably be disappointed.

I took one look at Caeliber Isaf and walked to the monument on Town Hill instead. Similarly, the padlocked gate to the track to the reservoir on Rhos Ymryson, and the presence of an uncooperative farmer there, provoked an amble to the 312m trig point.

Generally, I try to ask permission. In Wales this was granted for Carneddol, Hope Mountain, Cefn Cenarth and Rhiw Gwraidd, and simply to park my car for Mynydd Mawr, Moel Gyw, Carn Gafallt and Pen y Garn-goch. Permission was sought but refused for Upper Park, which I've not visited or counted. I simply kept a low profile on Mynydd Rhyd ddu and Foel Offrwm. On Allt y Main I was intercepted on my descent of the northern fields by the farmer on his all-terrain vehicle. I explained that I had found the right of way through the woods to be impassable and asked to return to the lane the way I had come, which was agreed to. I had real problems with farm dogs on the approaches to Mynydd Drumau, Craig y Castell, Pegwn Mawr and Foel Goch, where my wife was bitten in the presence of the farmer and his wife, because 'she was carrying a walking pole'.

Upper Park

ALAN DAWSON, SEPTEMBER 2003

This hill had acquired a reputation for not being welcoming, so I was keen to avoid any disturbance or confrontation. It was the last of six hills in a relaxed and largely enjoyable day, apart from being attacked by flies on High Vinnalls. I did some of the six on my own and some in company, and met up with two others for a dusk approach to Upper Park. The company and dim light helped us to feel quietly confident, the pheasants were also relatively quiet and we saw no-one. We tried to be inconspicuous, were able to avoid the use of torches and disturbed no birds, animals or people. We were and up and down by 9pm and enjoyed a minor celebration in a pub in Welshpool afterwards.

Number		Height	Name	Drop	Location	Summit
2161		752	Plynlimon / Pumlumon Fawr	526	SN 7897 8694	Trig
2166		560	Banc Llechwedd-mawr	161	SN 7754 8984	Cairn
2167		550	Drosgol	193	SN 7596 8786	Cairn
2169	M	506.1	**Disgwylfa Fawr *****	153.6	SN 7373 8473	Cairn
2205	M	611.0	Pen y Garn	194	SN 7985 7714	Grass
2170	L	489.7	Bryn Amlwg	171.0	SN 9216 9734	Knoll near trig
2172	M	482.0	Bryn y Fan	174.8	SN 9312 8849	Knoll near trig

Plynlimon

This is one of eleven hills in Wales with relative height over 500m. It is the highest and most prominent hill in Mid Wales, one of only three Marilyns over 600m high, along with Great Rhos and Drygarn Fawr. Its summit is much nearer the west coast than the English border yet it is within about 1.5km of the source of the River Wye and only about 5km from the source of the River Severn. Cadair Idris is the nearest higher summit, 30km to the north, but there is no higher summit in any other direction for almost 70km.

Disgwylfa Fawr

This hill was added as a Marilyn in the first revision in 1995. Its status was confirmed later after a summit survey by Myrddyn Phillips combined with Lidar data for its col.

ERIC YOUNG, SEPTEMBER 2010

I had puggled up Drosgol to enjoy the peaceful setting. An all-terrain vehicle with the organiser aboard turned up to collect the orienteering tri-flag and pin-punch. He had obtained grant funding for a new bridge over the Afon Llechwedd-mawr. There was an aluminium plank over Afon Hyddgen, 100 metres up from the confluence with Afon Henggwm, marked by an orange-topped pole. The route over Plynlimon and Drosgol, amongst others, had previously taken in Disgwylfa Fawr before returning to the visitor centre, until a competitor asked, 'who's the masochist that included that hill so late on in the marathon?' So Disgwylfa Fawr was once more left in peace.

Bryn y Fan (Myrddyn Phillips)

WM03 Pegwn-beacon

RHB sections 31B, 38A, 38B

OS maps 136, 137, 147

Number		Height	Name	Drop	Location	Summit
2182	M	585.3	Pegwn Mawr	301.5	SO 0239 8124	Cairn
2191	G	474.6	Gamallt	147.4	SN 9554 7094	Rock
2183	M	547.6	Beacon Hill	180	SO 1764 7679	Trig
2845	M	394.1	Sunnyhill	146.7	SO 3275 8380	Tussock by path
2188	G	498.1	Garreg Lwyd	205	SN 9421 7333	Rock
2192		460	Cefn Cenarth ***	155	SN 9690 7626	Grass
2189	L	477.3	Gwastedyn Hill	244.1	SN 9868 6614	Cairn
2197	M	441.7	Rhiw Gwraidd *	212.1	SO 0161 6343	Rock
2856	M	376.4	High Vinnalls	249	SO 4779 7240	Knoll
2846	M	358.2	Burrow	188.0	SO 3811 8308	Knoll
2202	AM	353.5	Caeliber Isaf	169.5	SO 2116 9341	Grass
2848	M	324.1	View Edge	170	SO 4227 8098	Grass

View Edge

ANN BOWKER, 1995

Not every hill in Dawson's book is worth climbing and View Edge, despite its name, is one which probably is not. We tried to follow a path but I returned to the car in almost total darkness, having encircled but not climbed the hill. Three days later I went back.

PHIL DANT, OCTOBER 2010

I took my two youngest children for a day's bagging. They loved the steep muddy ascent up through thick woods by a barbed-wire fence. It was easier going down, with tree trunks and trekking poles for support, but View Edge should really be called 'No View Edge', with the summit surrounded by trees.

Cefn Cenarth

GRAHAM MARETT, 2004

My map showed no footpaths and I climbed steadily along field edges. As I neared the top I heard a vehicle and saw the farmer, who was rushing over to see what I was up to. I was amused to see that he was riding an ancient pre-war motor cycle, which he reckoned was ideal for checking the sheep on his hills. At first he was suspicious that I was part of a gang of sheep thieves who had been operating in the area, but he soon realised I was a harmless nutcase, climbing his hill for a seemingly incomprehensible reason (to both of us).

High Vinnalls

PHIL DANT, OCTOBER 2010

We went up from near the castle, a road walk most of the way, but the last bit through the forest was delightful, with great views. The only disappointment was the mass of stinging nettles and a broken-down look-out tower surrounded by barbed wire at the top.

Garreg Lwyd

PAUL WHEELER, 2015

I have not enjoyed any Marilyns with wind farms, and tried to fit them in as a run or just not bother. Garreg Lwyd was the start of a wonderful walk above the Wye Valley as far as Gamallt, but why ruin the environment to try to save the environment, I don't get it.

Number		Height	Name	Drop	Location	Summit
2178	MT	660.0	Great Rhos	378.7	SO 1821 6390	Trig
2198	AM	440.7	Gilwern Hill	146.8	SO 0989 5829	Rock
2184	ML	542.1	Gwaunceste Hill	165.1	SO 1582 5555	Trig
2185	G	532.2	Llanfihangel Hill / Colva Hill	144.6	SO 1945 5540	Trig
2193	ML	451.3	Aberedw Hill	230.1	SO 0844 5077	Trig
2195	M	443.8	Carneddau	206.2	SO 0699 5519	Cairn
2199		415	The Begwns	157	SO 1550 4441	Trees
2853	M	426.9	Hergest Ridge	157.6	SO 2543 5626	Rock
2855	M	391.6	Bradnor Hill	179.0	SO 2823 5844	Cairn by tee
2858	ML	332.8	Wapley Hill	160.2	SO 3475 6244	Mound
2859		326	Shobdon Hill	172	SO 3819 6408	Woodland
2861	L	294.5	Burton Hill	198.3	SO 3941 4874	Woodland

This area straddles the Border, which is significant politically but not topographically. Shobdon Hill, Wapley Hill, Bradnor Hill and Hergest Ridge are all in England, but not by much. Burton Hill is more convincingly English though well west of the River Lugg, which forms part of the topographic boundary of the area.

Llanfihangel Hill

This hill was measured by G&J Surveys in 2015 so its height and drop are known to be accurate. It is one of four marginal Submarilyns, along with Fastheugh Hill in SS10, Monadh Mor in HE01 and Hill of Strone in HE11. Llanfihangel Hill is named Colva Hill in the OS trig point database, while on OS maps this name applies to the southern slopes and Llanfihangel Hill to the northern slopes. Both names seem to be equally applicable.

Bradnor Hill

ANN BOWKER, DECEMBER 1995

Offa's Dyke path crosses the eastern flanks of this hill but it does not visit the highest point, which is in the middle of a golf course. It seemed to be quite accepted that walkers should circumnavigate the hill, since we met others walking their dogs up there. Our only problem was to sneak up the 200 metres or so from the western escarpment to the top at a moment which avoided confrontation with either golfers or their balls.

The Begwns

CHATGPT, 2024

The Begwns is a range of rolling hills in Powys, Wales, located near the town of Hay-on-Wye. The name 'Begwns' is thought to derive from a Welsh word related to 'beacon', suggesting it was historically used as a signal or lookout point. The highest point of the Begwns is Begwns Roundabout, a circular clump of trees planted in the 19th century by the Maesllwch Castle estate to commemorate Queen Victoria's Diamond Jubilee. The Begwns are not particularly steep, making them a popular spot for gentle walking and enjoying panoramic views of the Black Mountains and the Brecon Beacons.

Aberedw Hill

Andy Tomkins, August 2012

Aberedw Hill was notable for the friendly farmer I met, who gave me directions when I lost the path and wandered into his field. On the way down I passed his house and was invited to enjoy a drink and a chat in the garden.

Hergest Ridge

Ann Bowker, December 1995

Offa's Dyke path runs across the top of this hill, cutting across the old racecourse but not quite visiting the summit, so we could not be quite sure that we had been to the summit when we had walked the path. In any case this is surely a ridge worth revisiting, its broad open grassy top giving great views and superb easy walking.

Dave Laing, 2000

Following the phenomenal success of his first album, Tubular Bells, Mike Oldfield bought a country home, The Beacon, on a hillside in Herefordshire in the west of England. Here he set up a 24-track studio and found the inspiration for his next large-scale composition. Described by one critic as a 'somnolent pastoral epic', Hergest Ridge was named after a ridge of hills nearby where Mike would fly his radio-controlled model glider. In an interview for Melody Maker, Mike emphasised the contrast between this album and its predecessor, describing Hergest Ridge as: 'smooth, uncluttered, no tube trains, very few car doors, lots of open countryside and well-being and non-hysteria, just a much nicer environment. It's basically not more than six different tunes and the tunes are related. If you want to get anything out of it, you've got to really listen to it.' When the interviewer remarked that Hergest Ridge has been criticised for the romanticism of its lyrics, Mike replied that 'the problem of the world today is that there's not enough romance.' He also described it as 'a different kind of record from Tubular Bells, more folky and orchestral'.

Hergest Ridge was recorded in 1974 and released in the September of that year. Mike played most of the instruments himself, adding woodwind by his brother Terry, oboe from Lindsay Cooper and vocals from Sally Oldfield and Clodagh Simmonds.

Virgin Records advertised the album on television, although the wording of the commercial had to be changed from 'available at Virgin and other immaculate record shops' to avoid religious controversy. Hergest Ridge went to number 1 in the UK charts immediately and stayed for three weeks. The album that took its place was Tubular Bells.

WM05 Drygarn-epynt

Number		Height	Name	Drop	Location	Summit
2203		645	Drygarn Fawr	259	SN 8629 5841	Cairn
2218	ML	331.4	Dinas	146.8	SN 7823 4668	Voutcrop
2207	M	592.8	Llan Ddu Fawr #	166	SN 7907 7042	Cairn
2209	M	487	Pen y Garn-goch	160	SN 8848 5028	Cairn
2270	M	475.7	Mynydd Epynt	198	SN 9612 4642	Post
2210	L	467.9	**Carn Gafallt *****	161.2	SN 9401 6464	Cairn
2211	M	460.9	Mynydd Mallaen #	201.7	SN 7221 4553	Cairn
2214	M	360.4	Hafod Ithel	156.0	SN 6106 6779	Trig
2219	T	329.5	Mynydd Cynros	221	SN 6206 3269	Mound by trig
2222		326	Pen-crug-melyn	184	SN 5027 2850	Trig
2221	L	323.4	Rhos Ymryson	160.8	SN 4604 5001	Grass by reservoir

Llan Ddu Fawr and Mynydd Mallaen

Llan Ddu Fawr was renamed from Waun Claerddu in 2006 and Mynydd Mallaen was renamed from Crugiau Merched in 2020. Lidar data and a survey by Myrddyn Phillips both indicated that the two summits of Llan Ddu Fawr are about the same height.

Mynydd Epynt

ALAN DAWSON, DECEMBER 2002

I chose to stack the odds in favour of success by nipping along the track from the main road in rain, mist and darkness two days before the new year. This worked well. I didn't think it would be a popular tactic but I subsequently discovered that Chris Upson was up there later the same night, when it was darker, wetter and mistier. I knew Chris quite well but was rather relieved that I didn't bump into him along the way.

MARK TRENGOVE, JANUARY 2003

Armed with my range pass from Sennybridge army camp, I took the traditional short stroll to the summit from the B4519. I could have made more of it if time had not been pressing. The sergeant at Sennybridge said they discouraged general rambling in this area on non-firing days because of the large number of shells lying around. He said the majority of people he met requesting access were not hill walkers but Druid types wishing to visit the standing stones that litter the plateau. I did have time to stop the car at a number of points along the B4519, to savour this marvellous wilderness area.

Pen y Garn-goch

CHRIS WATSON, OCTOBER 2010

Armed with an aerial photo from Google maps and a couple of useful implements, Andy Tomkins and I headed upwards. The promised weakness proved illusory, but ten minutes of pruning allowed us through to the summit clearing almost unscathed, with just a few pine needles in our pockets and none in any of our orifices. The main problems were entry and exit where the branches were at their densest, as it was possible to push through the middle ten metres or so. We also had trouble finding our way out as we had foolishly forgotten our yellow ribbons. This hill should become more comfortable in future, thanks to all those brave men who went before us.

WM06 Cwmcerwyn-brandy

Number		Height	Name	Drop	Location	Summit
2208	ML	536.5	Foel Cwmcerwyn	345.7	SN 0940 3115	Trig
2215	L	346.9	Mynydd Carningli	232.1	SN 0624 3723	Rock
2213	TL	394.8	Frenni Fawr	176.2	SN 2030 3491	Trig
2224	T	206	Brandy Hill	153	SN 2134 1338	Trig

Pembrokeshire could reasonably considered to be in South Wales rather than Mid Wales, but the topographic parent of Foel Cwmcerwyn is Drygarn Fawr in area WM05, which means that this area has to be included with region WM rather than WS.

The highest and lowest of the four hills illustrate the diverse nature of the Marilyns. The Mynydd Preseli offer some excellent hill walking but were excluded from traditional lists of hills because they are under 2000 feet high. Foel Cwmcerwyn is the 26th most prominent hill in Wales and is about 80km from any higher Marilyn. It is a dominant feature of the landscape and provides a classic example of the value of relative height as a measure of significance. In contrast, diminutive Brandy Hill seems to be an unfortunate consequence of the use of prominence. It is an ugly and awkward summit, guaranteed to be scorned by anyone who does not appreciate Marilyn bagging mentality or understand the perverse potential pleasure on offer from tackling ridiculous summits such as this.

Brandy Hill

Brandy Hill is next to a road but offers a challenge in ethics as well as gymnastics, thereby adding a ludicrous charm to the variety of Marilyn summits. It has drawn blood from several baggers, from hedge, barbed wire, fence, gate or other impediment. Brandy Hill was classed as a twin peak with Middleton Hill for several years, though they are about 7km apart and there is a separate 204m hill in between them. Both are shown as 205m on OS maps, but Lidar data has indicated that Middleton Hill is 204.8m while Brandy Hill is around 206m, though there is some uncertainty owing to the density of summit clutter. Successful ascent may be quietly celebrated with a glass of Courvoisier or similar tipple.

Jon Metcalf, 2003

In theory a drive-by summit, in reality quite hard as the trig pillar was deeply submerged in thorns, on a bank between a farmer's barbed-wire fence and a fenced communications compound. The trig on the bank overtops the entire compound, but a reservoir mound within an inner compound probably overtops the trig a little. Rather than commit gross vandalism on the two layers of fencing blocking the way to the reservoir, I counted this as a valid bag since my head was higher than the reservoir mound top when standing by the trig. I got back to the car with ripped clothes and leg, from barbed wire protecting the trig, to a chorus of 'why can't we have a normal dad?' from my two daughters.

Frenni Fawr

ChatGPT, 2024

On windswept heights of Frenni Fawr, where myths and mists entwine once more,
The echoes of the past still call, through bracken gold and shadows tall.

Frenni Fawr has an intriguing geological makeup, composed of ancient Ordovician rocks, which are over 450 million years old. The views from the top are spectacular.

——— South Wales ———

Land south of Afon Tywi and the upper Usk, south and west of the River Wye

Marilyns:	42
Highest and most prominent:	Pen y Fan, 885.7m, drop 676.4m
Lowest and least prominent:	Mynydd Dinas, 258.1m, drop 152.5m

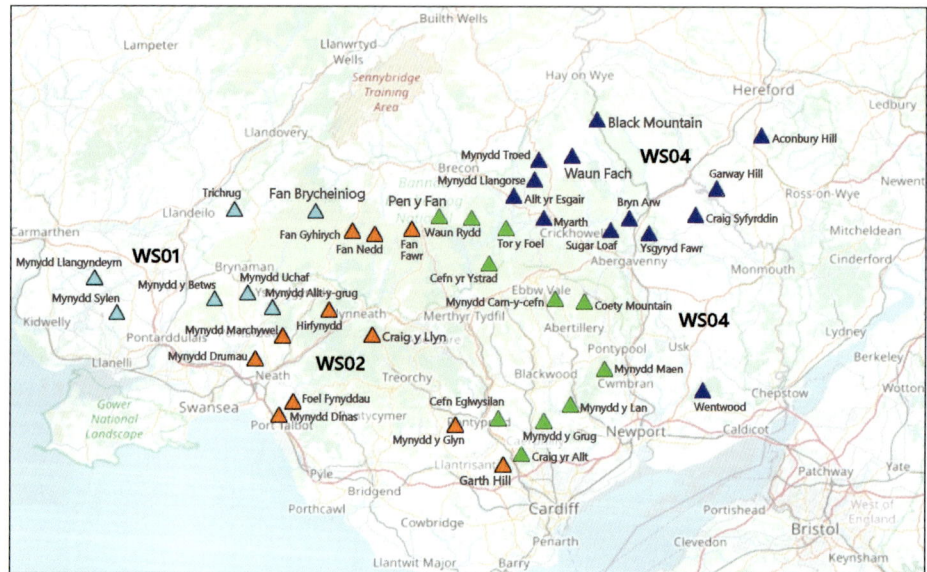

Looking down toward Mynydd Machen from the near the summit of Mynydd y Grug

Number		Height	Name	Drop	Location	Summit
5603	M	802.7	Fan Brycheiniog *	424.2	SN 8243 2206	Cairn
2279	T	415	Trichrug	191	SN 6989 2292	Wall by trig
2280	ML	373.2	Mynydd y Betws	208.1	SN 6649 0953	Tussock
2281	L	356.9	Mynydd Uchaf	181.9	SN 7156 1031	Tussock
2282	L	338.7	Mynydd Allt-y-grug *	190.3	SN 7533 0814	Rock
2283	MT	284	Mynydd Sylen	215	SN 5152 0800	Trig
2285	M	263.0	Mynydd Llangyndeyrn	172.4	SN 4823 1326	Outcrop by trig

Fan Brycheiniog

The summit of Fan Brycheiniog was moved 290 metres north of the trig pillar following a survey in 2011, to a point named as Twr y Fan Foel. In April 2023 it was announced that the Brecon Beacons National Park was to be renamed as Bannau Brycheiniog National Park. The benefits of this change to the landscape and the wildlife of the area was not immediately apparent. The official reason for the change was because the word 'beacon' was not compatible with climate change, an aspect not previously taken into account in naming hills or parks. Possibly the park intended to make the announcement on the first of the month but did not have the press release and the new signage ready in time.

Mynydd y Betws

One of the quickest and easiest of summits, it has a named antiquity to add interest for anyone feeling the need for extra justification for a short walk from the nearby road.

I did not expend much energy on Mynydd Allt-y-grug
It was over in ten minutes as it isn't very big
And so to try to satisfy a bit of an uppity fetish
My appetite was pacified on little Mynydd y Betws

Mynydd Llangyndern and Mynydd Sylen

ALAN DAWSON, NOVEMBER 2006

There can be many possible reasons for climbing a hill. Most hills have some aesthetic merit or a reasonable view or can offer interest or enjoyment somewhere along the way, but occasionally the only possible justification is the incentive to reach the summit in order to add one to the collection. This is hill bagging at its most brutally honest, with no self-deception.

It can be difficult to find uplifting beauty or transcendant tranquility on hills bearing ugly scars and suffering from the roar of trail bikes, particularly on a dull wet Tuesday in November. Five Marilyns would have been a fine haul for such a day, but when in basic bagging mode it can be tempting to push on for another. Two days earlier the total had been eight, so five did not seem quite enough. Mynydd Llangyndern was rather dark and rather wet but quick. On my own I would have settled for that but there were three of us and no-one said that six was enough. We seemed to delight in adding Mynydd Sylen. It was very dark and very wet yet somehow not at all miserable because it didn't take long and we were able to savour and share the absurdity of such bizarre behaviour.

Number		Height	Name	Drop	Location	Summit
2237		734	Fan Fawr	295	SN 9698 1936	Grass by cairn
2291	L	492	Mynydd Gethin	149	SO 0441 0255	Rock by platform
2238	A	726.1	Fan Gyhirych	281	SN 8805 1912	Tussock
2249	T	663.1	Fan Nedd	174	SN 9133 1841	Trig
2288	TL	600.1	Craig y Llyn	393.5	SN 9067 0317	Grass by trig
2277	L	482	Hirfynydd *	252	SN 8413 0754	Trees
2278	T	417.9	Mynydd Marchywel	264.3	SN 7682 0377	Trig
2284	LT	272.1	Mynydd Drumau	170.7	SN 7250 0018	Trig
2295		377	Mynydd y Glyn	189	ST 0319 8964	Cairn
2296	L	370.2	Foel Fynyddau	222.4	SS 7828 9360	Ground by trig
2301	G	258.1	**Mynydd Dinas *****	152.5	SS 7614 9153	Heather
2299	LT	306.9	Garth Hill	220.8	ST 1034 8350	Trig

Mynydd Dinas

This was added to the list in 1995 and its status later confirmed by GNSS survey. It is one of the Welsh hills that are said to sound Tolkienesque, along with Hafod Ithel and others. This claim has substance, as Welsh and Finnish were the two main languages used by J.R.R. Tolkien as inspiration for place names in The Hobbit and The Lord of the Rings.

Hirfynydd

ALAN DAWSON, JULY 2023

After driving south from Blaenau Ffestiniog and climbing two 600m hills along the way, I squeezed in an inspection of Hirfyndd in the gloomy dusk, as the forecast for the next day was dire. Lidar data showed the highest point to be in a plantation on a reclaimed spoil heap, over 200 metres from the trig pillar.

A straight track from Seven Sisters offered a direct approach, past listless youths messing about on trail bikes. The open-cast mine was easy to stroll through as it had been disused for many years, then there was a slithery shale slope up to the tree-line. I pushed through some thick branches, with wellies sinking into the bog, to reach a new track that passed within 100 metres of the estimated summit position. The trees were bigger and denser than expected but I backed my way up and through, hood up and eyes down, until I was within five metres of the Lidar location. It was an old-fashioned needling that could have almost been fun if it had not been almost dark. To make sure I went over the highest ground I carried on south to reach another track. This led back towards the trig, but the pillar was well hidden amongst trees and not easy to spot in the gloom.

Mynydd Gethin

ALAN DAWSON, JULY 2023

A desperately wet yet interesting umbrella walk, winding a way up along broad tracks from the huge mountain bike park on the southern fringe of Merthyr Tydfil. The trig pillar was slightly hidden in trees but easily overtopped by a man-made mound of earth and rock. This was a platform for riders to plunge off down one of the numerous colour-coded bike trails with wacky names. The drop from the summit mound is around 151m, but I concluded that the hill did not qualify as a Marilyn because the bare mound looked obviously man-made and did not resemble a permanent feature of the landscape.

Number		Height	Name	Drop	Location	Summit
2226	M	885.7	Pen y Fan	676.4	SO 0120 2158	Cairn
2233	M	769.2	Waun Rydd	169.7	SO 0621 2064	Grass
2260	M	617.4	Cefn yr Ystrad	177.5	SO 0869 1373	Trig
2267	M	551.0	Tor y Foel	157.0	SO 1145 1949	Ground by cairn
2289	L	576.5	Coety Mountain / Mynydd Coety	226.5	SO 2316 0799	Grass
2290	T	550.1	Mynydd Carn-y-cefn	176	SO 1871 0850	Grass near trig
2292	L	473.0	Mynydd Maen #	255.1	ST 2600 9784	Knoll near trig
2293	LT	382.5	Cefn Eglwysilan	233.6	ST 0971 9050	Trig
2294	L	381.3	Mynydd y Lan	221.7	ST 2090 9234	Mound
5273	A	374.2	Mynydd y Grug **	204.3	ST 1776 9066	Turf on gravel
2300	L	273.1	Craig yr Allt	154.9	ST 1333 8506	Rock

Pen y Fan

This is the third most prominent hill in Wales and seems to be the second most popular, after Snowdon. Carnedd Llewelyn is more prominent but is far less busy.

MARION MITCHELL, JUNE 2014

What I absolutely love is the sheer variety of hills awaiting us on our exploits. Marilyns can be very lonely hills so we just could not believe the massive crowds who tackled Pen y Fan in the Brecon Beacons on a fair-weather day in June. When we were told our route was called the Motorway we immediately knew why.

Tor y Foel

ALAN DAWSON, AUGUST 1996 AND NOVEMBER 2006

I recall this being one of the most enjoyable hills in South Wales, along with Ysgyryd Fawr and Garth Hill. It seemed short, straightforward, grassy and relatively effortless. It seemed not quite as good ten years later, possibly because it was a repeat ascent or possibly because it was one of 32 Marilyns climbed in six dank November days.

Mynydd Maen

This hill was renamed from Mynydd Twyn-Glas in 2022. A local hill walker, Trefor Beese, managed to convince OS to amend the position of both names on its maps.

Mynydd y Grug

ALAN DAWSON, MARCH 2024

This hill eventually superseded Mynydd Machen after a summit inspection and survey and then extensive cogitation. It was a reluctant promotion because much of the broad summit area did not look at all natural, though there were trees and shrubs growing near the top. The base of the trees was higher than the top of Mynydd Machen, which is eleven metres lower. Mynydd y Grug is a permanent feature of the landscape, its lower slopes are well wooded and entirely natural. Unlike on Hensbarrow Downs there seemed to be little revegetation of the barren summit area, making it look vaguely volcanic, though several drainage channels undermined this impression. Over time the summit area will presumably become more overgrown but this may be a long and slow process.

WS04 Waunfach-black

RHB sections 32A, 32C, 38B   OS maps 149, 161, 171

Number		Height	Name	Drop	Location	Summit
2229	L	810.6	Waun Fach	624.3	SO 2155 2999	Tussock and mud
2242	M	703.6	Black Mountain	154.5	SO 2552 3538	Tussock
2263	LT	608.5	Mynydd Troed	285.2	SO 1656 2923	Trig
2268	M	514.9	Mynydd Llangorse	160.3	SO 1593 2670	Heather
2266	L	595.6	Sugar Loaf / Y Fal	411.4	SO 2725 1877	Trig
2274	L	384.8	Bryn Arw *	161.4	SO 3015 2070	Rock
2269	T	486.2	Ysgyryd Fawr	343	SO 3311 1828	Rock by trig
2272	LT	423.3	Craig Syfyrddin – Edmund's Tump #	235.3	SO 4039 2106	Trig
2273	M	392.6	Allt yr Esgair	199	SO 1261 2435	Rock
2857	LT	366.6	Garway Hill	266.2	SO 4368 2507	Knoll by trig
2298	L	309.1	Wentwood	242.9	ST 4113 9431	Trig
2276	L	293	Myarth	164	SO 1709 2083	Cairn on stump
2864	LT	275.7	**Aconbury Hill *****	158.6	SO 5058 3300	Trig

Black Mountain

After extensive historical research and a summit survey, Myrddyn Phillips concluded that the summit of this long ridge is within Wales, although the border with England had not been very clearly defined. The highest point is about twelve metres west of the path. There are no Mountains in the list of Marilyns in Scotland or England but there are five in Wales: Coety, Holyhead, Hope, Long and Black Mountain, which is the only one over 600 metres high. Welsh names for them exist but are rarely used by hill walkers.

Black Mountain is also the name of a rock band from Vancouver and the title of their first album, released in 2005. Their fourth album, imaginatively called IV, includes their finest moment, a nine-minute epic called 'Space to Bakersfield'. Live versions are longer. The band name might derive from a college in North Carolina but guitarist and singer Stephen McBean is also in the Pink Mountaintops, so the nominal connection persists.

Waun Fach

BRIAN EDRIDGE, 2014

I had read of this being a wet hill, but after fifty years on the Scottish hills thought little of it. The ascent was fine but I was amazed at the huge quagmire of ankle-deep mud and water on the featureless summit plateau. In the thick mist I squelched around for ages looking for the highest point before deciding on the third visit to a solitary boulder that this was indeed the top.

Mynydd Troed

ALAN DAWSON, AUGUST 1988

One of the few hills I climbed for a reason other than reaching the summit. I had signed up for a weekend paragliding course and by the second day was getting the hang of flying and landing, though I found taking off difficult. On one occasion I failed to take off and was dragged along through the heather for several metres. The final flight from Mynydd Troed was the best, with a smooth and slow descent to the designated landing point, not far from a tree where one of the group ended up and needed a bit of help getting down.

Garway Hill

ANN BOWKER, 1995

No rights of way on this hill but the open area was criss-crossed by delightful grassy tracks. We came up on the footpath from the west then lost it and had to negotiate barbed wire to gain the open hill. Here were horse-riders, walkers and model plane operators, all enjoying the brilliant sunshine of a rapidly improving afternoon and the magnificent panorama from this hill at the westernmost fringe of England.

Aconbury Hill

Like Garway Hill, this is in England but included in area WS04 as it is west of the River Wye, which forms the topographic boundary. It was one of fifteen new Marilyns added in 1995, though four of these were later found to have less than 150m drop.

Ysgyryd Fawr

MARK TRENGOVE, JULY 2004

My best find of the year, diminutive in elevation but not in grandeur. This must be one of the finest of the lower hills of Wales, a real jewel, to be savoured often.

JIMMY WHITE, JULY 2006

I was on the summit ridge of Ysgyryd Fawr, watching a distant pair of common buzzards, when there was a sudden whoosh from behind and a buzzard came within inches of my head. I had never been mobbed by a bird of prey before, but fortunately I had a bit too much ballast to be food for young buzzards. For the next half hour I carried my walking pole pointing upwards above my head. It made the ascent of Bryn Arw through head-high bracken seem almost normal.

Myarth

GRAHAM MARETT, 2004

Myarth is an isolated, tree-covered hill near the River Usk in south Wales. As my wife and I passed the gamekeeper's lodge it seemed prudent to ask permission to proceed. The gamekeeper's wife had no objection to our continuing but clearly did not think we were wise. We soon found out why. The hill was not a pleasant climb, with no paths, and the broad, flattish summit was overgrown with dense bracken and scrub. After wandering about a bit and visiting what I thought must be the highest point, I found a rather easier route down following an old track. We had the misfortune to meet the gamekeeper himself on our descent, and he was not at all pleased to see us. He made it quite clear that permission would have been denied if he had been asked. This served to reinforce my normal policy of climbing hills first and asking questions later.

Craig Syfyrddin (Edmund's Tump)

DOROTHY WILSON, 2008

On the summit of Sugar Loaf I met a lady who was climbing the hill with her family to celebrate her 90th birthday. On Edmund's Tump a friendly farmer let me park in his field and warned me that a big party of children were having their school's annual outing and picnic on top of this hill. I met them on their way down so I had the summit to myself. The farmer had cut a path through the long grass all the way to the top and also cut all round the summit to give the children a picnic area, so walking couldn't have been easier.

——— Central England and Welsh Borders ———

Land south of the River Trent, east of the Dee and Severn, north of the Avon, Kennet and Thames

Marilyns:	22
Highest and most prominent:	Brown Clee Hill, 540.5m, drop 373m
Lowest:	Normanby Top, 168.0m
Least prominent:	Hegdon Hill, drop 154m

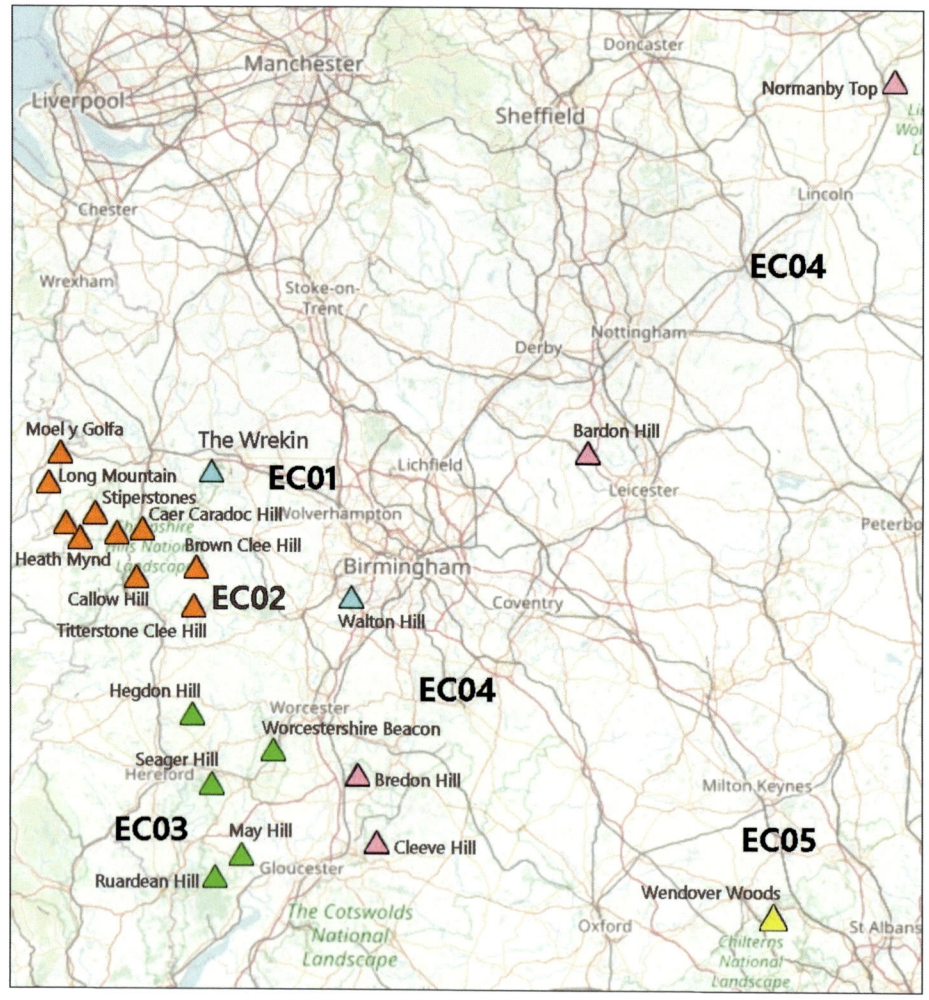

EC01 Wrekin-walton

Number		Height	Name	Drop	Location	Summit
2843	M	406.9	The Wrekin	310.4	SJ 6283 0819	Grass
2870	T	315.6	Walton Hill	210	SO 9426 7979	Grass by trig

The Wrekin

The Wrekin is a dominant feature of the landscape as the nearest higher Marilyn to the north or east is Kinder Scout around 60km away. It is one of only ten hills in England outside the Pennines or Lake District with relative height over 300 metres, but it is only the third most prominent hill in Shropshire, after Brown Clee Hill and Stiperstones. In 2015 a survey by Myrddyn Phillips found the highest ground on The Wrekin to be about 110 metres from the trig pillar.

ANN BOWKER

I don't know whether it is still common to use the phrase *I've been all round the Wrekin* to describe an occasion when one has been lost or taken a silly route, but it was one I used in my childhood long before I realised that it referred to a hill in Shropshire. When we lived in the Midlands we climbed this isolated hill several times, including one of my most memorable walks, an ascent by the light of the full moon. A more recent visit found it much spoiled with a track up to the radio mast on the summit ridge. I rather wished that I had not returned to pollute the memory of what used to be a pleasant grassy hill.

Walton Hill

ANN BOWKER

The Clent Hills lie so close to Birmingham that they can be overrun with people, horses and mountain bikes. The viewfinder was of little value on a hazy afternoon but the immediate surroundings were extremely pleasant and we enjoyed a splendid short circuit, shared with the crowds of a warm and dry Sunday afternoon in early spring.

Long Mountain (Myrddyn Phillips)

EC02 Clee-corndon

Number		Height	Name	Drop	Location	Summit
2837	M	540.5	Brown Clee Hill	373	SO 5937 8670	Mound
2839	M	533.2	Titterstone Clee Hill	233.0	SO 5913 7794	Trig
2838	M	536.9	Stiperstones	357.1	SO 3675 9864	Rock
2840	M	516.6	Long Mynd	190.9	SO 4151 9444	Trig
2841	M	459.5	Caer Caradoc Hill	274.2	SO 4774 9539	Rock
2842	M	452.6	Heath Mynd	191	SO 3355 9409	Heather by cairn
2847	ML	339.4	Callow Hill	157.2	SO 4608 8506	Grass by path
2187	M	513.6	Corndon Hill	203.1	SO 3060 9692	Rock by trig
2200	M	408.3	Long Mountain	305	SJ 2647 0582	Woodland by trig
2201	ML	403.2	Moel y Golfa	262.4	SJ 2907 1252	Rock

Titterstone Clee Hill

HAMISH BROWN, 2004

There was a lot of snow on the ground for Walton Hill, busy with sunny Sunday visitors, then it was on to a carnival atmosphere on Titterstone Clee Hill, with children sledging and a brilliant western sky, all in the blasted remnants of superquarrying. On top we so far forget ourselves as to embrace (to avoid hypothermia) and at the van had cake and champers – Jill had entered the Hall of Fame.

Caer Caradoc Hill

ANN BOWKER

It would be fanciful to liken Church Stretton to Chamonix yet it does have a certain similarity, lying in a deep valley with lovely hills on either side. The most striking hill, Caer Caradoc, was one of the first hills I climbed, because I stayed in my friend Jenny's cottage nearby and the ascent was one of our favourite walks. There is a cave just below the summit, which was supposed to be the place where Caratacus made his last stand against the Romans. Jenny used to sing a song about it.

Callow Hill

ANN BOWKER, 1995

The walk along Wenlock Edge was one I had wanted to do for a long time. As we walked I quoted A.E.Housman: 'On Wenlock Edge the wood's in trouble, his forest fleece the Wrekin heaves'. The wood was still there but the path had been upgraded to bridleway status and was badly churned up by horses. Apart from the mud, winter was the best time for the walk as there were glimpses of the view through the bare branches of the trees. We only walked a short section of the Edge and then turned sharply south-east to tackle Callow Hill, which lies off the main escarpment. We went straight up the steep public footpath.

Heath Mynd

ADRIAN RAYNER, OCTOBER 2005

During a visit to Shrewsbury to stay with friends I was able to sneak out after dinner to go over Stiperstones (a repeat) and then Heath Mynd in the dark, returning for coffee in polite company. The reaction of our hosts ranged from respect for my athletic qualities to downright puzzlement about my needing to climb some hill on a list.

EC03 Malvern-may

Number		Height	Name	Drop	Location	Summit
2854	ML	425.3	Worcestershire Beacon	335.7	SO 7688 4523	Rock near trig
2860	L	296.2	May Hill	217.1	SO 6952 2129	Knoll near trig
2862	A	290.8	Ruardean Hill	175	SO 6349 1691	Stone marker
2866	A	271.9	Seager Hill *	167	SO 6238 3794	Verge of track
2867	MT	254	Hegdon Hill **	154	SO 5852 5392	Hedge near trig

Worcestershire Beacon

ALAN DAWSON, 1974

My third Marilyn but my first in England, though I had climbed two hills with over 140m drop, Tennyson Down and Glastonbury Tor. I had driven past the Malvern hills a few times on my way between Wirral and Southampton and their outline appealed to me. At some point during 1974 I made it to the highest point for no particular reason, but it did not feeling anything special. I was a slow starter and late developer.

May Hill

ANN BOWKER, 1995

This hill belongs to the National Trust and a good track runs onto it from the south, but a quick stroll up the right of way and round the little wood at the summit was scarcely adequate as a walk for what was a pleasant little hill.

Ruardean Hill

ALAN DAWSON, AUGUST 1996

After strolling a few metres from the road to the trig I had an amusing encounter with a nosey neighbour who emerged to inform me that he owned the summit area. He had no objections, he just wanted me to know that I had trodden on his land. In 2019 I returned to survey the highest point, near a stone marking the highest point of the Forest of Dean.

Seager Hill

Lidar data indicated a summit relocation, and a survey in 2023 confirmed this. The eastern summit is nearer a road and easier to reach. It has no hostile notices and is 14cm higher.

Hegdon Hill

Grendon Green was superseded by Hegdon Hill in 1995 after detailed map study. Lidar data later confirmed the change but could not identify the exact summit of Hegdon Hill.

ANN BOWKER, 1994 AND 1995

I was sorry to see Grendon Green displaced as this gave us one of the most ridiculous episodes of the whole endeavour as we sprinted in turn across a featureless field to a trig point hidden in a hedge. The other person had to guard the car as we were unable to park anywhere nearby. Any observer would have regarded our behaviour with suspicion, not realising that it was simply a symptom of the incurable malady 'Marilyn madness'.

We resisted the temptation to drive to the summit of Hegdon Hill and approached on the bridleway through Durstone Farm. Although it was raining the views were pleasing across a rural landscape to the distant line of the Malvern Hills and towards Wales.

EC04 Cleeve-bardon

Number		Height	Name	Drop	Location	Summit
2869	LT	330.1	Cleeve Hill	234	SO 9969 2460	Fence near trig
2871	L	298.8	Bredon Hill	254.8	SO 9576 4026	Grass near viewfinder
2873	L	279.9	Bardon Hill	172	SK 4608 1319	Rock
2836	LT	168.0	Normanby Top #	162	TF 1211 9647	Trig by hedge

Cleeve Hill

GORDON INGALL, 2013

My reluctance to purchase OS maps covering one or two hills in an area I am unlikely to revisit has its drawbacks, and navigating by road atlas has its limitations. A visit to a local shop for a quick browse usually suffices for a drive-by bag. After strolling up Cleeve Hill on my way to North Wales, I arrived at a pillar and view indicator giving a height of 317.5m, whereas my road atlas showed it to be 330m. Suspiciously higher ground to the south added to my doubts and a quick look at a map in a local filling station confirmed the cock-up. The 330m trig pillar was 2km to the south. Maybe there is a moral here.

Bredon Hill

PAUL RICHARDSON, OCTOBER 1980

It was an easy climb to the summit and one of the most interesting hills I have been on. It stands like a stranded whale over the surrounding vales. As well as extensive views it has a large British hill fort, a squat seventeenth century tower, Parson's Folly, and a large limestone boulder, the Banbury Stone, in which mineral deposits were clearly visible.

Bardon Hill

JON METCALF, 2003

Utterly demoralising with trucks thundering past, surpassing even the gauche ruin of Dundry Down as an all-time low spot in my hill experience. It is the only prominence for miles around, so let's blow it away for road aggregate. It must have been beautiful once. The sorry remnants of this former haven could have been used to provide location shots for the fictional brutalisation of defenceless beauty in *The Return of the King*.

PHIL DANT, APRIL 2010

My favourite rubbish Marilyn. I loved it. I parked in a nice housing estate north of the hill, walked through a lane across a stream and then along a slightly muddy track into a lovely wood and was rewarded with great views of Leicestershire. The best bit was the summit 'ridge' with loads of boulders to scramble on and then finally the summit, with its fantastic steep drops into the quarry and no trucks about and the thrill of the tick.

Normanby Top (The Wolds)

ALAN DAWSON, MARCH 2010

My final Marilyn south of the border, reached at 8:30 on a damp grey Tuesday morning in March after driving through the night from Kent, with a short detour to Wendover Woods. The masts looming over the flat muddy fields, the ragged hedges and the half-hidden trig pillar seemed to encapsulate the morose feel of most of the summits of the previous few days. I could have done it differently, in better weather by better routes, but I was in bagging mode and did what needed to be done. After a largely sleepless night, alone with my thoughts, it was a fitting anti-climax to this part of the quest.

Number		Height	Name	Drop	Location	Summit
2874	L	267.5	Wendover Woods #	180	SP 8902 0898	Tree by road

Wendover Woods

This is the only Marilyn in a vast area of relative flatness. In 2001 it was renamed from Haddington Hill after reports from baggers who had been to the official summit, though it was hard to tell if it really was the highest point in the Chiltern Hills. Shotover Hill is not a Marilyn but has been co-opted into the area name on the grounds that it has an assonant name and has a relative height of over 100m so qualifies as a Hump.

ALAN DAWSON, MARCH 2010

On the way home from a funeral in Gloucestershire, via Dorset, the Isle of Wight and Kent, I reached the Tring ring road by 11pm. I drove all the way around Wendover Woods and failed to find a suitable spot to park up and rest for the night. After trying to figure out what to do, it took me a while to come up with the obvious answer, which was to leave the car by one of the barriers (designed to prevent people like me from driving up), and climb the hill in the dark. This turned an ordinary walk into an atmospheric and memorable one, as I enjoyed poking around various paths by torch-light in a brief spell of dry weather, looking for the summit marker stone and any other potential high points. Freed from the need to wait around in the south for daylight, I carried on driving north until I got near Lincolnshire, then dozed for a couple of hours in a lay-by outside Newark-on-Trent before heading sleepily toward the Wolds.

The relocated summit of Seager Hill near Hereford

——— Southern England and Isle of Wight ———

Land south of the Severn estuary, River Avon, River Kennet and River Thames

Marilyns:	32
Highest and most prominent:	High Willhays, 622m
Lowest:	Nine Barrow Down, 199.8m
Least prominent:	Brightstone Down, drop 150.6m

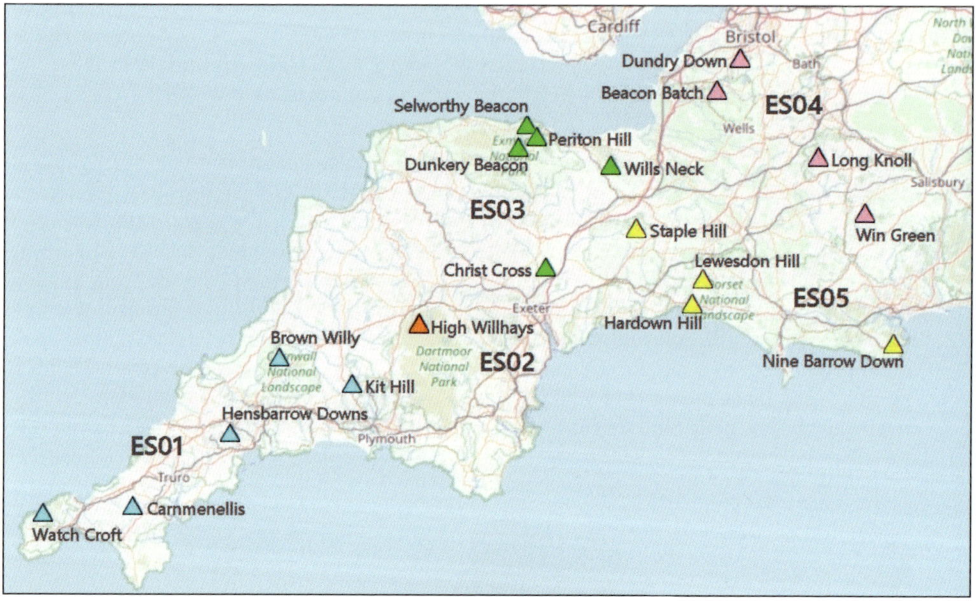

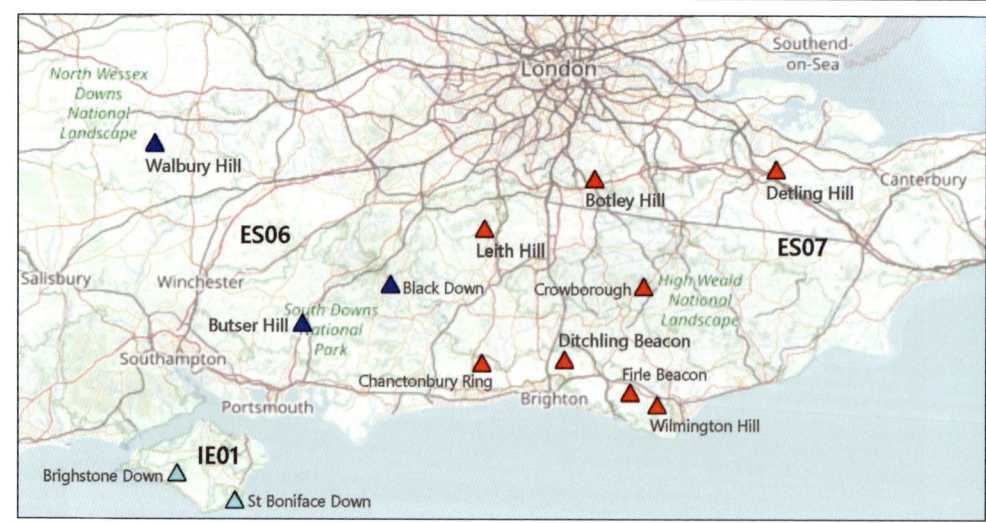

RHB section 40 OS maps 200, 201, 203

Number		Height	Name	Drop	Location	Summit
2881		420	Brown Willy	322	SX 1587 8000	Trig
19290	A	364.6	Hensbarrow Downs **	250.0	SX 0013 5747	Small rock
2883	L	334.1	Kit Hill	171.2	SX 3748 7134	Chimney
2886	LT	251.6	Carnmenellis	167.4	SW 6956 3644	Trig
2887	L	252.9	Watch Croft #	227.2	SW 4204 3570	Tor near trig

Brown Willy

ANN BOWKER, 1995

We had heard rumours of access problems but also read that there was a permissive path from Rough Tor. It was obviously a popular spot and on this splendid clear day the route was easy to find, although it would take some awkward scrambling to stand atop some of the many rough tors which give this hill its name. Soon we were standing on Cornwall's highest summit enjoying clear views of rolling moors beyond. We returned by a more northerly route to get a closer look at the remarkable stone formations on Showery Tor.

Kit Hill

ANN BOWKER, 1995

A toll road runs up from the east so we set out from the west, starting at Kelly Bray. Near the top we found open heathland but the summit was dominated by a tall chimney, with the banks of an earthwork and a big flat grassy area on which kids were playing football. In the lovely evening light the hill certainly lived up to its claim on the map to be a viewpoint, although the prospect was rolling rather than dramatic.

Hensbarrow Beacon

ANN BOWKER, 1995

This is without doubt the daftest hill in the tables as it was completely overshadowed by enormous spoil heaps from the china clay mines. We failed to find a parking spot nearby and it was raining torrentially, so we scampered 500 metres along a flat track as fast as we could. The mound of a tumulus gave a few feet of ascent to the trig point, while above us dumper trucks were depositing yet more spoil on this most unsatisfying summit.

Hensbarrow Downs

ALAN DAWSON, OCTOBER 2016

Dartmoor was out of bounds due to firing so I luckily had a spare day to investigate the state of this hill. I found it strangely thrilling to make my way up its very natural looking grassy slopes and try to locate the highest point. In thick mist it provided an atmospheric hill walking experience and I had no doubt that it was time to accept Hensbarrow Downs as the first obviously man-made Marilyn summit due to its fabulous transformation from eyesore to wild moor over the previous few years.

The new hill covers a wide area and its highest point is 52 metres higher than the trig on Hensbarrow Beacon. There are many lower man-made hills in the area, some with unusual profiles, that offer a varied and interesting scope for open-minded exploration.

Number		Height	Name	Drop	Location	Summit
2877	L	622	High Willhays	537	SX 5802 8922	Cairn on tor

High Willhays

This is one of only two Marilyns over 600m in England south of Lancaster, along with Kinder Scout. It is also the sixth most prominent hill in England, one of only seven with a drop over 500m. The second most prominent hill in Dartmoor, Mardon Down, has a drop of 141.4m. It is 357m high so would need a drop of 146.43m to qualify as a Submarilyn.

PAUL RICHARDSON, MAY 1986

I was delayed by having to walk the warden's dog as my hostel duty, so it was after 10am when I set off. I reached the edge of the moor to find hills rolling away into the distance, each indistinguishable from its neighbour. I decided to navigate by short legs between landmarks. My first landmark was to be a stone circle on the western side of Buttern Hill, but I couldn't find it until after a complete traverse of the hill. No Stonehenge this, but an incomplete circle of mostly buried stones a few inches high, then onward to Rival Tor.

The persistent mist descending on the featureless terrain of the moors was one of its great dangers, along with the numerous bogs and mires. The area around the source of Gallaven Brook, named Gallaven Mire, called to mind the stories of horses sweating with fear and refusing to go on. I never got near the brook. I sloshed around in a marsh that threatened to swallow me whole. With difficulty I retreated soggily and went in a big arc north and west toward Wild Tor, where cans and wrappers seemed to have been pushed into every crevice in the rocks. I found an ammunition box containing visitors' book and stamp – one of the famous Dartmoor letter boxes. I stamped the Wild Tor print in my notebook and set off for Hangingstone Hill, where there was an observation point for the firing ranges. A tin of beans, some teabags and slices of bread had been left inside.

Cloud smoked ominously around the highest tors and the higher hills were covered with hailstones. I crossed trackless moor towards the summit rocks and at last I was up. I was also wet, worried about the weather and generally rather miserable. It was almost unthinkable to climb Hill Willhays and not go on to the rather more attractive Yes Tor, but I felt pressed for time and set off hastily back the same way. It was very wet indeed.

Hensbarrow Beacon, with grassy Downs rising beyond

ES03 Dunkery-neck

RHB section 41   OS maps 181, 192

Number		Height	Name	Drop	Location	Summit
2889	L	519.9	Dunkery Beacon	414	SS 8915 4159	Cairn
2893	LT	308.5	Selworthy Beacon	192.1	SS 9188 4799	Trig
2894	L	297.4	Periton Hill	178.5	SS 9465 4416	Trees
2890	L	384.6	Wills Neck	268.2	ST 1648 3519	Gorse
2885	L	262.0	Christ Cross	173.2	SS 9640 0525	Tree near mast

Dunkery Beacon

ANN BOWKER

I was on holiday in Minehead with my parents and this was the first hill I ever climbed. I remember thinking I had done something significant, so it was disconcerting, when we went back there, to find it so ridiculously easy. A wide track runs up from Dunkery Gate to the enormous cairn, which gives a splendid panorama of the rolling hills of Exmoor.

ALAN DAWSON, SEPTEMBER 1980

I was on holiday in Minehead with my parents and this was the second hill I ever climbed with them, on our last holiday together. It did not feel significant, just cold and windy.

Selworthy Beacon and Periton Hill

ANN BOWKER

Selworthy Beacon was another hill which I had climbed on that Minehead holiday and I had a wonderful memory of springy turf, singing larks and sparkling ocean. It was a bit disappointing to find it so far from the sea and with more the atmosphere of a muddy cow pasture than a grassy down. It is a mistake to revisit those scenes of one's youth that hold some special magic, for the distorting mirror of memory is so easily shattered. Middle age has its own magic moments but they have a different aura from those of the child. Today we continued by East Lynch to Periton Hill. The tracks were confusing in the forest but we located the trig point and then wandered westwards to the higher but rather indeterminate summit. We returned by Wootton Courtenay, Huntscott, Blackford and the picturesque thatched village of Selworthy to Allerford. This made a very pleasant circuit, finishing over the pack-horse bridge whose picture was on our new map.

Wills Neck

ALAN DAWSON, MARCH 2010

This is the highest point of the Quantock Hills and the highest hill in Southern England apart from Cornwall and Devon. The nearest higher ground to the north in England is in the Malvern Hills. In theory it might have felt significant or offered a memorable walk, but I ended up simply climbing it by the shortest route to get another one in the bag.

A funeral in Cheltenham gave me the spur to spend a few days driving around the south of England. Overall I found it fairly dispiriting, so I could see why some people aimed to take longer routes to these hills, as the shortest route from road to summit rarely offered a satisfying walk. It seemed that there was always something to spoil a walk even if it was good in parts. On Wills Neck I had an excuse to be miserable as I had just been to a funeral, it was damp and getting dark, and I still had to find somewhere to spend the night.

ES04 Beacon-dundry

Number		Height	Name	Drop	Location	Summit
2891	LT	324.7	Beacon Batch	235.6	ST 4846 5727	Trig on tumulus
2895	LT	288.3	Long Knoll	173.0	ST 7861 3766	Grass near trig
2897	L	278.4	Win Green	159.1	ST 9251 2069	Copse
2900	L	233.0	Dundry Down	170.6	ST 5534 6672	Trig

Beacon Batch

This is the highest point of the Mendip Hills, which are higher than any hills to the east in Southern England. It is a minor tourist attraction compared to nearby Cheddar with its gorge, reservoir, cheese and biscuits. The grid reference refers to the trig pillar, which is located on top of a grassy tumulus over a metre high. This may not be on the highest natural ground but it is the highest point, it looks natural, and it is difficult to distinguish the natural from the unnatural on a broad plateau with several tumuli.

Mendips was the name of a house in Menlove Avenue in Liverpool where John Lennon lived from age 5 to 22. It is unclear whether Lennon walked in the Mendip Hills during filming of the Beatles' Magical Mystery Tour, but the tour bus did stop at a roundabout near Taunton. *The Fool on the Hill* was written by Paul McCartney and is thought to be about a mysterious, wise figure who is misunderstood by others but is content and observant.

Win Green

The highest point is in a small copse of trees about 50 metres from the trig pillar. Various paths cross the area but the summit can be reached by a simple stroll from a car park.

Long Knoll

ANN BOWKER, 1995

We had no map of this hill but memorised the rather obvious route from a quick glance at it in the library. The path to Kilmington via Long Knoll was signposted and ran through a small wood and then straight up the ridge onto the narrow, flat crest which it follows for about a mile, across a small dip, to the summit trig point at the very far end. Beyond this point the ground drops away sharply, giving this hill quite a dramatic feel despite the grassy terrain. Near the top was a collection of large burrows which we presumed to be a badger sett showing every sign of recent activity. The rolling scenery of the downs, pale hills and pale furrowed fields, is well appreciated from this hill, with misty grey dusk emphasising the chalky whiteness of the countryside.

Dundry Down

This has been regarded as the smelliest and ugliest Marilyn summit owing to the rubbish dump at the top. In a poll in 2009 it gained the most votes for worst hill of all.

ANN BOWKER, 1995

This was one of the least satisfying summits we have visited. The hill lies immediately south of Bristol and its slopes are dotted with villages and farms. We parked by the start of a bridleway that runs to the radio masts just north of the trig point. At the masts there were men with ferocious-looking dogs but these were behind a fence and not interested in our route. The day was rather misty so the probably impressive views across Bristol were muted and the most striking thing in the view was the tower of Dundry church.

Number		Height	Name	Drop	Location	Summit
2892	L	315.7	Staple Hill	213.8	ST 2404 1668	Woodland
2896	A	278.6	Lewesdon Hill **	187.2	ST 4377 0116	Mound
2901	G	206.6	Swyre Head	148.3	SY 9341 7846	Tumulus
2902	L	207.0	Hardown Hill	153.4	SY 4055 9426	Dyke
2903	A	199.8	**Nine Barrow Down ***	152.1	SZ 0084 8120	Fence

Nine Barrow Down and Swyre Head

These hills were promoted to Marilyns in 1999. They had been overlooked because Swyre Head has an ancient man-made summit and Nine Barrow Down has a man-made col, in a railway cutting. Swyre Head survived until 2015 when it was found to be lower than its 208m map height. The status of Nine Barrow Down was confirmed after an entertaining col survey, with the surveying equipment set up on the platform of a railway station. The approach to the summit was less fun, with a vast expanse of unavoidable cow mud.

Lewesdon Hill

This hill was omitted in error from the first edition, when Pilsdon Pen was listed as the Marilyn. In 2016 a survey confirmed Lewesdon Hill to be two metres higher.

ANN BOWKER, 1995

The 24-hour computer in the window of the tourist office in Bridport told us that Pilsdon Pen was the highest point of Dorset, but a recent communication from Alan Dawson said that Lewesdon Hill was two metres higher. As the two summits lie less than three km apart it seemed a good idea to combine the two in a circuit. We started from a lay-by south of Pilsdon Pen and soon dropped out of the mist. When we set foot on the south ridge of Lewesdon Hill we were on a delightful path through beech trees, reminiscent of the Cotswold escarpment. The summit was pleasant too, a grassy clearing in the trees, but we were back in thick mist. We veered left towards the unseen Pilsdon Pen and needed the compass to keep us on the right line before we reached a distinct bridleway, running between hedges. After a few minutes on the main road we turned north on a little lane to approach Pilsdon Pen. This brought us up onto the impressive ramparts of the hill fort. We were in the mist again, which gave the fort more atmosphere as we walked along its uppermost bank but deprived us of the reputedly magnificent view.

Staple Hill

ANN BOWKER, 1995

The map showed two picnic sites some 5km apart, with Staple Hill lying between them. We decided to use what we call the A B A principle whereby we would walk in opposite directions. Armed with a rough copy of the relevant paths, I set off from the western end. I had more or less abandoned the search for the trig point when I spotted it, only a few metres from where I stood but so covered in moss that it was scarcely visible amongst the green trees and undergrowth. Soon after this the waymarked path left the road and plunged into deep mud. It was difficult not to sink in above the tops of the wellies. When we met I was warned of even worse to come by my unfortunate companion who was far less suitably shod. The eastern picnic site had seats with views across the Vale of Taunton but thick mist meant we did not benefit from this reward for our troublesome traverse.

Number		Height	Name	Drop	Location	Summit
2906	L	296.8	Walbury Hill	188.7	SU 3734 6163	Trig
2908	L	280.8	Black Down	192.3	SU 9194 2963	Knoll near trig
2909	L	270.4	Butser Hill	156.5	SU 7168 2032	Trig
2911	G	254.9	Littleton Down	149.2	SU 9412 1494	Trees

Black Down

ALAN DAWSON, MARCH 2010

A bleak B&B in a bleak Portsmouth suburb was not the most inspiring way to start a tour of the summits of Sussex and Kent, but it meant that I got an early start for my second haul of eight Marilyns in a day (after eight in South Wales in November 2006).

Butser Hill might have been all right if I had been able to see it, but it was quick and the compass was useful. Black Down provided a pleasant walk in damp, atmospheric, woodland, but the trig pillar was surrounded by high trees and scrubby undergrowth.

Walbury Hill

ChatGPT, 2024

Walbury Hill, located in Berkshire, England, is interesting for several reasons:

- At 297 metres above sea level, Walbury Hill is the highest point in the south-east of England, offering stunning panoramic views over the surrounding countryside.

- The hill is home to an Iron Age hillfort, a historical site that dates back around 2500 years. This fortification offers clues about ancient life and defensive strategies in prehistoric Britain. The site is a designated Scheduled Monument, highlighting its archaeological significance.

- Nearby, there is a white chalk figure of a horse on the hillside, carved into the chalk, though it's not as well-known as some other white horses in the region, like the one at Uffington. These chalk figures are thought to be a form of ancient artwork or to have had ceremonial significance.

- The hill is part of the Ridgeway National Trail, a long-distance path that stretches across southern England and follows ancient routes used for thousands of years. The views from Walbury Hill are particularly scenic and provide hikers with a sense of the natural and historical beauty of the area.

- Walbury Hill is composed of chalk, which is common in this part of England. The surrounding area is part of the chalk escarpment of the North Wessex Downs, a region known for its geological features, such as exposed chalk ridges and valleys.

- Due to its elevation and location within an Area of Outstanding Natural Beauty, Walbury Hill is rich in flora and fauna. It supports a variety of wildlife, including rare species of birds and plants that thrive in the chalk grassland habitat.

Overall, Walbury Hill stands out as both a natural and historical landmark, offering insight into the ancient past, natural beauty, and cultural heritage of southern England.

Number		Height	Name	Drop	Location	Summit
2907	L	294.0	Leith Hill	247	TQ 1393 4318	Knoll near tower
3686	G	269.6	Botley Hill *	209	TQ 3871 5518	Tower
2912	LT	248.0	Ditchling Beacon	212.7	TQ 3316 1307	Trig
2913		242	Crowborough *	159	TQ 5105 3063	Road
2916	L	242.0	Chanctonbury Ring **	217.7	TQ 1392 1207	Mound
2917	L	218.4	Firle Beacon	197.7	TQ 4854 0593	Knoll near trig
2922	AL	164.3	Cliffe Hill ¬	149.8	TQ 4340 1071	Grass
2919	LT	214.7	Wilmington Hill	194.6	TQ 5485 0344	Mound near trig
2920	L	201	Detling Hill #	164	TQ 8037 5866	Trees
2921	AL	187.7	Cheriton Hill	149.7	TR 1978 3964	Grass

Botley Hill

The summit was relocated from one unsatisfactory summit to another in 2008, when the base of a water tower was found to be over two metres higher than the 267m trig point.

Cliffe Hill

There is no doubt about the summit of this hill, which was surveyed at night to avoid interfering with any golfers or golf balls. The key col seems to be in one of the ploughed fields in the vast and flat col area. Evidence from Lidar data is not entirely conclusive but indicates with 95% probability that the relative height is under 150 metres. Cliffe Hill has therefore been downgraded to Submarilyn status, but it can still be climbed anyway.

Leith Hill

ANN BOWKER, 1995

Our climb of Leith Hill was spoilt right from the start when we noticed we had parked next to a car which had been broken into. The side window had been smashed and glass was scattered over the seats. The owners soon appeared saying that they had only been away twenty minutes, so we rushed up and down the hill as fast as we could.

Ditchling Beacon

ANN BOWKER, 1995

It was completely dark but the friends with whom we were staying were not due back from work until 7pm. To utilise the time profitably we decided to drive to the car park near the summit of Ditchling Beacon. It was only a five-minute stroll to the trig point, with the lights of Brighton spread below us and a clear and starry sky above. Thus the walk, although ridiculously short, was a memorable and very beautiful one.

Chanctonbury Ring

ALAN DAWSON, MARCH 2010

This feature was found to be the highest point of Chanctonbury Hill after a line survey in 2007. It offered the nearest thing to hill walking I had found in the south of England since Dunkery Beacon. I was able to enjoy a relaxing and enjoyable stroll along a mostly good path, with a feeling of space and height that had been absent from all the intervening hills. The summit mound appeared to have had a fairly recent visit from someone with a flame thrower as there was little left of the gorse that had impeded the surveyors.

Detling Hill

This was renamed from North Downs in 1995. Its large and flat summit area includes car parks, buildings, paths, benches, trees, bushes and spoil heaps, making it difficult to identify the highest natural ground, even with a GNSS survey and Lidar data.

Cheriton Hill

This hill was added as a Marilyn in 1995 after extensive study of large-scale maps indicated it just about qualified, though locating the col was difficult. It survived for 25 years until Lidar data showed a more precise col location, giving a relative height of 149.7 metres.

ANN BOWKER, 1995

Although we had climbed all the English hills in Dawson's book, the discovery that Cheriton Hill had been added meant that our celebrations on Shillhope Law were fatally flawed. We decided that Cheriton Hill must be done but could hardly justify a special journey. A flight from Heathrow airport offered the excuse we needed. The plane was leaving at 7:30am on a Monday, making it essential to spend the night in the vicinity. We went clockwise round the London orbital motorway and by noon were mingling with the traffic heading for the continent. We parked up on the escarpment of the downs looking down on the vast concrete edifice which marks the entrance to the channel tunnel. After a short walk along the edge we turned inland on a narrow lane and left it on a delightful path through ripening corn. At the second track we turned left and soon found the trig point, overshadowed by a man-made reservoir. The official summit is further west but indeterminate in a flat field.

Crowborough

Crowborough epitomises the distinction between Marilyn bagging and hill walking. It offers a defiant antidote to the pompous twaddle that gets published by some outdoor writers with antipathy to summit bagging. Yes, it is a daft summit to visit, that's what makes it a prized addition to the collection. The desire to stand on its suburban summit is not all that different from the desire to reach the top of Snowdon or Ben Nevis.

Crowborough may be an unremarkable town but it provided a backdrop for the development of one of the most magnificently deranged and unsettling albums of the last century, one that is lyrically rich and ambiguous, with operatic themes of good and evil, hope and despair. Perhaps that is why it was so highly regarded in Italy. The music plunges dramatically from exceptional beauty to discordant chaos and back again, like a violent thunderstorm sweeping away a fabulous view and then leaving crystal clarity and sunshine in its wake. In 1971, the four members of Van der Graaf Generator arrived at a house in Crowborough – not a studio – to rehearse and refine the three tracks that were to appear on their third album, Pawn Hearts. It was labelled as prog rock but was more progressive than rocky, with little guitar but plenty of saxophone and organ, angelic piano and demented vocals. The dramatic centrefold photograph was taken in the garden of the house, though not the same house that now lies on the highest point of the town, where wheelie bins are recognised as the symbolic summit. Touching them is not usually a moment of transcendence but it can bring joy and satisfaction, a smile to the lips and another one to the total. The summit offers easy bagging but Pawn Hearts is not easy listening and it is not to everyone's taste. Not everyone likes Crowborough but it can be cherished by those able to embrace the contrasts that Marilyn bagging has to offer, with an openness to new experiences and a willingness to appreciate discord and harmony.

IE01 Isle of Wight

Number		Height	Name	Drop	Location	Summit
2914	L	242.0	St Boniface Down	242.0	SZ 5688 7852	Grass near fence
2918	A	213.7	Brighstone Down	150.6	SZ 4324 8472	Trig

The Isle of Wight has many attractive natural features but its Marilyns are disappointing. It is easy to drive almost to the top of the island, but access to its highest point can be awkward. Lidar data indicates that the summit lies inside the outermost compound but outside the innermost compound.

St Boniface Down

ANN BOWKER, 1995

The two Marilyns on the Isle of Wight gave us a splendid excuse to go to an island which otherwise we might never have visited. Starting from Wroxall we climbed first onto St Martin's Down and from here the flat-topped ridge swings in a great curve to the highest part. Dawson's grid reference was inaccessible, being occupied by a radar station behind a hostile fence. We reckoned the bumps and buildings therein to be man-made and hence not invalidating our claim to this summit. The trig point, at the end of the fence, is lower but opened up a pleasant vista westwards along the south coast of the island.

Brighstone Down

This was one of two hills named incorrectly in the original book, where it was listed as Brightstone Down. The other was Sgor Gaibhre in HC04, which was listed as Stob Gaibhre.

ANN BOWKER, 1995

A hazy day did not spoil the excellent walk along the Tennyson Trail from Brighstone Down to The Needles. We visited the summit first, an uninspiring spot since the trig point lies on a mound of grass, little elevated above a featureless plateau. The forest had been felled around it but this did little to improve a prospect. Rowland then set out towards the western tip of the island while I drove there and set out to meet him. The walk across Tennyson Down, with a memorial to the poet, was pleasant but unexciting.

The heavily vegetated summit of Brighstone Down

Psychology and philosophy

The list of Marilyns is a neutral catalogue of hills that meet the required criteria. That is its central point. It is not curated to include only walks that are pleasant or enjoyable in any conventional way. It does not offer concessions to accessibility or feasibility. Many hills are not suitable for an outing of any organised group unless it is a group of hill baggers. Most Marilyns do not offer good paths, stiles, benches or handy parking places. It may take under five minutes or over five hours to reach a summit, where there may or may not be a view. A determined and philosophical mentality is likely be useful.

Some hills can trap you or trip you up if you fail to find a good route. They may conceal hazards hidden within the deceptively simple contour lines of an Ordnance Survey map. Some people choose to give such hills a miss. For others, the uncertainty adds to the richness and variety of the quest and offers the possibility of succeeding where others have tried and failed, or not even tried.

The awkward hills form a small but important part of the list. To climb all the Marilyns, or all those on the mainland, it is likely that at some point you will find you are wading through bracken up to your armpits or having your trousers ripped by barbed wire, getting a bootful of muddy water or an earful of angry abuse from a landowner. You might be attacked by clegs or keds, dogs or midges, terns or skuas. You might get so frustrated that you swear out loud at the vegetation, the flies, the river, the wind, the rain, the bog, the trees or whatever hazard has pushed your tolerance beyond its threshold, until you get a grip and somehow find a way through and up, and safely down.

You may come to appreciate the positive aspects of such experiences when you look back at hills where you managed to succeed with cunning and determination, and those that rebuffed initial advances but were overcome when you returned better prepared or in better conditions. The challenge of problem solving is part of the appeal. Facing adversity and dealing with it. Getting to the summit despite the obstacles. Finding a way, rising to the challenge, showing persistence and perseverance, developing resilience. The qualities that can help you reach the summit of an awkward hill may also help you navigate through the problems of life in general, in theory at least.

Despite all that character-building stuff, the truth is that most Marilyns are pretty easy. You put on your boots or wellies, start off, keep going, get to the top, look at the view, relax, breathe deeply, have a rest and then go down. It is all so simple and yet somehow you feel different afterwards. You might feel better physically and mentally, with a sense of well-being and a pleasant ache in your thighs, a subtle reminder of the hills you have climbed. If you are able to share a drink and a meal with a few friends, possibly around a table near a log fire, the feeling is qualitatively different from a similar evening with food and drink but without the walk or the struggle.

On top of all that, you will have another hill or two or three in the bag. You haven't just been for a walk, you have risen to the challenge. At times it wasn't easy but you did it, you found a way and have taken another step toward your goal, whatever that may be. According to some writers and researchers, you have taken another step on the path to contentment, and possibly the path to meaning. What more could one ask for?

Many people in mainstream culture spend a lot of their time shopping or watching television or browsing social media. This is regarded as normal behaviour. Hill bagging is not normal behaviour. Some people call hill baggers sad, but you don't see many sad faces among those who have just reached the top of a summit or two on their target list.

Strategy and mentality

CAMPBELL SINGER, 2006

One big difference with reaching 600 Marilyns as opposed to climbing 282 Munros is that there is absolutely no sense of anti-climax following the event. There are plenty more to go at. It's rather like a marathon treasure hunt potentially lasting years, with next to no chance of ever reaching the finishing line. Perverse but true. It's amazing how what is essentially a book of lists can give so much enjoyment.

GAVIN THEOBALD, 2006

Not having a car, I am reliant on public transport. I go to an area and then blitz it over a number of days, doing as many hills as I can. I camp out in the hills for up to ten days at a time, self-sufficient, so most of my hills are done with a large pack on my back. I like to camp overnight on the summits, which is a good way of avoiding the worst of the midges. I moved to Scotland in 1999 and have been ticking off about 60 Marilyns a year.

JONATHAN DE FERRANTI, 2011

I guess there will always be those who deride or pity summit list tickers. There will also be those who deride the concept of relative height and reject anything that fails to attain a specific height above sea level. Well, each to their own, but ticking and counting summits is what gets me onto my feet and out into the wilderness, and stops me descending into vice. And, for me, it is relative height that makes a summit, regardless of height above sea level. It has been pointed out that the car park on Mount Washington is around 1900 metres above sea level, and so is a parking lot in Colorado Springs. I feel just as uplifted on a Fife Marilyn, or on the highest point of a island, as I do on a Munro.

And good for anyone who has climbed more relative hills than I have, who has climbed more relative hills in a day or year than I have, or who would leave me way behind in any hill race. I will tick my lists in my time and admire, but not attempt to compete with, others who tick lists in their time. I may not have been blessed with a bubbly, fun-loving and party-going nature, but I accept and search for the benefits of Asperger's syndrome rather than to attempt to cure it, as if it were a disease. I am fortunate that my circumstances allow me to do what I do best instead of being tied to organised employment, and to believe in what I believe, rather than commit myself to any form of organised religion. I hope to climb all the Marilyns and to continue to create digital elevation models, panoramic maps and lists of relative hills, and to make my work freely available to the world for many years to come.

MARTIN RICHARDSON, 2011

When AD first put forward the idea of P150 Marilyns, the sheer number of hills listed seemed daunting. However, it meant that it took the anarchy of the bumpiness of the British landscape and gave hill bagging a sense of order, a sense of possibility and the bonus of a wide geographical dispersal. Sure, the Marilyns list means that a number of gems can potentially be missed if baggers allow themselves to become too blinkered. I can see the merits of the P100 Humps as an additional list. For many of us, now, climbing the majority of the Marilyns is no longer quite so daunting, particularly with the improvements in the road network and increasing affluence in the last twenty years., so P100 hills fill the gaps between the Marilyns nicely.

Jon Metcalf, 2015

I found RHB in Nevisport Fort William on a biblically crap day and loved the absence of route descriptions, the liberation from Munros and introduction to islands. The Marilyns were clearly superior to the then recently subjectively re-revised Munros. What was not to like about a much larger, much more diverse and much harder challenge that could occupy a good part of a weekend explorer's life.

Many devotees were convinced they would never be finished, which did not detract from the pleasure one jot. Exploring new ground still beats repeat ascents and a couple of hundred remain to be visited. Marilyns have been a cornerstone of trying to cling to relative sanity, bagging an average of more than one a week for the 25 years I had lived in Scotland.

Adversity and absurdity

Alastair Matthewson, 2014

I like the exploratory satisfaction that can be achieved by climbing hills that are not mentioned in any guidebook and I make sure I avoid web research until after the event. It is not exactly Tilman and Shipton forging a route into the Nanda Devi sanctuary, but it keeps me happy and out of mischief.

My favourite hill tends to be the one I have just climbed. Some of the craggy west coasters south of Oban are amazing – wee bonsai hills, perfect miniatures of the mountain stereotype, offering an hour or two in the fresh air with the chance of spying a sea eagle. I quite enjoy the physical and mental challenge of a bit of forest bashing or knee-high tussocks. Sneaking past potentially irate landowners adds an attractive frisson to any expedition. However, wet shoulder-high bracken really gets me down.

Richard McLellan, 2015

The pursuit of Marilyns has taken me back and forth across Britain to some of its most wonderful places in the most varied of weather. There have been brief moments when trudging across bleak wet moorlands in darkness, or with fingers numbed by cold and fighting the wind to fold the map, when I have asked why.

The answer is never far away – perhaps a snipe unexpectedly taking flight or the ghostly curtains of greenish lights shimmering in the northern skies, or the friendships made through enjoyment and adversity and the excitement of exploring new places. But, most of all, it is standing on that piece of hallowed ground where so many others of the group have also stood, as have our ancestors before us – the highest point.

Colin Crawford, 2014

Standing atop Mount Eagle in near darkness, having struggled to locate the tree-moated grey trig in the failing light, I relished the sheer absurdity of what I was doing. How on earth would I have explained the purpose of this outing to someone who knew nothing of Marilyns. Any witnesses would have questioned my sanity, or indeed my possible criminal intent. And not for the first time. I well recall the bemused and suspicious stares from locals as I entered the compound on Ruardean Hill to touch the trig and ascend the water tank. Crazy, utterly absurd – the seductive facet of Marilyns which sets them apart from all other lists. What hill list can attain the heights of irreverence and downright impertinence scaled by certain relative hills.

For every A' Mhaighdean there is a Crowborough, for every Stac Lee a Bishop Wilton Wold. The juxtaposition of such extremes holds huge appeal for the lover of irony, cocking a snook at the smug seriousness of hardened Munro chasers. No Marilyn bagger could ever be accused of a sense of humour failure.

I didn't recognise this unique attraction immediately. The Relative Hills of Britain sat unattended on my bookshelf for several years before a casual tally of summits revealed the fact that I was over the 600 mark. Most of those 600 were a mixture of Munros, Corbetts, Grahams and English or Welsh 2000ers, with the occasional lower hill. Only when I began to explore Southern Scotland with a fresh eye did I discover such unlikely treasures as Belling Hill and Corse Hill. The latter was an isolated mound above a sea of conifers, involving a truly mind-numbing approach along endless forestry tracks. Belling Hill is only a few minutes from the nearest road, yet the summit is coy and elusive, unmarked near a crossroads of forest rides. Such non-hills removed the blinkers from my vision and ever since I have pursued the silly stuff with genuine fervour.

The snow-covered Cona Mheall treated me to an epic ascent several years ago, during which I escaped lightly after a series of foolish decisions, but for a genuine sense of menace it hardly compared to the clandestine bagging of Upper Park, where I had to crouch down in the trees to avoid being spotted by an armed and grim-looking gentleman on a quad bike. I lingered at the summit only long enough to ensure I had reached the highest point, keenly aware of possible watchers in the nearby summer house.

Then there was Billinge Hill, involving a flat stroll of a few hundred metres from the car to a graffiti-covered monument overlooking industrial detritus. Hutton Roof Crags was truly a voyage of discovery – an unsuspected labyrinth of rock and foliage and a genuine treat. Conventional hills? Hardly. To think that I might have missed out by restricting myself to the big beasts.

Summits blanketed by obscuring foliage, especially of the commercial variety, have an almost uniquely bad press. My least favourite anywhere was Airds Hill, a truly vicious example of the genre, whose actual summit I cannot claim to have bagged with pinpoint accuracy. Yet some forested summits have a perverse appeal. Locating the cairn on White Hill of Culreoch gave an immense degree of satisfaction. It has to be conceded that on a wet and blustery day the merits of an enclosed summit appear singularly obvious. Bucking the trend, the broad-leaved wildernesses of Creag Ghiubhais and Ord Ban held more conventional delights.

Several Marilyns lose out in the fame stakes to nearby honeypot tops. In some cases the obscurity is merited. On Bennachie, tedious Oxen Craig must receive a good deal fewer ascents than its lower but brasher neighbour Mither Tap. How many of the hordes who make the ascent of cocky little Ben A'an think to continue to the uninspiring moorland summit of Meall Gainmheach. Cairnpapple is another case in point – the lower top has a famous monument, with an interpretation centre, whilst the actual summit wallows in deserved neglect a few hundred metres south.

Teenage kicks

Rachael Metcalf, 2008

Who wants to toil through mud and ice, thorns and tussocks, rain and cold? Who wants to be lost and hungry in the middle of nowhere? Me for one, because the good parts of walking usually outweigh the bad ones. Some say that walking is an obsession. Well it can completely occupy my mind sometimes, but it isn't usually unhealthy, and any unpleasantness is short-lived compared to the good memories. It doesn't disrupt my life but rather gives contrast to the controlling routines of school and home, and gives something to look forward to when life is dragging. It isn't my only interest, or even my main one. It seems more rational to me than following bands or football teams, clothes trends or the latest movies, which many of my friends concentrate on. I do most of these as well of course, except for following football teams.

Hills give me a simple sense of freedom from the world, and some quiet time for thinking, without the hubbub of humanity. I love the peaceful feeling that surrounds you while hill walking, if you allow it to. I would never have expected examples of such beauty in the simple things around me, nor did I expect to enjoy hill walking as much as I do now. I used to hate walking and would scream and cry whenever my dad dragged me up a hill. Over time it has got under my skin. Now I sing instead of screaming.

Some of my best memories are of thrills and adrenalin rushes on hills. One of my favourites is An Teallach because of its scrambling, gorgeous looks, and of course its amazing sunbathing spots. My whole body hurt the day after, but I would not trade that day for anything. Some of my not-so-great memories are also from hills, for example falling on wet quartzite in the rain on Canisp. Even then the view of Suilven through a break in the clouds and the sense of achievement were pretty special.

Then there are the huts, some of which are cosy places to relax after a day in the hills. Others however are small, cramped, freezing and smelly, with paper-thin walls that are no defence against my dad's snoring. Luckily I become impervious to this when tired enough. I've met some brilliant hill people through clubs and my dad. There are also the perks of hill walking, like the time afterwards when you sit and just talk, or the events (meals, discos, dances, Baggershambles etc).

I don't always know where I am or the name of the hill I'm climbing or which direction I should be going, a trait I'm sure I've inherited from my dad. When climbing Corse Hill, my dad assumed that it would be an easy hill and that we wouldn't need the GPS. On reaching what we thought was the top, we couldn't find the trig point so we assumed we'd found the highest point instead. Later we found we'd entirely missed the top. But those are the situations you look back on and laugh at. I enjoy walking, but given the option of doing a second hill that is not part of the same walk I'll generally say no. You can spoil walking by doing too much. 'Planet Teenage' is also a major factor, particularly on a Sunday as I'd often much rather sleep in. In some cases this has resulted in bribery to get me up, for example a promise of coffee on the way home.

Hills haven't become ticks to me, nor is any list something I have to complete before I die. Hills are freedom, inspiration and a place to think and be alone (no matter how many others you're with). Maybe I can't read a map well yet and I'm not the fastest, but I love the sense of peace and undisturbed beauty (unless there is a wind farm that is) and I wouldn't give up hill walking without a fight. To take hills from me would be like taking away the odd glimmers of sun on a claggy day.

Aesthetics

AUDREY LITTERICK, 2012

Imagine getting to the top of a mountain that you know well and love, or perhaps one that you know is going to have a good view and would have done, yet you arrive there to be confronted with a forest of wind turbines, acres of trashed, drained peatland and miles of access tracks. If any of you still believe that wind farms can generate useful amounts of clean, green energy that is affordable, I can assure you that they can NOT. I can also provide an independent, scientific assessment of why wind farms are a serious waste of money as well as causing desecration of a sort that can never be fully reversed.

DAVID STALLARD, 2012

I'm interested in the wildlife, the geology, the history and the scenery you see when you go hill walking. Being on your own heightens your sense of all these things and just the feeling of being in the hills. There is so much more chance of getting this experience on the lower hills and I love finding my own way around hills which lack the obvious paths of the more popular hills. You tend to see a lot more wildlife, too. My eagle count on the lower hills is very much higher than on the Munros.

LIZ AND PETER HASTIE, 2012

One thing we have noticed with the Marilyns is how pleasant it can be to walk in forests. Looking at the maps before we committed ourselves to really tackling Marilyns as a project, we were a bit put off by the number of summits surrounded by trees, especially those with no apparent paths. It has turned out though that finding ways through the woods has proven to be generally more enjoyable than not. There has, however, been the occasional definitely never again.

JONATHAN APPLEBY, 2015

Marilyns have been a source of inspiration for me, opening my eyes to the beauty and interest to be found on the lower hills of Britain. I now do not consider any hill dull, no matter where it is. Even the conifer-infested lower summits that are sprinkled liberally across Scotland have some attraction to them. Maybe it is an age thing.

Ethics

ALAN DAWSON

Lots of sports have trouble with ethics, in areas where the rules are a little vague or old traditions are not universally accepted. Football has diving, cricket has ball tampering, cycling has doping, rugby has gouging and maiming, while golf has all sorts of arcane rules such as coughing without due care and attention. More recently, lots of sports have had trouble with gender definition and eligibility.

Hill walking has largely been free from ethical concerns. Most hill baggers regard their pursuit as a personal activity and have been content to follow their own rules and guidelines. No self-respecting bagger would claim a summit they knew they had not climbed, but there are grey areas. Some summits are awkward or indeterminate or may be fenced off from public access, such as Saxa Vord, Botley Hill and St Boniface Down. Any concerns about the validity of ascents have generally been regarded as a personal issue, where you were only cheating yourself if you claimed a doubtful bag, but the advent of league tables introduced a competitive element.

If some people apply one rule, such as touching the top, and others require standing on top or getting their head above it, then discrepancies can arise. This is minor stuff but can provide an element of scrutiny and amusement. Some hill baggers can get a minor thrill from overtaking someone in a league table, so the incentive is there for giving themselves the benefit of any doubt. There is also the matter of retrospective bagging, often known as armchair bagging, which raises issues of doubt and certainty. How can anyone be sure they went to the undisputed top of a hill several years earlier if they did not make a note or pay close attention at the time?

There are other types of ethical issue. Is it acceptable to hire a guide for the Cuillin? It has become more common in recent years. You still have to climb the hills yourself, even if you do get help from a tight rope. Ladders are used routinely on Everest so why not in Britain? A chair lift? Routine in the Alps, less acceptable for bagging Aonach Mor. Train up Snowdon? Surely not. Driving along forest tracks? Lots do, some don't.

Then there are summits with mildly technical issues such as Tryfan. Is it valid to reach up and touch the top? How many of those who have climbed the Inaccessible Pinnacle since its top fell off have managed to get their head above the new highest point?

Relatively few Marilyns raise technical or ethical issues compared to the vast lists of Humps and Tumps, where the problems of access might involve corporate compounds, private gardens, prisons, castles, guard dogs and razor wire. This goes beyond hill walking and becomes a different type of activity with its own challenges, rewards and ethics.

The main ethical issue for Marilyns concerns summit relocations, which range from trivial to considerable. The usual principle is that once you have climbed all the hills in a list then any subsequent changes do not affect the validity of completion. This has little relevance to Marilyns because few people manage to climb them all, so the nature of a relocation becomes significant. For example, Hail Storm Hill and Hoove both have a summit plateau where there is little height difference between the original grid reference and the current location identified by surveyors. Most baggers will feel no obligation to return for such trivial changes. By contrast, the new summit of Muncaster Fell is 70cm higher than the old one, it is about 500 metres away and there is over 30 metres drop between the two points. These look and feel like different summits, so most baggers will want to return at some point or accept losing one from their total.

Two unusual summit relocations are of specific interest. Hensbarrow Downs replaced Hensbarrow Beacon in 2017 and Mynydd y Grug replaced Mynydd Machen in 2024. These are the only two Marilyns with man-made summits that have added several metres to their height and resulted in them superseding the original summit, though lots of other summits have been disturbed by man in the distant or recent past, such as Snowdon, Tinto and Hirfynydd. Hensbarrow Downs were extensively treated with many tons of suitable soil to encourage natural regeneration. This was effective in transforming the large summit area from ugly spoil heap to grassy wildness in under twenty years. It looks and feels like a natural hill from most perspectives.

Mynydd y Grug is less satisfactory. It has lots of large trees on its slopes and looks convincingly natural below its largely bare summit area. It has not been covered with soil and in 2024 did not look natural, though there were trees and shrubs growing within about fifty metres of the highest point. It has become a Marilyn because it is a permanent feature of the landscape and is eleven metres higher than Mynydd Machen. Anyone not convinced by this change is entitled to include Mynydd Machen in their Marilyn total until Mynydd y Grug offers a more realistic impersonation of a natural hill summit.

Landmarks

Colin Crawford, 2007

Completion of a list, any list, is a curiously contradictory and bittersweet experience, with the satisfaction of a pilgrimage at an end, yet sadness that joyful episodes along the way will be no more. There is also the paradox that travelling is superior to arrival, for the moment of realisation can feel disappointingly flat. Anti-climax, I suspect, is more common than wild exhilaration. Perhaps that is a function of my own misanthropic tendency towards solitary ventures, but in discussion with those who have invited a large party, I detect a similar ambivalence. Such feelings may offer ironic justification to those who decry the list-ticking phenomenon as the antithesis of outdoor venturing, but there must be something about completing, as so many of us aspire to the condition.

That something, perhaps, is that we have attained a way-station in our lives, a notable landmark that serves to mark progress and initiate the beginning of a fresh adventure, though it may simply indicate an end in itself. I guess that those of us who continue to bag hills are the rolling stones of the outdoor world, not content with relaxed contemplation but in need of goals to tempt us forward on our quests. There are times when I am as satisfied with idle wool-gathering as any carefree rambler, but I confess to having a driven aspect to my personality that requires a succession of goals. It puzzles me that critics often opine that a list-ticking approach detracts from simply having a good day out. Yet how so? Even as I bag my summit, I can still linger to enjoy the sunset, marvel at wildlife sightings, revel in remoteness and soak up the invigorating ambience. The myopic hill nerd is surely a creature of myth. Adding a summit and recording the event later adds rather than subtracts from the experience.

So landmarks are important, yet completions are a relatively rare occurrence. Indeed, to be confronted with a large list of virgin hills can be daunting enough to deter serious engagement. Intermediate objectives are necessary to bridge such an enormous gap between start and finish. It is these minor landmarks, I'd guess, which motivate most of us to continue our activities on a regular basis. For the majority, this will involve hill walking by numbers. Fifty hills on a list seems significant, one hundred more so. This works especially well on chunky inventories like the Marilyns. The numbers game extends further of course. We all repeat hills, and a tally of total ascents of Munros, Marilyns etc offers other landmarks to aim for.

There are alternative methods of marking progress. The attainment of all summits in an area is one which will bear repeating as successive lists are tackled, and this one can be a matter of direct sensation. It is immensely gratifying to gaze out in all directions from a summit and consider that you have stood atop every eminence you can see. There will always be the odd virgin pimple on an even more obscure tabulation and a seemingly infinite number of trig points. Yet that visual survey of past experiences must surely evoke some justified conceit.

Islands are another wonderfully addictive delight and have their own series of landmarks. Even on islands I have visited frequently, I can always contrive a new goal to aspire to, an excuse for return. I harbour no hopes of reaching the majority of Britain's uninhabited islets, but I look forward to having visited as many as I can.

In terms of landmarks, I suspect that the surface I am scratching reveals only the faintest of etching. I am no innovator, and there must be a host of individual and creative ways in which folk record the progress of their outdoor endeavours.

Statistics and mathematics

Everyone knows that fresh air and exercise are good for you, physically and mentally. Mildly vigorous exercise, such as walking uphill, provides more health benefits than walking on flat ground. Hill walking is therefore seen as a healthy activity, but paying attention to the height and prominence of a hill may be regarded as eccentric and not so healthy. Some walkers dismiss an interest in hill data as contrary to the quality of the outdoor experience, but there is no need for any conflict between the numeric and the romantic when you can enjoy both.

An interest in numbers differentiates hill bagging from hill walking because it is a vital aspect of bagging. Hill data provide the structure for groups and lists of hills, while the numbers of hills in specific categories can provide a great incentive to climb more hills. In most activities there is a continuum from ignorance to lack of interest to healthy interest to passion to obsession. It is usually healthier to acknowledge and accept one's innocent interests than to suppress them. The numerical aspect of climbing hills can add an extra layer of motivation, satisfaction and enjoyment to the more mainstream aspects of walking in the hills. So let's have some more numbers.

There were 1542 Marilyns listed in 1992 but twelve of these have been found to have less than 150 metres drop and no longer qualify. Ten of these twelve are included in the tables as Submarilyns (all except Cunnigill Hill and Scafell). Since 1992, 25 new Marilyns have been discovered, taking the total to 1555, but the five Marilyns on the Isle of Man have been omitted because it is not part of Britain. A summary of these and other notable changes is given in the chapter on Revision on page 347.

There are 111 Marilyns over 1000 metres high but only three of them have over 1000 metres of relative height. Almost half the Marilyns are over 600 metres high but only 93 have over 600 metres of relative height. The median height of a Marilyn is 594 metres but median prominence is only 227 metres and over one third of Marilyns have relative height under 200 metres. High prominence is relatively rare, as the table below shows.

Metres	Number of Marilyns	
	Height	Drop
> 1200	7	1
> 1100	35	2
> 1000	111	3
> 900	237	11
> 800	392	30
> 700	596	52
> 600	767	93
> 500	984	154
> 400	1202	276
> 300	1373	480
> 200	1516	975
> 150	1550	1550

Distribution

There are 1218 Marilyns in Scotland, 173 in England and 159 in Wales, with 1318 on the mainland, 227 on Scottish islands, two on the Isle of Wight, two on Anglesey and one on Bardsey. The OS Landranger map with most Marilyns is sheet 33 which has 69, though 21 of these are also on maps 25 or 40. There are 67 Marilyns on map 50, 65 on map 41 and 62 on map 25. Only two 1km grid squares contain two Marilyns: NM9096 in Knoydart includes Sgurr na Ciche and Garbh Chioch Mhor, while NN9233 in Perthshire includes Meall nan Caorach and Meall Reamhar. This proximity does not necessarily make these the closest pairs of Marilyns, as adjacent hills may be in different grid squares. These appear to be the pairs of Marilyns nearest to each other, irrespective of grid square.

Area	Marilyn pairs	Distance apart
IR01	Ainshval (781m) and Trollabhal (702m)	0.88km
HS10	Meall nan Caorach (624m) and Meall Reamhar (618m)	0.92km
HW16	Sgurr na Ciche (1040m) and Garbh Chioch Mhor (1013m)	0.94km
SK01	Sgurr Alasdair (992m) and Inaccessible Pinnacle (986m)	0.98km
SK03	Sgurr na Coinnich (739m) and Beinn na Caillich (731m)	1.07km
IU01	South Lee (281m) and North Lee (263m)	1.09km
IX02	Mullach an Eilein, Boreray (384m) and Stac an Armin (197m)	1.10km
HW02	Mullach Coire Mhic Fhearchair (1015m) and Sgurr Ban (989m)	1.11km
HN06	Ben More Coigach (743m) and Sgurr an Fhidhleir (704m)	1.20km
IX02	Stac Lee (172m) and Mullach an Eilein, Boreray (384m)	1.22km
HC10	Meall a' Bhuiridh (1108m) and Creise (1100m)	1.24km

The Marilyns that are farthest from any other Marilyn are:
- Ward Hill on Fair Isle (83km from Fitty Hill on Westray)
- Wendover Woods in Buckinghamshire (70km from Walbury Hill)
- Normanby Top in Lincolnshire (67.6km from Bishop Wilton Wold)
- Bardon Hill in Leicestershire (61.5km from Walton Hill)
- Walbury Hill in West Berkshire (53.7km from Butser Hill)
- Bishop Wilton Wold in Yorkshire (50km from Urra Moor)

Proportional height

The statistics of Marilyns can be complex but the mathematics are simple, with the single criterion of 150 metres of relative height. The maths for Submarilyns are more interesting as the drop required for qualification decreases as the height increases. Hills 1000m high require 140m drop and this increases proportionally to 141m for 900m hills, 142m for 800m hills and so on, with 145m drop needed for 500m hills and 148m drop for hills 200m high. A hill exactly 150m high would need 148.5m drop to be a Submarilyn. The formula to generate the proportional results is: DROP < 150 AND DROP >= (150-(METRES/100)). This precision has been relaxed slightly to allow for inherent measurement uncertainty when surveying vegetated cols, and so four hills that are within 12cm of qualifying are included. These are Monadh Mor (HE01), Hill of Strone (HE11), Fastheugh Hill (SS10) and Llanfihangel Hill (WM04). Monadh Mor has only 138.8m drop but its 1113.4m height gives it landscape significance and enables it to qualify as the third highest Submarilyn, below only Cairn Gorm and Derry Cairngorm.

Social studies

The Relative Hills of Britain was published in April 1992 and the first update sheet was issued in 1995. Marhofn magazine was introduced in May 1999 and published annually until the final, full-colour edition in 2016. The magazine was well received by Marilyn baggers, particularly in its early years when it was the main source of information on lots of hills. It was funded entirely by voluntary contributions for eighteen years and provided a sense of community among people who had never met.

Circumstances have changed considerably since 1999. The main purpose then was to keep people informed about changes to the list – promotions, demotions, replacements and relocations. Tips for the tops were important as well. Many of the hills were rarely climbed and not much was known about them. As more people started to contribute to Marhofn, personal experiences and anecdotes became increasingly important.

Many of the contributions to this book have been drawn from early issues of Marhofn magazine, while the final edition afforded an opportunity for reflection. There were over 300 different contributors, including several who are no longer with us. Ashes to ashes, dust to dust, we all reach our final wall at some stage, but written memories may live on.

JENNY HATFIELD, 2016

Back in 2007 when I first saw the RHB book I recall being interested but not hooked on Marilyns, being focused on Corbetts at the time. It was seeing the subsequent Marhofn, and the personal stories of those climbing Marilyns, that got me hooked. My commitment to the Marilyns was largely down to the community that I found in the baggers. There is competition, then friendship and then camaraderie in even greater measure. I never thought I would get even close to 1000 let alone finish them. In all the new folk coming to the Marilyns I see the same thing, perhaps just a glimmer that things can be achieved.

TONY SMITH, 2016

So Marhofn reaches adulthood and is then, most disappointingly, about to be killed off. I shall mourn its passing and sincerely hope that it, or something equivalent, can continue to be produced in some similarly pleasing tactile format. Online just is not the same. I have kept all my copies and regularly refer to these to jog a failing memory. I do of course have my personal logs but for me Marhofn was really about the shared objectives and experiences, and yes, I admit there was also the competitive element.

JON METCALF, 2016

Marhofn introduced me to some kindred spirits who have gone on to become bagging mates on various trips, events and hills over the years. Islands, particularly the uninhabited ones, were a natural focus for tackling expensive objectives with a boat full of fellow eccentrics. I have kept my copies of the magazine, as it is interesting to see friends' progress into and through the Hall of Fame over the years.

Hall of Fame

The Marilyn Hall of Fame was inaugurated in 1996, when ten people were known to have climbed over 600 Marilyns, including three with over 1000. By the time the first edition of Marhofn was published in 1999 there were 37 members of the Hall of Fame, with Ann and Rowland Bowker having already climbed over 1500 Marilyns. The Hall was later extended to include a Corridor, for those with 400-599 Marilyns, a Cellar for those with under 400, and an Upper Hall for those with over 1000 Marilyns in their collection.

The concept of the Hall evolved from a daft little list to an opulent virtual meeting place for people who might never meet in person but shared a common eccentric interest. It became clear that some members valued the social aspect of Hall membership, which led to a series of annual gatherings and some small communal walks, as Marilyn baggers helped each other to celebrate reaching a landmark along the way. It was so rare for anyone to climb all the Marilyns that reaching a numeric or regional target could become an excuse for a summit celebration, usually involving whisky and cake, and sometimes a chant or a song. In this way the solitary nature of hill bagging could be transformed into a series of sociable occasions, to the surprise of some of those involved, who discovered they were not as anti-social as they had assumed. Lots of hill baggers chose not to participate, but everyone had a choice to do as they wished.

Membership of the Hall of Fame fluctuated as people joined, moved on to other interests or passed away. By the end of 2024 there were 332 current members out of 428 who had crossed the threshold at some stage and passed through the magnificent entrance portal. Reaching 600 Marilyns was the main objective for some, but others were spurred on by further intermediate landmarks such as 1000, 1200, 1500, the mainland Marilyns or all the Marilyns apart from those on St Kilda. In practice, climbing Conachair on Hirta is relatively feasible, so this target has become 1545, which could be rounded up to 1550 by those wishing to include the five Manx Marilyns or extended to 1644 by adding on the 99 Submarilyns.

By 2024, only eleven people had been able to climb all 1550 Marilyns in Britain: Rob Woodall, Eddie Dealtry, Alan Whatley, Michael Earnshaw, Martin Richardson, Tony Smith, Richard Tibbetts, Richard Mclellan, Jenny Hatfield, Rick Salter and Peter Ellis. Most of them later topped up their total after the discovery of new Marilyns Beinn Dearg and Rhinog Fach or replacements such as Foel Cedig and White Hill.

About thirty others are known to have climbed all the non-Kilda Marilyns, including several of the contributors to this book: Ann Bowker, Iain Brown, Anne Bunn, Ken Butcher, Bill Carr, Colin Crawford, Alan Dawson, Jonathan de Ferranti, Bill Forbes, Jim Fothergill, Alastair Govan, Liz Hastie, Peter Hastie, Alan Holmes, Graham Illing, Stewart Logan, George Morl, Tom Mundell, Chris Peart, Campbell Singer, Margaret Squires, Roger Squires, Gill Stephens, Ursula Stubbings, Andy Sutton, Norman Wares, Ken Whyte, Richard Wood and Eric Young. Some people have waited several years for the opportunity to climb Stac an Armin and Stac Lee in favourable conditions when access is permitted.

The annually updated Hall of Fame table was always an important part of Marhofn magazine. After the final edition in 2016, membership of the Hall was administered by the Relative Hills Society and publication of the annual table continued in the pages of Relative Matters, the journal of the society that arose from the ashes of Marhofn, with more colour, a new editorial team and a new style.

Thirty years after its inception, the Hall of Fame has evolved into a surprisingly sociable place, with meetings, dinners, boat trips, excursions, talks and communal walks with summit celebrations, as more people entered the Hall or reached another landmark. Gatherings have not been exclusive as all have been welcome regardless of how many summits they had reached, though some of the trips to St Kilda have had conditions applied for safety reasons. Despite the largely solitary nature of relative hill bagging, a distinctive, enthusiastic community has developed, with few formalities or obligations.

Nature study

CHRISTIAN HEINTZEN

Imagine a pleasant summer day on a high hill in Scotland, taking in the views and listening to the silence. Your mind is starting to drift when slowly a high-pitched hum starts reeling you back into the present. Like a Buddhist mantra the humming comes and goes but is too piercing to induce a state of meditative mindfulness.

Presently you have arrived back on solid ground but still perceive the world on scales of mountains and mountain ranges. Only gradually does your focus shift to closer realms. Then, as if by magic, a small creature appears on a lichen-covered stone. In the blink of an eye it is gone and just as quickly is back again, now 'singing' its song on a sun-lit boulder just a few feet away from you. Approaching slowly and avoiding casting your shadow on it, you may be rewarded with a close view. It may even tilt its head towards you as if to acknowledge your presence. You count six legs and two wings and are amazed by the size of its eyes. On account of your observations you decide it is a fly. Faultless like a freshly minted coin, it is a strikingly beautiful creature. Its wings are suffused with orange, its body a polished blue-black boldly marked with three pairs of cream-coloured stripes. It waits in idle gear, engine humming, wings folded back, vibrating at a high frequency. Then without warning it shoots off into the sky. Within milliseconds it has reached, investigated and chased off an interloper, and returned to its perch. There is the tilt of the head again – this time it looks more like a triumphant stance. For a few seconds the wings remain expanded, displaying its cream-coloured insignia to full effect. Then, wings folded, the humming starts again.

It is no ordinary fly that is serenading you. You have discovered royalty amongst the Diptera or two-winged flies: the hoverfly Sericomyia lappona. Its scientific name is much nicer that its vernacular name of white-barred peat hoverfly. Mountain tops are not the typical habitat for this hoverfly. Its larvae develop on much lower ground in boggy or peaty habitats (hence its name) and indeed you may find the adults there too, adorning various flowers whilst feeding on pollen and nectar.

So, what does it do at altitude, on the summits of the highest hills in Scotland? Is it exercising, seeking solitude or grand views? Probably not. The main purpose of this behaviour is thought to be that of finding a mate. Sericomyia lappona is one of many insects that is said to 'hill-top', which is the accepted term now used in the expanding literature on insects and other animals that actively seek out high ground. The earlier observations of 'hill topping' were interpreted as passive movements of insects carried on to the summits by up-drafts. Passive drifting is likely to play a role, but more recent research has shown that most of the hill-topping insects actively seek out summits to find mates. The vast majority of hill-topping insects one sees are males, a fact that seems to mirror observations for our own species found on the Scottish summits. I have yet to discover a single female hoverfly on hill tops.

The sex is easily determined by looking at the compound eyes: in males the eyes meet in the middle, in females they are widely separate. It is thought that the males congregate on the summits and compete for the attention of arriving females. Whether our hoverfly uses its 'song' – like birds do – to mark its territory or to attract females is not known but seems plausible. Once mating has taken place the females quickly descend to lower ground to lay their eggs in more suitable habitat, hence one rarely sees females on hill summits. In contrast, males stay put in wait for another chance.

Is it really necessary to go all the way up a high summit to find a mate? For our own species this is rarely an effective tactic. For many of the insects, however, flying to a mountain summit will greatly improve chances of finding a mate. Many hill-topping insects are scarce or live in widely scattered or isolated habitats. Congregating on summits concentrates numbers on a relatively small area, meaning chances for bumping into each other are much improved. Hoverflies are just one of many groups of hill-topping insects. Species of bot flies (Oestridae) and parasitic flies (Tachinidae) are frequent occupants of summits, and many species of bees, wasps, butterflies and beetles are also known to actively seek higher ground.

Whilst ascending to the rocky summit of Mount Adams (1766m) in the Presidential Range of New Hampshire, my wife and I were greeted by hundreds if not thousands of insects that were sitting or crawling over the summit rocks. Next to many hoverflies we noticed countless click beetles (Elateridae) of various species. They may have flown there to cluster for the purpose of hibernation. It is well known that certain species of ladybird converge in huge numbers on hill tops to hibernate. They probably seek areas of low temperature to induce a state of hibernation called diapause. Huddled together they survive the winter in suspended animation to breed in the following season.

The attraction to high summits is a widespread phenomenon that developed long before humans arrived on the scene. So much remains to be discovered about hill-topping insects and other summit-seeking animals that the keen hill bagger is well placed to add to our knowledge and understanding of this behaviour. So, next time you are up there, listen for the hum and take a closer look. It may guide you to a whole new world.

Male hoverfly Sericomyia lappona hill-topping on a lichen-covered rock at the summit of Beinn Fhionnlaidh (Christian Heintzen)

Painted Lady (Vanessa cardui) on Beinn Fhionnlaidh (Christian Heintzen)

Wild goats can sometimes be seen on summits, but not on Goat Fell. This one was by the coast on Islay.

Sport and games

ALAN DAWSON

From a young age, I always liked games. They were a small, self-contained bit of the world that you could understand, with clear rules, a start, a finish and a chance of succeeding. You could even make up your own games with a pencil and a piece of paper, or with nothing more than your own thoughts.

As I got older the world became even more confusing but I tried to understand it anyway. I found it difficult because most of it seemed to make little sense. The rules were arbitrary and unfair and everywhere seemed to have its own local rules. Even rules that I thought were fixed might suddenly change for no apparent reason. No wonder people turned to religion, it saved them having to think about lots of confusing stuff. I didn't do that because the evidence was elusive and I could not see the point in being almighty if you were going to be ineffective and so reluctant to use your power that it encouraged scepticism, which presumably was not what most deities wanted.

I thought I must be missing some important insight so at the age of 22 I decided to get help from academic experts and was accepted for a place to study philosophy and psychology at Lancaster University. It was a nice campus but a disappointing experience from an intellectual perspective. The main philosophy lecturer had a speech impediment that made him almost impossible to understand. One of the main political philosophy writers, Thomas Hobbes, had a literary impediment that made it difficult for me to understand what he was on about. Plato and others were little better. Nothing that I read seemed to make the world any less confusing yet I kept getting good marks. I assumed this was because I used a typewriter whereas other students submitted hand-written essays.

It took me a while to realise that being able to discuss issues in a thoughtful and literate way was enough to succeed in an academic environment, but that wasn't enough to satisfy my analytical mind. I wanted answers to Life, The Universe and Everything, and I wasn't getting them. Philosophy was sometimes defined as the pursuit of wisdom, but I didn't want to bother pursuing it if I was never going to find it. I gave it up after a year in favour of psychology and educational studies.

Psychology was not much better than philosophy. It seemed to be a pseudo-scientific study of knowing not much about how brains worked. In my third year I took a course about memory. I liked to strip things down to the basics, to look for the foundations or the framework and learn from there. When it came to memory, even the basics were missing. Where is it? Don't know. How does it work? Don't know. Is it reliable? Not really, sometimes maybe. How do I improve my memory? Er, have you tried keeping a diary? This was before personal databases and detailed brain scanning. Neuroscience has come a long way since the 1970s but I wasn't convinced that education had.

To make matters worse, the professor of psychology, the wise and well-dressed head of department and man of the world, said that he liked playing games. I could scarcely believe it. He may even have said that games were good for you. This made me reassess what little progress I had made. If this accomplished intellectual giant enjoyed playing games, I reckoned I might as well give up all the agonising and go back to playing Scrabble and book cricket. It was a huge disappointment but also a great relief. Was it acceptable for a so-called adult to enjoy playing games instead of trudging through dull texts about dialectical materialism, Cartesian dualism and anarcho-syndicalism?

The annoying thing was, I was quite good at sport, which was like playing games but with added exertion and co-ordination. If only I had allowed myself to join in, let go, play tennis and football and cricket, I might have had more fun, but I still stupidly thought that sport and games were a superficial waste of time. So I never scored a century. I did later get to 83 but the bowling wasn't very good and the umpire didn't know the rules. I was given out for having been in long enough already. It was annoying but I liked the spirit of the game, the not taking it too seriously.

Many years later I played a few games for Strathclyde University staff cricket team and once scored ten off the final over to win us the match by one wicket. The umpire ran down the pitch and gave me a big hug. The opposition didn't like that lapse in neutrality but the fielders were big enough to shake hands anyway. The spirit, the way you played the game, seemed at least as important as winning or losing. I didn't realise it at the time, but that final over turned out to be a useful source of solace when things weren't going well. Damn, the roof's leaking. Damn, stuck in the trees again. Damn, struggling down in the dark again. Never mind, I once scored ten off the final over to win a match and averaged 119 for the season. Unfortunately, our ragbag team got promoted thanks to my boundary off the final ball of the match and so we started playing some teams who took things more seriously than we did. Our best bowler stopped playing because the league table made it feel too competitive for him and so he no longer enjoyed the game.

Hill bagging is not really a sport but it is a game, a fine game that adds interest, reward, motivation and satisfaction to hill walking and landscape exploration. It is a game with endless scope and variety, a healthy mixture of co-operation and competition and an excellent set of rules that can be a little blurry around the edges to keep things interesting and deter complacency. It also has proven benefits for physical and mental health, with scope for creativity and problem solving. It is good for developing resilience in adversity and has a satisfying balance of the scientific and romantic, able to cater for intellectual and emotional needs. With all these benefits I sometimes wondered why more people didn't do it, yet it has remained a cult activity, a marginal subculture with its own eccentric allure, which seems to suit many of the participants. Perhaps that was why some of us liked to exaggerate the occasional awfulness, to help ensure it did not become so popular that it detracted from our experiences.

In 2005 I wrote a speculative article called 'Games baggers play', which began with a little philosophy, speculating on the point of hill bagging and the point of doing anything. I then suggested a few point-scoring games to add further interest to the numeric aspect of hill bagging. One of these games, Bilbo Baggins, is repeated here as it later led to an ambitious plan to push the game to its limits.

Setting records has never been part of the culture of Marilyn bagging, though some people do set personal targets for the year ahead. Yet it is inevitable that some of us will speculative about trying to set a record for something, as a personal challenge, a source of pride or to investigate what may be possible physically, mentally or logistically.

The following pages describe four record attempts of varying seriousness and strenuousness. One of them covers a year-long challenge and two describe contrasting 24-hour challenges. The other record attempt describes a whimsical quest that lasts as long as necessary until it is time to give up and go home, which probably best represents the usual Marilyn bagging mentality. By 2024 none of these records had been replicated, possibly because they are tough to beat or because no-one could be bothered to try.

Bilbo Baggins

Gist: To synchronise summit height with current Marilyn tally.
Scoring: One bilbo per baggins.
Example: Climbing 600m Black Combe as your 600th Marilyn.
Aim: To score at least one bilbo before you're bagged out.
Rewards: Shouting 'Bilbo' very loudly at the summit of a baggins.
Grey areas: Whether it's worth losing your friends just to try to score a bilbo.

Bilbo bagging

LEE NEWTON, 2007

The ancillary games suggested in Marhofn amused me such that I started keeping an eye out for the possibility of bagging a Bilbo Baggins. This under-used game presumably suffers from the fact that most players of such games have climbed so many Marilyns that they can no longer find a sufficiently high unclimbed hill. For me in the low 400s this was an altogether simpler matter. The opportunity presented itself on 30 December 2006, during a Christmas holiday visit to my family in Edinburgh, and that combination of timing and location turned up an unlikely possibility. I had randomly reached 421 the week before Christmas and was looking for number 422 somewhere around Edinburgh.

I was pleased to discover on perusal of the tables that Eildon Mid Hill (422m) was close by and could work out nicely as my 422nd. But as I checked out the maps and the other hills close by (the Eildons not being a full day out), I noticed the quite amazing possibility of a quintuple Bilbo. It seemed feasible, with an early start, to climb Eildon Mid Hill, Sell Moor Hill or Meigle Hill (both 423m), Rubers Law (424m), a conveniently placed spacer such as Cademuir Hill (415m) as number 425, and then to continue on to Broomy Law (426m) and White Meldon (427m), thus climbing six hills in the day, with five of them being Bagginses (taking the Tolkien plural). And the best thing was that I wouldn't have to run to accomplish it. My brother Jai was roped in as co-driver and company for the day, and the scene was set.

We arrived just after dawn at the foot of Eildon Mid Hill in less than ideal weather conditions. Nevertheless, we set off into a brisk wind under a leaden sky, safe in the knowledge that we had the necessary gear plus well-practised navigational skills if things deteriorated further. It only took 50 minutes up and down but it was already apparent that Jai wasn't firing on all cylinders. As we pulled up to the beginning of the path to Sell Moor Hill he decided to kip in the car while I walked up the hill. He was not one for complaining and was as strong as the proverbial ox, so I was a little concerned for him as I bent my head into the wind and admired the hazy view that emerged fitfully between squally showers.

When I returned to the car he said he would soldier on, so on we went. After another short drive we started off up Rubers Law on schedule, but it was clear that something was badly wrong with Jai. He waited in some trees below the summit while I topped out into what was now a gale-force wind. On the way down he was as white as a sheet and struggled to keep up, so back at the car the only decent thing to do was call it a day. We drove home slowly and Jai went straight to bed with a fever that lasted two days and kept him away from the Hogmanay celebrations. Bad luck, but I had still managed a triple Bilbo, possibly the first example of this obscure feat. The chance of the quintuple will not come again, and I doubt that a similar possibility exists at higher altitudes.

Binge bagging

ANDREW TIBBETTS, 2006

The catalyst for a record attempt was my move from Cambridge to Stirling in October 2005. My lifetime total of 271 Marilyns (as at 31 Dec 2005) comprised 95 Welsh, 95 English and 81 Scottish (only five below 600m). With so many unvisited summits on my doorstep, my first full year in Scotland seemed like the ideal opportunity to climb as many hills as possible. Transferring the mind-set of a hill walker based in East Anglia to one living in Stirling played a significant part in keeping the motivation going throughout the year. I had once climbed Bredon Hill and Cleeve Hill in the same summer evening after work, driving 125 miles from Cambridge and back again.

The final weeks of 2005 consisted of as much preparation as possible, poring over maps and walking guides, as well as picking the brains of experienced walkers for less well-known multi-hill hauls. I had a flexible choice of around 150 days of three hills or more, plus short or lower-altitude walks for the winter months and bad-weather days, long and higher-altitude outings for the summer months, traverses for two-car days, and a selection of 30 to 50 hills which I could probably climb after work on summer weekdays.

My three main holiday locations were the Outer Hebrides, the Northern Highlands and mid Wales. These were chosen for their impracticality for weekend visits as much as for their multi-bagging potential. These were the only trips that were planned and confirmed more than a week in advance. Flexibility is the key to a record attempt like this, not only planning based on weather conditions and daylight, but also factoring in fitness, tiredness and proximity of accommodation between walking days. The year contained 139 days off work (although eleven days yielded no new hills) and I was able to add 43 hills from 27 evening outings, reaching a total of 549 new Marilyns for the year.

Favourite hills
- The uncompromising thrust of rock that is An Grianan
- The wedding-cake tiers of An Lean-charn, also in the far north
- The steep rocky outposts of Ciste Dhubh, and steep and majestic Beinn Sgritheall
- Glorious and graceful Garbh Bheinn in Ardgour
- Sgurr na Ciche, something special to stand out from the crowd in a superb area
- The rocky rebel known as Suaineabhal on Lewis
- The rough rocky ridges of Stac Gorm near Loch Ness
- Scrambling in snow and ice on the ridges of Creag Dhubh in the Monadhliath
- The small but perfectly-formed Moel-y-Gest above Porthmadog

Least enjoyable hills
- Wading through bleak heather towards Creag nam Mial in Perthshire
- The uninspiring plateau of Carn Garbh near Helmsdale
- The heather and ditches of Beinn Uird, near Loch Lomond
- Slippery felled trees on the way up Beinn Lochain in Cowal
- Almost impenetrable wind-thrown trees on a poor route up Cnoc an t-Sabhail
- Driving rain, heather and head-high bracken ascending Bainloch Hill
- Poor ascent route, boggy ground and marauding bullocks on Cnoc nam Broighleag
- Tonnes of earth seemingly floating on a lochan on Knockan
- Several summer hills pursued by horseflies, clegs, etc

Marathon bagging

CHRIS UPSON, JUNE 2003

Applying the 150m drop criterion to various big hill rounds revealed that Jon Broxap's total of 29 Munros in 24 hours included 19 Marilyns, so I started wondering if it would be possible to climb 24 Marilyns in 24 hours on a route optimised to target only Marilyns. I learned that Chris Pearson made several attempts, with 18 Marilyns in 24 hours his best tally. If I wanted to do this, my only hope would be to get myself reasonably fit and to solve the problem of working out a 24-hill route that might be feasible on foot within 24 hours. I quickly whittled down the choices by selecting the Lake District, which has the advantage of good surfaces and plenty of paths.

Eventually I found a route that felt just about possible for someone of my ability, but I was conscious that this was still far bigger than anything I had done before. I spent the spring of 2002 checking some nine-hour sections in heatwaves, rainstorms and deep snow. At the end of each stage I was shattered. Two attempts were made at linking Pillar to High Stile before deciding this was a bad idea. These hills were deleted from my list and replaced by Baystones and the Harter Fell in Eskdale. I made an attempt at Lakes24, as I was now calling it, in June 2002, but soon abandoned it after just two hills, in torrential rain, low cloud and zero visibility. This only made me more determined.

My dad had taken me up Hallin Fell when I was five years old. Now he watched me disappear up the same hill from Martindale Hause at 5am on 14 June 2003. It was cool clear weather, ideal for running. I made good progress over Place Fell, High Street and Stony Cove Pike, and was 90 minutes ahead of schedule at the A592. I was keen to build a healthy margin on the early sections, knowing I would need it later. It was a glorious morning and I was enjoying myself over Red Screes and Fairfield, jogging along deserted fells. St Sunday Crag made eight hills in five hours and I was pleased with how easy I was finding it, but I fell in a quagmire at the outflow of Grisedale Tarn and my shoes filled with slimy mud. The grit would later turn my feet to a mass of blisters.

I reached the top of Helvellyn at 11:07am. It was becoming warm, so I begged water. Over Seat Sandal, hill ten, then down to the Traveller's Rest near Grasmere where I met my support team of Micky and Claire Ross for the first time. Feeling hot and frazzled, I made a mistake here: I should have changed socks, but preferred to keep going. It was warm on the road towards Loughrigg Fell, with traffic roaring past. Hordes of walkers were sunning themselves and enjoying leisurely rambles. Descending Loughrigg my legs were hurting and felt slightly unstable for the first time – not a good sign.

At Elterwater the support car was waiting outside the Britannia Inn. I guzzled Lucozade and munched bananas, then shuffled on down the road. I was feeling ropey in the heat, but managed to catch some shade before breaking out into sunshine again on Lingmoor Fell. Nine hours for twelve hills, so far so good, but I knew that the second half had bigger climbs and rougher hills, not to mention fatigue and darkness later on.

Micky joined me for Pike of Blisco, and having company made the going easier and helped me feel stronger. After Red Tarn there was a short climb across the shoulder of Cold Pike before a pleasant run down to Cockley Beck, where I took twelve minutes to rest and recover in the shade before feeling fit to face Harter Fell. An arrow of twigs left in March marked a short cut I had discovered through the forest, but it felt tough. I dropped Micky before the summit and cracked on to the Hard Knott road and the car.

Here I slumped to my lowest ebb. The remaining eight hills seemed an impossible task. The body was seizing up. I was slouching at the car, trying not to think of Scafell Pike, Great Gable, Kirk Fell. I was close to falling into a stupor. After fifteen minutes of prevarication I snapped out of it, shuffled eastward along the road for a few metres, then turned left, uphill. Hard Knott summit came in fifteen minutes but led to the daunting approach to Scafell Pike, where the ground was a roller-coaster of hidden dips and rises as I crossed the Great Moss. I was grinding to a halt, mind wandering, so it was a relief when the angle eased and I could boulder-hop across to the summit of England at 7:27pm. Now for the Corridor Route. It was familiar ground but today it was something else, with blisters causing pain on every foot strike.

Climbing Great Gable, hill 17, didn't bother me as I was always knackered here in the Borrowdale race, so it was no different. The descent was steep and awkward with plenty of scope for crocking myself. I looked back from Kirk Fell to see the evening light casting an orange glow across Great Gable's western flank. After Kirk Fell there was a runnable route to Honister, but blistered feet were now making running almost impossible.

I was falling off the pace. It was dark and midgey. Micky and Claire were concerned at my late arrival at Honister. I finally changed shoes and socks but the damage was done. Micky joined me over Dale Head and Robinson. Again the company helped, but I was not chatty. A red moon hung on the horizon, slowly turning orange then milky white. The descent from Robinson was steep but efficient, with a final grass precipice towards the headlights at Newlands Hause. Here Micky dropped out and I was faced with a 600m ascent of Grasmoor in the dark with burning feet. I knew this was the crux. It was dark, I was tired, and I hadn't properly checked the route. Just when I thought things couldn't get any worse, I realised the hill was plastered with deep bracken. On the brutal slog up Wandope I was losing all sense of time and perspective and grinding to a halt. The hill was so steep that the only way to keep any momentum was an all-fours technique.

On Grasmoor I tried to up the tempo but my feet were again making running difficult. I reached Grisedale Pike with two hours 22 minutes left for the last two hills. I thought I should be OK for time but then I attacked the descent and did something stupid. On hitting the first forest track at Whinlatter I had a mental block. Left then right? Right then left? No idea. Panic. I tried a short cut by a stream but ended up thrashing through forest in the dark. Ten minutes were lost before I found the road. I was so furious that I stormed up the hillside opposite without stopping for a drink and got confused in a labyrinth of paths and forest tracks.

I reached the summit of Lord's Seat at 3:52am but the safety margin had vanished. The descent eastward brought some hideous bog before the steep track down to the Swan Hotel. I had more or less given up. Having been so far ahead of time, I thought I had blown it. I reached the road and told Micky that I had had enough. My feet were agony and I had no intention of doing the final hill outside the 24 hours. Micky was upbeat and encouraging and said I could still do it. I thought it was 4:30am but my watch showed it was only 4:14. I jettisoned the bum bag and started sprinting along the road towards Braithwaite. My feet were forgotten. I focused on running technique and channelled energies for the closing moments. The road rolled by as I raced through the sleeping caravan park and reached the base of Swinside with twenty minutes in hand. A hurdle of the rusty fence, a thrash up through the undergrowth, and I was at the summit in 23 hours, 49 minutes and 40 seconds, after 112km with about 8900 metres of ascent.

Rally bagging

ROB WOODALL, 2005

At 02:41 the immaculate white Raw Head trig shows up in the torch light, right on cue. After the early-evening rain it's a perfect starlit night. Then I miss the descent route – one hill down and seven minutes behind schedule. Just early nerves, hopefully. Thirty minutes later I'm blundering about on Hope Mountain in the darkness – all gorse and cowpats. Third up, after a worryingly snowy drive, is Gyrn Moelfre, a late entry into the schedule. Tonight, keeping the torch off, tripping over a few branches and wondering where the route goes, the summit is pure magic by starlight with a sprinkling of snow. The concrete road to Mynydd-y-Briw is icy, but the grass makes for a swift, easy descent.

By Allt y Main it's 05:30 and there's a monochrome view, with enough light for a torch-less descent but no chance of being seen. Y Golfa produces the first proper view, and the first snow squall. By Upper Park it's 06:30 and fully light. There's more snow falling and no-one about. At the top a half-sun glows orange above a grey cloud bank. Such variety of hills, lighting and weather – it's great to be out, and it's good to be on safer ground with Stingwern Hill, a two-minute wonder and another nice view.

Moel y Golfa is frosty and superb, and I make an accidental time-saving short-cut. Long Mountain makes for an interesting snowy ascent and we're still in the car, with Brent in the driving seat. The first ten hills are in the bag in 5 hours and 25 minutes.

Caeliber Isaf kicks off the second ten, with a sprinkling of snow making the best of its prosaic view. In return for gate duty, Brent drops me at the base of Corndon Hill. The descent is into a biting wind, eyes streaming. Heath Mynd has nothing left of its bracken resistance and less of its heather after some recent burning. Then it's the superb Stiperstones tor. At 09:45 a single runner appears, the first sign of human life after a brown hare, a grey squirrel, countless rabbits and pheasants, a few fieldfares, the odd buzzard and sundry other creatures. Brent somehow manages to miss them all in 32 hours of driving.

By Caer Caradoc, uphill becomes hard work, so I need to slow down and dig in. I turn into more stinging wind-driven snow and trot down. For Callow Hill we take a chance on the ford at Strefford – no problem after a few dry days. View Edge still has the same weird contouring semi-path between the trees, but the open deciduous woodland makes a nice change. I get a welcome rest on the 29-minute drive to Brown Clee Hill, but the legs still don't have much to offer. Quickly giving up on the churned-up track, a short-cut makes a nice line across short grass, the feet just stay dry to the trig and then the heathery high point. More squally snow, and a grey view of sorts. The beeline descent doesn't take me quite to the car but repays the risk. At Titterstone Clee Hill the same snow squall catches me again. Twenty hills down, 10:26 elapsed – so far so good. Brent is regaining on the road the time I'm losing on the hills.

High Vinnalls is closed! Forest Enterprise have gone to a lot of trouble cordoning off paths and covering up waymarkers. All to no avail really. A slow ascent of Shobdon Hill, while Brent begs some more water for me. At Wapley Hill I manage to run a bit then go astray a bit on the way down. The Bradnor Hill golf course crossing is simple enough. Hergest Ridge has a biting wind and a fine view – such a great day to be on these hills. As usual I don't quite find the best way down though the gorse.

Fourteen hours in, Brent finally manages to miss a turning, en route to Burton Hill. The damage is less than five minutes. After the late-night bramble nightmare of our previous attempt, Burton Hill by daylight, with its comprehensive waymarking and summit track, puts up little resistance and I'm soon back at the waiting car. At Hegdon Hill I somehow make the one-metre ascent of the hedge bank to get my head above the reservoir. By Worcestershire Beacon my legs have finally woken up again. I catch a colourful afterglow and the usual icy wind.

The Hereford chippy is an essential two-minute diversion, then Aconbury Hill is an easy jog, thankfully avoiding the one-mile detour of our previous visit. At Garway Hill last time we had difficulty locating the top stile in the dark. This time Brent follows me up and lights the spot, although the bracken and gorse have gone. He outruns me on the way back to the car. That's thirty hills down in 17:09, but with a lot of driving to come.

Craig Syfyrddin is easier to climb than to spell (OS name for the trig is Serrerthin). By 20:20 the tiny sliver of moon is nearly down already. Ysgyryd Fawr is another late addition. We spend a few minutes finding the stile (amazingly, a farmer comes out and shows us). A bit more time is lost on the arable approach and the nose-bruisingly steep ascent, but it's a superb summit. Then it's on to the land of long drives and short hills – Ruardean Hill, May Hill, Wentwood. Now behind schedule, we sneak the car up the first steep part of the Mynydd Machen track. Brent reckons that descending the steep zigzag road above the lights of Ebbw Vale feels like bringing a plane into land, but he manages to avoid becoming airborne.

Finding the little road up to Mynydd-y-Lan proves to be tricky – the first of several little errors on these contorted roads. By now we're both tired. We have an idea to drive the first bit of the masts road, but there's a car parked – best not ask them to move. Reaching the masts I take a rough track south for the summit. Soon I realise that it's the wrong track, and after too much tussock-hopping I find the summit, nearly ten minutes later than intended. Descending the track, I see the headlights of the Vauxhall Corsa heading up to meet me: 37 hills down, 70 minutes left, so no chance now of 40 Marilyns inside the 24 hours. We place the two easiest hills next – Craig yr Allt and Garth Hill. The wind has dropped, the stars are out, and there's more than enough sodium light to dispel the darkness. I'm on Garth Hill 23 hours and 45 minutes after leaving Raw Head.

We decide to finish the planned 40 hills, in the wilder setting of Cefn Eglwysilan. This one is less easy than it was, as the 1:25000 map has the nearby Mynydd Twyn-glas as a twin summit. Arranging to meet Brent down at the track junction, I visit the trig then cross the (miraculously dry) col to the masts, reaching the 40 Marilyns in 24 hours and 23 minutes.

Descending to the rendezvous, I'm not greatly surprised to find there's no sign of the car. An easy walk back up the hill finds the car where I'd left it, with Brent sleeping soundly. So he does need sleep after all. With luck, and fewer errors, 40 Marilyns ought to be possible inside 24 hours. It was a great day out with many highlights, but overall, the chips at Hereford probably had the edge.

Arts and crafts

Maiden Pap (Klaus Schwartz)

Queen Loondie, depicting contours of Maoile Lunndaidh and Creag Toll a' Choin (Charles Everett)

Moelwyn Mawr, photo enhanced by Deep Dream Generator

Caer Caradoc Hill, photo enhanced by Deep Dream Generator

Music and navigation

Sport came first, music later, hills much later. These were the three foundations on which my life appeared to have been built and sustained. Other people had families, careers, skills, causes, life-long friendships and so on. I had tried other things, such as work, people, travel, books and films, and enjoyed aspects of all of them, but they had never managed to sustain the same long-term interest and variety as the big three.

Sport was there from a young age thanks to the influence of my father. I lost interest in horse-racing after leaving the family home, but football and cricket helped me to get used to a life of hope and disappointment, with occasional highlights. I later added golf and tennis to my portfolio, for playing as well as following, but they were second-tier sports and caused less emotional suffering. I hated rugby thanks to a snobby grammar school and being sent out to freeze in the long, desperate winter of 1963. It seemed to be a form of socially approved bullying with a stupid ball that I ran away from at every opportunity, not something to be inflicted on a timid ten-year-old during the most severe winter of the century. Even Latin was better than that.

Hills were slow-growing seeds that were planted without me noticing how or when. They did not flourish and flower until I was halfway to pensionable age. At school I had been an early developer, taking maths O-level at 13 and A-levels at 16, but the dark years of accountancy training and mundane clerical work set me back, so I turned into a late developer. I partly blamed school for that as well. Latin and rugby, sums and study, but no education in practical or social skills, and no exposure to nature, the outdoors or the hills. I was not keen on cubs and scouts either, with their military-style uniforms, church connections and camping in mud and rain. They were tolerable but I would rather have been playing football or cricket. Instead we played awful games like British Bulldogs, which was like a violent rugby scrum without rules or a ball.

I had to take a break from writing these words to observe a quartet of goldfinches that appeared on a bush above my garden fence. I was enjoying seeing the resident blackbirds and chaffinches stocking up on seeds that I threw out earlier, but the goldfinches were a new development. It was wonderful to see them so close, but such moments had not been enough to sustain long-term fascination. I was relieved that I did not have to record their presence in a notebook or database or try to photograph them. Seeing them was enough. Some people regarded hills in a similar manner and probably thought that was healthier than giving them obsessive attention. Perhaps, perhaps not. We were free to choose our approach, if we accepted that we had free will.

So it was music that sustained me through the desperate times of teens and twenties, particularly five years between school and university when I was earning a living from a series of office jobs until I could stand them no more and quit to travel around the coast, living in my £150 car, or to hitch-hike to Italy or sign on the dole and play golf on my own.

There was something elusive in both music and hill walking that occasionally made such a profound impression that I wanted to feel more of it, whatever it was. Sometimes it felt like a glimpse of meaning in an otherwise pointless existence. Sometimes it left a warm feeling of well-being, a sense that all was right with the world if such uplifting beauty could exist and induce feelings of euphoria or transcendence that I did not understand. Sometimes it could generate feelings of empathy, of warmth towards other people and creatures of this wonderful, spinning, overcrowded world that we all shared.

We were all just doing what we could to get by, even midges and mosquitoes. Yet such feelings soon faded and gave way to familiar thoughts of alienation from aspects of civilisation such as cruelty, violence, ignorance, intolerance, prejudice, greed, waste, the destruction of natural beauty and the disregard for wildlife.

Sometimes the uplifting feeling was simple escapism, a temporary transportation beyond the mundane world, away from the petty concerns of consumerism and celebrity culture and politics and sport, a sense of living for the moment, an escape to a world free from worry and responsibility. You always had to come down though. The song ended or the sunset faded, requiring a transition to some sort of normality, to find a way down a rough hillside in the dark or its metaphorical equivalent. Back down to the wonderful warmth and safety of civilisation, until the restless desire for escape returned.

Putting music and hills together was not easy in the days before MP3 players and portable cassette tape recorders. I could not carry my record player and speakers up a hill, and there was nowhere to plug them in anyway. I was not climbing hills in my twenties but I did sometimes go for a walk in the countryside. With no music available I tried to combine walks with literature. The idea was to find somewhere with a nice view away from people, sit down and read a book for a while. It rarely worked, because rain would wet the pages or things would crawl up my legs or I would get cold or restless.

When I started hill bagging I was so enthused by the new obsession that I had no need to bring music into it. Simply climbing and logging all those new hills was enough to see me through another week in the office. I could listen to music in the evenings or in the car on the way to a hill. The first memorable integration of music and hills occurred in Glen Scaddle in 1996 on my way to the Corran ferry after a tough weekend. I hoped to make a three-hour walk pass more quickly so I inserted a tape labelled Various I-J into my Sony Walkman. The song that transported me out of that glen and onto another plane was Sometimes, by James. This was from one of my favourite albums, Laid, but that song and swelling chorus had never before cut through with such uplifting intensity. The outdoor context, physical rhythm and absence of distraction amplified the impact.

I learned early on that the random element was vital. A portable MP3 player freed me from the constraints of tapes and generated numerous suitable soundtracks. I could not have predicted that Sinead O' Connor would be so effective in helping me up the snowy slopes of Stob Garbh on the way to Cruach Ardrain. Crampons on crisp snow helped me find a steady walking rhythm and Sinead made it feel effortless. The purity and clarity of her voice matched the snow and the slow rhythm matched my steps.

A few bursts of obscure punky rock from 1979 worked well on an otherwise uninspiring forest track in Argyll, where I became the first person to climb Beinn Dubh Airigh while listening to Best Thing I Ever Did by the Invaders and The Shape Of Things To Come by the Headboys. I could not have kept up the right speed going uphill, but the upbeat timing on the flat track was fine. The monotonous Teutonic rhythms of Can were more familiar to me and it was a Can track, Oh Yeah, that transported me up the east ridge of Merrick, on the way from Mullwharchar, with a slow rhythm and little conscious effort. On a more ethereal level, my ascent of Sgurr Mhurlagain from Loch Arkaig was made easier by the floaty vocals on Avenue and Marble Lions by Saint Etienne.

I remembered these details because the combination of hills and music had made a powerful impact on consciousness and left a strong impression on long-term memory.

If the pace of walking equated to the rhythm of the music then the view was the melody, the pretty highlight that came and went and usually made more immediate impression than rhythm. I liked a good melody and a good view but I could manage happily without them once I was attuned to the rhythm of the track underfoot and in my head. Classical music rarely seemed to have enough rhythm for stride synchronisation.

I liked other common elements of music and hills, such as progression and the occasional guest appearance, but it was rhythm that worked best for me, until I sat down on a summit and let silence, sensation and ambience take over. Atmospherics could be benign or menacing. In spring the contrast between dark violent showers and bright sunshine might be reminiscent of Van der Graaf Generator at their most discordant and melodious in the same track. Lyrics were usually irrelevant for creating atmosphere.

I had noticed that patterns of spatial awareness and methods of navigation were similar in walking and music. The two main methods when hill walking were map-based navigation and point-based navigation. I was used to being able to visualise a landscape from the contours on a map and took it for granted. Before I set off I already had a mental picture of what the terrain would be like, where the steep slopes and decision points would be, what to look out for and what to avoid. I used a map as I went along, but this was usually to see how far I had gone and to provide reassurance, not to find out which way to go next, because I already knew that. It was like having sheet music to confirm a piece I had already learned to play on piano.

The map-based method had served me well long before GPS technology. It allowed me to get a sense of when things did not feel right, perhaps because the angle of slope seemed wrong or it had taken too long to reach a lochan or other landmark. GPS made map-based navigation quicker and easier but it did not change the method, as I had maps on my GPS device. In contrast, a point-based method meant moving from one fixed point to another, often following instructions from a guidebook, such as to go west for half an hour, turn right at the fence then go uphill to the tree line. This was like following the voice in a car satnav. It worked well most of the time, until something went wrong and then you didn't know where you where or what to do next.

When playing music I could rarely get beyond the point-based method. I could follow the notes in sheet music if I went slowly, then learn the piece by a combination of brain memory and muscle memory, but if something went wrong I often didn't know where I was. I was playing one chord or bar at a time with a poor sense of the underlying pattern, often not knowing what would come next. I had no mental map of the overall piece, so I was poor at improvising or trying to play along with anyone else. I might have got better if I had tried harder and practised more, but I started too late, it never came naturally and was usually a struggle. I did not have the ear, the training or dedication to become an accomplished musician and pattern navigator. When I composed a tune I had to record the notes straight away to be able to repeat them in future.

I had heard tales of satnav woe from people who had been following instructions and ended up missing a vital turn or going a stupidly long way round. My first thought was to wonder why they had not looked at a map and then they would have soon realised when they had gone wrong and been able to put it right. Yet I was in the same situation when playing music. My musical navigation was poor because my mental model of the musical terrain was limited. That helped me sympathise with those who got lost in the hills or preferred to follow instructions rather than work things out from a map. These things were not easy to learn.

I could not remember how I had learned to visualise landscape and navigate from a map, but I was pleased that I had because it gave me the freedom to improvise and wander wherever I liked, knowing that I could find my way back or down from wherever I ended up. I had not followed a route in a guidebook since my early years of hill walking. The contours and scale had to be right for visualisation to work, and I always preferred the clarity of OS 1:50000 maps. On larger-scale maps there was too much detail, making it harder to see the big picture and visualise the landscape. Some OS 1:25000 maps were very poor, with paths and contour lines lost amidst a mass of unhelpful squiggles and symbols. No wonder people struggled to read them. Sadly, I was not keen on Harvey maps, although I liked the idea of a small company challenging the might and arrogance of Ordnance Survey. I didn't like the colour tones, the crag symbols or the 15-metre contour intervals. I wanted to like Harvey maps but I could not use them for visualisation.

As I try to finish writing this piece, a whole flock of goldfinches has arrived, dozens of them. Emboldened by reinforcements, they fly down onto the gravel and make a mass attack on the seeds, hopping right up to the slab by the window. No binoculars are needed for this colourful spectacle three metres from my seat. Another new track that I fail to recognise starts up, one of 40600 on the Brennan MP3 player. It adds atmosphere to watching finches feeding and turns out be called Name Taken, by Massive Attack. The track title was a fair suggestion, but I did not record the names of species because I knew where that sort of thing could lead. One hill bagger I knew had travelled around the planet bagging birds and had managed to spot every family and every genus, though not all 9000+ species and sub-species. I was pleased not to have to rush off to Tiree or Scilly for a glimpse of a rare migrant. Perhaps I did have free will, or maybe I was lucky.

It had been a few years since I had carried my MP3 player up a hill. Perhaps that was what I needed to encourage me to climb Meall nan Tarmachan more often. It was a great hill to have so close at hand, one I could walk to from home if I had the motivation. The only specifically relevant song I could think of was one I had written myself. I could load it along with two thousand other tracks and let the random element take over on a quiet evening. A sunset from the summit would be a fine thing, and the path down should be all right in the dark. I could think of lots of atmospheric tracks that might be appropriate and uplifting, such as Eternal Odyssey by Delerium, Saucerful of Secrets by Pink Floyd or Xerxes by William Orbit. Even if I did not reach that elusive transcendent state of consciousness, how wonderful might it be to walk slowly toward the summit of a high hill on a fine evening with the last two minutes of Shangri-La by the Electric Light Orchestra swirling through my head and making me feel as though I could keep going up into the air, to look down on the loveliness of the world below from a little fluffy cloud.

Even as I edit this paragraph, Conquest of Paradise by Vangelis has been served up on random play and sounds so perfect for hill walking that it makes me want to be up there, approaching a high, unspoiled summit with an endless horizon all around. However, the soundtrack would not be planned in advance. I would have to give a few thousand tracks a chance and see what the shuffle served up. If I was able to relax on the summit for an hour or so, perhaps I would finally see a ptarmigan on the top of Meall nan Tarmachan while listening to a suitable song. Synchronicity is a fine thing when the timing is right.

Extra-curricular activities

Viticultural bagging

Chris Crocker, 2003

Let's face it, not many hills in the south set the pulses racing. Visitors from afar can be forgiven for getting the job done with the minimum of effort, but those of us who live here need to make the most of our meagre assets. With a little effort, some of these hills can be made into decent walks. For example, Win Green, a 300-metre stroll from the car park, makes a fine horseshoe if approached from Tollard Royal. Other summits, like Detling Hill, seem beyond redemption. How do you turn those into a worthwhile outing?

My eventual solution can be traced back to a March weekend in the Black Mountains, when I spotted a sign to the Sugar Loaf vineyard on the A40. It's the only wine I've found which features a Marilyn on its label. So we paid the vineyard a visit, dumped our Abergavenny medium dry and Hiraeth Welsh sparkling wine in the car and ascended the rather pleasant hill. Sadly, the vineyard was up for sale and no longer open to the public.

A couple of similar incidents persuaded me that taking in a local vineyard would be a good way to enliven visits to these southern hills. I'd been round a fair number of English vineyards in the 1980s and found much of the wine indifferent, but things had moved on. Summers were warmer, wine-making had improved.

A wrong turning off the M25 en route to Botley Hill and another vineyard sign led me to Godstone vineyard on the Surrey / Sussex border. The wine was considerably more interesting than the hill and provided far more enjoyment. More vineyards followed. Wooldings followed the ascent of Walbury Hill. Elms Cross was combined with Long Knoll, while Avalon vineyard, home of Pennards organic wine, was visited on another west country trip. Pennards dry white was one of the best Seyval blancs I've had.

My main Somerset trip, to bag the four Marilyns in Exmoor and the Quantocks, came before I'd really got started, so I missed a golden opportunity to bag Dunkery vineyard, which lies at the foot of Periton Hill rather than Dunkery Beacon. It welcomed visits by appointment and had some interesting-looking red wines on its list.

The south-east may lack inspiring hills but it compensates by having the highest concentration of vineyards in the country. Baggers of the Kent and Sussex hills are spoilt for choice. Neither of the Isle of Wight vineyards lies near a Marilyn but we visited them both anyway. Brighstone Down is an undistinguished summit in forest, made more interesting by a through walk to Shorwell from Tennyson Down (better than either of the Marilyns) and a taxi back. St Boniface Down made a good little circuit. Adgestone vineyard was worth the detour, Rosemary less so.

Wales has a dozen or so vineyards but viticulture can be a struggle in the climate. Two vineyards which I've not visited are Gwinllan Eryi in Llanbedr (handy for the Rhinogs) and Gwinllan Pading in Anglesey (handy for Mynydd Bodafon). Few English vineyards at this latitude have survived, so I wish them luck. Bodenham is on the slopes of Hegdon Hill and is the largest vineyard in the Welsh Marches. Their Reichensteiner is said to have an incredible raisiny flavour.

There are certainly baggers in the viticultural world. I have encountered people attempting to collect labels from all the vineyards in Germany. There are about 2600 of them and the accepted rule is that you have to consume the contents to bag your label. I would be surprised if nobody was doing this in Britain.

Garden bagging

VAL HAMILTON, 2004

Over the years, accounts have been published of Marilyn bagging being combined with other pursuits such as football watching, whisky drinking, vineyard bagging and child minding. One topic not yet mentioned is garden bagging. A number of possible lists can form the basis for this. For example, there is the annual 'Yellow Book' of gardens open to the public. This blooms each February and features over 350 gardens open to the public on one or more days in the year. Some, such as Inverewe, are well known, but others are one-offs, urban or rural, giving a chance to glimpse a world behind fences, hedges and warning signs, and to sample some epic teas. The gardens are so widely distributed that there will always be one close to a Marilyn. The trouble with the Yellow Book as a target is that it is too variable, changing each year, and in many cases with only a single three-hour slot in which to get your tick. We combined Blath Bhalg with an impressive one-off arboretum near Bridge of Cally, and Deuchary Hill with the rarely open Murthly Castle, with its champion Picea Glehnii (a fancy spruce tree). Tree bagging, visiting the tallest or girthyest of each species, presents another possible challenge.

An attractive and more manageable subset is the Glorious Gardens of Argyll and Bute. The free pamphlet describing these nineteen gardens appears annually and most are open all summer, if not all year. They are located in some wonderful coastal locations with possibilities for interesting combinations. We linked Barguillean's Angus Garden (basically a large woodland round a loch, with no tea room or toilets but plenty of trees) with Deadh Choimhead, on which we managed to have a classic tree-fighting epic, trying to contrive a circular walk. The next day we made a much more successful circuit of Cruach nam Fearna followed by a wander round Arduaine.

Others on the list include Jura House, Ardkinglass near Stob an Eas or Cruach nam Mult, and An Cala on Seil, near little Beinn Mhor. If, after a day on Beinn Ruadh, Sgorach Mor or big Beinn Mhor, you cannot make the time to visit Ben More Gardens with its breathtaking giant redwood avenue, the tea room is worth a visit for good value food.

In the world of the one-off gardens there is almost limitless variety. Sometimes the ablutions are more interesting than the gardens, though similarly run down. I remember one wonderful Victorian creation with a chain which required such force to get any reaction that I thought the whole cast-iron water tank would come down on my head. At another garden the men were directed to a barn with a pile of straw bales.

For many people, however, the main reason for visiting these specially-opened gardens is to sample the teas. Most are reasonably priced and are a real treat, though there is the odd exception. We were seriously disappointed with the single Scotch pancake in the millionaire's village of Killearn (twinned with Earl's Seat). Generally the qualities and quantities of the food are the stuff of legend, although the drinks may require caution. Tea is king beverage and is usually of spoon-supporting strength. Coffee drinkers may wish to opt for orange squash rather than risk receiving a tepid mellow liquid. The main attraction is the home baking. Colintraive (twinned with Coraddie) was particularly memorable, but the spread which all others have to beat is that provided once a year at Aberarder, overlooking Loch Laggan and the gateway to Binnein Shios and Binnein Shuas. Its fairytale setting and the huge array of sandwiches, cakes, scones and tray-bakes makes Aberarder worth an annual pilgrimage.

Bagging with a toddler

LYNDA WOODS, 2002

This article covers several mental diary entries during weekend breaks and our summer holiday in Wales in 2002, the first holiday when Daniel was officially too heavy for the backpack. It aims to show that you can still climb Marilyns if new tactics are employed. As luck or good planning would have it, our first week was spent with my mother, uncle and aunt, with a few days at my cousin's. This offered scope for the first tactic:

Tactic 1 – leave toddler with someone else

Jonathan and I had days out on our own on Mynydd Carningli, Frenni Fawr and Foel Cwmcerwyn. A lot of the Marilyns in Wales were reasonably close to a road – virtually unknown in Scotland in my experience. Therefore we didn't need to leave Daniel for too long, so the babysitter's goodwill remained for another day and another hill.

Tactic 2 – take toddler with you

We employed this tactic on May Hill, which involves a bit of ascent but, bribed with jam tarts, Daniel made it to the top. A game of hide-and-seek ensured his progress through the trees to the trig point. We also got him 'up' Ruardean Hill and Mynydd y Betws.

A good supply of chocolate is useful. On Daniel's first Marilyn, Cairnpapple in May 2002, I surreptitiously put a Bob the Builder lollipop on the trig point, having bribed him to climb up to see what the fairies had left at the top. Now the poor child expects there to be one on each summit. I will have a lot to answer for when he realises that I am the hill fairy – the tooth fairy's worst enemy. On the other hand, the skills sometimes needed to get him up a hill could get me a negotiating job with the UN. When I was little I promised myself I would not lie to my own children. However, 'it's not really far now' has, I regret to say, passed my lips. Getting the toddler to walk up on his own is a good opportunity to make getting up a hill fun, so hills become associated with pleasant experiences. I would recommend good weather so you can stop and admire things. It may take longer than usual but the toddler is being initiated gently and enjoyably into the art of hill walking. It also helps if some hills are very near the road, e.g. Mynydd Sylen, which we got my mum up too. A good variation, if the terrain allows, is to take the toddler in an ATP (All Terrain Pram), as on my 700th, Burgiehill, which we reached via forest tracks. However, the most commonly used tactic, when relatives have been exploited and you have run out of toddler-friendly hills, is the relay.

Tactic 3 – the relay

We first employed this tactic on Hunt Hill. It has variations depending on whether you both want to climb the hill. We found it the best way for two of us to get up some hills, e.g. Black Mountain, Mynydd Llangorse and Mynydd Troed, where we had good weather and both managed to walk or run up while the other fed Daniel and played, had a little walk, admired sheep, wild ponies, paddled about in streams etc. Great fun. Descending Mynydd Llangorse I had full view of the family by the car, and I did wonder at Jonathan's warming-up tactics when he suddenly dived off at speed down the steep road, but then I realised that Daniel's ball had started to roll off down the hill. This method is good but takes longer than other tactics and is weather-dependent, so you don't end up sitting in the car with the rain lashing outside listening to endless Postman Pat stories on tape. Although that is better than having the toddler explore mobile phones or car controls. Sunk in a Postman Pat-induced stupor, I once realised that Daniel had started the car.

A few extra minutes can seem a lifetime to the person stuck in the car with Postman Pat. At new year, Jonathan went up Troweir Hill with the dogs in windy, squally weather, leaving us in the car scenically parked opposite Ailsa Craig. In the first five minutes on the beach Daniel had gone over the top of his wellies in the sea and demanded that we stay in the car. Jonathan was later than he anticipated as he had to detour around cows.

If employing this tactic, always ensure you both have a set of car keys. Once I ran up Cnoc Mor near Strathpeffer while Jonathan and Daniel, well wrapped up in waterproofs (and with the car keys) set off for the maze in the forest. I was waiting by the car for 30 minutes in pouring rain before they came back.

However, if you pick your hill and parking spot, and the weather is good, toddlers can be amused quite happily for ages and you might have time to walk up and down rather than running. Sometimes you can strike lucky in unpromising parking spots. During a relay up Meall Mor from the side of the A9, I noticed that a couple were looking under their car bonnet (Daniel was asleep and Jonathan had gone first). Nipping over to ask what the trouble was, it so happened that my car had had the same problem two weeks earlier, so for once I knew what I was talking about car-wise. They were from Barra, and as we had been there the year before, the conversation soon flowed while I lent them my phone and gave them AA details. Daniel woke up and played with their kids, Jonathan came down and swapped places with me, and I went up the hill.

A variation on this tactic is when only one person goes up. This is handy for picking up brownie points, especially if stuck in the car in bad weather. I amassed quite a few points when pleurisy kept me off the hills and I stayed behind with Daniel. The bagger will be reminded later that they need to give back 'time in lieu' at some stage.

Tactic 4 – the drop off

If only one wants to do a hill it may be possible to drop off and meet up at another spot later. This tactic is no use if both wish to climb a hill on the same day, but is useful for partners who do not like lurking in cars with Postman Pat and insist that toddlers need more quality time than learning to start the car or looking at insect life in ditches.

This approach worked well on Harris when I dropped off Jonathan and he ran up and over Beinn Dhubh and met me on the beach later. It worked less well at Alness where Jonathan dropped off Daniel and me to go swimming while he did Cnoc Ceislein. The pool was reached by walking over a footbridge, and Jonathan had driven away before I had read the note on the door saying the pool was closed. I had a swimming bag, limited outdoor clothing, a disappointed toddler and two hours to kill in Alness, so I was grateful to the recently-planted Jubilee gardens and its play area, where we spent the two hours.

Lamington Hill lends itself to this tactic, with an excellent play area where Jonathan and Daniel spent a happy time while I went up the hill. At Golspie, Daniel and I spent an interesting time at Dunrobin Castle and grounds, where there was an excellent falconry display. While we watched owls flying up and over our heads, Jonathan ran up and over one of the hills nearby. This tactic also worked well near Poolewe on a rainy afternoon in May, when I took Daniel swimming and Jonathan went up Meall an Doirein. He wasn't allowed to leave the car park until I had checked the pool was open. The next day I did the same hill in the sun while Jonathan played with Daniel and walked as far as the river.

Whatever tactic is employed, the main thing is to make it fun for the toddler and plan carefully, taking weather into consideration. Hill walking with toddlers is a delicate operation, balancing your own enjoyment of the hills with the possibility of introducing them to something they may, or may not, want to do themselves at a later stage.

Broadcasting

TOM READ (M1EYP)

SOTA – Summits on the Air – is a popular amateur radio awards scheme, launched in 2002 by John Linford G3WGV (Cumbria) and Richard Newstead G3CWI (Cheshire). The idea is to climb a hill and 'activate' it by making a minimum of four ham radio contacts from the summit.

When devising the programme, one of the first considerations was eligibility criteria for the hills and mountains to include. In order to avoid inevitable debate, something objective rather than subjective was required. Inclusion in an existing list would not be sufficient, as the plan was always for the scheme to be scalable internationally.

The founders discovered the Relative Hills concept and soon realised that the P150 approach would offer an excellent variety of hills and mountains spread throughout the UK. Summits in Devon and Cornwall, along the South Downs, Shropshire etc would make a nationwide scheme viable. Furthermore, with the objective definition throwing up curiosities such as Crowborough, Ruardean Hill and Bishop Wilton Wold, the SOTA programme could be considered to be genuinely inclusive.

Many of the early participants in SOTA purchased a copy of The Relative Hills of Britain, and the SOTA scheme officially launched on 2 March 2002, with associations in England and Wales. Scotland, Isle of Man and Northern Ireland were added shortly after. The programme has since grown to cover over 200 associations in over 90 countries, on all continents of the world. Some larger countries, like USA and Brazil, are broken down into multiple associations to keep things manageable.

Obviously, the Relative Hills approach is suited to the hills of Britain. Developing something that could be used consistently throughout the world without deviating too far from the 150m prominence approach has proved challenging. Generally speaking, we have been able to apply P150 internationally, but there is an exception for countries with less than one P150 summit in 2000 square kilometres. These may be permitted to use a P100 list, and so Belgium, Netherlands, Luxembourg, Jersey and Guernsey are all able to participate in the SOTA scheme.

SOTA has been remarkably successful in its first 23 years, and now has over 34000 registered participants globally. Over 11 million QSOs (ham radio contacts) have been logged and recorded as taking place from summits. The most popular SOTA summit in the programme is The Cloud (SOTA reference G/SP-015) on the Cheshire – Staffordshire border, with over 2400 activations having taken place from its summit.

Lots more statistics, facts, figures and resources are available via the SOTA website at www.sota.org.uk, including honour rolls of the leading activators and chasers for each association. Chasers are those who try to make contact with mountaineers from their home radio shack. The summit list for each association is also available, along with photographs, articles, tracks and tips from activators.

Globalisation

The total number of Marilyns worldwide can never be known precisely owing to volcanic activity, man-made activity and measurement uncertainty. Research by Andrew Kirmse in 2017 and 2023 generated a massive global dataset of all points likely to have prominence over 30 metres. The data indicated that between 800000 and 850000 of these summits have relative height over 150 metres. Most of these are likely to be unnamed and unclimbed.

Humping and Tumping

Humps extend the principle of classifying hills by relative height regardless of height above sea level. In 2009, Mark Jackson published 'More Relative Hills of Britain' which listed 2987 hills with 100m of relative height, including by definition all the Marilyns. He also started work on the Tumps, which require only 30m of relative height. The Humps and Tumps magnify the scale, the advantages and disadvantages of Marilyns, with problem solving becoming as significant as hill walking. Some Humps are extremely difficult to climb and some Tumps are practically impossible. On the other hand, there are Tumps almost everywhere, so prolific hill baggers can have extra incentives to explore their local area after they have climbed all the Marilyns within easy reach of home. Humps and Tumps have been officially adopted by the Relative Hills Society and there are Halls of Fame for both. Many British hill baggers also extend their activities to Ireland, which has 454 Marilyns and 832 Humps as well as its own series of hill lists.

Mountaineering

The highest mountains on Earth are over six times as high as Ben Nevis, so the term 'mountaineering' is rarely applied to British hills, but hundreds of hills are referred to as mountains even though they may not be prominent enough to qualify as Marilyns or Submarilyns. The most comprehensive objective list is the Simms (Six-Hundred Metre Mountains) which have thirty metres of relative height, so they are a subset of Marilyns, Humps and Tumps. Worldwide, there are lots of local lists of mountains, such as the 4000-metre peaks of the Alps and 14000-feet summits of Colorado, but until recently there was no comprehensive, objective worldwide list of peaks. Advances in technology and data availability have led to extensive research and publication of *The Relative Mountains of Earth: The Ribus*, by Daniel Patrick Quinn. This book catalogues the 7150 most prominent peaks on the planet, all with over 1000 metres of relative height. Other lists based on prominence are available for specific areas, on websites such as Europeaklist, Summits on the Air and Gunung Bagging, and there is a book on the 100 most prominent summits of the Iberian Peninsula, by José Martínez Hernández.

Island bagging

This has become one of the most significant extensions to hill bagging in recent years and has taken on a life of its own, attracting a wider range of people. The need to hire boatmen and share costs for group trips has given an incentive for more people to join The Relative Hills Society and has helped to support several independent boat-based businesses. Interest in island bagging began for many people after 1996 and publication of *The Scottish Islands*, a lavish hard-back book by Hamish Haswell-Smith. Interest from hill baggers was further stimulated by compilation of two large, overlapping lists covering the whole of Britain: Tumps and Sibs. There are only 59 islands with Marilyns, but about 760 out of over 17000 Tumps are the highest point of an island or sea stack. Most of these islands are uninhabited and rarely visited, with many of them difficult to land on, so there is endless scope for frustration as well as exploration and adventure.

The Significant Islands of Britain (Sibs) comprise a more selective set of around 600 islands, including several that qualify by area rather than height but excluding sea stacks and rocky islands that are impractical for the majority to reach or climb. Hill baggers naturally aim to reach the highest point, but some island baggers are content with a landing, while a few regard an overnight stay as the best way to tick off an island.

Lighthouse bagging

This relatively new activity has attracted several enthusiasts in recent years. The main stimulus has been publication in 2019 of Sarah Kerr's book *The British Lighthouse Trail: A Regional Guide*, which catalogues, classifies, describes and illustrates over 600 lighthouses. The range of interesting coastal locations is one of the main attractions, along with some fascinating stories and tragedies. Methods of bagging a lighthouse range from sighting to touching to circumnavigating to ascending. It coincides with and complements island bagging in many coastal areas.

Trigpointing

There are around 6500 OS triangulation pillars in Britain but most of them are not on the summits of relative hills, so there is more divergence from hill bagging than overlap with it. For those more interested in trigs than hills, Trigpointing is a well-established and distinct activity with its own minutiae, eccentricities and websites. There are fallen trigs, vanished trigs, Vanessas, rebuilt trigs, undiscovered and rediscovered trigs, plus a range of Ordnance Survey paraphernalia such as benchmarks and buried blocks.

Fallen trig pillar on Nine Barrow Down

Beyond the fringe

Several other activities may have some overlap with relative hill bagging, such as hill running, long-distance walking, orienteering, geocaching and so on. There are also lots of hill lists with no objective definition, based on historical, political, personal or arbitrary criteria. Some of these are far more popular and fashionable than relative hill bagging, but there is no need to go into detail about these lists and activities as they have been well covered by other publications and websites. For discerning Marilyn baggers, scientific validity and topographic significance carry far more weight than popularity, while for a few, the search for truth has led to another extra-curricular activity.

Surveying

The process of surveying using GNSS is the same in principle as using a hand-held GPS device or GPS on a phone. You climb a hill, press a button or touch a screen, then look at the height reading and grid reference. It is a complex and remarkably accurate system that is simple to use. There are three main reasons why surveying with specialist GNSS equipment is far more accurate than with a hand-held GPS device:

- The equipment can record multiple satellite data readings every minute.
- Complex software can be used to process the data, apply models of the Earth and its atmosphere, then calculate the weighted average from numerous readings.
- The network of Ordnance Survey base stations (OS Net) is used to provide control data, so that multiple readings from a point with unknown height (a summit or col) can be compared with readings taken simultaneously from several points for which the precise height is known. This process is called Differential GNSS because it calculates differences between readings at survey points and reference points.

Satellite signals are subject to interference as they pass through the atmosphere, but the use of OS Net and suitable software minimises the effect of atmospheric conditions and allows most sources of error to be eliminated.

There is more to hill surveying than pressing a few buttons. You have to carry the equipment to the point you want to survey. If it is a summit, you have to identify the highest natural point. This may be beneath a cairn, on top of a tor or somewhere on a heathery plateau. On lower hills it may be in a forest or next to a wall or building that impedes satellite signals. You have to set up the equipment so that it is stable, measure how far it is positioned above (or below) the highest point, then wait around to collect data for as long as you judge necessary. You pack up and move on and then, if you want to find out the relative height, you have to locate the relevant col and measure that too, which is often more difficult. When you get back you have to download the relevant OS Net control data and process the data sets using complex software to get the final results.

Surveying requires better weather than walking. The equipment can cope with rain and darkness but wind is an issue. The antenna is designed to be screwed on to a pole or tripod that needs to be fairly still for best results. Temperature does not affect the equipment but it is a big issue for the surveyor. Warmth soon slips away from hands and feet when waiting at summits or cols. Frozen fingers make it difficult to press the right buttons and write notes. Snow may blow off summits but it often piles up at cols, making it impossible to locate the optimum survey point. Mist does not affect satellite signals but it can render a laser level useless for helping to identify the highest point of a summit. If there is no snow, wind or rain, there is a fair chance that there will be midges, which can be more maddening than ever when you are required to stay in the same place for half an hour or more. Midges can be harder to cope with than tough terrain or terrible weather.

Surveying hills can be a difficult challenge and an endurance test but it can also feel worthwhile and satisfying. By the time of publication, the summits of 770 Marilyns had been surveyed using GNSS, and 318 key cols, as well as the summits of 140 potential Marilyns. The accuracy of the revised list is a substantial improvement on the original book, partly owing to better mapping and Lidar data but mainly due to GNSS surveying.

Most prominent Marilyns

Area	Number	Height	Name	Drop	Location	Map
HC01	278	1344.7	Ben Nevis	1344.7	NN 1668 7128	41
HW10	803	1182.8	Carn Eighe	1145	NH 1235 2619	25
WN02	1963	1084.7	Snowdon / Yr Wyddfa	1039	SH 6099 5437	115
SK01	1239	992.0	Sgurr Alasdair	992.0	NG 4500 2078	32
HS08	26	1173.9	Ben More	986	NN 4327 2441	51
IM01	1301	966.9	Ben More	966.9	NM5257 3307	47, 48
HW04	953	1054.8	Liathach - Spidean a' Choire Leith	957	NG 9293 5796	25
HE02	518	1309.3	Ben Macdui	950	NN 9890 9894	36, 43
HC15	141	1214.3	Ben Lawers	915	NN 6355 4143	51
HW03	1040	1108.9	Sgurr Mor	913	NH 2032 7181	20
EL03	2359	978.1	Scafell Pike	912.2	NY 2154 0721	89, 90
HC11	232	1127.1	Ben Cruachan	880	NN 0696 3047	50
IA01	1472	875.0	Goat Fell	875.0	NR 9913 4154	62, 69
HS03	65	1131.4	Ben Lui	874	NN 2663 2629	50
HW22	1349	888.4	Sgurr Dhomhnuill	873	NM 8896 6788	40
HM01	658	1128.1	Creag Meagaidh	868	NN 4183 8754	34, 42
SK02	1255	928.8	Blabheinn	862	NG 5299 2174	32
HW06	987	895.7	Beinn Bhan	850	NG 8036 4503	24
HC08	191	1149.4	Bidean nam Bian	844	NN 1434 5421	41
HW09	926	1151.9	Sgurr na Lapaich	841	NH 1610 3512	25
HW19	773	983.2	Gulvain	840	NN 0027 8758	41
HW16	730	1040.2	Sgurr na Ciche	839	NM 9022 9668	33, 40
HN05	1183	998.9	Ben More Assynt	838	NC 3183 2015	15
HS11	17	985.3	Ben Vorlich	834.3	NN 6291 1891	57
HS12	32	973.7	Ben Lomond	820	NN 3670 0286	56
HW08	884	1083.7	Sgurr a' Choire Ghlais	819	NH 2588 4300	25
HN04	1165	962.1	Ben Klibreck	819	NC 5853 2992	16
IR01	1292	812	Askival	812	NM 3931 9522	39
HN07	1062	1081.7	Beinn Dearg	807.5	NH 2594 8118	20
LH01	1587	800.0	An Cliseam	800.0	NB 1547 0732	13, 14
HW15	731	1019.4	Ladhar Bheinn	796	NG 8240 0398	33
HC10	233	1107.9	Meall a' Bhuiridh	795	NN 2506 5034	41
HW12	862	1119.2	A' Chraileag	785	NH 0942 1479	33
IJ01	1449	785.2	Beinn an Oir	785.2	NR 4980 7494	60, 61
HC04	345	1147.7	Ben Alder	783	NN 4962 7186	42
HW21	1333	883.3	Beinn Odhar Bheag	774	NM 8465 7787	40
HN02	1123	927.2	Ben Hope	772	NC 4775 5014	9
HW14	683	1035.1	Gleouraich	767.8	NH 0394 0534	33
HC02	287	1129.4	Binnein Mor	759	NN 2121 6635	41
HW01	1003	1062.6	An Teallach - Bidein a' Ghlas Thuill	757	NH 0689 8436	19
HW23	1373	853.0	Creach Bheinn	754	NM 8705 5765	49
WN04	1965	1064	Carnedd Llewelyn	750	SH 6836 6437	115
HC07	195	1024.2	Beinn a' Bheithir - Sgorr Dhearg	729	NN 0568 5584	41
HW05	981	960.7	Sgorr Ruadh	723	NG 9590 5050	25
HC13	103	1083.3	Schiehallion	714	NN 7138 5476	42, 51, 52
EL05	2515	949.8	Helvellyn	713.4	NY 3424 1511	90

Area	Number	Height	Name	Drop	Location	Map
HS04	68	1012.2	Beinn Ime	713	NN 2549 0848	56
SK03	1279	739.1	Sgurr na Coinnich	712.5	NG 7624 2226	33
HW13	684	1026.6	Sgurr a' Mhaoraich	708	NG 9839 0656	33
EL01	2319	930.7	Skiddaw	706	NY 2604 2908	89, 90
SS04	1688	843	Merrick	705	NX 4275 8554	77
HS06	1424	741.5	Beinn Mhor	700.2	NS 1078 9081	56

Least prominent Marilyns

Area	Number	Height	Name	Drop	Location	Map
HC12	140	466.3	Meall Chomraidh	150.9	NN48395567	42,51
LH05	1577	261.9	Beinn Bhragair	150.9	NB26684326	8
HS10	11	637.4	Creag Gharbh	150.8	NN 6323 3272	51
HS10	14	456.8	Creag na Criche	150.8	NN 9857 3507	52, 53
HW04	979	383.0	Sithean Mor	150.8	NG 8359 7401	19
EP04	2832	328.7	Gisborough Moor	150.8	NZ 6324 1241	94
EL06	3321	159.1	Arnside Knott	150.8	SD 4561 7747	97
WM01	2171	484.9	Garreg-hir	150.7	SN 9987 9792	136
SS07	1823	423.9	Sell Moor Hill	150.7	NT 4803 4446	73
HN01	1117	423.8	Beinn Dearg	150.7	NC 2797 6581	9
IE01	2918	213.7	Brighstone Down	150.6	SZ 4324 8472	196
HC15	163	925.6	Meall a' Choire Leith	150.5	NN 6124 4388	51
IA01	1482	479.7	Sail Chalmadale	150.5	NR 9143 4009	62, 69
SC02	1675	228.9	Cairnie Hill	150.4	NO 2793 1548	59
SS07	1944	217.1	Lamberton Hill	150.4	NT 9444 5865	67, 74, 75
HC09	218	688.3	Beinn Molurgainn	150.3	NN 0195 4006	50
SS04	1691	786.8	Kirriereoch Hill	150.2	NX 4209 8695	77
WN07	2051	304.9	Mynydd y Cwm	150.0	SJ 0730 7673	116
SS03	1798	240.1	See Morris Hill	150.0	NX 9029 7795	84

Most prominent Submarilyns

Area	Number	Height	Name	Drop	Location	Map
HW10	810	1112.7	Tom a' Choinnich	149.8	NH 1640 2733	25
ES07	2922	164.3	Cliffe Hill	149.8	TQ 4340 1072	198
ES07	2921	187.7	Cheriton Hill	149.7	TR 1978 3964	179, 189
HW18	778	895.3	Beinn Gharbh	149.6	NM 8820 8766	40
HS05	1428	658.4	Stob na Boine Druim-fhinn	149.5	NN 1688 0253	56
WN10	5622	383.1	Pared y Cefn-hir	149.4	SH 6619 1488	124
HC01	344	231.1	Cruim Leacainn	149.4	NN 1666 8074	34, 41
IS01	1545	171.3	Faan Hill	149.4	HU 3447 8020	1, 2, 3
SS04	1734	295.6	Troweir Hill	149.3	NX 2112 9602	76
EL06	2537	779.0	Harter Fell	149.2	NY 4597 0932	90
HS06	1437	568.4	Cruach Bhuidhe	149.2	NN 1252 9470	56
ES06	2911	254.9	Littleton Down	149.2	SU 9412 1494	197
EP02	2734	674.8	Lovely Seat	149.1	SD 8790 9504	98
HC03	340	571.4	Meall na Duibhe	149.1	NN 2265 6232	41
HM03	635	833.6	Marg na Craige	149.0	NN62069732	35
HC01	334	712.4	Meall an t-Suidhe	149.0	NN13947299	41
HS09	53	674.0	Meall Cala	149.0	NN50831277	57
HN06	1213	587.5	Sgorr Tuath	149.0	NC11030749	15

Revision

Since the first edition, 25 new Marilyns have been discovered. There was an initial flurry in the first few years after publication, with eleven additions by 1995. Six of these were in Wales, where OS Landranger maps with tightly-packed contour lines did not provide enough clarity to identify all the relevant hills. Three more were later identified in Wales making nine in all, compared to only four in England, six in the Scottish Highlands, four in Southern Scotland, one in Lewis and one on Arran. However, there has been a lot more uncertainty in England, where seven hills in the original list have since been demoted, as well as six that were added between 1995 and 1999 but were later found to be just short of qualification. A further five Marilyns in England have been superseded by nearby higher hills. This means that there are eighteen former Marilyns in England but only two in Wales, which have both been replaced rather than demoted. Nine of the demoted or temporary Marilyns in England still qualify as Submarilyns and are included in the Tables. These figures do not include relocated summits that have their original name.

New Marilyns

These are the new Marilyns that have been added since 1992.

Year	Area	Number	Height	Name	Drop	Location	Map
1995	LH05	1577	261.9	Beinn Bhragair	150.9	NB 2668 4326	8
2018	HN01	1117	423.8	Beinn Dearg	150.7	NC 2797 6581	9
2014	HN04	1182	260.9	Creag an Amalaidh	151.2	NH 7587 9752	21
2015	HW04	979	383.0	Sithean Mor	150.8	NG 8359 7401	19
1995	HE05	1503	491.2	The Bochel	154.9	NJ 2325 2325	36
2005	HC12	140	466.3	Meall Chomraidh	150.9	NN 4839 5567	42, 51
2009	HS10	14	456.8	Creag na Criche	150.8	NN 9857 3507	52, 53
2008	IA01	1482	479.7	Sail Chalmadale	150.5	NR 9143 4009	62, 69
2013	SS03	1799	239.7	Killyleoch Hill	151.6	NX 8785 8203	78
2015	SS04	1691	786.8	Kirriereoch Hill	150.2	NX 4209 8695	77
1995	SS07	1823	423.9	Sell Moor Hill	150.7	NT 4803 4446	73
2013	SS07	1944	217.1	Lamberton Hill	150.4	NT 9444 5865	67, 74, 75
1995	EL02	2513	244.8	Swinside	151.9	NY 2433 2244	89, 90
2005	EL06	3321	159.1	Arnside Knott	150.8	SD 4561 7747	97
2013	WN01	1960	191.4	Mynydd Anelog	151.0	SH 1519 2722	123
1995	WN06	2049	389	Mynydd Rhyd ddu	165	SJ 0545 4774	116
2009	WN07	2051	304.9	Mynydd y Cwm	150.0	SJ 0730 7673	116
2021	WN09	2062	711.6	Rhinog Fach	151.0	SH 6648 2701	124
1995	WN10	2158	321	Moel Fynydd (Craig y Castell)	153	SH 6978 1620	124
1995	WM02	2169	506.1	Disgwylfa Fawr	153.6	SN 7373 8473	135
1995	WM03	2192	460	Cefn Cenarth	155	SN 9690 7626	136, 147
1995	WM05	2210	467.9	Carn Gafallt	161.2	SN 9401 6464	147
1995	WS02	2301	258.1	Mynydd Dinas	152.5	SS 7614 9153	170
1995	WS04	2864	275.7	Aconbury Hill	158.6	SO 5058 3300	149
1999	ES05	2903	199.8	Nine Barrow Down	152.1	SZ 0084 8120	195

Replacement Marilyns

These are the replacement Marilyns that have superseded hills listed in 1992.

Area	Number	Height	Name	Drop	Location	Replaced
IB02	19345	197	Sron an Duin	197	NL 5486 8023	Sotan
HW07	891	1005.3	Creag Toll a' Choin	402	NH 1308 4532	Maoile Lunndaidh
HW13	713	885.5	Buidhe Bheinn	161.0	NG 9633 0904	Sgurr a' Bhac Chaolais
HE03	596	863.0	Creag an Dail Bheag	211	NO 1573 9815	Carn Liath
HS06	1440	519	Coraddie	371	NS 0500 7786	Beinn Bhreac
HS11	3937	708.3	Creag na h-Eararuidh	353	NN 6851 1900	Beinn Dearg
SS02	13420	249.7	White Hill	164.4	NY 0383 8333	Hightown Hill
SS06	1809	565.9	East Cairn Hill	168	NT 1280 5931	West Cairn Hill
EP03	3682	507.8	Cracoe Fell	310	SD 9931 5883	Thorpe Fell Top
WN10	19413	667.5	Foel Cedig	180.1	SH 9817 2833	Cyrniau Nod
WS03	5273	374.2	Mynydd y Grug	204.3	ST 1776 9066	Mynydd Machen
EC03	2867	254	Hegdon Hill	154	SO 5852 5392	Grendon Green
ES01	19290	364.6	Hensbarrow Downs	250.0	SX 0013 5747	Hensbarrow Beacon
ES05	2896	278.6	Lewesdon Hill	187.2	ST 4377 0116	Pilsdon Pen
ES07	2916	242.0	Chanctonbury Ring	217.7	TQ 1392 1207	Chanctonbury Hill

Demoted Marilyns

These hills were listed in 1992 but have under 150 metres drop. All except Cunnigill Hill and Scafell qualify as Submarilyns.

Year	Area	Number	Height	Name	Drop	Location	Map
1994	IS01	1543	176	Cunnigill Hill	127	HU 4323 6752	2, 3
1995	HN06	1213	587.5	Sgorr Tuath	149.0	NC 1103 0749	15
2015	HS05	1428	658.4	Stob na Boine Druim-fhinn	149.5	NN 1688 0253	56
1995	HS06	1437	568.4	Cruach Bhuidhe	149.2	NN 1252 9470	56
2014	SS04	1734	295.6	Troweir Hill	149.3	NX 2112 9602	76
1995	SE01	2306	714.4	Hedgehope Hill	147.3	NT 9438 1980	80
1995	SE01	2309	616.2	Cushat Law	148.7	NT 9282 1374	80
1994	EL03	2360	963.9	Scafell	132.2	NY 2068 0647	89, 90
1996	EL06	2537	779.0	Harter Fell	149.2	NY 4597 0932	90
1996	EL06	2607	486.9	Baystones	147.7	NY 4031 0514	90
2009	WN08	2828	227.1	Raw Head	148.4	SJ 5084 5484	117
2024	ES07	2922	164.3	Cliffe Hill	149.8	TQ 4340 1071	198

Baystones was listed in 1992, demoted in 1996, reinstated in 2001 and demoted again in 2010 after a definitive GNSS survey. Troweir Hill was found to be about the same height as Saugh Hill, which is 1.1km further north. Owing to the nature of the summits it was not possible to be certain which is higher. Neither qualify as a Marilyn but Troweir Hill is nominated as the Submarilyn.

A survey of Cliffe Hill in 2016 showed its drop to be over 150 metres, but the col area is vast and flat so it was impossible to be sure of its exact location, with several ditches between fields adding to the uncertainty. Lidar data later identified the key col to be in a slightly different location and indicated that Cliffe Hill was probably not quite a Marilyn.

Relocated Marilyns

Lots of hills have new grid references owing to relocation of the summit to a nearby point, but the name remains the same. The summits listed below are at least 150 metres away from the original location.

Area	Number	Name		From		To	Map
LH03	1569	Guaineamol	405.1	NB 262 135	405.2	NB 2604 1339	13,14
HN04	1177	Creag a' Ghobhair	345.0	NH 655 939	345.4	NH 6597 9406	21
HN07	1085	Breac-Bheinn	462	NH 500 950	464	NH 4981 9507	20
HN08	1111	Hill of Nigg	203	NH 828 713	205	NH 8206 7053	21
HW05	996	Beinn na Feusaige	625.0	NH 093 543	626.8	NH 0900 5424	25
HW13	688	The Saddle	1011.2	NG 934 131	1011.5	NG 9361 1312	33
HW15	744	Sgurr nan Eugallt	894.9	NG 931 045	897.5	NG 9271 0486	33
SK03	1290	Sgurr nan Caorach	280.9	NG 587 029	281.2	NG 5937 0301	32,39
IM01	1321	Beinn Chreagach	377.2	NM 517 216	378.5	NM 5198 2170	48
IJ01	1460	Cruach na Seilcheig	296	NR 684 980	304	NR 6781 9847	55,61
HM02	651	Meall an Tarsaid	492.0	NH 490 132	492.3	NH 4915 1306	34
HC09	228	Na Maoilean	349.8	NM 971 369	352.6	NM 9753 3721	49
HS03	84	Meall nan Gabhar	743.4	NN 235 242	744.0	NN 2357 2402	50
HS03	1396	Dun Leacainn	359	NN 035 015	360	NN 0336 0161	55
SE02	2318	Housedon Hill	267.5	NT 902 329	268.3	NT 9021 3270	74,75
EL03	19242	Muncaster Fell	231.4	SD 112 993	232.1	SD 1155 9866	96
EL06	2665	Lambrigg Fell	338	SD 586 943	339.6	SD 5868 9418	97
EP01	2773	Hoove	554	NZ 003 071	554.6	NZ 0018 0691	92
WN10	2145	Maesglase	675	SH 823 152	678.5	SH 8169 1500	124,125
WM03	2197	Rhiw Gwraidd	442	SO 009 634	442	SO 0161 6343	147
WS01	5603	Fan Brycheiniog	802	SN 825 218	802.7	SN 8243 2206	160
WS01	2282	Mynydd Allt-y-grug	338.2	SN 751 079	338.7	SN 7533 0814	160
WS02	2277	Hirfynydd	481	SN 839 076	482	SN 8413 0754	160
WS04	2274	Bryn Arw	381	SO 303 197	384.8	SO 3015 2070	161
EC03	2866	Seager Hill	271.7	SO 613 390	271.9	SO 6238 3794	149
ES07	3686	Botley Hill	267	TQ 396 553	269.6	TQ 3871 5518	187
ES07	2913	Crowborough	240	TQ 511 307	242	TQ 5105 3063	188

G&J Surveys measured the old summit of Rhiw Gwraidd to be 7cm lower than the new one.

Excluded Marilyns

These hills are no longer included as they are on the Isle of Man, which is not part of Britain. They should not have been included in the original listing, but it is still possible to climb them. The status of Mull Hill is marginal.

Area	Number	Height	Name	Drop	Location	Map
XM01	1945	621	Snaefell	621	SC 3977 8808	95
XM01	1947	488	Slieau Freoaghane	153	SC 3408 8836	95
XM01	1948	483	South Barrule	436	SC 2577 7592	95
XM01	1949	233	Bradda Hill	196	SC 1942 7114	95
XM01	1950	169	Mull Hill	151	SC 1899 6767	95

Temporary Marilyns

Years	Area	Number	Height	Name	Drop	Location	Map
1995-2021	IJ02	1468	317.4	Giur-bheinn	148.9	NR 3798 7286	60,61
1995-2014	HC01	344	231.1	Cruim Leacainn	149.4	NN 1666 8074	34,41
1995-2010	EP02	2734	674.8	Lovely Seat	149.1	SD 8790 9504	98
1996-2006	EP03	2798	609.3	Horse Head Moor	31.4	SD 8943 7698	98
1997-1999	EC02	2863	283.4	Abberley Hill	144.5	SO 7519 6722	138,150
1999-2015	ES05	2901	206.6	Swyre Head	148.3	SY 9341 7846	195
1997-1999	ES06	2872	294.3	Milk Hill	146.3	SU 1042 6431	173
1995-2021	ES07	2921	187.7	Cheriton Hill	149.7	TR 1978 3964	179,189

Horse Head Moor superseded Birks Fell in 1996, which had only a 608m spot height on large-scale OS maps, but in 2006 G&J Surveys found that Birks Fell was 610.4m and so had always been higher than Horse Head Moor. Abberley Hill was promoted owing to the depth of its col, which was in a cutting under a bridge. This col was filled in soon after its promotion, as part of work to reinforce the road, meaning that the bridge was no longer a bridge and Abberley Hill was no longer a Marilyn. Several hills were classified as twin peaks until a GNSS survey confirmed which one of the pair was higher. In most cases the summit originally listed retained its Marilyn status. Exceptions, such as Buidhe Bheinn and Creag an Dail Bheag, are listed in the table of replacement Marilyns.

Giur-bheinn on Islay on the day it was demoted after 26 years as a Marilyn

Pared y Cefn-hir, found to be 9cm higher than Bryn Brith but 60cm short of Marilyn status

Renamed Marilyns

Numerous hill names have been changed as new information has come to light.

Area	Number	Original name	Current name
IS01	1534	Dalescord Hill	Button Hills
HN07	1077	Meall Dubh	Beinn Bhreac
HW06	995	Meall an Doireachean	Beinn a' Chlachain
HE08	416	Creag an Loch	A' Chaoirnich
HC04	374	Beinn Pharlagain - Meall na Meoig	Meall na Meoig
HS04	82	Binnein an Fhidhleir	Stob Coire Creagach
HS09	47	Ceann na Baintighearna	Beinn Stacach
HS10	5	Ciste Buide a' Claidheimh	Shee of Ardtalnaig
SS06	1827	Cairnpapple Hill	Ballencrieff Hill
SE01	2317	Ros Hill	Ros Castle
EL02	2504	Long Barrow	Dent
EL04	2668	Lowick High Common	Kirkby Moor
EP03	2804	Ilkley Moor	Rombald's Moor
IW01	1961	Yr Arwydd	Mynydd Bodafon
WN10	2104	Foel Rhudd	Esgeiriau Gwynion
WN10	2155	Mynydd Cwmcelli	Craig Goch
WN10	2159	Ffridd Cocyn	Foel Cocyn
WM05	2207	Waun Claerddu	Llan Ddu Fawr
WM05	2211	Crugiau Merched	Mynydd Mallaen
WS03	2292	Mynydd Twyn-glas	Mynydd Maen
WS04	2272	Edmund's Tump	Craig Syfyrddin
EC04	2836	The Wolds	Normanby Top
EC05	2874	Haddington Hill	Wendover Woods
ES01	2887	White Downs	Watch Croft
ES07	2920	North Downs	Detling Hill

This table does not include numerous hills that have had their names amended on Ordnance Survey maps, notably in the Western Isles. Some of the changes have removed unconvincing Anglicisations, such as changing Caiteshal to Caiteseal and Ben Corodale to Beinn Choradail, while Bla Bheinn on Skye has become Blabheinn. Some hill names have been through a few iterations, such as Trallval on Rum changing to Trollaval and then Trollabhal, and Ben Scrien on Eriskay, which has evolved via two alternatives to become Beinn Sgritheann. In most cases Gaelic pronunciation has not changed despite the impression given by some of the revised names.

Various mainland hills with Gaelic names have also had updates and adjustments, such as Ben Aden becoming Beinn an Aodainn, A' Chralaig changing to A' Chraileag, Stuchd an Lochain to Stuc an Lochain, Ben Challum to Beinn Challuim and Meall a' Ghiubhais to Meall a' Ghiuthais. Some instances of Bidein have been changed to Bidean, some instances of Choinich have become Choinnich, and several occurrences of Sidhean have been amended to Sithean, such as An Sithean in area HW08 and Sithean na Raplaich in area HW23.

Timetable

1986	Idea for the definition of all hills by relative height, on a walk over Skiddaw.
1989	Sample chapters sent to Cicerone Press and confirmation of publication.
1992	*The Relative Hills of Britain* is published, retail price £8.99.
1993	The name of the subset of Marilyns referred to as Elsies is changed to Grahams.
1995	First update sheet is published, listing 15 new Marilyns, with six deletions, three replacements, seven relocations and seven name changes.
1995	First online mailing list is set up (using Onelist). First booklet in the series of TACit Tables is published (The Murdos).
1995	First landmark celebration, as Rowland Bowker reaches 1000 Marilyns on Turner Cleuch Law on 18th March.
1996	The first Marilyn Hall of Fame is compiled, recording details of those who have climbed over 600 Marilyns. There are eight members.
1999	First edition of Marhofn is published, a six-page newsletter. First gathering of Marilyn baggers, at Corpach, first island trip (Carna), first AGM (two minutes long). The community of relative hill baggers is established.
2008	Sail Chalmadale on Arran is surveyed using GNSS, by G&J Surveys. It is the first new Marilyn to be discovered using satellite-based technology. Scientific research on the relative heights of hills enters a significant new phase.
2009	*More Relative Hills of Britain*, by Mark Jackson, is published. It lists all hills in Britain with 100m drop, to be known as Humps (Hundred Metre Prominences).
2012	First use of Leica RX1250 GNSS survey equipment, on Fastheugh Hill.
2013	Lamberton Hill near Berwick is the first new Marilyn found using the RX1250.
2014	Programme of detwinning to identify the higher of hills listed as twin peaks.
2014	Rob Woodall reaches the top of Stac Lee and becomes the first person to climb all Marilyns listed in the book, followed a few minutes later by Eddie Dealtry.
2015	The most successful St Kilda expedition, with several more people climbing Stac an Armin and Stac Lee. These are the final Marilyns for some of the party.
2016	The final edition of Marhofn magazine is published, in colour.
2016	The Relative Hills Society (RHSoc) is established. The informal community of Marilyn baggers has evolved into a formal society.
2016	Hensbarrow Beacon is superseded by a man-made but well-vegetated summit.
2018	Beinn Dearg near Cape Wrath is found to qualify as a Marilyn following a GNSS survey by Jon Metcalf. It is the last new Marilyn to be discovered in Scotland.
2020	The first Marilyn found by Lidar data, which shows White Hill near Lockerbie to be higher than Hightown Hill. The finding was later confirmed by GNSS survey.
2021	Rhinog Fach near Harlech is found to qualify as a Marilyn following a GNSS survey by Myrddyn Phillips. It is the last new Marilyn to be discovered in Wales.
2021	Pedantic Press is established and the first book published.
2024	Isle of Man is excluded, Cliffe Hill is demoted. Mynydd Machen is superseded by the man-made summit of Mynydd y Grug.
2025	The Revised Relative Hills of Britain is finally published.

Literature

Clements, E.D. *The Hewitts and Marilyns of Ireland*, TACit Press, 1997

Dawson, Alan. *The 1033 High Hills of Britain*. Pedantic Press, 2021

Dawson, Alan and Bowker, Ann. *Tales from the Grahams: 231 Medium-sized Hills of Scotland*. Pedantic Press, 2022

Drummond, Peter. *Scottish Hill Names*. Scottish Mountaineeering Trust, 2010 revision

Haswell-Smith, Hamish. *The Scottish Islands: A Comprehensive Guide*, Canongate, 1996

Jackson, Mark. *More Relative Hills of Britain*, Lulu, 2009

Kerr, Sarah. *The British Lighthouse Trail: A Regional Guide*, Whittles Publishing, 2019

Leonelli, Lucy. *A Year In The Life: Adventures in British Subcultures*. Unbound, 2022

Parrado, Nando. *Miracle in the Andes*. Orion Books, 2006

Quinn, Daniel Patrick. *The Relative Mountains of Earth: The Ribus*. Pedantic Press, 2024

Smith, Ken. *The Way of the Hermit: My 40 Years in the Scottish Wilderness*. Pan Books, 2023

Weldon, Craig. *The Weekend Fix*, Sandstone Press, 2021

Websites

ChatGPT: chatgpt.com
Deep Dream Generator: deepdreamgenerator.com
DOBIH: Database of British and Irish Hills: www.hills-database.co.uk
Europeaklist: sites.google.com/site/europeaklist
Gunung Bagging: www.gunungbagging.com
Hill Bagging: www.hill-bagging.co.uk
Kirmse global hill dataset: everymountainintheworld.com
OpenStreetMap: www.openstreetmap.org
Peakbagger: www.peakbagger.com
Pedantic Press: www.pedantic.org.uk
Relative Hills Society: www.rhsoc.uk
Scotland's Gardens Scheme: scotlandsgardens.org
SIBS: www.hill-bagging.co.uk/hill-list/the-sibs
SOTA: Summits on the Air: www.sota.org.uk
Trigpointing UK: www.trigpointing.uk
Viewfinder Panoramas: www.viewfinderpanoramas.org
World Ribus: worldribus.org and worldribus.pythonanywhere.com

Contact details

Please send any comments or enquiries about this book or about any other Pedantic Press publications to press@pedantic.org.uk

Glossary and key

***	New Marilyn added since the first edition in 1992
**	New hill name and location, replacing a hill listed in the first edition
*	Same hill name but a significant relocation to a new grid reference
#	Different hill name at the original location
¬	Hill that was listed as a Marilyn in 1992 but is now a Submarilyn
DOBIH	Database of British and Irish Hills
GNSS	Global Navigation Satellite System
GPS	Global Positioning System
Grahams	Scottish Marilyns between 600m and 762m high
Humps	Hills of any height with at least a Hundred Metres of Prominence
RHB	The Relative Hills of Britain
RIB	Rigid inflatable boat
Ribus	Mountains worldwide with at least 1000 metres of topographic prominence
SIBs	Significant Islands of Britain
Simms	Six-Hundred Metre Mountains with 30 metres of prominence
Tumps	Hills of any height with Thirty and Upward Metres of Prominence

Acknowledgements

This book is the outcome of several years of meticulous topographic research along with a wide range of contributions from numerous people. For additional stories, paragraphs, anecdotes and articles, sincere thank you to all the contributors, including those who could not be contacted before publication, and to Daniel Patrick Quinn and Bert Barnett for proof-reading and helpful comments.

For topographic research, thanks to the other GNSS surveyors John Barnard, Graham Jackson, Jon Metcalf and Myrddyn Phillips. All the diligent survey work has been valuable and at times revealing. For digital research using large-scale mapping and Lidar data, thanks to the team behind the Database of British and Irish Hills, notably Jim Bloomer, Chris Crocker, George Gradwell and Dave Marshall. Specific acknowledgement also to Simon Edwardes and others involved in developing and sustaining the Hill Bagging website, and to the team behind the development of OpenStreetMap for the mapping that has been used as background for the hill distribution maps.

Thanks also to all those who have been in touch over the past thirty years with helpful comments and suggestions, and to all friends and hill companions for their tolerance, company and support. Hill walking, surveying, researching, writing and editing have usually been solitary activities, which has made occasional encounters with sentient and intermittently intelligent beings all the more welcome.

Index

The names of Submarilyns are indented, not listed under their parent Marilyn.

355

Beinn a' Charnain, Pabbay	LH06	22
Beinn a' Chearcaill	HW04	71
Beinn a' Chlachain	HW06	75
Beinn a' Chlachair	HC04	165
Beinn a' Chlaidheimh	HW02	66
Beinn a' Chochuill	HC11	178
Beinn a' Choin	HS08	201
Beinn a' Chreachain	HC12	180
Beinn a' Chrulaiste	HC06	169
Beinn a' Chuallaich	HC05	167
Beinn a' Chuirn	HC11	178
Beinn a' Chuirn	HW13	87
Beinn a' Chumhainn	HC04	165
Beinn a' Ghlo	HE09	150
Beinn a' Ghraig	IM01	119
Beinn a' Mhadaidh	HN03	51
Beinn a' Mhanaich	HS07	199
Beinn a' Mheadhain	HW11	83
Beinn a' Mheadhoin	HW10	82
Beinn a' Mhonicag	HM02	131
Beinn a' Mhuinidh	HW02	66
Beinn Achaladair	HC12	180
Beinn Airigh Charr	HW02	66
Beinn Akie	HN01	45
Beinn Alligin - Sgurr Mor	HW04	71
Beinn an Aodainn	HW16	91
Beinn an Dothaidh	HC12	180
Beinn an Eoin	HN05	54
Beinn an Eoin	HN06	58
Beinn an Eoin	HW04	71
Beinn an Lochain	HS05	195
Beinn an Oir	IJ01	123
Beinn an t-Sidhein	HS09	202
Beinn an Tuim	HW18	94
Beinn an Tuirc	HS02	187
Beinn Bhac-ghlais	SK05	114
Beinn Bhalgairean	HS03	193
Beinn Bhan	HS03	193
Beinn Bhan	HW19	97
Beinn Bhan	HW06	75
Beinn Bharrain	IA01	213
Beinn Bheag	HS06	197
Beinn Bheag	HW03	68
Beinn Bheag	HW22	103
Beinn Bheigier	IJ01	124
Beinn Bheoil	HC04	165
Beinn Bheula	HS05	195
Beinn Bhragair	LH05	22
Beinn Bhreac	LH03	22
Beinn Bhreac	HW21	101
Beinn Bhreac	SK05	114
Beinn Bhreac	IJ01	123
Beinn Bhreac	SK01	107
Beinn Bhreac	IJ01	123
Beinn Bhreac	HS03	193
Beinn Bhreac	IA01	213

Beinn Bhreac	HN07	59
Beinn Bhreac	HS07	199
Beinn Bhreac	HE08	148
Beinn Bhreac-liath	HC14	182
Beinn Bhrotain	HE01	137
Beinn Bhuidhe	IM01	119
Beinn Bhuidhe	HW15	89
Beinn Bhuidhe	HS03	193
Beinn Chabhair	HS08	201
Beinn Challuim	HC14	182
Beinn Chaorach	HS07	199
Beinn Chaorach	HC14	182
Beinn Chapull	HS01	185
Beinn Chlaonleud	HW23	105
Beinn Chliaid	IB01	33
Beinn Choradail	IU01	29
Beinn Chreagach	IM02	121
Beinn Chreagach	SK05	114
Beinn Chreagach	IM01	119
Beinn Chuirn	HS03	193
Beinn Churalain	HC08	172
Beinn Clachach	HW13	87
Beinn Conchra	HW07	77
Beinn Damh	HW05	74
Beinn Damhain	HS04	194
Beinn Dearg	HN01	45
Beinn Dearg	HS12	206
Beinn Dearg	HS03	193
Beinn Dearg	HC13	181
Beinn Dearg	HW04	71
Beinn Dearg	HE08	148
Beinn Dearg	HN07	59
Beinn Dearg Bheag	HW02	66
Beinn Dearg Mhor	SK03	111
Beinn Dearg Mhor	SK02	109
Beinn Dearg Mor	HW02	66
Beinn Dhorain	HN04	52
Beinn Dhubh	LH04	22
Beinn Direach	HN01	45
Beinn Domhnaill	HN04	52
Beinn Donachain	HC11	178
Beinn Donn	HC08	172
Beinn Dorain	HC12	180
Beinn Dronaig	HW07	77
Beinn Dubh	HS12	206
Beinn Dubh Airigh	HS03	193
Beinn Dubh an Iaruinn	HW09	80
Beinn Dubhain	HN03	51
Beinn Dubhchraig	HS03	193
Beinn Duirinnis	HC09	175
Beinn Each	HS11	205
Beinn Eich	HS07	199
Beinn Eighe - Ruadh-stac Mor	HW04	71
Beinn Eilde	HC04	165
Beinn Eilideach	HN07	59
Beinn Enaiglair	HN07	59

Beinn Eunaich	HC11	178	Beinn na Drise	IM01	119
Beinn Fhada	IM01	119	Beinn na Duatharach	IM01	119
Beinn Fhada	HW11	83	Beinn na Feusaige	HW05	74
Beinn Fhionnlaidh	HC08	172	Beinn na Gainimh	HS10	204
Beinn Fhionnlaidh	HW10	82	Beinn na Greine	SK05	114
Beinn Gaire	HW21	101	Beinn na Gucaig	HC02	162
Beinn Gharbh	HW18	94	Beinn na h-Eaglaise	HW05	74
Beinn Ghlas	HS03	193	Beinn na h-Eaglaise	HW13	87
Beinn Ghlas	HS01	185	Beinn na h-Iolaire	SK06	115
Beinn Ghlas	HS03	193	Beinn na h-Uamha	HW23	105
Beinn Ghobhlach	HW01	65	Beinn na h-Uamha	HW22	103
Beinn Ghuilean	HS02	187	Beinn na Lap	HC03	164
Beinn Iaruinn	HM02	131	Beinn na Lice	HS02	187
Beinn Ime	HS04	194	Beinn na Muice	HW08	79
Beinn Iutharn Mhor	HE10	152	Beinn na Seamraig	SK03	111
Beinn Lagan	HS05	195	Beinn na Seilg	HW20	99
Beinn Lair	HW02	66	Beinn na Sreine	IM01	119
Beinn Leamhain	HW22	103	Beinn na Sroine	HC14	182
Beinn Leoid	HN05	54	Beinn nam Ban	HW01	65
Beinn Liath Mhor	HW05	74	Beinn nam Beathrach	HW23	105
Beinn Liath Mhor a' Ghiuthais	HW03	68	Beinn nam Fuaran	HC14	182
Beinn Lochain	HS05	195	Beinn nan Aighenan	HC10	176
Beinn Lora	HC09	175	Beinn nan Cabar	HW18	94
Beinn Luibhean	HS04	194	Beinn nan Caorach	HW13	87
Beinn Lunndaidh	HN04	52	Beinn nan Carn	SK03	111
Beinn Maol Chaluim	HC08	172	Beinn nan Eun	HN08	61
Beinn Mhanach	HC12	180	Beinn nan Imirean	HC14	182
Beinn Mheadhanach	LH02	21	Beinn nan Lus	HC10	176
Beinn Mheadhoin	HM04	134	Beinn nan Oighreag	HC15	183
Beinn Mheadhoin	HW08	79	Beinn nan Ramh	HW03	68
Beinn Mheadhoin	HW23	105	Beinn Narnain	HS04	194
Beinn Mheadhoin	HE02	138	Beinn Odhar	HC14	182
Beinn Mheadhonach	HC09	175	Beinn Odhar Bheag	HW21	101
Beinn Mheadhonach	HC09	175	Beinn Ra, Taransay	LH06	22
Beinn Mheadhonach	HE08	148	Beinn Raimh	HW07	77
Beinn Mhealaich	HN04	52	Beinn Reidh	HN05	54
Beinn Mhialairigh	HW13	87	Beinn Resipol	HW22	103
Beinn Mhic Cedidh	HW21	101	Beinn Ruadh	HS05	195
Beinn Mhic Chasgaig	HC10	176	Beinn Ruigh Choinnich	IU01	29
Beinn Mhic Mhonaidh	HC11	178	Beinn Sgeireach	HN05	54
Beinn Mholach	LH05	22	Beinn Sgluich	HC08	172
Beinn Mholach	HC05	167	Beinn Sgritheall	HW13	87
Beinn Mhor	IU02	29	Beinn Sgritheann	IU01	29
Beinn Mhor	HS01	185	Beinn Sgulaird	HC09	175
Beinn Mhor	IJ01	124	Beinn Sheasgarnaich	HC14	182
Beinn Mhor	HM05	135	Beinn Shiantaidh	IJ01	123
Beinn Mhor	LH03	21	Beinn Spionnaidh	HN01	45
Beinn Mhor	IU01	29	Beinn Stacach	HS09	202
Beinn Mhor	HS06	197	Beinn Stumanadh	HN02	49
Beinn Molurgainn	HC09	175	Beinn Suidhe	HC11	178
Beinn na Caillich	HW15	89	Beinn Talaidh	IM01	119
Beinn na Caillich 731	SK03	111	Beinn Tangabhal	IB01	33
Beinn na Caillich 732	SK03	111	Beinn Tarsuinn	IA01	213
Beinn na Cille	HW23	105	Beinn Tarsuinn	IA01	213
Beinn na Cloiche	HC03	164	Beinn Tarsuinn	HW02	66
Beinn na Cro	SK03	111	Beinn Tart a' Mhill	IJ01	124
Beinn na Croise	IM01	119	Beinn Teallach	HM01	129

Beinn Tharsuinn	HW07	77
Beinn Tharsuinn 692	HN08	61
Beinn Tharsuinn 711	HN08	61
Beinn Trilleachan	HC09	175
Beinn Uamha	HS12	206
Beinn Udlaidh	HC14	182
Beinn Udlamain	HC05	167
Beinn Uird	HS12	206
Belig	SK02	109
Belling Hill	SE02	238
Ben Aigan	HE05	143
Ben Alder	HC04	165
Ben Armine	HN04	52
Ben Aslak	SK03	111
Ben Avon	HE03	140
Ben Bowie	HS07	199
Ben Buie	IM01	119
Ben Chonzie	HS10	204
Ben Clach	HS11	205
Ben Cleuch	SC02	210
Ben Cruachan	HC11	178
Ben Dearg	SK04	112
Ben Donich	HS05	195
Ben Dreavie	HN05	54
Ben Garrisdale	IJ01	123
Ben Geary	SK05	114
Ben Griam Beg	HN03	51
Ben Griam Mor	HN03	51
Ben Gulabin	HE10	152
Ben Hee	HN01	45
Ben Hiant	HW20	99
Ben Hiel	HN02	49
Ben Hope	HN02	49
Ben Horn	HN04	52
Ben Hutig	HN02	49
Ben Inverveigh	HC11	178
Ben Klibreck	HN04	52
Ben Laga	HW20	99
Ben Lawers	HC15	183
Ben Ledi	HS09	202
Ben Lee	SK05	114
Ben Lomond	HS12	206
Ben Loyal	HN02	49
Ben Lui	HS03	193
Ben Macdui	HE02	138
Ben Meabost	SK02	109
Ben More	IM01	119
Ben More	HS08	201
Ben More Assynt	HN05	54
Ben More Coigach	HN06	58
Ben Nevis	HC01	161
Ben Newe	HE05	143
Ben Oss	HS03	193
Ben Rinnes	HE05	143
Ben Shieldaig	HW06	75
Ben Stack	HN05	54

Ben Starav	HC10	176
Ben Tee	HW17	93
Ben Tianavaig	SK05	114
Ben Tirran	HE13	157
Ben Vane	HS04	194
Ben Venue	HS12	206
Ben Vorlich	HS04	194
Ben Vorlich	HS11	205
Ben Vrackie	HE09	150
Ben Vuirich	HE09	150
Ben Wyvis - Glas Leathad Mor	HN08	61
Benaquhallie	HE04	142
Benarty Hill	SC02	210
Benbeoch	SS03	220
Beneraird	SS05	225
Bengairn	SS03	220
Bengray	SS04	223
Bennachie	HE06	145
Bennan	SS03	220
Benvane	HS09	202
Bidean Bad na h-Iolaire	HC02	162
Bidean nam Bian	HC08	172
Bidein a' Chabair	HW16	91
Bidein a' Choire Sheasgaich	HW07	77
Bidein a' Ghlas Thuill	HW01	65
Bidein Clann Raonaild	HW05	74
Billinge Hill	EP06	257
Bin of Cullen	HE05	143
Binnean nan Gobhar	HS12	206
Binnein Beag	HC02	162
Binnein Mor	HC02	162
Binnein Shios	HC04	165
Binnein Shuas	HC04	165
Binsey	EL01	241
Biod an Athair	SK05	114
Biod an Fhithich	HW13	87
Biod Mor	SK01	107
Bioda Buidhe	SK04	112
Bioda Mor, Dun	IX01	35
Birks Fell	EP03	253
Birnam Hill	HS10	204
Bishop Forest Hill	SS03	220
Bishop Hill	SC02	210
Bishop Wilton Wold	EP04	254
Blabheinn	SK02	109
Black Combe	EL03	245
Black Craig	HS06	197
Black Down	ES06	304
Black Hill	SS07	229
Black Hill	SS06	227
Black Hill	EP07	258
Black Mount	SS06	227
Black Mountain	WS04	290
Blackcraig Hill	SS03	220
Blackhope Scar	SS07	229
Blacklorg Hill	SS03	220

Blackwood Hill	SE02	238	Cairn Toul	HE01	137
Blaeloch Hill	SS01	217	Cairn William	HE04	142
Blake Fell	EL02	242	Cairnharrow	SS04	223
Blath Bhalg	HE09	150	Cairnie Hill	SC02	210
Bleabhal	LH04	22	Cairnkinna Hill	SS03	220
Blencathra	EL01	241	Cairn-mon-earn	HE14	158
Blotchnie Fiold, Rousay	IO03	18	Cairnpapple Hill	SS06	227
Bogrie Hill	SS03	220	Cairnsmore	SS04	223
Botley Hill	ES07	305	Cairnsmore of Carsphairn	SS03	220
Boulsworth Hill - Lad Law	EP06	257	Cairnsmore of Fleet	SS04	223
Bowfell	EL03	245	Caisteal Abhail	IA01	213
Bradnor Hill	WM04	282	Caiteseal	LH03	21
Braeriach	HE01	137	Calf Top	EP03	253
Braigh Coire Chruinn-bhalgain	HE09	150	Calkin Rig	SS10	234
Braigh na h-Eaglaise	HN03	51	Callow Hill	EC02	294
Braigh nan Uamhachan	HW19	97	Cam Chreag	HC12	180
Brandy Hill	WM06	285	Cam Chreag	HC14	182
Breabag	HN05	54	Canisp	HN05	54
Breac-Bheinn	HN07	59	Capel Fell	SS10	234
Bredon Hill	EC04	296	Carleatheran	SC01	209
Brighstone Down	IE01	307	Carlock Hill	SS05	225
Brimmond Hill	HE04	142	Carn a' Bhodaich	HW12	85
Broad Law	SS08	231	Carn a' Chaochain	HW12	85
Broomy Law	SS06	227	Carn a' Chlamain	HE08	148
Broughton Heights	SS06	227	Carn a' Choin Deirg	HN07	59
Brown Carrick Hill	SS04	223	Carn a' Choire Ghairbh	HW12	85
Brown Clee Hill	EC02	294	Carn a' Chuilinn	HM02	131
Brown Cow Hill	HE04	142	Carn a' Ghaill	IR01	117
Brown Muir	HM05	135	Carn a' Gheoidh	HE10	152
Brown Willy	ES01	299	Carn a' Ghille Chearr	HE02	138
Bryn Amlwg	WM02	280	Carn a' Ghobhair	HW16	91
Bryn Arw	WS04	290	Carn a' Mhaim	HE02	138
Bryn y Fan	WM02	280	Carn an Fhidhleir	HE08	148
Buachaille Etive Beag	HC08	172	Carn an Fhidhleir Lorgaidh	HE08	148
Buachaille Etive Mor	HC08	172	Carn an Fhreiceadain	HM03	133
Buckden Pike	EP03	253	Carn an Righ	HE10	152
Buidhe Bheinn	HW13	87	Carn an Tionail	HN01	45
Burach	HW14	88	Carn Bad a' Chreamha	HW11	83
Burgiehill	HM05	135	Carn Ban	IM01	119
Burnhope Seat	EP01	251	Carn Ban	HN07	59
Burrow	WM03	281	Carn Bhac	HE10	152
Burton Hill	WM04	282	Carn Breac	HW05	74
Butser Hill	ES06	304	Carn Breugach	IC01	127
Button Hills	IS01	11	Carn Chuinneag	HN08	61
Bwlch Mawr	WN01	265	Carn Daimh	HE05	143
Bynack More	HE02	138	Carn Dearg	HM01	129
Cacra Hill	SS10	234	Carn Dearg 770	HM02	131
Cadair Berwyn	WN08	274	Carn Dearg 817	HM02	131
Cadair Idris	WN10	277	Carn Dearg	HM03	133
Cademuir Hill	SS08	231	Carn Dearg 1034	HC04	165
Caeliber Isaf	WM03	281	Carn Dearg 941	HC04	165
Caer Caradoc Hill	EC02	294	Carn Dearg	HS01	185
Cairn Gorm	HE02	138	Carn Dearg Mor	HE08	148
Cairn Hill	SS02	218	Carn Duchara	HS01	185
Cairn Pat	SS05	225	Carn Ealasaid	HE05	143
Cairn Table	SS02	218	Carn Easgann Bana	HM02	131

Garbh Bheinn	HC06	169	Great Whernside	EP03	253
Garbh Bheinn	HW22	103	Greatmoor Hill	SS11	235
Garbh Chioch Mhor	HW16	91	Green Hill	SS02	218
Garbh-bheinn	SK02	109	Green Lowther	SS02	218
Garn Boduan	WN01	265	Grey Hill	SS04	223
Garreg Lwyd	WM03	281	Griomabhal	LH02	21
Garreg-hir	WM01	279	Grisedale Pike	EL02	242
Garth Hill	WS02	288	Groban	HW03	68
Garway Hill	WS04	290	Guaineamol	LH03	21
Gathersnow Hill	SS09	233	Gulvain	HW19	97
Geal Charn	HW17	93	Gummer's How	EL06	248
Geal Charn	HE02	138	Gun	EP07	258
Geal Charn	HC04	165	Gwastedyn Hill	WM03	281
Geal-charn	HC05	167	Gwaunceste Hill	WM04	282
Geal-charn	HC04	165	Gyrn Ddu	WN01	265
Geal-charn Mor	HM03	133	Gyrn Moelfre	WN08	274
Geallaig Hill	HE03	140	Hafod Ithel	WM05	284
Ghlas-bheinn	HN01	45	Hail Storm Hill	EP06	257
Gilwern Hill	WM04	282	Hallin Fell	EL06	248
Gisborough Moor	EP04	254	Hard Knott	EL03	245
Giur-bheinn	IJ01	124	Hardown Hill	ES05	303
Glamaig	SK02	109	Hare Cairn	HE11	154
Glas Bheinn	HW13	87	Hart Fell	SS09	233
Glas Bheinn	IJ01	124	Hartaval	SK04	112
Glas Bheinn	HC12	180	Harter Fell	EL03	245
Glas Bheinn	IJ01	123	Harter Fell	EL06	248
Glas Bheinn	HN05	54	Heabhal	IB01	33
Glas Bheinn	HC03	164	Healabhal Bheag	SK05	114
Glas Bheinn 635	HW22	103	Healabhal Mhor	SK05	114
Glas Bheinn 731	HW17	93	Heath Mynd	EC02	294
Glas Bheinn Mhor	SK02	109	Heacla	IU01	29
Glas Bheinn Mhor	HC10	176	Hedgehope Hill	SE01	237
Glas Maol	HE11	154	Hegdon Hill	EC03	295
Glas Mheall Mor	HC05	167	Heileasbhal Mor	LH04	22
Glas Tulaichean	HE10	152	Heiseabhal Mor	IB01	33
Glas-bheinn Mhor	HW12	85	Helvellyn	EL05	247
Glas-charn	HW18	94	Hensbarrow Downs	ES01	299
Glasgwm	WN10	277	Hergest Ridge	WM04	282
Gleouraich	HW14	88	High Raise	EL03	245
Glyder Fawr	WN03	267	High Rigg	EL03	245
Goat Fell	IA01	213	High Spy	EL02	242
Gometra	IM02	121	High Stile	EL02	242
Gormol	LH03	22	High Street	EL06	248
Goseland Hill	SS09	233	High Vinnalls	WM03	281
Graig Syfyrddin	WS04	290	High Willhays	ES02	300
Grange Fell	SS10	234	Hill of Arisdale, Yell	IS02	11
Grasmoor	EL02	242	Hill of Clibberswick, Unst	IS02	11
Grayrigg Forest	EL06	248	Hill of Fare	HE04	142
Greabhal	LH04	22	Hill of Foudland	HE06	145
Great Coum	EP03	253	Hill of Garvock	HE14	158
Great Gable	EL02	242	Hill of Goauch	HE14	158
Great Knoutberry Hill	EP03	253	Hill of Nigg	HN08	61
Great Mell Fell	EL05	247	Hill of Persie	HE10	152
Great Orme / Y Gogarth	WN06	272	Hill of Stake	SS01	217
Great Rhos	WM04	282	Hill of Strone	HE11	154
Great Shunner Fell	EP02	252	Hill of the Wangie	HM05	135

Hill of Tillymorgan	HE06	145	Lingmoor Fell	EL03	245
Hill of Wirren	HE13	157	Linton Hill	SE01	237
Hirfynydd	WS02	288	Little Conval	HE05	143
Hods Hill	SS02	218	Little Mell Fell	EL05	247
Holme Fell	EL04	246	Little Wyvis	HN08	61
Holyhead Mountain	IW01	263	Littleton Down	ES06	304
Hoove	EP02	252	Liuthaid	LH01	21
Hope Mountain	WN07	273	Llan Ddu Fawr	WM05	284
Housedon Hill	SE01	237	Llanfihangel Hill	WM04	282
Hownam Law	SE01	237	Lochnagar - Cac Carn Beag	HE12	156
Huiseabhal Mor	LH01	21	Long Crag	SE01	237
Hunt Hill	HE13	157	Long Knoll	ES04	302
Hutton Roof Crags	EL06	248	Long Mountain	EC02	294
Illgill Head	EL03	245	Long Mynd	EC02	294
Inaccessible Pinnacle	SK01	107	Longridge Fell - Spire Hill	EP05	255
Ingleborough	EP03	253	Lord Arthur's Hill	HE06	145
Innerdouny Hill	SC02	210	Lord's Seat	EL02	242
Keelylang Hill	IO02	18	Loughrigg Fell	EL03	245
Kerloch	HE14	158	Lovely Seat	EP02	252
Killyleoch Hill	SS03	220	Low Fell	EL02	242
Kinder Scout	EP07	258	Lowick High Common	EL04	246
King's Seat	HE15	159	Luinne Bheinn	HW15	89
Kirk Fell	EL02	242	Lurg Mhor	HW07	77
Kirkby Moor	EL04	246	Maesglase	WN10	277
Kirkland Hill	SS02	218	Maiden Pap	HN03	51
Kirriereoch Hill	SS04	223	Maireabhal	IU02	29
Kisdon	EP02	252	Mam Hael	HC09	175
Kit Hill	ES01	299	Mam na Gualainn	HC02	162
Knap of Trowieglen, Hoy	IO01	18	Manod Mawr	WN05	271
Knock Hill	HE05	143	Maol Ban	IM01	119
Knock of Braemoray	HM05	135	Maol Chean-dearg	HW05	74
Knock of Crieff	HS10	204	Maol Domhnaich	IB02	33
Knockan	HE05	143	Maovally	HN05	54
Knockdolian	SS04	223	Marg na Craige	HM03	133
Knott	EL01	241	Marsco	SK02	109
Ladhar Bheinn	HW15	89	May Hill	EC03	295
Ladylea Hill	HE05	143	Meadie Ridge	HN02	49
Lamachan Hill	SS04	223	Mealaisbhal	LH02	21
Lamberton Hill	SS07	229	Meall a' Bhainne	HW22	103
Lambrigg Fell	EL06	248	Meall a' Bhainne	HC03	164
Lamington Hill	SS09	233	Meall a' Bhuachaille	HE02	138
Largo Law	SC02	210	Meall a' Bhuiridh	HC10	176
Larriston Fells	SE02	238	Meall a' Chaise	HN04	52
Law Kneis	SS10	234	Meall a' Chaorainn	HN07	59
Leagag	HC12	180	Meall a' Chaorainn	HW03	68
Leana Mhor 677	HM01	129	Meall a' Choire Bhuidhe	HE10	152
Leana Mhor 684	HM02	131	Meall a' Choire Leith	HC15	183
Leathad an Taobhain	HE08	148	Meall a' Chrathaich	HW12	85
Leathad Mor	HC12	180	Meall a' Ghiuthais	HW04	71
Leith Hill	ES07	305	Meall a' Mhaoil	SK02	109
Lendrick Hill	SC02	210	Meall a' Mhuic	HC12	180
Leum Uileim	HC03	164	Meall a' Phubuill	HW19	97
Lewesdon Hill	ES05	303	Meall Alvie	HE03	140
Li a' Deas	IU02	29	Meall an Doirein	HW04	71
Li a' Tuath	IU02	29	Meall an Fheadain	HN06	58
Liathach	HW04	71	Meall an Fheur Loch	HN05	54

Meall an Fhithich	HS01	185	Meall na Suiramach	SK04	112
Meall an Fhuarain	HN01	45	Meall na Teanga	HW17	93
Meall an Fhuarain	HN06	58	Meall nam Maigheach	HC15	183
Meall an Fhudair	HS04	194	Meall nan Caorach	HS10	204
Meall an Tarsaid	HM02	131	Meall nan Clach Ruadha	HN02	49
Meall an t-Seallaidh	HS08	201	Meall nan Con	HW20	99
Meall an t-Slamain	HW22	103	Meall nan Damh	IA01	213
Meall an t-Suidhe	HC01	161	Meall nan Damh	HW22	103
Meall Ban	HC08	172	Meall nan Each	HW20	99
Meall Bhanbhaidh	HW19	97	Meall nan Eagan	HC04	165
Meall Blair	HW17	93	Meall nan Eun	HW15	89
Meall Buidhe	HS10	204	Meall nan Eun	HC10	176
Meall Buidhe	HC12	180	Meall nan Gabhar	HS03	193
Meall Buidhe	HC12	180	Meall nan Subh	HC15	183
Meall Buidhe	HW15	89	Meall nan Tarmachan	HC15	183
Meall Cala	HS09	202	Meall Odhar	HS03	193
Meall Chomraidh	HC12	180	Meall Odhar a' Chire	HE08	148
Meall Chuaich	HE07	147	Meall Onfhaidh	HW19	97
Meall Coire an Lochain	HN06	58	Meall Reamhar	HS10	204
Meall Corranaich	HC15	183	Meall Sguman	HW10	82
Meall Dearg	HS10	204	Meall Tairbh	HC11	178
Meall Dheirgidh	HN07	59	Meall Tairneachan	HC13	181
Meall Doire Faid	HN07	59	Meall Uaine	HE10	152
Meall Dola	HN04	52	Meallach Mhor	HE08	148
Meall Dubh	HW14	88	Meallan a' Chuail	HN05	54
Meall Fuar-mhonaidh	HW12	85	Meallan Chuaich	HW03	68
Meall Gainmheich	HS09	202	Meallan Liath	HN02	49
Meall Garbh	HC11	178	Meallan Liath Coire Mhic Dhughaill	HN01	45
Meall Garbh	HC15	183	Meallan nan Uan	HW07	77
Meall Ghaordaidh	HC15	183	Meallan Odhar Doire nan Gillean	HW09	80
Meall Glac Tigh-fail	HW01	65	Meigle Hill	SS07	229
Meall Glas	HC14	182	Meikle Balloch Hill	HE05	143
Meall Greigh	HC15	183	Meikle Bin	SC01	209
Meall Horn	HN01	45	Meikle Conval	HE05	143
Meall Innis an Loichel	HW09	80	Meikle Says Law	SS07	229
Meall Liath Choire	HN07	59	Meith Bheinn	HW18	94
Meall Lighiche	HC08	172	Mellbreak	EL02	242
Meall Lochan a' Chleirich	HW04	71	Mendick Hill	SS06	227
Meall Luidh Mor	HC03	164	Merrick	SS04	223
Meall Meadhonach	HN01	45	Mickle Fell	EP01	251
Meall Mheinnidh	HW02	66	Mid Hill	IO02	18
Meall Mor	HM04	134	Mid Hill	HS07	199
Meall Mor	HC10	176	Mid Ward, Muckle Roe	IS01	11
Meall Mor	HE11	154	Middlefield Law	SS01	217
Meall Mor	HC08	172	Mile Hill	HE11	154
Meall Mor	HC01	161	Milldoe	IO02	18
Meall Mor	HN08	61	Millfore	SS04	223
Meall Mor	HS08	201	Millstone Hill	HE06	145
Meall na Duibhe	HC03	164	Minch Moor	SS08	231
Meall na Faochaig	HW07	77	Mochrum Fell	SS03	220
Meall na Fearna	HS11	205	Moel Cynghorion	WN02	266
Meall na h-Aisre	HM02	131	Moel Eilio	WN02	266
Meall na h-Eilde	HW17	93	Moel Famau	WN07	273
Meall na h-Eilrig	HW12	85	Moel Fynydd	WN10	277
Meall na Leitreach	HC05	167	Moel Gyw	WN07	273
Meall na Meoig	HC04	165	Moel Hebog	WN01	265

Moel Llyfnant	WN05	271	Mynydd Llangorse	WS04	290
Moel Siabod	WN05	271	Mynydd Llangyndeyrn	WS01	287
Moel y Dyniewyd	WN05	271	Mynydd Machen	WS03	289
Moel y Gamelin	WN07	273	Mynydd Maen	WS03	289
Moel y Golfa	EC02	294	Mynydd Mallaen	WM05	284
Moel y Gydros	WN05	271	Mynydd Marchywel	WS02	288
Moel Ysgyfarnogod	WN09	275	Mynydd Mawr	WN01	265
Moel-ddu	WN01	265	Mynydd Nodol	WN05	271
Moelfre	WN09	275	Mynydd Rhiw	WN01	265
Moelwyn Mawr	WN05	271	Mynydd Rhyd ddu	WN06	272
Moel-y-Gest	WN01	265	Mynydd Sylen	WS01	287
Mona Gowan	HE04	142	Mynydd Troed	WS04	290
Monadh Mor	HE01	137	Mynydd Twr	IW01	263
Monamenach	HE11	154	Mynydd Uchaf	WS01	287
Moncreiffe Hill	HS10	204	Mynydd y Betws	WS01	287
Mor Bheinn	HS11	205	Mynydd y Cwm	WN07	273
Morrone	HE10	152	Mynydd y Glyn	WS02	288
Moruisg	HW07	77	Mynydd y Grug	WS03	289
Morven	HN03	51	Mynydd y Lan	WS03	289
Morven	HE04	142	Mynydd-y-briw	WN08	274
Mount Battock	HE14	158	Na Maoilean	HC09	175
Mount Blair	HE11	154	Newtyle Hill	HE09	150
Mount Eagle	HW08	79	Nine Barrow Down	ES05	303
Mount Hill	SC02	210	Nine Standards Rigg	EP02	252
Mount Keen	HE14	158	Normanby Top	EC04	296
Mountbenger Law	SS08	231	Norman's Law	SC02	210
Muaitheabhal	LH03	21	North Berwick Law	SS07	229
Muirneag	LH05	22	North Lee	IU02	29
Muldoanich	IB02	33	Noss Head	IS03	11
Mullach an Eilein, Boreray	IX02	35	Nutberry Hill	SS01	217
Mullach an Rathain	HW04	71	Oireabhal	LH01	21
Mullach Buidhe, Shiant Islands	LH07	22	Ord Ban	HE01	137
Mullach Coire Mhic Fhearchair	HW02	66	Orval	IR01	116
Mullach Coire nan Geur-oirean	HW19	97	Pap of Glencoe	HC06	169
Mullach Fraoch-choire	HW12	85	Pared y Cefn-hir	WN10	277
Mullach Mor	IR01	116	Peel Fell	SE02	238
Mullach Mor	IA02	213	Pegwn Mawr	WM03	281
Mullach na Carn	SK06	115	Pen Llithrig y Wrach	WN04	268
Mullach na Dheiragain	HW10	82	Pen y Fan	WS03	289
Mullwharchar	SS04	223	Pen y Garn	WM02	280
Muncaster Fell	EL03	245	Pen y Garn-goch	WM05	284
Mwdwl-eithin	WN06	272	Pen-crug-melyn	WM05	284
Myarth	WS04	290	Pendle Hill	EP06	257
Mynydd Allt-y-grug	WS01	287	Penvalla	SS06	227
Mynydd Anelog	WN01	265	Penycloddiau	WN07	273
Mynydd Bodafon / Yr Arwydd	IW01	263	Pen-y-ghent	EP03	253
Mynydd Carningli	WM06	285	Periton Hill	ES03	301
Mynydd Carn-y-cefn	WS03	289	Pibble Hill	SS04	223
Mynydd Coety	WS03	289	Pike of Blisco	EL03	245
Mynydd Cwmcelli	WN10	277	Pikethaw Hill	SS10	234
Mynydd Cynros	WM05	284	Pillar	EL02	242
Mynydd Dinas	WS02	288	Place Fell	EL06	248
Mynydd Drumau	WS02	288	Plynlimon / Pumlumon Fawr	WM02	280
Mynydd Enlli	IW01	263	Pressendye	HE04	142
Mynydd Epynt	WM05	284	Pumlumon Fawr	WM02	280
Mynydd Gethin	WS02	288	Queensberry	SS02	218

Quinag - Sail Gharbh	HN05	54	Sgiath Chuil	HC14	182
Raw Head	WN08	274	Sgor Gaibhre	HC04	165
Red Screes	EL05	247	Sgor Gaoith	HE01	137
Rhialgwm	WN10	277	Sgor Mor	HE02	138
Rhinog Fach	WN09	275	Sgorach Breac	SK03	111
Rhinog Fawr	WN09	275	Sgorach Mor	HS06	197
Rhiw Gwraidd	WM03	281	Sgorr a' Choise	HC08	172
Rhobell Fawr	WN05	271	Sgorr an Fharaidh	IR01	117
Rhos Ymryson	WM05	284	Sgorr Craobh a' Chaorainn	HW22	103
Roan Fell	SS11	235	Sgorr Dhearg	HC07	171
Robinson	EL02	242	Sgorr Dhonuill	HC07	171
Rogan's Seat	EP02	252	Sgorr Mhic Eacharna	HW22	103
Roineabhal	IU01	29	Sgorr na Diollaid	HW09	80
Roineabhal	LH01	21	Sgorr nam Faoileann	IJ01	124
Roineabhal	LH04	22	Sgorr nam Fiannaidh	HC06	169
Roineval	SK05	114	Sgorr nan Lochan Uaine	HW05	74
Rois-Bheinn	HW21	101	Sgorr Ruadh	HW05	74
Rombalds Moor	EP03	253	Sgorr Tuath	HN06	58
Ronas Hill	IS01	11	Sgreadan Hill	HS02	187
Ros Castle	SE01	237	Sgribhis-bheinn	HN01	45
Royl Field	IS01	11	Sguman Coinntich	HW09	80
Ruadh Stac	SK02	109	Sgurr a' Bhealaich Dheirg	HW11	83
Ruadh Stac Mor	HW02	66	Sgurr a' Chaorachain	HW06	75
Ruadh Stac Mor, Beinn Eighe	HW04	71	Sgurr a' Chaorachain	HW07	77
Ruadh-stac Beag	HW04	71	Sgurr a' Chaorainn	HW22	103
Ruardean Hill	EC03	295	Sgurr a' Choire Ghlais	HW08	79
Rubers Law	SE02	238	Sgurr a' Choire-bheithe	HW15	89
'S Airde Beinn	IM01	119	Sgurr a' Gharaidh	HW05	74
Sabhal Beag	HN01	45	Sgurr a' Mhaim	HC02	162
Sail Chalmadale	IA01	213	Sgurr a' Mhaoraich	HW13	87
Sail Ghorm	HN05	54	Sgurr a' Mhuilinn	HW07	77
Sail Mhor	HW01	65	Sgurr Alasdair	SK01	107
Sandness Hill	IS01	11	Sgurr an Airgid	HW11	83
Saugh Hill	SS04	225	Sgurr an Doire Leathain	HW13	87
Saxa Vord, Unst	IS02	11	Sgurr an Fhidhleir	HN06	58
Scafell Pike	EL03	245	Sgurr an Fhuarain	HW16	91
Scald Law	SS06	227	Sgurr an Utha	HW18	94
Scalla Field	IS01	11	Sgurr Ban	HW02	66
Scaraben	HN03	51	Sgurr Beag	HW16	91
Scaw'd Fell	SS10	234	Sgurr Bhuidhe	HW16	91
Schiehallion	HC13	181	Sgurr Breac	HW03	68
Scrae Field	IS01	11	Sgurr Choinnich	HW17	93
Scrinadle	IJ01	123	Sgurr Choinnich Mor	HC01	161
Seaforth Island	LH07	22	Sgurr Coire Choinnichean	HW15	89
Seager Hill	EC03	295	Sgurr Cos na Breachd-laoidh	HW16	91
Seana Bhraigh	HN07	59	Sgurr Dearg	IM01	119
Seana Mheallan	HW05	74	Sgurr Dhomhnuill	HW22	103
Seat Sandal	EL05	247	Sgurr Dhomhuill Mor	HW21	101
Seatallan	EL02	242	Sgurr Dubh	HW05	74
See Morris Hill	SS03	220	Sgurr Eilde Mor	HC02	162
Sell Moor Hill	SS07	229	Sgurr Fhuaran	HW11	83
Selworthy Beacon	ES03	301	Sgurr Fhuar-thuill	HW08	79
Sgairneach Mhor	HC05	167	Sgurr Fiona	HW01	65
Sgaoth Aird	LH01	21	Sgurr Gaorsaic	HW10	82
Sgarbh Breac	IJ01	124	Sgurr Ghiubhsachain	HW22	103
Sgiath a' Chaise	HS11	205	Sgurr Innse	HC01	161

Sgurr Marcasaidh	HW07	77	Sron an Duin, Berneray	IB02	33
Sgurr Mhic Bharraich	HW13	87	Sron Romul, Scarp	LH06	22
Sgurr Mhurlagain	HW16	91	Sron Smeur	HC04	165
Sgurr Mor, Beinn Alligin	HW04	71	St Boniface Down	IE01	307
Sgurr Mor	HW16	91	St Sunday Crag	EL05	247
Sgurr Mor	HW03	68	Stac an Armin	IX02	35
Sgurr na Ba Glaise	HW21	101	Stac Gorm	HM04	134
Sgurr na Ciche	HW16	91	Stac Lee	IX02	35
Sgurr na Ciste Duibhe	HW11	83	Stac na Cathaig	HM04	134
Sgurr na Coinnich	SK03	111	Stac Pollaidh	HN06	58
Sgurr na Dubh-chreige	HW16	91	Staple Hill	ES05	303
Sgurr na Feartaig	HW07	77	Steele's Knowe	SC02	210
Sgurr na h-Iolaire	SK03	111	Steygail	SS02	218
Sgurr na h-Ulaidh	HC08	172	Stingwern Hill	WM01	279
Sgurr na Lapaich	HW09	80	Stiperstones	EC02	294
Sgurr na Ruaidhe	HW08	79	Stob a' Choin	HS09	202
Sgurr na Sgine	HW13	87	Stob a' Choire Mheadhoin	HC01	161
Sgurr na Stri	SK01	107	Stob a' Choire Odhair	HC10	176
Sgurr nan Caorach	SK03	111	Stob an Aonaich Mhoir	HC05	167
Sgurr nan Ceannaichean	HW07	77	Stob an Eas	HS05	195
Sgurr nan Ceathramhnan	HW10	82	Stob Ban	HC01	161
Sgurr nan Clach Geala	HW03	68	Stob Ban	HC02	162
Sgurr nan Cnamh	HW22	103	Stob Binnein	HS08	201
Sgurr nan Coireachan	HW16	91	Stob Breac	HS09	202
Sgurr nan Coireachan	HW18	94	Stob Choire Claurigh	HC01	161
Sgurr nan Conbhairean	HW12	85	Stob Coire a' Chearcaill	HW22	103
Sgurr nan Eugallt	HW15	89	Stob Coire an Albannaich	HC10	176
Sgurr nan Gillean	SK01	107	Stob Coire Creagach	HS04	194
Sgurr Thuilm	HW18	94	Stob Coire Easain	HC01	161
Shalloch on Minnoch	SS04	223	Stob Coire Raineach	HC08	172
Sharp Haw	EP03	253	Stob Dearg	HC08	172
Shaw Hill	SS04	223	Stob Dubh	HC08	172
Shee of Ardtalnaig	HS10	204	Stob Dubh	HC10	176
Shillhope Law	SE01	237	Stob Ghabhar	HC10	176
Shining Tor	EP07	258	Stob Mhic Bheathain	HW22	103
Shobdon Hill	WM04	282	Stob na Boine Druim-fhinn	HS05	195
Sighty Crag	SE02	238	Stob na Cruaiche	HC06	169
Sithean a' Bhealaich Chumhaing	SK04	112	Stob na Doire	HC08	172
Sithean Mor	HW04	71	Stob Odhar	HS02	187
Sithean Mor	HW18	94	Stony Cove Pike	EL06	248
Sithean na Raplaich	HW23	105	Strathfinella Hill	HE14	158
Skiddaw	EL01	241	Streap	HW18	94
Slat Bheinn	HW15	89	Stronend	SC01	209
Sleteachal Mhor	LH01	21	Struie	HN08	61
Slioch	HW02	66	Stuc a' Chroin	HS11	205
Smean	HN03	51	Stuchd an Lochain	HC12	180
Snowdon / Yr Wyddfa	WN02	266	Stulabhal	IU01	29
Sotan (Sron an Duin), Berneray	IB02	33	Stulabhal	LH01	21
South Lee	IU02	29	Suaineabhal	LH02	21
Spartleton	SS07	229	Sugar Loaf / Y Fal	WS04	290
Speinne Mor	IM01	119	Suilven	HN05	54
Spidean a' Choire Leith	HW04	71	Sunnyhill	WM03	281
Spidean Coinich	HN05	54	Swinside	EL02	242
Spidean Coire nan Clach	HW04	71	Swyre Head	ES05	303
Spidean Mialach	HW14	88	Tal y Fan	WN04	268
Sron a' Choire Chnapanaich	HC12	180	Tap o' Noth	HE05	143
Sron a' Choire Ghairbh	HW17	93	Tarn Crag	EL06	248

Tarren y Gesail	WN10	277	Walbury Hill	ES06	304
Tarrenhendre	WN10	277	Walton Hill	EC01	293
Tathabhal	LH02	21	Wapley Hill	WM04	282
The Begwns	WM04	282	Ward Hill, Fair Isle	IS04	11
The Bochel	HE05	143	Ward Hill, Hoy	IO01	18
The Brack	HS05	195	Ward Law	SS10	234
The Buck	HE05	143	Ward of Bressay	IS03	11
The Calf	EP02	252	Ward of Scousburgh	IS01	11
The Cheviot	SE01	237	Ward's Stone	EP05	255
The Cloud	EP07	258	Watch Croft	ES01	299
The Cobbler	HS04	194	Watch Hill	EL02	242
The Coyles of Muick	HE12	156	Waughton Hill	HE06	145
The Fara	HC04	165	Wauk Hill	SS03	220
The Fruin	HS07	199	Waun Fach	WS04	290
The Saddle	HW13	87	Waun Rydd	WS03	289
The Slate	HS02	187	Well Hill	SS02	218
The Sow of Atholl	HC05	167	Wendover Woods	EC05	297
The Stob	HS08	201	Wentwood	WS04	290
The Storr	SK04	112	West Lomond	SC02	210
The Wiss	SS10	234	Wether Hill	SS03	220
The Wrekin	EC01	293	Wether Law	SS06	227
Thacla	IU01	29	Wetherlam	EL04	246
Tighvein	IA01	213	Whernside	EP03	253
Tinto	SS02	218	Whitbarrow	EL06	248
Tiorga Mor	LH01	21	White Coomb	SS09	233
Titterstone Clee Hill	EC02	294	White Grunafirth	IS01	11
Todun	LH01	21	White Hill	SS02	218
Toll Creagach	HW10	82	White Hill	EP05	255
Tom a' Choinnich	HW10	82	White Meldon	SS06	227
Tom an t-Saighdeir	HS01	185	White Top of Culreoch	SS04	223
Tom Bailgeann	HM04	134	Whitfell	EL03	245
Tom Meadhoin	HC02	162	Wideford Hill	IO02	18
Tom na Gruagaich	HW04	71	Wild Boar Fell	EP02	252
Tom nam Fitheach	IM01	119	Wills Neck	ES03	301
Top o' Selside	EL04	246	Wilmington Hill	ES07	305
Tor y Foel	WS03	289	Win Green	ES04	302
Torlum	HS11	205	Windlestraw Law	SS07	229
Torr Achilty	HW03	68	Windy Hill	IA03	213
Tosson Hill	SE01	237	Windy Standard	SS03	220
Trahenna Hill	SS06	227	Winter Hill	EP06	257
Trichrug	WS01	287	Wisp Hill	SS10	234
Triuirebheinn	IU01	29	Woodhead Hill	SS03	220
Trollabhal	IR01	116	Worcestershire Beacon	EC03	295
Troweir Hill	SS04	223	Y Fal / Sugar Loaf	WS04	290
Trum y Ddysgl	WN01	265	Y Garn	WN09	275
Tryfan	WN03	267	Y Garn	WN03	267
Tullich Hill	HS07	199	Y Gogarth / Great Orme	WN06	272
Turin Hill	HE15	159	Y Golfa	WM01	279
Turner Cleuch Law	SS10	234	Y Llethr	WN09	275
Uamh Bheag	HS11	205	Y Lliwedd	WN02	266
Uisgneabhal Mor	LH01	21	Yarlside	EP02	252
Uisinis	LH03	22	Yewbarrow	EL02	242
Upper Park	WM01	279	Yr Aran	WN02	266
Urra Moor	EP04	254	Yr Arwydd / Mynydd Bodafon	IW01	263
Valla Field, Unst	IS02	11	Yr Eifl	WN01	265
View Edge	WM03	281	Yr Wyddfa / Snowdon	WN02	266
Vord Hill, Fetlar	IS02	11	Ysgyryd Fawr	WS04	290